D1241882

Regulating a New Society

Regulating a New Society

*Public Policy and Social Change
in America, 1900–1933*

Morton Keller

Harvard University Press
Cambridge, Massachusetts
London, England
1994

Copyright © 1994 by Morton Keller
All rights reserved
Printed in the United States of America

This book is printed on acid-free paper, and its binding
materials have been chosen for strength and durability.

Library of Congress Cataloging-in-Publication Data

Keller, Morton.
    Regulating a new society : public policy and social change in
America, 1900–1933 / Morton Keller.
        p. cm.
    Includes bibliographical references and index.
    ISBN 0–674–75366–6 (acid-free paper)
    1. Social change—United States. 2. United States—Social policy.
3. United States—History—20th century. 4. Progressivism (United
States politics) I. Title.
HN57.K38 1994
303.4′0973′0904—dc20
93–47567
        CIP

LIBRARY
ALMA COLLEGE
ALMA, MICHIGAN

For David and Sonia

Have friends. 'Tis a second existence.

Contents

Preface

Now, at the end of the twentieth century, there is a growing interest in American public life during the century's early years, the time of the Progressive movement. Then, as today, there was a widespread belief that, despite the lack of major threats from abroad or economic depression at home, things were deeply wrong with the nation's politics and government, its economic institutions, and its social system. This sense of malaise focused on systemic corruption in public and private life, and on a social fabric so weakened by rapid change that, it was feared, the center would not hold.

The issues that concerned politically active Americans then—political corruption and government inefficiency; the concentration of economic wealth and power; the state of the family, the home, and the child; social welfare; conservation of the environment; cultural and racial diversity—are the issues that concern them today. And then as now programs for change emerged, most notably from the chattering classes: intellectuals and academics, socially conscious businessmen and professionals, journalists and reformers, who sought to secure their goals not primarily through the major political parties but through special-purpose organizations designed to lobby politicians and influence public opinion.

By their lights, early twentieth-century Americans did in fact accomplish a great deal. A flood of new local, state, and national laws, four constitutional amendments in six years, court decisions, and new administrative procedures substantially changed American public life. They had a will, and found ways, to effect change that might readily excite envy and admiration in our own clotted time. But while much was done, much of that (or so it appears in historical retrospect) would have been better left *undone*: strengthened and formalized racial segregation, the repression of dissent during World War I, Prohibition, and immigration restriction based on national origins.

In the early decades of the twentieth century we can see the American polity beginning to come to grips with the full force of modern society—modern in its scale, diversity, and complexity. Is this a time best understood as the one in which a modern American state emerged? Or (as proposed here) is it best seen as a period dominated by the clash between new issues and old institutions, *both* invigorated by the pressures of social and economic change? From either perspective, the story has a special relevance at the century's end.

This is the second of a three-volume study of early twentieth-century American politics, law, and government, which together will constitute a sequel to my *Affairs of State: Public Life in Late Nineteenth-Century America* (1977). *Regulating a New Economy: Public Policy and Economic Change in America, 1900–1933* (1990) explored the ways in which American law, politics, and government responded to the rise of a corporate/consumer economy. The present volume examines a comparably wide range of social policies, responses to no less dramatic and portentous changes in early twentieth-century American society.

The rise of big business, new technologies, and a consumer-based economy shaped the regulatory response to the early twentieth-century American economy. Similarly, changing conditions in American life—a more urban society, massive new immigration, an ever larger, more diverse public opinion—shaped social policy. The character of those policy responses is the subject of this book.

I am well aware that to speak of "a new society" or of "modern times" raises the question of just what those slippery words "new" and "modern" mean. Let me briefly make my case for the view that early twentieth-century American society, like the economy, can meaningfully be described as "new" by repeating what I said in *Regulating a New Economy:*

> There are grounds for holding that around the turn of this century, much of Western society experienced change at a pace, and on a scale, far beyond what had been seen before—or, arguably, since. It was then that modernity came with a rush. The historian Eric Hobsbawm reminds us [in *The Age of Empire*, 1987] that "so much of what remained characteristic of our times originated, sometimes quite suddenly, in the decades before 1914." Norman Stone [in *Europe Transformed*, 1984] makes the same point more dramatically: "In 1895 the novelist Henry James ac-

quired electric lighting; in 1896 he rode a bicycle; in 1897 he wrote on a typewriter; in 1898 he saw a cinematograph. Within a very few years, he could have had a Freudian analysis, travelled in an aircraft, understood the principles of the jet-engine or even of space-travel." Mark Sullivan [in *Our Times*, 1926] recalled some of the words unknown in 1900 but very much part of the American language a quarter century later: "The newspapers of 1900 contained no mention of . . . jazz, nor feminism, nor birthcontrol. There was no such word as rum-runner, nor hijacker, nor bolshevism, fundamentalism, behaviorism, Freudian, . . . Rotary, . . . cafeteria, automat . . . they would not have pictured boy scouts . . . nor traffic cops, nor Ku Klux Klan parades . . . nor one-piece bathing suits, nor advertisements of lip-sticks, nor motion-picture actresses, for there were no such things."

A word as to the research on which this volume (like its predecessor) rests. I concluded early on that to draw largely on traditional primary sources—manuscript collections, government documents, statistical data, and the like—in a synoptic study such as this would be the scholarly equivalent of trying to empty the sea with a slotted spoon. Yet to rely primarily on the work of other historians would imprison me in their sense of what mattered and what it meant, and remove me from the freshness and immediacy of contemporary observation. So I immersed myself not only in the very substantial body of historical writing on early twentieth-century American social policy but also, and most especially, in the relevant periodicals of the time. These popular, scholarly, and technical journals trained their sights on the society around them on a previously unmatched scale. Their bequest to us is a rich, comprehensive, and often insightful record of the public life of those years.

As before, I have important obligations to record: to the Harvard and Brandeis libraries, and to supportively critical colleagues and friends: Nancy Cott, Aïda Donald, David Fischer, Ellen Fitzpatrick, Lawrence Friedman, Mary Ann Glendon, Fred Hoxie, Harold Hyman, Jacqueline Jones, Linda Kerber, James Kloppenberg, and Stephan Thernstrom. What I owe to Phyllis Keller belongs not here but in the book of life.

Regulating a New Society

Introduction

Regulating a new society—using government and law to control the behavior of institutions, individuals, and groups—was a conspicuous feature of that outburst of state activism that we call the Progressive movement. Much ink, and almost as much thought, has been spent on the sources, character, and consequences of Progressivism. Was there an agenda, explicit or implicit, that gave it shape?

At one time it was enough to attribute the Progressive movement to a general desire to do good, to remedy some of the inequities and human suffering that came with big business, large cities, and massive new immigration. But the reform impulse of the time was more complex than that. For decades now, historians have been finding other motivations. One is that a middle class confronting big politics, big business, and organized labor turned to political, economic, and social reform. Another is that corporations and the middle class sought to impose greater social controls on an urban-immigrant industrial working class thought to be dangerously susceptible to radicalism and/or social disorder. Yet another approach stresses the degree to which public policy was shaped by the evolution of the United States from a dispersed and localized to a nationally organized society.[1]

This medley of explanations has led to doubts as to whether there was in fact a distinguishable Progressive movement. But abundant evidence suggests that major new impulses entered into social (as they did into economic) policy-making after 1900. The several explanations of the Progressive impulse—that it was a multiclass response to a variety of political, social, and economic evils or a middle-class revolt against the consequences of organization or a corporate revolt against the consequences of *dis*organization—are not mutually exclusive but varying perspectives on a larger, more complex whole.

1

This impression gains strength from a comparative view. Many of the social issues that are the subject matter of this book figured largely in other Western nations as well. Variants of American Progressivism, distinguished as much by their differences as by their similarities, can be seen in Britain's New Liberalism, German Social Democracy, and the Republican-Radical governments of early twentieth-century France.[2]

Still, American social policy is best understood as a product of the distinctive character of the nation's public life. Before 1900 that public life was shaped by the values of classical liberalism: strong popular nationalism; a commitment to representative government and a weak central state; a belief in personal freedom (however vitiated in theory and practice by race, gender, and class prejudice); and the assumption that the natural laws governing society (like those governing the economy) were not readily altered by public policy.

The massive economic and social changes occurring around the turn of the century inevitably led to new ways of viewing the structure of American society. In particular, the passion for classification that was so much a part of Darwinian biology had a profound effect on social thought. The prevailing trend was to sort human beings into distinct racial, ethnic, and social groups. The creation and the character of particular social types is the central theme of seminal works such as Frederick Jackson Turner's essay on the effects of the American frontier (1893), Thorstein Veblen's *Theory of the Leisured Class* (1898), and William Graham Sumner's *Folkways* (1906). This was in keeping with Herbert Spencer's diktat that the basic course of evolution was from simplicity to complexity, from homogeneity to heterogeneity.

The urge to classify pervades social commentary during the early 1900s. Class analysis now entered into American social science with the work of Charles Beard and others, as did the interest-group approach to politics with the appearance of Arthur F. Bentley's *Process of Government* (1908). One social taxonomist came up with "clingers" (conservatives), "sensualists" (risk takers), "stalwarts" (utopians committed to the Bible, the Constitution, and moral law), and "mugwumps" (the professional classes, shielded from the struggle for existence, wedded to criticism over action). The sociologist Franklin H. Giddings identified social outlooks with geographically defined character types: the ideo-motor (forceful, to be found on the seacoasts, in the mountains, and on the Great Plains); the ideo-emotional (convivial, clustered in the South); the dogmatic-emotional (austere, dwelling in New England); and the critical-intellectual (rational and conscientious, to be found in the cities). Only 1.5 percent of the population fit that final category (Giddings's own, as it happened), which of course was the highest evolutionary form.[3]

Early twentieth-century American social policy-making was not shaped primarily by class conflict. It is true that Progressives often expressed their common social outlook by identifying themselves, explicitly or implicitly, with—and as—the middle class. They sought to distinguish themselves from aristocracy, conservatism, and plutocracy on the one hand, and the proletariat and radicalism on the other. But this was more an encompassing than a restrictive or exclusionary label. To speak of the middle class, as most Progressives saw it, was but another way to speak of the people. It was, said one of them, "to the common people after all, to the so-called middle class of our citizens, that the reformer must chiefly look for aid and support . . . The wealthier classes, the multi-millionaires, will not do it; the low, ignorant, and vicious cannot and should not do it."[4]

This was a peculiarly American attitude. The concept of the average man (the "middle American") was alien to most European social thought, either as a reality or as an ideal. European reformers tended rather to speak of national types or characteristics that might transcend, but hardly obscured, class distinctions.[5]

The distinctive tone, and the frequent ambiguities, of the Progressive mind-set are evident when one looks at a representative figure, the sociologist Edward A. Ross. Was he a man of the right or of the left? There are two answers to that question: he was both, and neither. Ross's *Social Control* (1901) used that term not in its current meaning of elites holding sway over the powerless, but as a label for the universe of rules, formal and informal, public and private, by which people socially organized themselves. Like his European counterparts Henry Maine, Ferdinand Tönnies, and Emile Durkheim, Ross sought a *mode d'emploi* for the study of modern society. And by "modern society" he, like so many of his generation of social thinkers, had in mind a shift of emphasis from community to society, from ethnic and other tribalisms to larger social units, from a natural, unconscious order to a conscious social one—one subject to social control.[6]

Ross was no socialist. Nor, despite the fact that his support for prohibition and immigration restriction rested on his belief in hereditary as well as environmental sources of social pathology, can he be called a racist. He once observed: "To the scholar the attributing of the mental and moral traits of a population to heredity is a confession of defeat, not to be thought of until he has wrung from every factor in life its last drop of explanation." He thought that "race," like "sex," as a category of social analysis was "the fetich of the lazy."[7]

What most characterized Ross and others of his Progressive generation was their belief in, and search for, policies designed to restore an American social cohesion whose loss they regarded as a major casualty of modern times. One of them asked a question that nagged at many of his fellows: "If . . . individualism is in practice rejected and doctrinaire Socialism is not adopted, upon what social philosophy are we proceeding?" His answer had wide resonance: "The principle of order and organization," applied to the improvement of individuals and institutions.[8]

Here we come to the heart of Progressivism. However varied were the goals of social policymakers, they had a shared sense that the good society was efficient, organized, cohesive. Historians tend to sort out early twentieth-century public thought and action on either side of the fault line of right and left. But it is important to recognize how much overlap there was in social ideologies during the early 1900s. The sense that a new society, turbulent, full of different sorts of people, problems, and ideas, had come into being was as widespread as the awareness that big business, consumerism, and new technology were creating a new economy. Regardless of their place on the ideological spectrum, thinkers and doers sought to cope with this overriding social reality.

They shared as well a belief in progress, and even in the best way to achieve it: through a better-organized, more uniform, more efficient social order. The British Spencerian Benjamin Kidd, by any reasonable measure a social conservative, spoke in language familiar to Progressives everywhere when he equated the success of a society "with the ethical and moral conditions favorable to the maintenance of a high standard of social efficiency, and with those conditions only." J. A. Hobson, the English liberal economist whose writings on imperialism influenced Lenin, spoke in similar terms of the "organic unity of the problem of social progress," of "a scientific harmony of the claims of socialism and individualism." American social thinkers, too, put a high value on "the principle of order and organization"; they believed that "potentially, the greatest producer, recorder, interpreter and user of social fact is an efficient democracy."[9]

This characteristically Progressive attitude faced two powerful counterforces. First, in issue after issue, the search for ways of enhancing social conformity ran head-on into the fact of American pluralism. An ever-greater variety of people, ideas, interests, and institutions emerged from the same economic and social developments that fed the Progressive taste for unity and efficiency. There was a subliminal message of sorts in the fact that *The Encyclopedia of Social Reform* (1897), designed for "general workers and students in social reform," traversed a vast and varied social landscape that stretched from abandoned farms to urban zones. The other countering force was the weight of the past, the persistence—even the strengthening—of traditional social values and beliefs. This found expression in a variety of forms: localism, individualism, religious fundamentalism, laissez-faire.[10]

The interplay among these elements—Progressivism, pluralism, persistence—defined much of the content and led to many of the conflicts that shaped early twentieth-century American social policy-making. The historian Richard Hofstadter was right. This was indeed an "age of reform," but reform infused with scientific, instrumentalist language and ways of thinking; internally subdivided and several-minded as to means and ends; consistently inhibited by the sheer scale and diversity of modern America and the legacy of the American past.

World War I was a traumatic event in modern European history. It meant much less to America, given the brevity of the nation's involvement. In historical retrospect its impact lay more in the realm of sentiment and attitude than in substantial institutional, economic, or social change. The war was at once a revelation as to how people, goods, and beliefs could be mobilized and organized for an overriding public purpose—the embodiment of the Progressive ideal—and a definitive demonstration of the social conflict and damage that could issue from so bold a venture in purposeful public policy.

What followed was . . . the twenties, which the American memory persists in recalling as a decadal romp between war and depression, a national wallow in xenophobia and irresponsibility, a time set apart from the Progressive past and the New Deal future. But as our historical perspective lengthens, we can see more clearly that the notion that the First World War sharply split the early twentieth century into two periods is a strained and artificial one. The prewar, wartime, and postwar years together are more properly seen as a whole, to be differentiated from the Great Depression–New Deal–World War II years to come.

In the wake of the war a number of intellectuals and policymakers tried to foster a movement of postwar economic and social reconstruction. They were influenced in part by an analogous English effort, but most of all they drew on the ideas and spirit of Progressivism. Their goal was "to furnish a scientific basis for progressive, in distinction from revolutionary or reactionary, social reconstruction." This movement had no chance of succeeding, given the postwar hostility to continued government economic and social control. But the episode suggests that what happened in the 1920s was not so much the replacement of the prewar triad of Progressivism, traditionalism, and pluralism, as a shift in the balance of public power among them.[11]

Even more than in the prewar years, social analysts during the 1920s dwelt on the tension between individualism and collectivism in modern mass society. There was much discussion of the need for collective social forms imposed by technology and the conditions of modern life. A 1926 civics text concluded: "You cannot mistake the direction of the movements we have been studying. They aim chiefly at the good of collective society . . . Daily the web of human life is being bound closer and closer together."[12]

The Progressive quest for social efficiency and order went on in the 1920s. But the legacy of the war gave that pursuit a darker cast. The prewar emphasis on more inclusive humanitarian policies and on institutional and structural reform now gave way to an American version of the mind-set evident in much of the postwar world: cultural traditionalism, xenophobia, institutional rigidity, and the assertion of authority by social and economic elites. As we will see, in area after area of public policy these repressive impulses faced (though they were hardly defeated by) countering social values. American government in general moved not in the direction of growing power and control—the prevalent tendency elsewhere—but in quite the opposite direction. Old individualism and a new pluralism conjoined to check the outward reach of the state.

This slowdown had its price. Economic regulation and social policy innovation slowed or stopped. Those seeking to check the power of big business found little assistance in the instruments of government; though so, too, did those seeking to enforce social conformity. The

Progressive ideal of a new America, run by experts and characterized by efficiency and cultural cohesion, gave way before the prevailing reality of a weak state, strong corporations, and an eclectic public opinion. The labor economist Leo Wolman lamented in 1927: "Within less than a decade those who have faith in the uses of a controlled society have seen an elaborate structure of social control disintegrate before their very eyes."[13]

By the end of the 1920s many Progressives (and younger social commentators as well) had an elegiac sense of the gulf that separated the prewar from the postwar years. This was a perception that the depression intensified, and that is still with us today. The prototypical Progressive Edward A. Ross reflected that attitude when he worried about "world drift" in 1928. He saw a planet in the grip of an ever-intensifying capitalism and a growing cultural conflict between the advanced West and the backward East. There were some hopeful signs: better public health, more education, more social equality and freedom of association for men and women. But the declining fertility of the American native stock, and strikes ever more damaging to an economic system heavily invested in its industrial plant, made him fear for the future.[14]

Frederick Lewis Allen's *Only Yesterday*, which appeared in 1932, most evocatively put forth what came to be the popular view of the twenties. As early as 1930 Allen had it firmly in mind that the "Post-War Period in American history" was over, that the country was at "the end of an era." And what did he take to be the defining characteristics of the decade now past? Disillusion first: cynicism had replaced the idealism of the war (and, by extrapolation, the high hopes of domestic Progressivism). This disposition emerged in a variety of forms: Menckenian debunking; the reduction of human behavior to biological causes; the sexual replacing the romantic in gender relations (for the young, sexual experimentation had taken the place that socialism once occupied). What else? Science enthroned, religion dethroned; a get-rich-quick ethos in commerce and laissez-faire in government, both feeding on and fed by the prosperity of the decade.[15]

Yet the continuity between prewar and postwar social thought was clear when Herbert Hoover in 1929 created the President's Research Committee on Social Trends, headed by the Progressive-minded social scientist William F. Ogburn. This body was charged to survey the American social scene and come up with an answer to the question:

Whither America? The committee's report, *Recent Social Trends*, appeared in 1933, an epitaph of sorts for an American era now rapidly fading into the realm of the once-was.

Committee monographs, directly descended from the Progressive mode of social inquiry, explored population trends, communications and their social impact, education, urban and rural life, races and ethnic groups, women's issues, labor, recreation, the arts, health and the environment, and public administration and the federal government. The committee concluded that modern life had a special character, "everywhere complicated, but especially so in the United States, where immigration from many lands, rapid mobility within the country itself, the lack of established classes or castes to act as brakes on social changes, the tendency to seize upon new types of machines, rich natural resources and vast driving power, have hurried us dizzily away from the days of the frontier into a whirl of modernisms which almost passes belief."[16]

The weighty presence of the Progressive past was evident as well in the lack of any reference to the Great Depression, and in the committee's undiluted belief (in 1933!) that the "outstanding problem" facing the nation was "bringing about a realization of the interdependence of the factors of our complicated social structure, and of interrelating the advancing sections of our forward movement so that agriculture, labor, industry, government, education, religion and science may develop a higher degree of coordination in the next phase of national growth." Not surprisingly, the committee looked back longingly to that Progressive epiphany, the American effort in the First World War: "In retrospect it offers a significant illustration of the rapidity and the success with which a people can recast its basic institutions at need."[17]

The coming of a new society had several—conflicting—consequences: a search for greater national cohesion through various forms of social engineering; the demands of a new social and cultural pluralism; an American traditionalism paradoxically given new vitality by social change. The complex policy results are explored in this book. It is a story of high expectations robustly raised and rudely dashed, of fertile new possibilities and stubbornly persisting constraints.

We will observe the playing out of this drama first in the realm of major social *institutions:* the family, religion, and education. Then we will look at major social *issues*, most as old as the Republic, but assuming a new urgency in modern times: libel and slander, privacy and mental suffering (what came to be called the rights of personality), and the basic civil liberties of freedom of speech and of the press; the regulation of mores (in particular gambling, prostitution, drug-taking, and drinking); the causes of crime and the treatment of criminals; and social welfare, which in the early twentieth century focused on poverty, public health, and the conditions of labor. Finally, we will examine an area of social policy that assumed a notably new vigor after 1900, affecting the status and rights of *groups:* immigrants and aliens, blacks, Indians, and women.

As in *Regulating a New Economy,* the goal of this book is to provide a comprehensive overview of the rich, complex setting of ideas, interests, and issues that gave shape to early twentieth-century American public policy. To give an old saw new teeth, to be ignorant of the texture of the past is to be condemned to misunderstand it.

I · INSTITUTIONS

Let us begin with the institutions that law and custom regard as fundamental to the social order: the family; forms of voluntary association, most particularly religion; and education. Insofar as they were subject to a common regulatory policy, it was: hands off. To live your own family life, to associate and worship as you chose, to educate your young according to your (or at most your community's) lights: these were, however flawed in practice, major components of the core definition of American freedom.

The new turn-of-the-century American society upped the stakes of state intervention in these institutions. But here as elsewhere the impulse to order, unify, and improve the social conditions of modern life collided with two powerful counterforces: past traditions of liberty and individualism, and the present reality of a pluralist society.

1 ▪ The Family and the State

No social institution carried a greater burden of civic responsibility than the family. And yet, other than the church, none could make a stronger case for its autonomy, its right to be free from the authority of government. Modern times further complicated this relationship. The family's claim on its independence steadily eroded. The growing public recognition of wives' civil rights, and the state's increasing stake in marriage, child rearing, and divorce, gave the family an ever-larger place on the public policy agenda.

The national government had little voice in that agenda. As the Supreme Court observed in 1930: "Domestic relations of husband and wife and parent and child [are] matters reserved to the states." And for all the new pressures, family policy continued to be dominated by two powerful traditional beliefs: that the role of the state should be minimal, and that the husband/father should be predominant. These attitudes (more often strengthened than eroded by the new immigrants) meant that the regulatory impulse, whether to foster the independent status of wives or children or to fend off threats to family stability, found heavy going in early twentieth-century America.[1]

The Matrix of Marriage

Nineteenth-century American family law and legislation were notably liberal for their time. The common law presumption that marriage created one person—the husband—continued to prevail in Britain (with some parliamentary modification). French marriage law remained in thrall to the Napoleonic Code of 1804, which sustained the place of the husband/father at the head of the family. Its primary purpose was to protect "the social interest in the maintenance of the integrity of the legal system. The next important interest seems to be the social interest in the maintenance of the family. All other interests, individual, public and social, seem to be subordinated to, and will be sacrificed for, these two."[2]

Early twentieth-century American marriage law reflected wider tensions: the conflicting goals of social order and cultural uniformity; the maintenance of traditional values in the face of dramatic socio-economic change; and the reality of a new social pluralism. Licensing and prohibition, the favored instruments for state control of marriage, were applied as well to drinking, prostitution, and gambling, where (as with marriage) the object of regulation was a mass of small-scale transactions rather than large vested interests.

The major nineteenth-century marriage issue was the property rights of married women. After 1900 it was the making and breaking of marriages. To get married, or to get divorced, came to be regarded less as a private matter between the parties and more as a transaction, like those between capital and labor or between business interests, demanding the attention of the polity. Wide acceptance of the view that social behavior was linked to heredity, and the belief that divorces and desertions were rapidly increasing—the same sorts of perceptions that fed efforts to eliminate prostitution and prohibit the sale of liquor—spurred restrictions on entry into and exit from marriage.[3]

Polygamy, which aroused widespread concern in the nineteenth century, continued to be an object of public attention. The election of Mormons to Congress—Brigham H. Roberts to the House in 1900, Reed Smoot to the Senate in 1902—kept alive a debate between critics who dwelt on the immorality of the practice and apologists who stressed civil liberty and religious freedom. Although polygamy was banned in the major Mormon states of Utah and Idaho, calls continued for a constitutional amendment forbidding the practice.[4]

Antimiscegenation laws were another nineteenth-century legacy that persisted, indeed flourished, after 1900. By 1905 twenty-six states forbade unions between whites and blacks, six banned unions of whites and "Mongolians," four of whites and Indians. Other eugenics-minded constraints multiplied as well: sixteen states prohibited marriages between first cousins; by 1912 thirty-four forbade marriages between lunatics; some included epileptics. In 1912 and 1913 Oregon, Pennsylvania, and Wisconsin passed such "efforts to prevent by law injury to the race."[5]

The marriage contract itself came under closer scrutiny and more detailed regulation. Laws requiring a premarital medical inspection and a marriage license steadily spread: by 1916 two thirds of the states had marriage registration requirements. States gradually raised the age of consent from the traditional common law standard of fourteen for males and twelve for females. By 1913 twelve states had set the age of female consent at eighteen, one at seventeen, twenty-two at sixteen, and two at fifteen.[6]

Before 1900 New York law regarded marriage as a civil contract, and accepted almost any arrangement agreed on by the parties. A revised marriage law in 1901 reclassified it as a type of civil contract requiring authentication to be legal: if not by a clergyman or magistrate, then at least by a notary. Future marriages in the state would not be contractually valid unless they met the new specifications, which included a written marriage contract signed by both parties and two witnesses.[7]

The sexual dimension of marriage was a matter of special delicacy in the nineteenth century. Courts and legislatures touched on it very gingerly. Almost all courts around the turn of the century held that impotence was not ground for annulment, unless fraud could be proven. But there were very few pre-1900 cases that passed on whether or not venereal disease justified an action for breach of the marriage contract. A few American courts held that it was against public policy to enforce a marriage entered into under such conditions, and that a divorce might be granted on grounds of cruelty if the disease was communicated, the plaintiff was ignorant of its existence or nature, or the defendant infected his partner knowingly or willfully.

States began to prohibit marriages if one of the parties had VD. Effective implementation was difficult: a 1913 Pennsylvania law set down a number of grounds for denying a marriage license but left its enforcement to licensing clerks. Wisconsin forbade marriage licenses to males who failed to produce a physician's certificate that they were free from venereal disease. But the law prescribed an unrealistically low doctor's fee of three dollars, thereby earning the hostility of the state medical society. It was challenged in the courts for interfering with religious freedom and unreasonably restraining the right to marry. But the state supreme court upheld the law, on the ground that while the great majority of women were "pure" before marriage, a "considerable percentage" of men were not, and "society has a right to protect itself from extinction and its members from a fate worse than death." The view that the state had a proper interest in seeing to it that procreation was not tainted by venereal disease would be greatly strengthened by the First World War army experience, and came to be widely accepted by the 1920s.[8]

The question remains whether these restrictions stemmed primarily from a "modern" quest for social control, the product of social science and/or class tensions, or from a more traditional, religion-based social morality. True, "the course of modern legislation has tended very generally to do away with the fiction of the common law that by marriage a husband and wife become one legal person." But it was no less true that "at her marriage . . . a woman walks into a complicated legal net whose meshes entangle her the more closely with every step she takes." A number of states in the South and West, as well as Wisconsin and the District of Columbia, had not yet authorized married women to enter into contracts of their own by the end of the nineteenth century.[9]

Attitudes did not rapidly change, but the variety of husband-wife relations, and of public responses, steadily increased. One example was the ever-greater inadequacy of the common law rule that a husband was entitled to benefit from his wife's services, not only in the home but from what she earned outside. Although the spread of separate property acts undermined this doctrine, the courts were reluctant to break new ground. They struck down agreements in which husbands compensated wives for their housekeeping and allowed them to collect accident damages paid to their wives. In many states a husband still could recover for the loss of his wife's services in the home. Some commonwealths recognized the doctrine of relinquishment—that a husband could donate to his wife his right to her services. Many others continued to deny it.[10]

Over time the service doctrine eroded. But consortium, the legal obligation of each marriage partner to provide the other with society, companionship, affection, and protection, was if anything strengthened by the view of marriage as an institution based on mutual obligations. To preserve that relationship, courts turned with increasing frequency to the injunction. In theory this was an attractive remedy, for it served to continue rather than to end the marital relationship, a desirable social end. But judges found it difficult to intervene in so personal a realm of life unless some clear issue of property or monetary rights, and thus of measurable damages, was at stake. And in practice they were not likely to sustain a view of marriage in which the wife was a coequal partner.

For instance, in Texas a husband sued his wife's lover for alienation of her affections and asked a state court to enjoin the lover from having any future association with her. The court granted the injunction; the lover violated it, was cited for contempt, and challenged the court's power to enjoin him. The state supreme court upheld the injunction, citing the right of a husband to his wife's service and consortium.

A New Jersey woman estranged from her husband had an illegitimate child, and obtained a birth certificate on the false claim that her husband was the father. He asked the court to enjoin this, arguing that his wife improperly sought to secure the rights of a legitimate child for her offspring. The court upheld the husband on the ground that he had a property interest in his paternity.[11]

But when a wife brought suit in New York in 1896 against the woman who was living with her husband on the ground that the usurpation of her husband's name was an "assault upon the identity and individuality of the plaintiff, distressing to her" and endangering her community standing, the court refused to grant relief.[12]

Similarly, an Ohio woman in 1924 sought an injunction to keep her husband's lover from associating with him, arguing that this threatened her property right in her husband's consortium. The court refused: "The decree in this case is an extreme instance of government by injunction. It attempts to govern, control, and direct personal relations and domestic affairs."[13]

In a few instances judges were willing to extend the conception of the separate personality of the wife to areas beyond the realm of property. The common law rule that a wife could not be a witness against her spouse gradually was limited to criminal law alone. The rationale was that as the family shifted from a producing to a consuming unit, it was no longer necessary to sacrifice individual justice to the ideal of family unity. And there was a growing readiness (spurred in good part by automobile accidents) to allow wives to sue their husbands.

Nevertheless, the view persisted that too ready access to litigation threatened the tranquillity of the home. An estranged wife in Minnesota set out on a systematic campaign to make life miserable for her husband, publicly charging him with immorality, attacking him on the street and in church, and causing his expulsion from several clubs. The state supreme court refused to grant the husband relief, on the ground (tenuous indeed, given the facts of the case) that torts between a husband and a wife should not be allowed to disturb "the tranquillity of family relations" or "the welfare of the home, that abiding place of love and affection."[14]

American marriage law in 1920 was a bewildering mix of old and new, with substantial variation among the states. Twenty-six states still fully recognized common law marriage, and six partially recognized it. Seventeen still had no fixed minimum age of marriage; nine, including Massachusetts, Missouri, and Pennsylvania, relied on the common law rule of fourteen for males, twelve for females. Only eight states required the filing of a notice of intention to marry. Because of this diversity, the courts held that the law of the place of marriage prevailed when disputes arose over the domicile of the partners.[15]

Not much had changed by the early 1930s. The Commissioners on Uniform State Laws proposed a Marriage and Marriage License Act in 1907; only Wisconsin (and in a modified form Massachusetts) had adopted it by 1930. True, all but three states now required formal marriage licenses. But the freeing up of mores (and the mobility that came with the automobile) in the 1920s fostered the spread of "marriage market towns" where hasty unions could be made: fifty-seven of them in twenty-nine states, according to one survey. Only fourteen states had time limits restricting hasty marriages in 1932. Bills requiring physical examination of potential husbands for venereal disease were regularly defeated in state legislatures. And the courts tended (unless legislation dictated otherwise) to let marriage partners determine their own fitness for union.[16]

Traditional values persisted as well in community property law. California, Louisiana, and Texas, which at one time had been subject to Spanish civil law, adhered to the rule that property ownership was equally divided between the partners to the marriage. But as in common law, the husband was the managing agent of the property.[17]

Common law marriage, another inheritance from the American past, came under growing criticism. The Supreme Court in 1878 had given legal sanction to these unions in order to legitimate their offspring. But the fear that unrecorded alliances could jeopardize property titles, the growth of marriage regulations, and the fact that common law marriages often were followed by formal unions with other partners fed doubts as to their social desirability. New York's new marriage law of 1901 appeared to end the validity of common law marriages in that state. In 1907, however, a general revision of the state's domestic relations law inadvertently repealed its ban on common law marriage. Not until 1933 was the ban restored. By the end of the 1920s the states were evenly divided between those that allowed common law marriages and those that forbade them.

The legal uncertainties surrounding common law marriage were highlighted by the experience of the Bureau of War Risk Insurance in the First World War. About 110,000 soldiers sought to be exempted from compulsory support of wives and children on the ground that theirs were common law marriages. Resolving problems of insurance compensation for common law wives and children made the bureau in effect the world's largest court of domestic relations.[18]

The tension between old verities and new realities in the realm of marriage was evident as well in the law's treatment of emotional issues such as breach of promise, criminal conversation (a third party having sex with a husband or wife), and alienation of affection. While the states remained reluctant to extend the right to sue for loss of consortium, by the 1920s almost every one of them allowed a wife to sue for alienation of affection or her husband's adultery. Some courts regarded the resulting loss of consortium as the deprivation of a property right.[19]

Juries at times awarded substantial compensation to women who claimed breach of promise to marry. Male amour propre was threatened by these often highly publicized cases. The reaction to them was outsized: by 1935 New York, Illinois, Indiana, Michigan, Pennsylvania, and New Jersey had passed laws forbidding "heart balm" suits by women over twenty-one. Indiana's statute was titled "An Act to Promote Public Morals." These laws were justified on the ground that heart balm suits lent themselves to fraud and blackmail, and that to measure damages was difficult.[20]

It appears that the regulatory relationship between husbands and wives did not markedly change during the early twentieth century. In the conflict between the new (and struggling) impulse to expand the separate identity of the wife and the traditional inclination to preserve the patriarchal family, it is not surprising that stasis prevailed. Public policy was devoted more to regularizing the institution of marriage than to redefining the rights of its parties.[21]

The Dilemmas of Divorce

The same social concerns that tightened the terms of entry into marriage made exit from that relationship—the process of divorce—a source of even greater anxiety. The scale of American divorce was in a class by itself. The British divorce rate in 1901 was 2 per 100,000 marriages; the French, 23; the American (in 1900), 70.

Divorce was an issue in early twentieth-century British public life as well; but unlike America, the prevailing concern was with the difficulty, not the ease, of ending a marriage. Reform proposals multiplied, and a Royal Commission on Divorce was appointed in 1909. Its 1912 report recommended that adultery, desertion, cruelty, lack of maintenance, incurable insanity, habitual drunkenness, and imprisonment under a commuted death sentence be the acceptable grounds for divorce. But it paid little attention to the obstacles to working-class divorce; and an 85,000-strong Mothers' Union was against easing the existing law.[22]

A strong current of public opinion in turn-of-the-century America looked on divorce not as in need of liberalization but as a source of social danger. Carroll Wright of the Bureau of Labor Statistics published a disturbing report on American marriage and divorce in 1889 which concluded that the United States granted more divorces than the rest of the Western world combined. A Divorce Reform League lobbied for tighter laws, and in 1896 changed its name to the more evocative League for the Protection of the Family.[23]

Divorce gained a place on the inventory of concerns that gave shape and substance to Progressivism. As with crime, drink, prostitution, political machines, and trusts, a flood of inquiry and speculation dealt with its causes and what might be done about it. Theodore Roosevelt gave the issue national visibility. He told an Inter-Church Conference: "Questions like the tariff and the currency are of literally no consequence whatsoever compared with the vital question of having the unit of our social life, the home, preserved." In January 1905 he called for the updating of marriage and divorce statistics, and proposed a uniform national marriage and divorce law. A special Census report on marriage and divorce found that almost three times as many divorces had been granted between 1887 and 1906 as between 1867 and 1886.[24]

This increase was due to the push of changing social conditions, not to the pull of easier laws. Among those new sources were the insecurities and frustrations of workers in an urban industrial setting, and heightened tensions between affluent couples over the spending of family income. Adultery, desertion, and drunkenness, the staples of nineteenth-century divorce law, now appeared to be giving way to incompatibility and cruelty (though desertion led the causes of divorce in 1916: it and cruelty were responsible for 65 percent of more than 100,000 recorded separations in that year).

Sociologist Edward A. Ross ascribed the rising divorce rate to the growing number of working women who could support themselves. In the North, seven out of ten divorces were initiated by wives (though often with the complicity of their husbands: about nine in ten divorces were consensual). The rising age of marriage also was a factor: the older the age at marriage, the more likely a divorce. Extrapolating from existing figures, Ross predicted that one in four marriages would end in divorce by 1950, and one in two by 1990. He hastened to add: "No one who understands the vital role of the family in a healthy society anticipates any such deplorable outcome." (The actual 1950 figure was one in three; in 1990 almost one in two).[25]

Defenders as well as critics of divorce became more conspicuous. The rising rate, said one observer, was "but the outward manifestation of underlying social evils, a part of the movement for social liberation which has been gaining strength and volume since the days of the Reformation." Another thought that it represented a yearning for better things made necessary by the ease of matrimony: "The greatest social evil in our country is the marrying habit. There is practically no check on marriage." The woman's suffrage leader Elizabeth Cady Stanton icily observed that male judges and clergymen were the primary advocates of a uniform divorce law. Its effect, she warned, would be to make it more difficult for wives to escape unhappy marriages. She proposed instead the continuation of the common law view that marriage should be regarded as a civil contract, entirely under state law, and that the states should be laboratories in which varying views as to the acceptable terms of divorce might be tested.[26]

Most of the rise in divorce occurred despite the considerable tightening of state law. The number of legal causes declined: by 1900 only Washington, Kentucky, and Rhode Island retained "omnibus" provisions permitting courts to grant divorces for any reason they deemed proper. State residence requirements increased, as did restrictions on remarriage. Compared to the still lax marriage laws, divorce regulation embodied "the whole modern theory of social control."[27]

The variety of state divorce provisions was as offensive as the frequency of the practice. They ranged from South Carolina, which flatly forbade divorce, and New York, which allowed it only for adultery, to the more common triad of adultery, cruelty, and desertion. South Dakota went against the grain by adding to its already liberal provisions a reduction of its residence requirement from ninety to sixty days, foreshadowing Nevada's later pursuit of the divorce dollar.

A widely supported (and typically Progressive) solution was the Uniform Divorce Act, approved in 1907 by the Commission on Uniform State Laws. This was supposed to discourage forum shopping by parties seeking a quick and easy parting of the ways. In fact, over 80 percent of divorces occurred in the home state of the parties. And state and federal courts were likely to void divorces from jurisdictions where the plaintiffs were not, in their judgment, bona fide residents, even though they had resided there for the statutory term. Nor was a uniform list of causes of divorce readily acceptable in so theologically and culturally diverse a society. Only Delaware, New Jersey, and Wisconsin had adopted the Uniform Divorce Act by 1930.[28]

At one time it was the legislatures that granted divorces, but they had long since turned this role over to the courts. In a time of attempts to improve the fit between the structure of government and the issues generated by a new society, it is not surprising that what concerned the courts most was conflicting state jurisdiction, "the vexatious question of domicile."[29]

Most courts at the turn of the century held to the view that a marriage valid where it occurred was valid everywhere. But divorce was another matter. Its uncertain social acceptability strained the principle of comity—that a state accepted the judgment of its fellows. Nettlesome questions abounded. For example: If the offending party in a divorce action could not remarry in the state where the divorce took place, could he or she go to another place and remarry? Pennsylvania's supreme court held that this was invalid on grounds of public policy and good morals.[30]

Jurisdictional conflict over divorce came to a head in the 1906 Supreme Court case of Haddock v. Haddock. The Haddocks got married in New York in 1868 but quickly separated. Mrs. Haddock moved to Connecticut, secured a divorce there in 1881 (after pro forma notice to her husband, which he apparently never received), and remarried in that state. A number of years later she sued for divorce in New York as well. The New York court found the Connecticut divorce invalid, arguing that its basis was not acceptable under New York law. The Supreme Court by five to four affirmed the New York decision. The majority presumably wanted to make dubious divorces, such as one obtained without the other party's knowledge, harder to secure. The state in which the marriage took place was the only jurisdiction competent to dissolve it: a triumph of federalism—and an impediment to divorce—in the modern age.

One expert celebrated the result as a victory for husbands: "The husband and wife are for the first time in the history of the common law put upon an absolute equality so far as a right to a divorce is concerned." Others warned that the decision threatened the legitimacy of the children of subsequent marriages, that it cast a cloud over property rights, and that it weakened the constitutional obligation of each state to give "full faith and credit" to the laws of its sister commonwealths. Justice Oliver Wendell Holmes, one of the dissenters, was less apocalyptic. He doubted "that civilization will come to an end whichever way this case is decided." And in fact *Haddock* was widely ignored in subsequent American divorce cases.[31]

Subtly but visibly divorce came to hold a different place in the public consciousness of the 1920s than in the prewar years. Concern over its spread, and the impulse to increase its accessibility, abated. Instead there occurred, as so often was the case with social policy during the twenties, a regularization of the existing order of things.

This was in sharp contrast with the situation in Britain, where the problem of divorce took on new urgency, and a special poignancy, in the wake of the First World War. Failure to enact the reforms proposed by the Royal Divorce Commission in 1912 led to the rapid growth of separation as the only viable alternative. It was estimated in 1917 that half a million couples had parted in the course of the war. Unable to remarry, they were unlikely to produce the children necessary to counter a falling birthrate and the casualties of the battlefield. A 1917 Matrimonial Causes Act sought to make separation convertible into divorce after three years, as French law had done in 1908, and to make easier the legitimation of children conceived or born before wedlock— as, again, wartime France had done in 1915. A Poor Persons' Act, providing state aid for divorce to those needing it, assisted 2,351 of 5,763 divorces granted in 1919.

The British Matrimonial Causes Act of 1923 allowed both sexes access to the same causes for divorce. Previously adultery was the only ground available to a wife. And in 1926 a Court for Divorce and Matrimonial Causes made a judicial divorce available (to those who could afford the legal fees). Before this, only an ecclesiastical divorce or an Act of Parliament could sunder a marriage. The leading legal text on the subject, published in 1910, now had to be largely rewritten.[32]

The myth of the Roaring Twenties notwithstanding, divorce in America still was far from being the everyday event it is today. The rate per 1,000 population changed little: 1.6 in 1920, 1.7 in 1930. The wife remained the party more likely to seek an end to the marriage, and cruelty continued to gain on adultery among the major causes of divorce. Desertion, "the poor man's divorce," surpassed its legal counterpart in frequency. Desertion rates in American cities ranged from 28 to 203 per 100,000; there were an estimated 200,000 instances in 1929.

The frequency of divorce varied widely on the basis of state law, race, religion, class, age, and region (highest in the West, lowest in the East). A study of Minnesota divorce cases in 1921 and 1922 found that it was often the last resort of older people, who had tried to adjust their differences over a number of years. Four out of five times both husband and wife were foreign-born—a measure of the social strain of immigration.[33]

Federalism and the lack of national standards reinforced diversity. A few eastern and southern states continued to have notably archaic provisions, which led to most conflict of laws controversies. Maryland, for example, did not recognize cruelty (mental or physical) as acceptable grounds for divorce; North Carolina did not accept failure to provide, cruelty, or drunkenness; New York allowed only adultery (with two witnesses). Georgia required two jury trials in separate terms of court; Virginia granted a divorce only after three years of separation. While most states gradually liberalized their ground rules and recognized divorces granted elsewhere, those with hard-line policies such as New York, Pennsylvania, Georgia, and the Carolinas relied on the *Haddock* rule to deny the validity of divorces from other jurisdictions. Divorces obtained in Reno and Mexico were particularly frowned upon. The consequence, thought some experts, was patternless chaos.[34]

Divorce reform continued to arouse some muted interest. But potent cultural taboos stunted its development. Even the feminist Charlotte Perkins Gilman called divorce a necessary evil, like a surgical operation. Kansas Senator Arthur Capper led a desultory attempt in the early 1920s to secure a national divorce law (if necessary through a constitutional amendment) with five causes for separation. Among its endorsers were the General Federation of Women's Clubs and the Daughters of the American Revolution. But the existing structure of state regulation, as well as Catholic and much Protestant church opposition, doomed the proposal—just as the child labor amendment went nowhere.[35]

Meanwhile, out in the world of day-to-day life, unhappily married couples made their own adjustments. A study of divorces in Wisconsin's Dane County from 1927 to 1931 found that recrimination, a traditional legal doctrine which held that a countercharge of marital misconduct could void a divorce action, was pled (unsuccessfully) only in 44 of 567 cases, even though both parties appeared to have been at fault in 90 percent of them. What this suggested was that connivance had become the norm in a divorce, despite the legal assumption that it was an adversarial action.[36]

Much as New Jersey and Delaware amended their corporation laws to attract trusts and holding companies around the turn of the century, so did a few states, Nevada most notably, tap the growing market of out-of-state affluents seeking a quick and easy separation. Divorce mills existed in the nineteenth century, but not on the scale, or with the notoriety, that Nevada attained. In 1927 the state reduced the period of time necessary to establish residence from six to three months. Rushed through the legislature, this law was a response to the competition of cheap and quick Mexican divorces, and to the danger that another western state might pass a similar act. The great majority of Nevada newspapers criticized the new law. But there was no arguing with success: forty-eight divorces were granted in the first forty-eight hours after the law was passed.

When Arkansas and Idaho followed suit in 1931, Nevada countered with the six-weeks' residency requirement and closed-door hearing that made Reno the divorce capital of the world. Divorces quickly doubled in number, and the city provided detailed information on how to secure a separation. But the legality of a Reno divorce remained doubtful in a number of states.[37]

On a more theoretical level, too, old assumptions were changing. A "clinical notion of divorce," which called on the courts to play a conciliatory, even therapeutic role, now came into vogue. The legal theorist Karl Llewellyn observed that in the past, economic necessity and social change had forced couples to stay together; now those forces tended to drive them apart. The rise of divorce thus did not necessarily signify the decay of marriage; there were more particular causes such as family convenience or economic necessity. Llewellyn did not want divorce to be too easy, but he thought that mutual consent should be an acceptable basis for separation. Although practice would lag by decades, legal and social thinking by 1930 was well on the road that led from the view that a divorce proceeding was a means of determining legal fault to the view that it was an instrument of social adjustment.[38]

Parent and Child

Public policy affecting parents and children followed a course very similar to that affecting husbands and wives: a gradual increase in the role of the state, tempered by a persisting belief in the essentially autonomous nature of the relationship.

Something analogous was going on in Great Britain. The Children's Act of 1908 codified a long-term evolution from the view that the state enforced the rights but not the duties of the father to the view that government could enforce those duties, restrain parents from abusing their authority, and if necessary take over the responsibilities of parenthood.

French family law remained in thrall to the Napoleonic Code. It was modern in the sense that the rights of the child had more explicit standing than in British common law: "The basis of the French system is not the rights of the father, but the interests of the children. The latter need direction and support, which it is the duty of their parents to afford them." But the parental obligation of support was intimately linked to the child's duty to serve and obey. Sons could not enter into marriage without parental consent before the age of twenty-five, daughters before the age of twenty-one; parents could turn over unruly children to the criminal justice system.[39]

The social worker Sophinisba Breckinridge claimed in the 1930s: "There is no branch of the law which has been more completely revolutionized by statutory amendment than the law of husband and wife and the law of father and child." But she had in mind regulations such as child labor and compulsory education laws. The more intimate aspects of the parent-child relationship were more likely to come before the courts.[40]

What change there was occurred in slow, subtle, halting fashion. Judges appear to have been increasingly responsive to the claims of children even at the cost of property rights, and to have modestly eroded the superior standing of fathers as against mothers. One observer called the process a shift from the old common law assumption of the absolute rights of the parent to a relationship where the child was, as it were, held in trust by the parent.[41]

Thus, a child's contracts came to be voidable if not to its advantage. And common law assumptions about the degree to which a parent was due his or her child's service inevitably came in for a buffeting, given the conditions of modern life. A Georgia father in 1919 obtained an injunction forbidding his daughter's lover from associating with her; but the court relied on the reputation of the family rather than on the traditional ground of a father's right to service. The trend away from the legal fiction of loss of service went hand in hand with a growing sensitivity to the child's own interest. Yet courts were reluctant to reject completely the loss-of-service theory, in part because it was so well ensconced in the law, in part because they feared that to do so would encourage parents to feign injury and engage in other devious practices to keep the service of their children.[42]

The character of the obligation to support one's child also was changing. By the 1920s the great majority of states had made it a general legal duty, not dependent on the child's obligation to provide service. But enforcement was very lax, and almost nowhere before the First World War could a child enforce that right by a legal action against a parent. It was held to be against public policy to encourage suits between child and parent, as between husband and wife. Kansas in 1923 took an important step forward when its court held in a case involving the father of an illegitimate child that the duty to support was enforceable by legal action.[43]

Nineteenth-century American family law had adopted the principle that in custody cases the welfare of the child, and not just the paternal claims of the father, should be taken into account. In practice this meant a greater regard for the rights of the mother than was the case in traditional common law. Yet by 1900 only nine states and the District of Columbia had given statutory sanction to equal guardianship. And the economic disabilities of divorced or separated mothers worked against their pleas for custody. It is a measure of the torpor afflicting family law that not until the mid-1920s did the phrase "for the best interest of the child" enter into general use.[44]

Change came gradually, often in response to public opinion. In 1909 a South Carolinian (the son of Senator Ben Tillman) gave custody of his two daughters to his mother, and then told his wife what he had done. The state legislature responded to public outrage with a law safeguarding the mother's right to her children, and the South Carolina Supreme Court held that Fourteenth Amendment due process protected a child's right against so blatant a misuse of parental authority. But even this incident paled beside Massachusetts's *Narramore* case. An indigent husband gave custody of five of his children to a stranger and consigned the sixth child and his wife to a poorhouse. The distraught mother killed her six children and herself—and the legislature passed an equal guardianship law.[45]

So the doctrine took root, in both courts and legislatures, that the mother had a more than equal right to the custody of her children. A skeptic might note that this change in preference suspiciously paralleled the transformation of children from economic assets to liabilities. But it is clear that the courts were powerfully swayed as well by concern over the welfare of the child, which for younger children usually meant a preference for the custody of the mother. By 1930 most states had made a father's failure to support his minor child a criminal offense (though in so decentralized a polity, enforcement was notably lax).[46]

Acts penalizing parents for failing to obey compulsory education laws or contributing to the delinquency of minors added to the legal proscriptions that defined the parental role. A number of states followed Colorado's 1907 lead in making parents guilty of a misdemeanor if their child was delinquent—although, again, enforcement lagged far behind the intent of the law. Typical of the new concern for children was a 1905 New York law that made child abandonment a felony. Before then it was punishable only as disorderly conduct, and guilty parties could not be extradited from other states. But the traditional judicial reluctance to interfere in family affairs weakened its effect. The New York court held that no felony existed if the abandoned child had been left at home; and charges often were dropped if the delinquent parent agreed to provide maintenance.[47]

The Progressive effort to institutionalize neglected, destitute, or delinquent children and to establish separate children's courts has often been noted (and its intentions questioned). Yet traditional views of parental autonomy maintained a strong hold on popular opinion. The most important constitutional interpretations of the period touching on the family reinforced the autonomy of the parental tie as against the authority of the state. These were the Supreme Court's Meyer v. Nebraska and Pierce v. Society of Sisters decisions during the 1920s, which recognized parents' authority over their children's education in striking down state laws that prohibited foreign-language and private schooling.[48]

The parent-child relationship became more ambiguous in the realms of illegitimacy and adoption. Nineteenth-century American courts and legislatures protected the status of children in these conditions more than was the case in Europe: a republican conception of the family modified traditional attitudes toward blood ties. But those ties gained new strength from Victorian morality and the growing amount of property at stake in family inheritance. By the turn of the century, decisions dealing with the testamentary and other rights of adopted children were notably diverse.[49]

As with divorce, disputes involving illegitimacy or adoption most often took the form of conflict of laws cases. When the domicile of the child was different from that of the father, difficulties arose. The courts in general held to the view that the rights of illegitimate and adopted children, no less than those of their legitimate and natural counterparts, should prevail whenever possible. Usually a court allowed a child living within its jurisdiction to be adopted even though the adopting parents had their residence elsewhere. There was a practical reason for this: the state where the child was domiciled had an interest in its being recognized and cared for by its father. A number of states permitted the legitimation of children in ways other than the subsequent marriage of their parents, and allowed them full inheritance rights at a time when this still was under debate in England.[50]

Norway pioneered in Europe with its relatively liberal bastardy act of 1910. The strongly Scandinavian state of North Dakota followed with a 1917 statute declaring that in the eyes of the law every illegitimate child had full legal standing as the offspring of its natural parents—though it did not provide for adequate supervision or administrative machinery. Minnesota in the same year sought to secure for illegitimate children the care, support, and education that would be their due if they were legitimate. In 1922–23 alone thirteen states established a procedure for the legitimation of children with unwed parents.

But traditional morality and the property rights of legitimate children made further progress in this area difficult. Thirty-nine states had mothers' pension laws by the mid-twenties, yet only Michigan and Nebraska (and, more ambiguously, Wisconsin, with its provision for a "mother without a husband") included unwed mothers.[51]

In 1922 the National Conference of Commissioners on Uniform State Laws proposed a standard illegitimacy act. But it was narrowly framed, focusing on compulsory support for the children. The commissioners had to drop a provision that the offspring of voided marriages should be considered legitimate. Even so, only five states (New York, the Dakotas, Nevada, and New Mexico) adopted the act in some form by 1930. Most courts gave illegitimate children some claim to support, education, and inheritance; and they tended to enforce state legitimation laws fully. Otherwise the treatment of illegitimate children drew more on the model of poor relief than of coequal descent.[52]

The adopted child also bore the weight of traditional constraints. Eight states still did not provide for inheritance by such children by 1930, and there was wide statutory variation in the others. For the most part adopted children could inherit from both their natural and adopting parents, but not from the latter's relatives. The overall impression, as in the case of illegitimacy, is of relatively little change in the legal and policy understanding that existed at the turn of the century. It is a measure of this immobility that with its Legitimacy and Adoption of Children Acts of 1926, British law drew abreast of its American counterpart.[53]

Birth control—Margaret Sanger and others coined the term around 1914—was the most intimate (and the most explosive) family policy issue of the early twentieth century. In one sense it was the quintessential expression of the Progressive search for both social control and social betterment. It promised with little cost and less oversight a solution to poverty and its attendant social evils. But because it sought to regulate human processes as fundamental as conception and birth, the movement evoked a commensurately intense reaction.

Like many turn-of-the-century social causes, the birth control movement was an Anglo-American phenomenon. It began with Britain's Malthusian League, established in 1877. As its name suggests, the League sought to counter the danger of overpopulation, particularly by the poorer and presumably less capable portion of society. At the same time these neo-Malthusians *opposed* the use of birth control by the best and the brightest because they were dangerously limiting the size of their socially desirable families.

Reducing the fertility of the poor majority while increasing that of the elite was not, on the face of it, a vote-winning issue. Conservative Prime Minister Arthur Balfour refused to appoint a royal commission to look into the subject. But in 1911 the regnant Liberals agreed to include questions in that year's census designed to elicit information on the fertility of marriages. (The figures, not published until 1923, showed that in fact widespread family limitation was practiced.) A National Birth-Rate Commission established by the National Council of Public Morals reported in 1916 on the declining birth rate while ignoring the rapid rise of illegitimate births.

The alignment of forces on these issues was complex. The Marxist Social Democratic Federation opposed the neo-Malthusians; the Fabians were more sympathetic. Advocates of birth control listed doctors, churchmen, and especially socialists as their major enemies. But as the human costs of the First World War escalated, many from the same social class that had initially welcomed birth control as a way of reducing the size of poor families now supported spurs to family creation. A National Baby Week (modeled on an American effort) was proclaimed in July 1917.

As the memory of the war faded, so too did British opposition to birth control. Marie Stopes's Society for Constructive Birth Control and Racial Progress, formed in 1921, was dedicated to bringing the gospel to the lower classes; its first clinics were aimed at the working poor. By 1930 the British medical profession was lending its support, the Ministry of Health had accepted it as a legitimate concern of local welfare officials, and the Church of England at its 1930 Lambeth Conference reluctantly sanctioned the practice. In essence the British struggle for birth control had been won.[54]

Nineteenth-century American law identified birth control with pornography and blasphemy. The Comstock Act of 1873 included birth control information and devices among obscene materials barred from the mails. Over half the states followed suit with Little Comstock Acts that made their sale and use illegal. These restrictions were varied, haphazard, and capriciously enforced.[55]

The years after 1900 saw the rise of the nation's first overt pro–birth control movement, centered on the fiery person of Margaret Sanger, a vivid embodiment of the social style welcomed by one sociologist in 1908: "Virtue no longer consists in literal obedience to arbitrary standards set by community or church but rather in conduct consistent with the demands of a growing personality." Sanger very much resembled Marie Stopes, the doyenne of the British movement, in her cultural radicalism and her stress on sexual enjoyment (which may have been why the two were such bitter enemies).

Sanger's National Birth Control League had a conspicuous place in the feisty world of early twentieth-century American social and economic radicalism. The Post Office banned issues of the socialist *New York Call* because it carried articles by her that called on working women to practice contraception. Her pamphlet *Family Limitation* also was excluded from the mails; the Free Speech League and prominent reformers Hutchins Hapgood and Lincoln Steffens defended her.[56]

As in Britain, the social objectives of the American birth control movement were far from clear. Some—such as Margaret Sanger in the early stage of her career—saw in it hope for greater social justice and material well-being for the poor. One couple, declaring that "socialism and eugenics go hand in hand," predicted that a socialist society would make the ability to earn a living a prerequisite for becoming a parent. Others—such as Margaret Sanger in the later stages of her career—questioned the effectiveness of birth control as a cure for poverty, and dwelt instead on the need to improve the national stock: "Birth control is recognized today as a factor in eugenic control."[57]

For all its similarity, the American birth control movement had a very much more difficult time of it than did its British counterpart. In both countries the strong Catholic component of the working class was a major obstacle, but far more so in the United States. The AFL opposed national pro–birth control legislation as hostile to the working class; a pro-immigrant spokesman linked it with the Ku Klux Klan and immigration restriction as an expression of racist nationalism; the American Medical Association did not declare contraception medically safe until 1937.[58]

The grid of state laws against contraceptive devices and information was another formidable obstacle. By 1930 some twenty-six states had anti–birth control laws on their books, ranging from complete prohibition in seven of them to restrictions on sales and advertising. New Jersey's law was splendidly ambiguous: it forbade the supplying of contraceptives "without just cause." And enforcement depended mightily on local attitudes and prosecutorial zeal. By 1926 only thirty-one indictments for disseminating birth control information had been brought under the federal Comstock Act of 1873, twenty-one of them in New York. Nine of these were dismissed, six defendants were freed, five were fined, two were sent to the workhouse, ten were jailed.[59]

The Cummins-Vale bill, designed to repeal the Comstock Act, failed to pass in 1923, as did eleven similar legislative efforts, spearheaded by Margaret Sanger's National Committee for Federal Legislation for Birth Control, between 1930 and 1936. The first significant reversals came when federal courts held that contraceptives were not obscene products (1930), allowed them to be shipped through the mails (1933), and exempted doctors from the Comstock Act's provisions (1936). But full legitimation of birth control had to await the new morality of post–World War II America, the *Griswold* decision of 1965, and the incorporation of sexual privacy into the Constitution.[60]

Even more sensitive—and less respectable—was the related effort to legalize abortion. Antiabortion legislation grew in pace with late nineteenth-century antidivorce and anti–birth control laws. Between 1880 and 1900 the United States changed from a country without abortion laws to one where abortion was legally barred by statute or common law in every state.

The courts broadly defined criminal abortion as any interruption of a pregnancy with intent to destroy the fetus. The only common exception was when it was necessary to save the life of the mother. Only three jurisdictions—Colorado, New Mexico, and the District of Columbia—allowed abortion to preserve the mother's health. As in so many areas of social control, popular reluctance to see the state involve itself too obtrusively in private or family affairs made enforcement difficult. Persistent complaints were leveled at the paucity of prosecutions and juries' unwillingness to convict. But not until after the Second World War would a large-scale assault on antiabortion sanctions be politically and legally feasible.[61]

The most ambitious—and intrusive—act of state interference with procreation was the sterilization of men and women deemed unfit to bear children. Its rationale came from the "science" of eugenics, a belief in the hereditary sources of social behavior. Like so many social policies of the time, it reflected both a desire for social control stoked by class and ethnocultural tensions, and confidence in the capacity of social science–driven public policy to create a purer, more rational society.

Eugenics figured in early twentieth-century social policy-making on both sides of the Atlantic, and appealed as much to the left as to the right. Its British advocates included right-wing elements fearful of the geopolitical implications of a declining birthrate and an inferior citizenry, and liberal and left-wing advocates of genetically engineered social betterment. The Fabians—Sidney and Beatrice Webb, H. G. Wells, George Bernard Shaw—were much taken with this instrument of social planning, as were Harold Laski and John Maynard Keynes.

But for all the intellectual appeal of eugenics, popular distaste prevented its having more than a very limited impact on British public policy. Its major achievement was the Mental Deficiency Act of 1913, the consequence of a 1908 report by a Royal Commission into the Care and Control of the Feeble-Minded. The act increased the authorities' power to detain and segregate such persons, but fell far short of granting the power that advocates such as Winston Churchill called for.[62]

The First World War and its aftermath gave new life to eugenicist thinking in Europe. The staggering loss of life in the war weakened support for population restriction through birth control. But concern over the quality of the surviving population and hope for eugenics as a form of social engineering mounted. The progressive social scientist Edward A. Ross observed that the war had destroyed much of "the sounder portion of the belligerent people." Because of "this immeasurable calamity that has befallen the white race," eugenics was no longer an academic matter: "The fear of racial decline provides the eugenist with a far stronger leverage than did the hope of accelerating racial progress." Both German Nazism and Soviet Bolshevism found much that was compelling in the "science" of eugenics.[63]

The Marxist British geneticist J. B. S. Haldane decried the fact that "the growing science of heredity is being used in this country to support the political opinions of the extreme right, and in America by some of the most ferocious enemies of human liberty." Still, he thought that there was useful work to be done in countering the tendency of the best and the brightest to move into the richer classes while their duller fellows filled the more rapidly procreating ranks of the poor. His remedies: an end to hereditary property, as well as free compulsory education, better housing, and birth control for the poor. But it remained difficult to translate eugenics precepts into law in Britain. Parliament in 1931 defeated a bill to legalize the sterilization of mental defectives. It was in the United States that eugenics had the greatest impact on public policy.[64]

Concern over the genetic makeup of the American people, and the lure of eugenicist remedies, persisted like a low fever in social policy-making during the early twentieth century. Indiana in 1907 enacted a law declaring that since "heredity plays a most important part in the transmission of crime, idiocy, and imbecility," a board of two surgeons and the chief physician of a mental institution could authorize the involuntary sterilization of inmates. Other states followed suit—fourteen of them between 1909 and 1922.

These laws ran into a thicket of opposition. Doctors questioned the utility, lawyers the constitutionality, and many people the humanity of "legalized homicide." Pennsylvania's eccentric governor Samuel Pennypacker vetoed a sterilization law in 1905. (He later reminded a raucously hostile political audience: "Gentlemen, gentlemen! You owe me a vote of thanks. Didn't I veto the bill for the castration of idiots?") The governor of Vermont refused to sign a sterilization act in 1913, warning "against unnecessary and dangerous nostrums in legislation," and the *Nation* detected a "decided reaction from the first fine frenzy of the militant eugenicists."[65]

A number of state courts struck down eugenics laws as violations of the Constitution's equal protection guarantee. New Jersey's high court held that the sterilization of epileptics bore no reasonable relation to its policy object and denied equal protection: "The case in hand raised the very important and novel question whether it is one of the attributes of government to essay the theoretical improvement of society by destroying the function of procreation in certain of its members who are not malefactors against its laws."[66]

Only Indiana and California seriously tried to enforce their statutes. By 1915 some two hundred operations had been conducted in the former state, about three hundred in the latter. But even there, doubts persisted. A committee of the American Institute of Criminal Law and Criminology found "great reluctance on the part of the responsible officials" in the two states "to proceed under the law." Indiana's governor in 1915 thought that the statute was unconstitutional and suspended its enforcement.[67]

Nevertheless, the sterilization of mental defectives won growing acceptance in the 1920s and especially during the early 1930s. It is evident that the fears feeding Prohibition and immigration restriction were at work here as well. Between 1909 and 1927, about one in twelve mental patients was sterilized under California's law, males over females by a three-to-two margin, with no manifest racial or nationality discrimination, and in steadily increasing numbers during the 1920s. Wisconsin sterilized 499 people from 1913 to 1933; 451 were female, in what was defended as an assault on sexual promiscuity. By 1929 more than 5,800 such operations had been performed in California, four times as many as in the rest of the world combined.

The practice of sterilization expanded rapidly during the depression. On January 1, 1928, the cumulative number was 8,515; on January 1, 1932, 12,145; on January 1, 1935, 16,056.[68]

The courts became more receptive to the practice during the 1920s. Michigan enacted a new sterilization law in 1923, and the state supreme court approved it. Noting that "biological science has definitely decided that feeblemindedness is hereditary," the chief justice regretfully observed: "It is an historic fate that every forward step in the progress of the race is marked by an interference with individual liberties." Still, the judicial score by 1929 was that of the ten state eugenics laws challenged in the courts, three had been upheld and seven found to be unconstitutional.[69]

With a brief and "unusually platitudinous" opinion by Justice Oliver Wendell Holmes, the United States Supreme Court by an eight-to-one margin upheld Virginia's law in Buck v. Bell (1927). Holmes's famous rhetorical flourish—"three generations of imbeciles are enough"—nicely summed up the social engineering impulse that fueled sterilization policy. Revealing, too, was the identity of the odd Justice out, the conservative Catholic Pierce Butler, father of eight children, who dissented without an opinion.[70]

Twenty-four states had sterilization laws by 1930. Half a century later twenty still did, though they were severely hedged in by federal regulations. Attempts in the wake of the *Buck* decision to pass sterilization laws in Kentucky, Louisiana, and Pennsylvania failed. An observer concluded in 1927: "The movement to add sterilization to the list of punishments for crime common to the United States has made no headway. On the contrary, the tendency has been to condemn punitive asexualization as repugnant to our institutions."[71]

Sterilization was even harder to justify when it was not a criminal punishment. Opposition stretched from civil libertarians to Catholics, one of whom warned: "The most drastic means so far adopted for the extinction of the individual is sterilization." Many xenophobic native-born Protestants found modern science, genetics, and social engineering—the eugenicist mind-set—unpalatable. The same social values that made it so difficult to legalize the right of a mother to abort the birth of her child limited the power of the state to destroy the capacity to procreate.[72]

There is a notable disjunction here between the scale of public concern about marriage and divorce, the status of children, birth control and abortion, and the degree to which public policy responded. Legislation, and the decisions of the courts, tinkered with and modified but did not substantially alter the laws that governed husband-wife and parent-child relations. Why was this so?

The explanation lies in the deeply ambivalent attitude during the early twentieth century toward the role of the American state. Public interest in family issues clearly grew in intensity, due no doubt to the rise of an urban-industrial, culturally polyglot society. But the belief persisted that the active state was as likely to weaken as to foster the autonomy of the individual, the sanctity of the family, the supremacy of the husband and father. The result: heightened public concern, conflicted and relatively static public policy.

2 · Church and State, School and Society

Churches, other voluntary associations, and schools rank with the family as major American social institutions. Given their importance, one might expect them to have attracted special attention at a time when there was a heightened sense of the need to secure a more cohesive and unified society. But, as in the case of the family, established traditions of individualism, localism, and hostility to state authority, reinforced by the new social reality of a growing pluralism, blunted the force of public policy.

Government intervention in the affairs of voluntary associations was severely limited by historical legacy and constitutional constraint. Courts traditionally did little more than (reluctantly) arbitrate disputes over membership rights; legislatures confined themselves to minimal regulation of what were usually unincorporated bodies.

The changing conditions of life in the early twentieth century raised new issues. In 1930 civil rights expert Zechariah Chafee took up the question of how the new legal interest in individual rights applied to members of voluntary associations. Expulsion might be contested on the ground of a property interest in membership (a view more common in English courts). Or the argument might be made that entry into an association was in effect a form of contract, and thus legally protected. Chafee was bothered by the strained and artificial quality of these approaches. Yet the alternative model—that the relationship between a member and his or her association was equivalent to that between a principal and an agent or a master and a servant—did not seem any more satisfactory.[1]

In practice, noninterference continued to hold sway over regulation. Thus, courts refused to find against the Massachusetts American Legion for censuring an officer who had written a newspaper article attacking his commandant, or Bryn Mawr College for dismissing a student for theft without formal charges or a hearing. Voluntary associations continued, as in the past, to have substantial immunity from oversight by courts and legislatures.[2]

Church and State

Given the social tensions of an urban industrial society and the flood of non-Protestant immigrants, church-state relations might reasonably have become more heated in the early twentieth century United States. Certainly this was the case in England and France, where the interplay of church, state, and school produced major political conflicts.

At the turn of the century there were more than twelve thousand public-supported, church-based schools in Great Britain, all but about a thousand of them owned and operated by the Church of England. The Education Act of 1902 perpetuated the tax-based financing and ecclesiastical management of these schools. A passive resistance movement, led by Welsh Nonconformists, refused to pay taxes for the maintenance of church schools. Thousands of people were summoned to appear before local police courts, and about a hundred wound up in jail.

After their sweeping 1906 electoral victory, the Liberals passed a new law responding to Nonconformist grievances. This act put all elementary schools under public control, eliminated religious tests for teachers and headmasters, and forbade the teaching of the catechism during school hours. But most Tories, the Church of England, Irish Nationalists, Jews, and the Catholic church opposed this attempt to exclude religion from the schools; the House of Lords substantially amended the bill, and it remained stillborn.[3]

Conflict over the relationship of church and state was even sharper in France. The Dreyfus affair emboldened secularists to launch an assault against Catholic schools. The Republican bloc won a sweeping victory in the 1902 election, and Emile Combes, the new premier, adopted a strongly anticlerical policy. During the three years of Combes's government, from 1902 to 1905, one in three Catholic private schools, educating in sum about a quarter of the nation's pupils, was forced to close.

Moderates protested; Bretons rioted. But Combes firmly held to the supremacy of the state: "Liberty of education is not one of those essential rights which are inseparable from the person of the citizen . . . [but] a concern of the social power, which has the right to regulate its usage." A commission under the leadership of Aristide Briand worked out more conciliatory legislation, passed in 1905, which preserved a religious presence in French education—a settlement that would still be a source of conflict in the 1980s.[4]

The experience of the United States was very different. The federal government, which had little say over education, had even less over religion. And when the states sought to regulate religious education, both law and custom weighed heavily against them. Indeed, issues that had a prominent place in nineteenth-century American public life—Bible reading in the public schools, state aid to religious institutions—faded into quiescence during the early 1900s. The Progressive commitment to public policies that in principle transcended class, religion, ethnicity, and region diluted clashes between religious groups and between church and state. And a more secular attitude emerged with the new turn-of-the-century society. As a *Readers' Guide to Periodical Literature* heading succinctly put it: "Infidelity. See Skepticism."

Required school readings from the King James Bible, a contentious nineteenth-century issue, now seemed to be resolved. The Wisconsin Supreme Court held in 1890 that Bible reading in the public schools was unconstitutional, and a survey in 1902 concluded: "There is a growing tendency . . . on the part of the courts to adopt an interpretation . . . which will give the largest possible freedom in the exercise of religious belief." New state constitutions around the turn of the century, and laws in Ohio, Nebraska, Kansas, Mississippi, and Wisconsin, prohibited sectarian instruction in the public schools.[5]

True, there was still much public recognition of religion. A number of states barred atheists from holding office; the Sabbath was widely recognized; some restrictions on blasphemy still stood. Church property was almost universally tax exempt, even when church funds were used for nonreligious purposes. But as one observer remarked, "it is only in a very limited sense that Christianity can be said to be a part of our common law."[6]

Elimination of state aid to religious institutions went hand in hand with doctrinal neutrality. The appropriation of public funds for the benefit of religious schools was forbidden in Massachusetts, Minnesota, Wisconsin, Michigan, Indiana, and Oregon, though this legislation was anti-Catholic in intent, as well as an effort to foster the separation of church and state. And challenges to Sunday laws by Jews and others usually were rejected on the ground that what was at stake was not religious freedom but the state's police power to safeguard the health and welfare of its people. The same argument was applied to the Salvation Army when it opposed police regulations affecting its use of the streets: "The right of the state to protect itself as it sees best is clear."[7]

In an age increasingly conscious of the power of corporations, and of the need of the state to regulate them, religious associations were not immune. New Jersey in 1898 affirmed that its religious denominations had a legal personality. A number of states limited both the amount and the use of church property; Congress put a $50,000 cap on the value of church property in the territories. Most states (New York and Wisconsin were exceptions) held to the view that a bequest to a church for masses for the soul of the donor was illegitimate.[8]

For the most part, however, the American polity kept its distance from the internal affairs of religious organizations. This is evident when one compares the British and American responses to dissenting congregations that challenged the decisions of their church hierarchies. Some Scottish Free Church congregations refused to accept the merger of their sect with the United Presbyterian church, and resisted an attempt to remove them from their church property. The Law Lords of the House of Lords deeply involved themselves in the theological aspects of the dispute, to the extent that one counsel expostulated: "But, my Lords, we are dealing with a subject which requires learning!" They finally decided in favor of the dissenters, on grounds of both public policy and church doctrine.[9]

In America the union of the Cumberland and Northern Presbyterian churches led to similar challenges by Cumberland church congregations. But most state decisions adhered to the Supreme Court's Watson v. Jones (1872) rule that in hierarchical sects the decisions of the superior authority should be allowed to stand.[10]

Perhaps the most sensitive church-state issue at the turn of the century involved the burgeoning sect of Christian Scientists. Their disbelief in the material basis of disease, like Mormon polygamy in the nineteenth century, bred conflict with the authorities. The Nebraska Supreme Court concluded in 1894 that Christian Science therapy belonged under state regulation of medicine and surgery. But the growth of the sect made regulation impolitic, and in 1905 the governor vetoed a law aimed at Christian Science practitioners. Colorado's governor in

1903 vetoed a similar act on the ground that it interfered with the freedom of citizens to choose the medical technique they wanted, and gave state protection to "a trust or combination of certain schools of medicine." The New York and Massachusetts legislatures refused to pass bills subjecting Christian Science practitioners to the states' medical regulations; North Carolina and Illinois specifically exempted them. And the United States Supreme Court held in 1902 that since the effectiveness of mental healing was a "matter of opinion," postal authorities could not treat it as fraudulent.[11]

The growing authority of organized medicine gradually eroded this view. Most courts held that, in general, religious beliefs had to give way to the state's police power over public health. The Pennsylvania Supreme Court in 1903 upheld the denial of a charter of incorporation as a healing body to a Christian Science church. The justices agreed with the finding of a court-appointed master that "the common faith of mankind relies, not only upon prayer, but upon the use of means which knowledge and experience have shown to be efficient."[12]

Two cultural trends—quite opposite in direction but closely related in origin—put new strains on the American church-state relationship during the 1920s. One was the increasing secularization of modern urban middle-class life. The other was a resurgent fundamentalism: in part a response to modernism, in part an instance of the cyclical recurrence of the evangelical impulse in American religion.

These conflicting tendencies confronted each other in the realms of education (most notably in the Scopes antievolution trial) and politics (in Al Smith's 1928 presidential campaign). Conflict increased as well over Sunday blue laws, and over the old issue of compulsory Bible reading in the public schools. Efforts to introduce religious teaching picked up after the First World War, in part because of the belief that "the Bible teaches recognition of, and obedience and respect to the law and established government." Jews and agnostics joined Catholics in opposition. The courts wrestled fitfully, but to no fixed conclusion, with the question as to which parts of the Bible were religious and which were not.[13]

For all this controversy, religion as a public issue did not regain its nineteenth-century level of intensity. The forces of modernity and social pluralism, and the constitutional tradition of separation of church and state, were too strong. The American political response to the Great Depression would be conspicuous for its relative lack of appeals to religious bigotry.

School and Society

Education was an especially rich setting for the swirl of ideas and interests old and new that gave early twentieth-century American public policy its distinctive tone. The family, voluntary associations, and religion had a relatively marginal relation to government. In contrast, if measured by scale of expenditure, extent of popular involvement, and social significance, education might properly lay claim to being the most important function of state and local government during the early twentieth century. Spending on schools absorbed a quarter of nonfederal government expenditure in 1902, a third in 1922, 30 percent in 1932.

Concurrent British experience suggests how the same social problem—the adaptation of schooling to the new conditions of urban industrial life—assumed a distinctive form in each national culture. Education policy in turn-of-the-century Britain was stoked by the need to respond to the economic challenge posed by Germany and the United States, by concerns over national fitness raised by the Boer War, and by a popular demand for greater social equality and opportunity. Compulsory primary education was in place by 1900. But more students were in denominational than public schools, and fees still were charged. The result, according to a Cabinet memorandum, was that the poor "have had to bear a burden which has never been imposed before upon their class in this country."[14]

Nevertheless, the first new educational reform effort had more elite concerns in mind. The Liberals' Royal Commission on Secondary Education, chaired by Lord Bryce, called in 1894 for expanding scientific and technical instruction. Conservative Unionist Prime Minister Salisbury feared that "ornamental, or, as it is now called, technical education" would replace instruction in religion. But the more insistent view favored a "National System of Education . . . What the nation wants is coordination and levelling up all round." John Gorst, the Conservatives' leading educational spokesman, declared: "It is essential to the welfare of the nation that the elementary education given in the voluntary schools should be made as efficient as possible."[15]

The Education Bill of 1902 (introduced the day after the end of the Boer War) replaced local school boards with bodies supervised and in part appointed by borough, county, or town councils. The *North American Review* called the act "a great step towards efficiency," and it was backed by a coalition including Prime Minister Balfour and

Fabians such as the Webbs, who saw in it a greater opportunity for the talented of all classes to get to secondary school. But the Trades Union Council and religious Nonconformists fiercely opposed a bill that did so little for free secular education.[16]

An American magazine observed that the "supreme belief in education as the indispensable ladder to success which pervades and animates America appears, by contrast, to be all but inoperative in England." There, it seemed, "the school system is deliberately intended to keep some down while helping others up." A distinctively British educational mix of state and voluntary schools, separate primary and secondary systems, and continued direction from the central government, with schooling universal, compulsory, and free but "based primarily upon that which is chiefly suitable for the literary class," would persist to our own time.[17]

The politics of education in America was very different. The provision of free, secular education was all but unchallenged public policy. "No other great nation . . . thinks it worthwhile to train everybody for everything—and nothing!—and to do it at public expense," said one observer. Then as now this had its price. American education appeared to be less rigorous than its foreign counterparts. After touring American schools in 1908, the German education expert Friedrich Paulsen chastised them for their weakness and effeminacy, and stressed the need for three educational imperatives: "Learn to obey! Learn to apply yourself! Learn to repress and overcome desires!"[18]

A more efficient, rationalized, and economical school system, so tempting a goal in Britain, had great appeal in the United States as well, for a number of reasons: the interest of American, like British, policy intellectuals in greater national efficiency; the belief that more specialized curricula better prepared students for a complex urban industrial society; the assumptions that ignorance, waste, and corruption were fostered by localized political domination of schools, and that education had to take on the daunting task of "Americanizing" new immigrants and their children. But the politics of the selection, makeup, and activity of urban school boards, of compulsory attendance and other school policy, and of the structure and content of the curriculum were determined by more than the dictates of economy, efficiency, and social control.[19]

Educational policy was very much a national issue in Europe. In

America it was almost entirely decided on the state and local levels. And, as in other areas of social policy, the politics of education was not so much a confrontation along clearly delineated fault lines—the people versus elites, localism versus centralization—as it was an issue shaped by new congeries of interests and ideas. A heightened interest in efficiency and organization did not replace traditional values, but interfused with them in complex ways.

Another element in the turn-of-the-century American educational scene that had no major European counterpart was the sheer size and diversity of the immigrant masses flooding into American cities—and their schools. The constant inflow and outgo (some 250,000 students left school each year, according to a 1910 estimate) of a population ever on the move added to the turmoil. These social facts, and the overwhelmingly local character of school policy-making, gave the politics of American education a special intensity. Educators, reformers, politicians, parents, and voters were in constant, complicated conflict over school policy.[20]

Vocational and secondary education is an example. In Britain as in America the primary issues were curricular (should there be more emphasis on technical training?) and social (should there be expanded popular access?). But the range and depth of dispute was altogether more extensive in the United States. A number of state commissions studied vocational and industrial education, and by 1911 five commonwealths (New York, Massachusetts, Connecticut, New Jersey, and Wisconsin) had "voc. ed." systems. Meanwhile, controversy raged over whether vocational education replaced an undemocratic, unitary curriculum with one that recognized social diversity, or was a device by employers to ensure a trained and docile work force. High schools, too, were regarded either as a highway to a better life for all young people, or as an education subsidized by the many for the benefit of the few: "dead-beat socialism."[21]

The rhetoric of educational reform at times echoed Britain's elite reformers: "The fundamental demand in education, as in everything else, is for efficiency—physical efficiency, mental efficiency, moral efficiency." In 1909 the Russell Sage Foundation's Leonard P. Ayres proposed an arithmetical "Index for Efficiency of Public School Systems," based on the ratio of expenditures to pupil retention, to determine the optimum number of pupils per grade. Another efficiency study concluded that at least 51 percent of high school, 15 percent of elementary, and 35 percent of normal school teachers should be men. A discussion titled "The State and Education" called for a blend of German efficiency with English liberty.[22]

But when John Dewey, the godfather of American progressive education, spoke of "nationalizing education" in 1916, he had in mind "a nationalism which is the friend and not the foe of internationalism" and would recognize the complexity and diversity of the American people. This was Progressivism in its most expansively inclusive mode. Comprehensive high schools open to a wide range and number of students; compulsory attendance laws; curricular and institutional reforms designed to bring all young people into the great assimilating institution of public schooling: these were responses to the demands of a diverse and aspiring population as much as they were instruments of social control. It was this heterogeneity of sources and purposes that gave early twentieth-century educational reform its considerable momentum—and fed its no less substantial limitations.[23]

The effort to change the composition of city school boards from large numbers of ward-based, boss-chosen members to a small number of prominent public figures tells a revealing story. It embodied the Progressive view that politicized, locally controlled education was inadequate (and too expensive, too out of control) for a modern urban society. But local politics, the decentralized nature of the American educational system, and the tradition of popular control of education were not to be lightly shunted aside. "The great problem of public school administration," said one observer, "is to take the schools out of politics and still maintain popular control."[24]

By 1900 a "surprising unanimity" had been attained in the organization of the larger city schools. Only Philadelphia, Pittsburgh, and New York City still had their old systems of local school boards, and these soon gave way to single citywide bodies. The impulse everywhere was to centralize and depoliticize. Municipal courts were empowered to appoint the new school boards in Philadelphia and Washington, D.C. Cleveland's model was the federal government, with an executive (a seven-member board, headed by a director and elected at large), a legislature (a school council), and a professional superintendent.[25]

This trend was not limited to cities. Uncoordinated, expensive country school district systems, and the trustees or directors who ran them, came under growing assault. In Illinois 45,000 school officers and trustees (about one out of every thirteen adult males) employed and supervised 12,000 teachers. Connecticut had 2,100 school officials and 5,100 teachers. According to one observer in 1914, "throughout the state and municipal systems there may be seen a gathering up of the scattered threads of power; instead of the large, unwieldy commissions formerly appointed, the newer bodies are of smaller size."[26]

Consolidation did not go unchallenged. Thousands of Connecticut teachers opposed it in 1917 and 1918. Critics warned that reliance on general rules endangered variety and experimentation, fostered red tape and bureaucracy, and valued efficiency over learning. But for all its apparent uniformity of purpose, the consolidation movement in fact varied substantially from place to place. Nor was it strictly the product of elites seeking efficiency, economy, and social control. School reform was supported in St. Louis not only by professional educators and community leaders but also by the Missouri Child Labor Commission, the general secretary of the Building Trades Council, the Socialist Labor party, and immigrants who saw in compulsory attendance laws a guarantee of their children's free education.[27]

Boston's corrosive Yankee-Irish conflict colored the struggle over that city's schools. A. Lawrence Lowell, a future Harvard president, was elected to the Boston School Committee in 1896. He pressed for a superintendent of schools who would be a true executive officer. Edwin P. Seaver in 1898 sought to be just that, introducing civil service principles in the selection of teachers. But when Lowell's term on the board ended, neither party renominated him. And the board's reformers, under attack as anti-Catholic and for importing teachers into the city, lost control in 1903.

In 1905 the school committee was reduced from twenty-four to five members as part of a more general assault on the ward bosses' political power. The old system had grievous faults. It was estimated in 1901 that about a third of Boston's education tax money was eaten up by waste, inefficiency, and corruption. Favoritism and kickbacks in the selection of teachers and textbooks (Charlestown had its own geography text) were endemic. School reform was defended as "simply a concentration of authority and responsibility for the sake of efficient administration"—but with a caveat: "Concentration for efficiency can never in America be applied, as in Germany it is applied, to the extent of taking the control of the schools out of the hands of the people." Unresolved, the clash between the center and the neighborhoods, between the Irish and other groups, would continue in Boston for the rest of the century.[28]

Chicago's ethnic mix was more varied than Boston's, and educational issues were not so sharply drawn along ethnic or religious lines. But this hardly removed the school board from politics. A 1901 law drafted by the Chicago Civic Federation reduced that city's board from twenty-one to nine members. The new superintendent of schools, Edwin J. Cooley, like his Boston counterpart Seaver, began to appoint teachers on the basis of competitive examinations, and the board sought to strengthen the public school system by adopting free textbooks and opposing support for parochial schools. Progressive reformer Edward F. Dunne, elected mayor in 1905, staffed the board with Jane Addams and two other women, Single Taxer Louis F. Post, and the muckraking journalist Raymond Robins. This unusual group sought to apply John Dewey's progressive education principles to the school curriculum. In 1909 Ella Flagg Young, a student of Dewey's who believed in "scientific method applied to the art of teaching," became the first female school superintendent of a major American city.[29]

A variety of interests gradually blunted the edge of school reform. Superintendent Cooley, chiefly interested in efficiency, resisted the progressive ideas of the board's reformers. The Chicago Teachers' Federation, led by Margaret Haley, which supported Dunne in his race for mayor and was at the peak of its influence, put pressure on the board to renegotiate leases on land in the Loop (the remnants of the original federal land grant for education) so as to increase the revenue available for teachers' salaries. But the board refused to do so.

The progressive complexion of the board faded in the face of political, economic, and ethnic pressures. In the same year the board was restored to its previous size, and teachers were made subject to annual reappointment. Hostility from new board members, Mayor Carter Harrison, and teachers antagonized by Young's policies forced her to retire in 1913. In 1916 the board fired over fifty instructors for belonging to the Teachers' Federation. Soon thereafter it became embroiled in the fevered politics of the era under Mayor William H. ("Big Bill") Thompson, and machine politics superseded progressive educational reform.[30]

Baltimore underwent a strikingly similar experience. Charter reform in 1899 created a new nine-member board of school commissioners—unpaid distinguished citizens—to replace the old ward-based board. Superintendent James H. Van Sickle tried to professionalize his teaching staff, but he faced powerful opposition from politicians, textbook company agents, and teachers seeking higher salaries and fewer promotion exams. Democratic mayoral candidate James N. Proctor in 1911 promised to "popularize the schools"; after his election he quickly removed Van Sickle and the remaining school board Progressives.[31]

This by-now familiar scenario played itself out in New York City as well. The legislature's Davis bill of 1900 centralized educational administration in the newly consolidated city and sought to establish a reliable tax base for the schools. A single citywide board of education of forty-six members was created in 1902. *School* magazine accurately predicted that as a result "the public schools of the entire city will pass into the direction and control of a vast bureaucracy," and so they remain to this day.[32]

But New York's school wars went on. Reformers and politicos clashed over education. Nicholas Murray Butler, editor of the *Educational Review* and soon to be president of Columbia, and William H. Maxwell, Butler's coeditor at the *Review* and the first superintendent of the newly consolidated New York City school system, had experiences similar to those of Lowell and Seaver in Boston. In the name of greater administrative efficiency, the legislature in 1917 reduced the size of the board of education to seven and enlarged the powers of the superintendent. Meanwhile, familiar clashes of interests persisted. Real estate and other economy advocates tried to limit the board of education's authority over teachers' salaries; the board in turn controversially enforced a policy of firing female teachers who married or became pregnant.[33]

There was another element that, while present elsewhere, was so pervasive in New York City as to be unique. This was the ceaseless pressure of the vast immigration of the time, abetted by compulsory education and child labor laws. The elementary school population almost doubled between 1895 and 1915; that of the high schools increased fivefold. There were times when tens of thousands of students could find no place in the schools at all. Despite the expenditure of more than $100 million on new buildings, over 140,000 pupils, twice the 1900 number, still attended school part-time in 1915.

School policy was shaped in large degree by the need to deal with this torrent of students. In 1905 the city's board of education cut back on manual training and domestic arts in an attempt to concentrate more on the three R's. More often the response was to add specialized educational services: kindergartens; classes for mental defectives and crippled, deaf, blind, and anemic children; schools for truants, for older immigrants, for industrial training.[34]

The city also tried to adopt the Gary system, a quintessentially Progressive response to the problems of urban immigrant education. William Wirt, Gary, Indiana's, school superintendent, sought to apply his University of Chicago teacher John Dewey's educational theories, but to do so in a way designed to gladden the heart of the most tightfisted advocate of educational economy. He tried to make maximum use of space by devices such as staggered sessions and frequent study hours. Teachers, organized into departments according to subject, processed relays of students throughout the day. And the curriculum was rich in woodworking, home economics, and other activities intended to prepare pupils for life in an urban industrial society. Between 1914 and 1920 the Gary approach was introduced into 136 schools in 37 cities.[35]

This yeasty mix of Deweyite reform and educational efficiency won the praise of Progressives. Muckraker Ida Tarbell spoke well of it, as did Dewey himself in his *Schools of Tomorrow* (1915). The "Gary System," wrote an admiring Randolph Bourne in the *New Republic* in 1915, was "to treat the public school as a public service, and apply to it all those principles of scientific direction which have been perfected for the public use of railroads, telephones, parks and other 'public utilities.'" Bourne was attracted by the Gary plan's communitarianism, its emphasis on the utilitarian, its attempt to inculcate resourcefulness and self-reliance in immigrant children (and their parents: a rich diet of evening school courses was an integral part of the Gary approach to the school as a community center). But Paul Shorey, author of a traditionalist tract, *The Assault on Humanism*, criticized Bourne for writing socialist propaganda masquerading as a philosophy of education. Another critic darkly warned: "The assumption at Gary is that a child knows better what is good for him than the teacher."[36]

The Gary plan strongly appealed to New York's new mayor, John Purroy Mitchel, an Irish-Catholic lawyer and reformer who had been elected in 1913 as a Fusion candidate pledged to a Progressive platform of economy, efficiency, and home rule. He went to Gary in the spring of 1914, and with the financial support of John D. Rockefeller's General Education Board brought Wirt in to establish his plan in a dozen Bronx immigrant schools.

The result was a firestorm of opposition. Tammany politicians attacked the experiment as an elitist manipulation of pupils, linked to Gary's steel mills and Rockefeller money. This was a major theme of the Hearst press and Democratic candidate John M. Hylan in the 1917 mayoral campaign. At the other end of the political spectrum, school superintendent Maxwell was unhappy with a decentralized reform experiment not under his control. A Catholic observer of one of the Gary system schools charged that the study hours were "merely a storage room for surplus children," and that the system stressed arts and crafts at the cost of the three R's. The result, he thought, would be untrained, characterless children; but "what is the welfare of the child compared with the success of a great, new, wonderful System?" Parent protests escalated to near-riots; a 1918 review of the Bronx Gary system schools by the General Education Board was critical of the results, and the experiment was abandoned.[37]

This episode says much about the complexities—and the realities—of early twentieth-century social policy. It suggests that there was no simple division between Progressives and traditionalists along class lines, and that it is a mistake to assume that the drive for social control swept all before it. Finally, it reminds us once again of how persistent are the issues—the fault lines—in twentieth-century American public life, how rich and complex are their alignments, and how elusive is their resolution.

The social goals that stoked Progressive educational reform were initially reinforced by America's entry into the First World War. John Dewey welcomed the opportunity for "constructive social engineering" which he thought the war provided. One of his more enthusiastic followers proclaimed: "Regulation, cooperation, control are the new catchwords of statesmen, social philosophers and educators, and these are the guides to future action." The expectation was that there would be a postwar "reconstruction" of schools as of other American institutions. There was talk of a new social studies curriculum designed to enable pupils to understand a complex modern society. Not just facts would be taught but social policies as well. The question, according to a Teachers' College professor in 1922, was whether American nationalism would "be left instinctive, crude, and emotional, or be made thoughtful, rational, tolerant, and instructive."[38]

But this Progressive instrumentalism was overborne by the war's darker heritage: xenophobia, illiberalism, pressure for conformity. John J. Tigert, a Kentucky psychology professor who became Warren Harding's commissioner of education, exemplified the trend. A protégé of Interior Secretary Albert B. Fall, he was an active American

Legion member who dwelt on the mission of the schools to Americanize their students, a task that he equated with antiradicalism.

The assault on civil liberties during and after the war left its mark on the schools, most notably in attempts to rid them of pro-German or radical teachers and to prohibit teaching the German language. In New York City, where nearly two thirds of the sixty thousand high school students were foreign-born or the children of foreign-born parents, the board of education launched an inquiry into the loyalty of their teachers. The director said that its purpose was "to see how we can make the people more patriotic and more willing to serve in the army when their time comes." Three teachers were suspended for having subversive views, and after a farcical "trial" their dismissal was recommended. Another half dozen were transferred.[39]

More substantive and long-lasting was the assault on the teaching of German in the public schools. The National Security League took the lead, and received wide cooperation from local boards of education. New York City's board ordered on May 29, 1918, that no classes in German be offered for the duration of the war, and state laws in Nebraska and elsewhere forbade its teaching until the Supreme Court found them unconstitutional. Even without these spurs, the teaching of German went into sudden and irrevocable decline.[40]

The war had another legacy as well: a higher estimate of the social value of education. The primary goal in postwar Britain was not more conformity but greater popular access. The Education Act of 1918 was supposed to enact this admirable objective into law. But it was a severely limited piece of legislation, disappointing labor spokesmen and other advocates of major change. It left undisturbed the 1902 settlement regarding the place of church schools. In theory it extended the minimum leaving age to fourteen; but in 1920 the right to suspend that provision was granted to school authorities. The 1921 report of the Geddes Commission on governmental economy advised against more spending on the schools. And the suspicion and hostility of local authorities dashed hopes for centrally directed expansion. Wasting conflicts over education estimates continued during the 1920s, part of the ongoing Labour-Conservative political strife of the decade.[41]

National education policy—what there was of it—in postwar America focused on the attempt to establish a Cabinet-level Department of Education—"part of the general movement towards the nationalization of all our institutions"—and on a related effort to provide federal support for schools. The Smith-Towner Act, drafted by the National

Education Association (NEA), proposed a Department of Education and expenditures (on a matching basis with the states) for a number of attractive purposes: $50 million for equalizing educational opportunity by improving rural schools; $20 million for health and physical education; $15 million for teacher training; $25 million to help educate immigrants and illiterates. Participating states would have to have school years of at least twenty-four weeks, a minimum school leaving age of fourteen, and required instruction in the English language.[42]

A wide range of groups supported this legislation, including the NEA of course, but also the General Federation of Women's Clubs (who saw in an education department a way of getting a woman in the Cabinet), the American Federation of Labor, hundred of chambers of commerce and Rotary clubs, and the Daughters of the American Revolution. More weighty in the end—for the Smith-Towner bill never passed—were the forces in opposition: leading university presidents, Catholics, educational conservatives, and above all a widespread public disinclination to subject America's schools to the dictates of the national government. Smith-Towner, said one critic, "involves centralization of education in America on a scale that has been hardly dreamed of until now." Yale president Arthur T. Hadley objected to its "Prussian" spirit; the liberal Catholic journal *Commonweal* called it "Mussoliniism."[43]

A subsequent proposal by the Harding administration for a Department of Public Welfare responsible for education, health, social services, and veterans' relief fared no better. Educators feared that education would be engulfed in this portmanteau department. *School and Society* reminded its readers of the dark history of politicized education; warnings abounded that the schools should be kept from "federal bureaucratic control."[44]

The idea of a Department of Education and Welfare continued to lead a half-life during the 1920s. University presidents condemned it at a congressional hearing in 1924. In 1929 it resurfaced; a proponent argued the need for a department "so that all the people . . . without regard to race, creed, or color, shall have larger educational opportunities and thereby abolish illiteracy." But advocates of states' rights, those suspicious of a larger bureaucracy, and a massive state and local educational establishment already in place defeated these efforts.[45]

To more evident effect, the war reinvigorated the search for educational efficiency. Educational surveys, an increasingly regulated teaching profession, and more bureaucratic school administration proliferated. A 1927 Index of Holding Power found that the Washington and Oregon school systems had the strongest grasp on their students, South Carolina and Georgia the weakest. The goal of this exercise was to provide a way of judging profit and loss in the education business. *Bankers' Magazine* responded to a report that Americans spent more on automobiles than on primary and secondary education, more on chewing gum than on schoolbooks, and that day laborers earned more than teachers: "We pay the day laborer more than the teacher because he is worth more—because he produces a service of great value to society—just as the corporation-manager is paid more than the preacher."[46]

In response to the rapid growth of high schools, the federal Bureau of Education in 1918 sponsored a study by the NEA's Commission on the Reorganization of Secondary Education. This body produced a report that has become a black classic in the literature of Progressive education. It listed seven objectives for secondary school curricula: health, home membership, vocational training, citizenship, the use of leisure, ethical character—and what it called "command of fundamental processes": reading, writing, and arithmetic. Its chief recommendation was that objective most dear to educational (or any other) bureaucrats: reorganization—in this case into six years of elementary and six years of secondary education. The commission explained in its opaque prose that "increased attention to specialization calls for more purposeful plans for unification," and prescribed the expansion of "electivism"—which turned out to mean more vocational training. It added, almost as an afterthought: "Provision should also be made for those having distinctively academic interests and needs." A Catholic critic noted that the report ignored the educational value of language teaching, and had nothing to say about inculcating clear thinking, judging, reasoning, developing the imagination, or cultivating taste.[47]

The forces that worked against prewar educational reform persisted throughout the 1920s. A movement in Delaware, with Pierre du Pont taking a prominent role, sought centralized educational administration, a longer school year, and higher school taxes, and a 1919 law was designed to achieve these ends. But a strong popular reaction headed by Daniel J. Layton, a Democratic politician, led to a revised law in 1921 that restored some of the powers previously given to the county boards.[48]

More important than abortive attempts at federal regulation or a persisting belief in the lodestones of efficiency and the whole child was the response of the postwar schools to the rapidly mounting day-to-day demands placed on them by a modern urban industrial society. More varied, specialized education increased; steadily larger sums were spent by states and localities on teachers and school buildings; and high schools began to take on the universality that had previously been limited to the primary schools. Elementary and secondary school expenditures more than doubled, from $1 billion to $2.3 billion between 1920 and 1930. Staff expanded from 700,000 to 900,000; the proportion of seventeen-year-olds with high school diplomas went from 16.8 percent to 29 percent.[49]

The adaptation of American education to a more diverse clientele began before the 1920s, but it became a characteristic feature of educational policy and practice during the postwar decade. The massive number of articles on education listed in the *International Index to Periodicals* for the years 1924–1927 dwelt not on large issues of policy but on adjusting, expanding, and improving an already complex system. About 1,200 education laws were passed in the United States between 1926 and 1928. Many of these revised and codified existing statutes; often they were the result of surveys and investigations; the trend was to vest greater responsibility in state boards of education.

Educational policy in prewar New York City had been dominated by the sheer scale of its immigrant inflow and the consequent issues of expansion and social control. The city's school population tapered off after 1924, the result of immigration restriction, a declining birthrate, the growth of the suburbs, and increasing private and parochial school enrollments. Education issues in consequence became more qualitative and organizational.[50]

This trend was evident in rural education as well. The most notable development was continued school consolidation, hastened by the proliferation of better roads, buses, and autos. Iowa had 17 consolidated schools in 1913 and 340 by 1920, with more being added at the rate of one a day. The county became the key unit in educational affairs outside the large cities, taking over power from local school districts.[51]

The courts frequently dealt with issues of transportation in the new consolidated school districts. They rarely questioned the constitutionality of state school transportation laws, even though these eroded the traditional autonomy of local school districts. Judges regarded the transportation of pupils as a way of equalizing educational opportunity, but to be used with discretion. Some held that only districts getting state funds could transport children. The Kansas and Iowa courts decided that their states' busing laws applied only to grade school children, the Texas court that its law did *not* apply to them. The Colorado Supreme Court held in 1931 that long waits for buses and substantial distances traveled—products of the state's ambitious consolidation movement—violated the constitutional requirement to maintain a public school in each school district. But in general the massive consolidation of rural school districts proceeded without judicial hindrance.[52]

Certification of school superintendents became common. A 1919 Iowa bill "to legalize the profession of superintending" was justified on the ground that "it is apparent that the only way in which a strong profession respected enough and with opportunities enough to induce worthy red-blooded young men to enter it for a life work . . . is by setting up standards and legalizing them." At the same time, consolidated school boards lost the more representative social character of their local predecessors. A 1928 study found that half of a sample of male board members were proprietors, half were members of the professions.[53]

For all this, educational politics proceeded along familiar paths. School superintendents in Terre Haute, Indiana, and Newark, New Jersey, were driven from office by political pressure. Atlanta's superintendent Willis Sutton fought constantly against the economy and efficiency inclinations of the city's business elite. Democratic mayor William Dever made William McAndrew Chicago's school superintendent in 1923. Dever's Republican adversary William Hale Thompson regained the mayoralty in 1927, attacking the British-born McAndrew for fostering too pro-British a tone in the history taught in the city's schools. The school board dutifully conducted a highly publicized "trial" of McAndrew, which was still under way when the superintendent's term ended in January 1928.[54]

Teachers had an increasingly difficult time raising (or even preserving) their status. They remained torn between their desire to be regarded as professionals and the need to defend their interests through unionization. Female teachers in particular faced severe cultural pressures. Even in the late 1920s more than half of America's larger cities required them to leave when they married; and almost no American public schools hired married women. New York City's board of education had a longtime policy of refusing to appoint or reappoint married women and of firing those who had children. "It goes without saying," an observer concluded, "that a school board in employing teachers can discriminate as it pleases on the basis of marriage, religion, or politics."[55]

Standards regarding the physical appearance, dress, health, speech, and "personality" of teachers increased during the 1920s. The American Federation of Teachers and local unions fought this trend, but the going was hard. Three Fresno members of California's Teachers' Federation were fired for "incompetency" in 1921, and superintendent of schools Jesse Cross announced that it was time "to use base ball bats, or perhaps gatling guns" in dealing with the federation's leaders. Reformers sought to overthrow the school board, but the city's leading newspapers supported it; superintendent Cross was reelected; and five more teachers were fired for being active in the election campaign.[56]

The Seattle school board required its teachers to sign "yellow dog" contracts pledging not to join the American Federation of Teachers. The state supreme court in 1931 upheld this stipulation on the ground that it was "immaterial whether the reason for the refusal to employ . . . is because the applicant is married or unmarried, is of fair complexion or dark, is or is not a member of a trade union . . . The board is not bound to give any reason for its action. It is free to contract with whomever it chooses." School board elections were fought out over the union issue, and finally the board dropped its antiunion rule.[57]

The courts were comparably reluctant to recognize the rights of students. Dress codes and other regulations were regularly upheld. The Arkansas board of education banned transparent hosiery, low-necked dresses, clothing styles tending to immodesty, and cosmetics ("face paint"). A Miss Pugsley insisted on wearing talcum powder despite this ukase, and was suspended; the state supreme court refused to reinstate her.

Still, deference to parental scruples and to a student's vested right to an education carried weight. When a California school board added dancing to its curriculum, a judge refused to let a pupil be expelled for refusing to participate on religious grounds. And when a diploma was denied because of a student's refusal to wear a cap and gown at graduation, the Iowa Supreme Court ordered that both diploma and transcript be delivered to the miscreant. Courts in general inclined to the view that a student's residence in a school district, even if the legal domicile was elsewhere, guaranteed access to the local school.[58]

The overtly contractual basis of the student-school relationship in private colleges fostered some reluctance to allow them free rein in expulsions. When Syracuse University sought to reserve to itself the right to dismiss a student without giving a reason, a New York court held this void, as against public policy. But the Pennsylvania Supreme Court refused to compel the readmission of a Bryn Mawr student expelled for "undesirable conduct" as defined by the school's president.[59]

The rapid spread of high schools created another substantial new realm of educational controversy. Illinois high school districts began to tax and issue bonds, with irregularities and controversies following as the night the day. The state supreme court held that the directors of a high school district did not have the power to levy a tax, and that many of these districts in fact were illegal. The legislature responded in 1921 with nine "Curative Acts" designed to legitimate "compact," "compact and contiguous," and "community" high schools. About twenty high school cases came before the court in 1921–22, and it bowed to the inevitable by agreeing that the legislature could retroactively authorize a high school district to levy taxes. But it was evident that new school laws were needed to handle board elections, revenue, relations with municipal corporations, and other issues raised by the creation of these new districts.[60]

Money, not ideology, was at the heart of school politics during the 1920s and 1930s. A dramatic expansion of the American educational system coexisted with deep antitax attitudes. Education policy evolved in close conjunction with financial adequacy. The New York legislature in 1919 linked minimum salaries for teachers in urban schools to expanded compulsory education and the extension of night and factory schools to Americanize the foreign-born. Governor Al Smith in 1925 justified the improvement of rural schools and equal pay for male and female teachers by the need to increase educational efficiency. But he vetoed a flock of bills giving a mandatory salary increase to New York City teachers, accepting the argument of city authorities that they did not have the money to pay for it.[61]

Increased spending had the effect of magnifying the differences between better- and worse-off districts. State school support had declined from almost 24 percent of the total in 1890 to 16.8 percent in 1918; local and county aid took up the slack. Now, in the 1920s, almost every state tried to lessen internal disparities by expanding state aid to poorer communities and by creating larger school districts. Delaware was by far the leader in state-collected school revenues during the mid-1920s: 92 percent as against a national average of around 20 percent.[62]

The need for additional funds fostered reliance on the techniques of modern public relations. Supporters of a new school bond issue waged an intense, highly organized campaign in San José, California, in 1924. Pamphlets and fliers were printed in high school print shops and distributed by students. On election day voters were polled by telephone, cars were mobilized to bring voters to the polls, school bands paraded. Of 18,000 registered voters, only 602 opposed the measure.

Los Angeles's 1927 school bond campaign was the largest and most successful of the period. The assistant superintendent of schools boasted: "We conducted our publicity campaign very much the same as a business firm advertises a new product." Private funds and organized labor were used in the campaign; students were mobilized to remind their parents to vote. The nearly $35 million bond issue was approved by a two-to-one margin.[63]

For all the national pressures changing the scale and scope of American education, its basically local character altered little. An observer concluded in 1931: "Despite a certain degree of progress in matters of centralization, administration, and control, and despite utterances of educational threats and court decisions to the contrary, schools in the United States continue to be in fact local institutions dominated by the traditions and policies of district and town systems." But this did not lessen the tension between old social values and new social realities. The pervasive ethnocultural conflict of the 1920s gave as distinctive an ideological tone to education policy as the Progressive desire for progress, efficiency, and order had in the prewar years.[64]

A study of state laws regulating curricula found that in 1904 there were few prescriptions except "prohibition of the teaching of religion and the religion of the teaching of prohibition." But by 1924 eight times as many laws prescribed what should be taught, including language (English only), American history, Americanization, fire prevention, first aid, kindness to animals, conservation, and thrift. One observer noted how little in the way of constitutional rights protected school curricula from the pressures of conformity.[65]

One thing changed little: racial segregation and discrimination. The pattern so firmly imposed during the late nineteenth and early twentieth centuries did not alter in the 1920s, despite the large-scale flow of blacks out of the South and into the cities. When thirty-four black children sought admission to a new school in Toms River, New Jersey, in 1927, a separate school was set up for them in the one-room African Methodist church. The pupils refused to go: most were Baptists, and the building and facilities provided were inferior. They were charged with truancy. The authorities argued in extenuation of the students' exclusion from the regular school that they were behind their peers, since most were from families newly arrived from the South (an argument not applied to other recent immigrants).

The coming of widespread secondary education only strengthened educational separatism. Twelve hundred of the 1,900 white students in the Gary, Indiana, high school walked out to protest the enrollment of black students in 1927. The city council appropriated $15,000 for the immediate construction of a temporary school for blacks. The three black members of the council opposed this, to no effect. Although the *Chicago Tribune* criticized the strikers and the city council as un-American, the authorities went ahead with plans to build a separate high school for black pupils.[66]

The hoary Protestant-Catholic clash over educational issues also continued during the 1920s. Massachusetts in particular was a battleground. That state's Catholic hierarchy opposed state aid to education as long as a constitutional ban against aid to private (read: parochial) schools prevailed. It frowned as well on compulsory physical education, which it saw as a cover for sex education. And while Massachusetts, New York, and Pennsylvania forbade religious tests for public school teachers, Ohio and other states did not, and discrimination against Catholic and Jewish applicants for teaching jobs was widespread.[67]

The most highly visible conflicts over educational policy pitted the culture of a modern, urban industrial, pluralistic society against the older, more unitary localistic culture that it was superseding. This is evident in confrontations which raised important questions about the character of American education. The issues at stake—religion and education, immigration and ethnicity, the respective powers of parents and professionals, local preferences and national opinion—made these emblematic confrontations. But their results support neither those who define the educational history of the period as the triumph of corporate-elite social control or those who see the 1920s as the time of the triumph of American nativism.

One of the most enduring issues in American education is the place of English and other languages in the school curriculum. It stretches back well before 1900, and forward into the late twentieth century.

The First World War and after seemed an ideal time for an English-only policy. The Rhode Island legislature passed a bill in 1921 providing that an old English-language-only law (directed primarily at French-Canadian parochial schools) be enforced in all private institutions. The law went into effect in 1922, and became a major issue in the November election. The Democrats, victorious in the Assembly, proposed a new law easing the English language requirement in private schools. A coalition of respectables, including the *Providence Journal*, the League of Women Voters, the state board of education, the Veterans of Foreign Wars, the American Legion, the Unitarian Laymen's League, and the Federation of Women's Clubs rose up against modification. The entrenched rural, Protestant Republican Senate majority rejected the measure, and the more restrictive language law remained on the books.[68]

But the result was different when the language issue entered the national scene. The Supreme Court in Meyer v. Nebraska (1923) reviewed wartime Nebraska, Iowa, and Ohio laws that forbade the teaching of German in public and private schools. In this first Supreme Court decision on educational policy, Justice James C. MacReynolds's majority opinion struck down the laws on the idiosyncratic grounds that they interfered with freedom of occupation by depriving German teachers of their livelihood without due process, and that experience taught that proficiency in a foreign language was "not injurious to the health, morals or understanding of the ordinary child." Hence its prohibition was beyond the police powers of the state. The conservative MacReynolds avoided what to him would have been the embarrassment of applying the First Amendment. Holmes dissented, defending the right of state legislatures to shape their educational systems as they chose.[69]

An even more evocative controversy swirled around a 1922 Oregon law that made public education compulsory. Endorsed by the largest majority in the history of the state's vaunted popular initiative system, this assault on Catholic parochial schools was the product of a coalition dominated by the Ku Klux Klan, the Masons and other white Protestant fraternal associations, and the Federated Patriotic Societies. Their campaign dwelt on the elitism of private schools, and on the common school as a universal melting pot in which "one flag, one school, one language" (a chilling foretaste of the Nazis' "ein Land, ein Völk, ein Führer") would be taught. A substantial coalition fought the bill, including Catholics and other sects with a stake in church schools; businessmen fearing the taxes that an expanded public school system would bring; and the press, both secular and religious, bothered by the substance of the bill and by the unfavorable notoriety that it brought to the state. The *Literary Digest* observed: "Whose is the child? So far as its education is concerned, Oregon has answered that it is the state's."[70]

The Oregon school law came before the Supreme Court in Pierce v. Society of Sisters (1925). Amicus briefs in support of the plaintiffs were filed by the Episcopal church, the Seventh-Day Adventists, and the American Jewish Committee. As in Meyer v. Nebraska, McReynolds struck down the law on grounds that emphasized rights of property rather than First Amendment freedoms. The decision was unanimous, and so was press comment in favor of it. There was a line between state and church, and a pluralistic character to American education, that could not be readily denied.[71]

The most notorious case of the decade, in which educational, religious, and cultural conflict conjoined to stunning dramatic effect, was the Scopes trial in Dayton, Tennessee. In 1925 that state's legislature passed a law forbidding the teaching of Darwinian evolution in the schools. John Thomas Scopes, a young Dayton schoolteacher, was charged with violating the statute. His trial became a cause célèbre for conflicting views over local and state control of education, science and religion, modernism and fundamentalism, urban and small-town American culture. With William Jennings Bryan representing the state as the voice of fundamentalist Creationism, and Clarence Darrow representing Scopes as the voice of the new urban rationalism, the trial became a resonant expression (like the Hoover-Smith election of 1928) of the ethnocultural conflict that dominated American public life during the 1920s.[72]

This was no simple, straightforward confrontation between the forces of light and the forces of darkness. There was a strongly democratic, populist strain in the fundamentalist position. Bryan made much of "the right of the people to have what they want in government including the kind of education they want." Legislators, not boards of education or scientists or teachers, were the most direct spokesmen of the popular will. A British commentator observed that farmers and villagers elsewhere in the world knew no more of science, "but in other countries I doubt if these people insist on their beliefs so independently. In the American body politic it is not enough to state a fact upon the highest authority. It is necessary to convince the majority."[73]

Twenty-one state legislatures considered forty-one antievolution laws between 1921 and 1929, though Mississippi and Arkansas were the only states besides Tennessee to adopt them. Sixty-three percent of Arkansas voters endorsed that state's law in a 1928 initiative. The vote overrode variables such as number of Baptists, level of illiteracy, and degree of rural population, and the law stayed on the books for forty years, until the United States Supreme Court found it unconstitutional.[74]

Support for the Tennessee antievolution law came from a variety of sources. A Catholic lawyer was conscious of the danger of anti-Catholic bigotry and the invasion of civil and religious liberty that it posed. But he regarded evolution as a doctrine unfit to be taught to young people, and was bothered by Darrow's blasphemous approach to the teaching of religion. Reform-minded lawyer David Lilienthal, who would run the Tennessee Valley Authority in the 1930s, had some doubts as well. The states had long acted as social laboratories. But now it was being argued on constitutional grounds that Nebraska could not ban the teaching of German, that Oregon could not forbid private schools, that Tennessee could not exclude the teaching of evolution.[75]

The major organs of opinion, both secular and religious, supported Scopes. Modern-minded religious leaders accepted that the authority of the Bible could not be ensured by legislation. Judges and lawyers questioned the constitutionality of the Tennessee law; a *Tennessee Law Review* article argued that the statute did not come under the state's police power because it dealt with fact and opinion, not health or morals. Another critic warned that to teach Creationism was to provide state aid for sectarian instruction and to ignore "the trend of scientific and scholarly elevation, and . . . the consensus of opinion of specialists in education who have chosen teaching as their profession."[76]

The press, taking its cue from H. L. Mencken's caustic account of the trial, subjected Bryan and his views to national ridicule. A Kentucky antievolution bill failed to pass by one vote; similar laws were defeated in Missouri, in North Carolina, and (overwhelmingly) in Georgia. Nor did other attempts to inject religion into the curriculum fare any better. Bills in Indiana and Ohio providing for Bible reading and instruction in the schools were vetoed; a proposal that the Ten Commandments be read in New York City's public schools was condemned by clergymen of all faiths.[77]

The ultimate disposition of the Scopes case reveals how insecure was the cultural support on which the Creationists relied. The Dayton judge found Scopes guilty. Tennessee's supreme court in 1927 upheld the antievolution law, but decided that the $100 fine imposed on Scopes was unconstitutional because he had not had a jury trial. It suggested that the prosecuting attorney drop the matter: "We see nothing to be gained by prolonging the life of this bizarre case. On the contrary, we think the peace and dignity of the state . . . will be better conserved by [its dismissal." And so it ended, not with a bang, or even a whimper, but with a wheeze.[78]

More significant than these attempts to control education from a religious—or any other—point of view was their paucity and lack of success, even in so culturally tense a time as the 1920s. For all its transforming power, the Great Depression also failed to alter decisively the shape and substance of American schooling. The leading work on the subject concludes: "The history of the public schools in the Great Depression might be summarized as one of short-term dislocation and long-term continuity."[79]

Advocates of educational Progressivism thought to find in the depression an opportunity denied them during the 1920s. Dewey's disciple George S. Counts of Columbia Teachers' College wanted the schools to dedicate themselves to "social reconstruction," a yeasty mix of collectivism, expertise, science, and technology. American education needed to be centrally directed; teachers should organize themselves into a national profession; school boards should be made up of people "whose position in society rests not on property but on some form of labor or service."[80]

The right had its own way of coping with hard times: by 1936 twenty-one states required teacher loyalty oaths, fourteen of them since the beginning of the depression. But as always, the bulk of teachers and administrators were indifferent to political indoctrination from the left or the right, dwelling instead on the timeless issues of school finances, facilities maintenance, and that always fragile vessel, the character of youth.[81]

It was in the realm of these bread-and-butter concerns, not in the loftier reaches of ideology, that the depression was most strongly felt.

By 1932–33 budget cuts ranged from 3 percent in the North Atlantic states to 16 percent in South-Central cities. The poorer states and districts suffered most. By April 1934 about twenty thousand rural schools had closed, affecting almost a million students. Black education in the South, already minimal, was further devastated: funds for black schools sank to levels not seen since Reconstruction.

The sharpest reductions in city schools affected not teacher-pupil ratios so much as the special programs added in recent decades— Americanization and adult classes, summer and night schools— though the impact of these cuts was lessened by the decline in the number of immigrants. At the same time, secondary education continued to grow, helped now by the lack of jobs. There were 3.9 million high school students in 1929 and 5.7 million in 1934, owing in part to a sharply higher retention rate.[82]

What shielded education from the full force of the depression? The virtual end of immigration and a declining native birthrate left its mark. So did the inertial force of the school system, helped by the popular belief in children as the society's future (and in the schools as social safety valves). In 1933–34, 133 communities voted on whether or not to exceed state-mandated minimum school budget increases; all but one favored doing so. Hard times were eased, too, by a substantial shift from local to state financing. The share of school budgets supported by the states nearly doubled during the 1930s. Often this was the result of a potent political alliance of the schools with homeowners, farmers, realtors, county supervisors, local tax leagues, and others with a stake in seeing education costs shifted to a higher level of government.[83]

While much of the schools' depression experience was determined by the national economic disaster, local conditions varied widely. Affluent districts of course did better than poor ones. But leadership and political culture also made a difference. Thus, in both Chicago and Detroit the already substantial power of local banks and business leaders over school budgeting became even greater in the face of impending municipal insolvency. Corrupt politics and the risibly low valuation of commercial buildings on school-owned land had put the Chicago schools in jeopardy even before the depression hit. The city's teachers had payless paydays as early as December 1929, and by May 1932 the city owed them $20 million in back salaries. In July 1933 the school board voted to fire 1,400 teachers, 10 percent of the city's staff. Teachers, parents, women's clubs, and other groups formed a Save

Our Schools Committee and got 350,000 signatures on a petition of protest, to no avail. Detroit was a different matter. Superintendent of Schools Frank Cody was a skillful politician and publicist; Mayor Frank Murphy was sympathetic; firings were avoided, and the city's educational program was preserved.[84]

The traditional character of American education was no more altered by the New Deal than by the Great Depression. The new political dispensation led the National Education Association and other groups to resurrect the phoenix of federal aid. Their hopes were dashed, for a revealing set of reasons. First, New Dealers shied from trying to work within the existing structure of schools, and sought instead to innovate in their own agencies, such as the Civilian Conservation Corps, the Works Progress Administration, and the National Youth Administration. Also, Congress continued to be highly resistant, for (unlike welfare, public works, or agricultural and industrial policy) direct federal aid to education raised enormous political problems: the question of parochial schools, the threat to racially segregated education, the powerful tradition of local control. Only vocational education, with well-established links to Congress, was able to secure direct federal aid.[85]

Inevitably, education policy in early twentieth-century America reflected the changing public mood: the Progressive fixation on efficiency and social cohesion before the First World War, similar values in a more xenophobic and repressive guise during the 1920s. But through it all, other social facts asserted themselves: the continuing influence of past principles and practices; an increasingly pluralistic culture; perhaps, above all, the pressing day-to-day realities of paying for and operating increasingly complex and expensive school systems that were intensely local and intensely political. Who, then, controlled—"ran"—the schools? In the larger, sweeping sense, no one: they were too local, too numerous, too varied. In the more immediate, on-the-ground sense: the complex, ever-changing American mix of interests and ideology, old ways and new circumstances.

II · ISSUES

Cutting across the structure of institutions were social issues defined by politics, law, and government. Some of these were as old as America, as old as society itself; some were products of the new society. Old or new, they took on a distinctive tone in early twentieth-century American public life.

The most important social issues of the time reflected the dominant concerns of a new urban industrial society. They ran the gamut from suddenly more important, and primarily legal, issues of identity and expression—involving the interests of personality (slander and libel, privacy, mental suffering) and civil liberties (freedom of speech and of the press)—to old challenges to peace and good order, now heavy with new social meaning: sins of the flesh (drinking, drugs, gambling, prostitution); crime and what to do about it; poverty and welfare. Here were played out many of the most passionately contested and socially meaningful policy conflicts of the early twentieth century.

3 · Private Rights and Civil Liberties

The conditions of modern life changed the social context of individual rights. Larger, more impersonal settings—factories and offices, distended cities, a culture shaped increasingly by mass media and mass consumerism—brought with them fresh threats to the integrity of the self. But the new facts of modern urban industrial life did not mean that collective social values effortlessly displaced a more individualistic American past. Instead, the challenges of the new society compelled the polity to reconsider an old issue: the place of the individual in society.

The Interests of Personality

Torts—the harms suffered by one person because of the negligence of another—were as old as the common law. The rise of a machine civilization greatly expanded the character and number of the injuries to which not only flesh but the spirit might fall victim. True, the anonymity of the factory or the city could mean freedom: escape from the constraints of the farm, the small town, the neighborhood, the extended family. But the new social environment brought its own fresh dangers as well, among them threats to the "interests of personality," a phrase coined by the Harvard law professor Roscoe Pound in 1915.

Pound noted that "injury to the nervous system, mental injury, and injury to sensibilities, where there is no physical injury or no injury to substance or to any relation is a new problem of modern law." The issue here was not the relation of the individual to the state, but the more subtle and elusive question of the infringement of one person's rights by the actions of another. In the past it had been necessary to distinguish individual from corporate or public interests. So now was it necessary to define "the expanded individual life."[1]

The injunction, which before 1900 had served primarily to restrain strikers and close down saloons and brothels, now was invoked as well to protect the rights of personality. In order to do this, the courts had to find some basis for rooting these grievances in material interest and loss, to define them as "rights of substance." Legal tradition opposed the use of equity courts to protect personal rights, and finding a common law basis for the interests of personality proved to be a difficult task. The only feasible means of doing so, before the expansion of constitutional protection in the present day, was to find that the violation of a personality interest—in reputation, in privacy, in emotional security—entailed some material or physical loss. Free speech champion Zechariah Chafee, Jr., declared in 1920 that "the extension of equitable jurisdiction for the protection of human dignity and peace of mind has been made easier through the ever widening meaning attached to the conception of property."[2]

It was no easy matter for courts to think this way, and by the 1930s they were far from having integrated the interests of personality into the law's customary concerns. It is revealing that when Pound first spoke of the interests of personality in 1915, he saw them as natural rights: "The law does not create them, it only recognizes them." A decade later he was less certain of that natural law basis, and defined them instead as claims by individuals or groups that society must recognize. It was now a matter not so much of meeting or responding to particular interests as of weighing competing ones. Modern times, it appeared, brought not the obliteration of personality, nor its reaffirmation in ways that took full account of the new society, but the ambiguous beginnings of an awareness that there *was* a new legal problem—and a strong desire to deal with it in familiar ways.[3]

Defamation of character—slander and libel—was the interest of personality most fully recognized in law. The rise of a popular press and electoral democracy in the nineteenth century, and the decline of the aristocratic (indeed, tribal) contexts that gave defamation its earlier meaning, made this issue a notable instance of "the pressure of continual adjustment between the needs of society and the protection of individual rights." The problem here, as elsewhere, was how to adapt a traditional legal grievance to the new conditions of life in modern mass society.[4]

In theory, libel law was essentially the same in Britain as in America. But libel was more vigorously prosecuted, and juries were more likely to find for the plaintiff, in the mother country. English common law had ample room for actions against defamation, spoken or written, for the British class structure put a high value on reputation. The Judicature Act of 1883 empowered the Court of Chancery to issue injunctions against libelous publications; the Slander of Women Act (1891) made the imputation of adultery to a married woman an actionable offense.

By the turn of the century, said one observer, the English law of defamation read like a series of exceptions to freedom of speech. The English doctrine that published words, regardless of the writer's intent, were libelous if reasonable men might take them to apply to the aggrieved party reached its peak in Hulton v. Jones (1910). In that case a newspaper had printed a story about a fictitious Artemus Jones and a woman not his wife. A county court judge, whose only connection with the article was that he happened to have the same name, successfully sued for libel.[5]

In hundreds of "hopelessly irreconcilable" decisions, nineteenth-century American courts wrestled with the question of what if any limits might be imposed on the journalistic treatment of public (and, increasingly, private) persons. Yet despite the continuing increase in the size and sensationalism of the press, libel suits were relatively rare. State laws protected the reporting of gossip and private affairs when it was done without malice and in the belief that the information was true.[6]

Still, the need to prove the truth of what was said if libel was charged was an ever-present threat to newspapers. A notable incident occurred in Pennsylvania, where Governor Samuel J. Pennypacker's behavior and appearance made him a juicy object of ridicule by reporters and cartoonists. Pennypacker assailed press sensationalism as a spur to crime, vice, divorce, and political corruption, and secured a law that allowed for damages from libels "resulting from negligence in the ascertainment of facts, and in making publication affecting the character, reputation, or business of citizens." Caricatures and cartoons as well as prose came under the act. But its only immediate consequence was a fresh series of cartoons and articles ridiculing Pennypacker, and it was repealed in 1907.[7]

Theodore Roosevelt also was highly sensitive to press criticism. In his December 1908 annual message to Congress, he accused the *New York World* and the *Indianapolis News* of defaming his administration by accusing it of underhanded dealings in its acquisition of the Panama Canal Zone. He instructed the attorney general to begin proceedings against the papers; indeed, he wanted a charge of sedition included as well, on the ground that the *World* was distributed at West Point. But the court threw out the suit. After he left the White House, Roosevelt successfully sued a Wisconsin newspaper editor for suggesting that he had a drinking problem, and in turn was accused (and acquitted) of libeling New York Republican state chairman William Barnes, Jr., by calling him a corrupt political boss.[8]

The appearance of radio in the 1920s created a new context for reconsidering old issues. Was broadcast defamation slander or libel? Did the unique character of radio transmission require a change in the ground rules of privileged communication and liability? In the pioneering case of Swenson v. Wood (1932) the Nebraska Supreme Court held a radio station liable for defamatory utterances. While it equated radio broadcasting with journalism, the court observed that the 1927 Radio Act did not make radio transmission a form of privileged expression, and it took note of the vast spread (and hence capacity for defamation) of radio messages.[9]

The traditional law of slander and libel thus took on new contexts; but it was hardly clarified by the experience. A 1915 study found that the courts were totally unclear as to the admissibility of evidence proving malice in a libel suit. The pure civil libertarian view was that the courts should protect an individual only from malicious defamation and pay no heed to other considerations such as the need to preserve "peace and good order." Instead, judges developed concepts— "constructive malice," "legal malice," "implied malice"—which had the effect of easing the evidentiary rules for proving malicious intent.[10]

Legislation did so as well. A 1901 Texas law broadened libel to include exposing the subject "to public hatred, ridicule or financial injury." New York required that to avoid being libelous a defamatory publication not only had to be true but had to have been published "with good motives and for justifiable ends." The Illinois court upheld a similar standard in that state's constitution, taking the occasion to attack the "yellow press." Juries were inclined to determine not only the intent of a publication but also how its readers were likely to interpret it.[11]

The belief grew that the consequences of an act were more important than its intention. Thus the nineteenth-century rule that an action could not lie for group defamation because this inflicted no specific harm on another person was gradually modified in the early twentieth century. Another new and increasingly productive source of libel suits was a "malicious tort," defamation which had a clearly material basis, as in business competition or labor-capital disputes.[12]

Yet for all these instances of a broader and more varied concern for injured feelings, it appeared by 1930 that "the trend of legislation relating to the law of libel has been largely in the direction of widening defenses and minimizing damages." Another expert thought that in general the scope of immunity and privilege allowed in public discussion had been enlarged during the early twentieth century. The larger truth was that defamation had become enmeshed in the heightened interplay of private and public interest characteristic of modern times. What it meant to be defamed was the product of a "continuous comparison of the social value of the interests involved and the probable effect thereon of license or restraint upon statement and discussion. Immunity is granted or withheld on the principle of the residuum of social convenience deriving from the protection of one interest at the expense of another." Thus it was their social importance that made public figures vulnerable to even intentional defamation. At the same time, a growing sensitivity to the interests of the individual personality in mass society fed a recurrent unhappiness with the idea that truth was a sufficient defense against the charge of libel.[13]

Privacy was the most evocative new interest of personality in the early twentieth century. The view that there might be a distinct, definable "right to privacy" came into prominence in 1890, when Louis D. Brandeis and his law partner Samuel Warren published a pioneering article in the *Harvard Law Review* which argued for the existence—or, more precisely, for the *need* for the existence—of a tort of violation of the right to be let alone.

The authors tried (with doubtful success) to ground their view in traditional common law. What made their argument fresh and important was that they sought to establish a right of privacy distinct from a property or other material basis: "Not rights arising from contract or from special trust, but . . . rights as against the world." Whether or not there was indeed a legal right to privacy, and if so how to define that right, came to be a particularly meaningful question in dealing with the issue of individual identity in a complex modern social order. Yet courts found it difficult to address the problem. A legal system solidly rooted in the measurement of material considerations could not readily cope with less tangible interests.[14]

New awareness of a legal right to privacy was not limited to the United States. In turn-of-the-century France the unauthorized use of a surname led to litigation redolent of Belle Epoque honor and social status. A publisher announced a forthcoming directory of French Jews in 1896. A Lyonnais named Dreyfus got an injunction barring its publication, on the ground that the book's appearance at the height of the furor over the Dreyfus affair might damage his reputation as well as his business. At the same time French photographers got the courts to block unsanctioned reproductions of their work; one of these decisions produced the first French judicial attempt at a general theory of privacy.

In Germany, Count Ferdinand von Zeppelin successfully sued over the unauthorized use of his portrait and name on a cigar band. Similar actions arose in England, where the courts relied on existing principles of common law—breach of trust, literary property rights, trade secrets, libel—rather than recognize a new right of privacy. European judges in general appear to have been content to define privacy as a particular kind of property.[15]

As early as 1869 the American constitutional theorist John A. Jameson turned his attention to the commercial use of photographic likenesses, which he thought violated "a sort of natural copyright, possessed by every person of his or her own features." But the courts found it difficult to overcome the national commitment to free expression and the law's discomfort with nonmaterial interests. Thus, when the widow of Michigan politician John Atkinson tried to prevent the sale of cigars with his name and likeness, much as in the Zeppelin case in Germany, the court could not find legal ground for an injunction. And in Schuyler v. Curtis (1895), New York's Court of Appeals refused to forbid an artist from exhibiting a bust of the deceased philanthropist Mrs. George M. Hamilton Schuyler at the Chicago World's Fair. Nor did a federal court grant relief to the family of the inventor George Corliss, who sought to block an unauthorized biography and photo. It concluded that the First Amendment and the public character of the subject did not allow it to do so.[16]

The new century saw increasing judicial sensitivity to the issue. When a newspaper made unauthorized use of an actor's photograph in a circulation-building popularity contest, the court found for the plaintiff: "An individual is entitled to protection in person as well as property, and now the right to life has come to mean the privilege to enjoy life without the publicity or annoyance of a lottery contest waged without authority."[17]

But there was an inherent tension between the need to recognize a right to be let alone and the need to root that right in material interest. The first important case to reflect this was Roberson v. Rochester Folding Box Company, decided by the New York Court of Appeals in 1902. The company had distributed twenty-five thousand cards advertising a brand of flour, featuring an (unauthorized) lithographic likeness of a young woman, who was labeled "The Flower of the Family." The subject sought damages for shock and humiliation. Judge Alton B. Parker wrote the majority opinion, arguing that he could not restrain an unauthorized publication that offended only a person's feelings. There had to be manifest harm to property or reputation. Dissenting justices found that a property right—the right to profit from one's likeness—had indeed been violated. The press dwelt more on the presumed suffering of the plaintiff. The *New York Times,* not unmindful of the implications of the case for freedom of the press, loftily observed: "A woman's beauty, next to her virtue, is her earthly crown, but it would be degradation to hedge it about by rules and principles applicable to property in lands and chattels."[18]

A strong popular reaction against the decision led the state legislature to pass a law prohibiting the use of a person's name or picture for advertising purposes without the subject's consent. The Court of Appeals upheld the statute but hedged it with limitations designed to keep it from interfering with freedom of the press; the law was rarely applied. As one commentator observed: "The right of privacy, so called, represents an attractive idea to the moralist and social reformer, but to the law-maker, who seeks to embody the right in a statute, the subject is surrounded with some serious difficulties."[19]

When Thomas Edison sued a patent medicine company for using his photograph and a purported endorsement by him of their product, the New Jersey court enjoined this enterprise on traditional grounds. The justices found it "difficult to understand why the peculiar cast of one's features is not also one's property, and why its pecuniary value, if it has one, does not belong to its owner rather than to the person seeking to make an unauthorized use of it." In another widely noted case involving the intrusion of advertising into American life, the Georgia Supreme Court was more innovative. An insurance company ran an ad showing the consequences of buying or not buying its policy: in the first case a healthy figure of a man ("Do it now. The man who did"); in the other a sickly, ill-dressed specimen ("Do it while you can. The man who didn't"). The ill-portrayed plaintiff, whose permission had not been secured, successfully brought suit; the court for the first time spoke of privacy as a natural and not just a property right.[20]

The identification of privacy with human personality was endorsed in Vassar College v. Loose-Wiles Biscuit Company (1912). The firm sold Vassar Chocolates, packaged with a version of the college's seal. But "Always Fresh" replaced the school's commitment to "Purity and Wisdom," and in the center of the seal a young lady in academic gown munched on the product. The college sued, but a federal district court in Missouri held that as a corporation it had no personality to be injured.[21]

Violated privacy differed in kind from the harms to reputation traditionally remedied by the common law of slander or libel, breach of contract, or assault and battery. The intrusions of photography and advertising had an impersonality that was part of a new world of mass media and mass markets. The courts feared that to be too generous in defining a right of privacy would, in a common phrase of the time, "open the floodgates of litigation." And they found themselves confronted by an ever-denser thicket of conflicting interests and rights: between the violated individual and freedom of expression; between the known world of property, contractual, and other material rights and the unknown world of inner emotional harm. The problem, according to one authority, was that "the civil law is a business system, dealing with tangible property and contractual rights, and does not undertake to redress psychological injuries."[22]

A 1918 *Yale Law Journal* article grandly declared: "New discoveries in the art of photography and reproduction, the growth of a journalism which considers nothing sacred or immune from public scrutiny, and an increased importance which an advancing civilization gives to things emotional and spiritual, require that the law should grow away from the notion that only the physical welfare of the individual can receive legal protection." Brave words! And the spread of advertising, sensational journalism, and the movies and radio added to the importance of being able to maintain a private self in an ever more intrusive world.[23]

A poignant instance of this intrusion of modern technology into private lives occurred in California, where a former prostitute—happily married, her previous life a well-kept secret—found that her name and occupation, taken from the court record of a murder trial, had been used in a movie. The court held for the plaintiff, not on grounds of privacy but because her (state-guaranteed) constitutional right to life, liberty, and happiness had been violated.[24]

Occasionally a right of privacy was recognized *faute de mieux*. In Georgia the victim of an attempted rape, unable to plead assault and battery because of some evidence of consent, successfully argued that her right of privacy had been violated. A Kentucky garage owner posted a large sign in his window accusing one of his patrons of failing to pay his bill. Libel could not be pled, since truth was an acceptable defense in that state's law, but the plaintiff successfully claimed damages for the violation of his right of privacy.[25]

By 1930 it seemed that privacy had a secure place in American law. An observer detected a new vigor in the right of privacy "after a period of apparent stagnation." It was, he thought, more securely recognized, less limited in application. "The courts have already given extensive protection to feelings and emotions," another expert concluded in 1936. "They have shown a notable adaptability of technique in redressing the more serious invasions of this important interest of personality."[26]

Nevertheless, judges continued to have difficulty in defining privacy as a purely personal right without the buttress of a property interest. The great majority of cases involving privacy claims were decided primarily on other grounds: breach of trust or contract, the violation of a property interest, libel. Only four state courts—Georgia, Kentucky, Missouri, and Kansas—explicitly recognized a separate and distinct law of privacy by 1930. Another four—Michigan, New York, Rhode Island, and Washington—explicitly refused to do so.

The division here between rural and industrial states suggests that recognition of the right of privacy was as much the product of traditional values (such as a regard for what were assumed to be the special sensibilities of women) as of a modern concern for individual rights in mass society. Roscoe Pound noted that "the present status of the right, even in jurisdictions where it has been recognized, is a tenuous one; the 'new chapter in the law of torts' is not long." And a 1936 review concluded: "Today, the right of privacy is, in the minds of those who make our law, on the bench and in the legislatures, the same formless embryo which Brandeis and Warren observed forty-six years ago." Not until 1965 would Supreme Court Justice William O. Douglas discover a constitutional right of privacy, like a previously unknown moon of Jupiter, blushing hitherto unseen in the penumbras of the First, Fourth, and Fifth Amendments.[27]

Mental suffering had a close relation to privacy as an evocative (if elusive) interest of personality in modern life. The established British common law rule was that "mental pain or anxiety the law cannot value, and does not pretend to redress, when the unlawful act complained of causes that alone." A changing material environment did not necessarily alter that view. As one commentator put it in 1902: "There is no legal right to absolute peace and quiet; such an ideal existence cannot be enjoyed amidst a complex civilization." The great majority of judges, like those on the Pennsylvania court in 1905, were reluctant to allow the tort of negligence to "cover so intangible, so untrustworthy, so illusory and so speculative a cause of action as mere mental disturbance." Still, of necessity the courts were obliged to consider the sources and physical effects of fright engendered by the technology and the living conditions of modern society.[28]

By 1920 it appeared to an observer that "the field within which damages for mental suffering are allowed in cases of breach of contract is, in general, much broader than is usually realized." The subject matter of mental suffering cases is revealing: emotional consequences stemming from artifacts of modern society such as misdelivered or undelivered telegrams and functioning (and malfunctioning) horse cars, elevators, and automobiles. Three decisions handed down in New York between 1896 and 1931 reflect both the changing conditions of urban life and an evolving legal sensibility. The fact that each of them involved a female plaintiff (as did several of the privacy cases) suggests the presence of a gender dimension in this realm of law. That dimension is perhaps best described as male paternalism (in the words of a recent analysis, "The law's category of emotional harm was gendered as female"), tempered by a judicial reluctance to equate fright-based harm with physical injury suffered from more visible and substantive causes.[29]

The plaintiff in the 1896 case was standing at a crosswalk in Rochester, New York, waiting to board a horse car when another car suddenly bore down on her, stopping so close that she found herself standing between the horses' heads. She fainted, and sometime later suffered a miscarriage and subsequent illness. The court, fearful that a decision in the plaintiff's favor would open "a flood of litigation," denied her damages on the ground that the event itself caused "no immediate personal injury."[30]

By 1914 the perils of urban life were making a greater claim on the sympathy of the courts. The plaintiff in our second case lived on the ground floor of an apartment house owned by the defendant, a realty company. The building's elevator stood at that floor, its doors open, its operator temporarily absent. Two of the plaintiff's children made their way into the elevator while their mother's attention was turned elsewhere for a moment, closed the doors, and started it up. The mother turned to see the elevator rising with her children inside. She rushed to the open shaft, fainted, and fell into it. This time the court followed the chain of cause and effect back to the negligence of the realty company and allowed recovery for her injuries.[31]

Judicial readiness to find cause, and liability, for injury wrought by mental anguish stretched still further in Comstock v. Wilson (1931). The plaintiff was a passenger in a car driven by her husband. He had a minor collision with another car; the other driver was to blame. His wife, uninjured by the crash, stepped out to write down the license number of the other car. While doing so she was overcome by the stress of the event, fainted, fractured her skull on the curb, and died twenty minutes later. By earlier standards the liability of the driver of the other car (and thus of his insurance company) would have seemed remote. Now the court held that liability did indeed exist.[32]

By the 1930s most jurisdictions were allowing recovery in fright cases—but only so long as there was a direct link with physical injury. At the end of the decade a torts expert found over a hundred decisions dealing with the infliction of mental suffering. Nevertheless, the courts remained reluctant to extend legal protection to peace of mind per se; the belief persisted that this "would open up a wide vista of litigation in the field of bad manners, where relatively minor annoyances had better be dealt with by instruments of social control other than the law."[33]

Mental suffering had a doctrinal history much like that of privacy. In the one case as in the other, judges were reluctant to modify the rule that there had to be a tangible cause of tangible harm. Although modern times brought a greater awareness of the interests of personality, the courts were stubbornly resistant to giving those interests a legal identity of their own.

Civil Liberties and Social Change

Freedom of speech and press were another matter. They had been issues in American public life from the nation's earliest days. But major controversies were few (over the Alien and Sedition Acts of 1798, over press restrictions during the Civil War), and focused more on the powers of government than on the First Amendment rights of individuals.

Civil liberties became a more conspicuous issue in the early twentieth century. Why? In part because new economic and social tensions heightened class and ideological conflict: criticism and hostility to criticism of American institutions grew together. In part, too, because the Progressive impulse of the time was so ambivalent, dedicated on the one hand to uncovering the deficiencies of American society and on the other to enhancing social unity and order; the result was both a spur to outspokenness and a fear of its consequences. And in part because the character of the new society itself—an ever-richer mix of new people, new ideas, new technologies—put fresh strains on the old American ideal of free expression.

Civil liberties issues usually are seen as clashes between political or other kinds of radicalism and the forces of social and economic conservatism. This was an important part of the story, but far from all of it. Like the interests of personality, conflicts over freedom of speech and the press came to reflect the social situations of a new American society.

Nineteenth-century rural and small-town America inclined to regard freedom of speech as a matter of local self-determination. Very few cases involved the First Amendment. The Supreme Court held in 1900 that the privileges and immunities clause of the Constitution did not necessarily embrace the Bill of Rights. Roscoe Pound observed of the first ten amendments in 1913: "Such provisions were not needed in their own day, they are not desired in our day."[34]

But civil liberties became a more substantial and visible public issue in pace with the increasing variety of interests, issues, and ideas characteristic of modern American life. A growing awareness of social problems and the erosion of Victorian mores widened the range of permissible (and actual) speech. At the same time it strengthened the social anxieties that fed attempts to limit free expression. Sociologist Edward A. Ross noted the entry into public opinion of broader, more diverse themes, and the consequent suppression of free speech by local authorities. The creation of the American Association of University Professors in 1913 to protect academic freedom, and a 1915 report, "Free Speech and Its Limits," by the National Civic Federation's Free Speech Commission, reflected both a new awareness of and new threats to civil liberties.[35]

A growing number of local ordinances required licenses for meetings on streets and in other public places. This was a response not only to the labor unrest of the time but also to crowded and chaotic urban life. A leading authority on municipal law distinguished between "purely private rights" such as gambling or drinking in private, which were free from official interference, and the at times justifiable regulation of expression in the public sphere.[36]

Judges generally endorsed these constraints as appropriate exercises of the state and municipal police power. In 1895 Oliver Wendell Holmes, sitting on the Massachusetts Supreme Judicial Court, upheld a Boston ordinance requiring a permit from the mayor for public addresses: "For the legislature absolutely or conditionally to forbid public speaking in a highway or public park is no more an infringement of the rights of a member of the public than for the owner of a private house to prohibit it in his house"—a sentiment approvingly quoted two years later by the United States Supreme Court.[37]

It was freedom of the press rather than freedom of speech that produced the first significant body of First Amendment law. A revolution in American journalism around the turn of the century, evident in the Hearst-Pulitzer "yellow press" of the 1890s and muckraking in the early 1900s, led to a variety of legal conflicts over what was permissible in the print media.

The tradition of a free press remained strong. Governor Charles Evans Hughes could not get the New York legislature to pass an act requiring publication of the names of those responsible for the contents of newspapers so that aggrieved parties might know to whom they might respond—or sue. A similar California law, passed in 1900, quickly became a dead letter. And the Missouri court struck down a 1908 law that required organizations judging the character and qualifications of political candidates to publish the facts on which they based their conclusions, and the names and addresses of their sources.[38]

Some courts and legislatures held that the public interest was best served by full discussion of the activities and qualifications of public officials, and that commentators had a "qualified privilege": they need not prove the truth of what they said but only that no "actual malice" was intended. The Kansas court in Coleman v. MacLennan (1908) upheld this larger view of press freedom because of

> the modern conditions which govern the collection of news items and the insistent popular expectation that newspapers will expose . . . actual and suspected fraud, graft, greed, malfeasance and corruption in public affairs . . . The press as we know it today is almost as modern as the telephone and the phonograph. The functions which it performs at the present stage of our social development . . . are magnified many fold, and the opportunities for its influence are multiplied many times.[39]

More often courts held that the item in dispute did not involve the public welfare, and thus was not privileged. As one authority put it: "Subjects that are proper for public information and discussion are only those in which the public has an interest. The fact that a large number of people may have a private interest in the matter will not make it . . . proper for public investigation." A 1910 survey of British and American decisions concluded that they "would seem to leave little, if any, more practical freedom in the discussion of matters of public interest than that which is permitted in the discussion of the conduct of a private person. It leaves the law very much in the attitude of saying, 'You have full liberty of discussion; provided, however, you say nothing that counts.'"[40]

States and communities had broad authority to restrain publications on the ground that they endangered public morals and safety. The Connecticut Supreme Court upheld an 1895 law aimed at newspapers specializing in criminal and other sensational news. Denying that this violated the rule against prior restraint, the court argued: "The notion that the broad guaranty of the common right to free speech and free thought contained in our constitution is intended to erect a bulwark or supply a place of refuge in behalf of the violators of laws enacted for the protection of society from the contagion of moral diseases belittles the conception of constitutional safeguards, and implies ignorance of the essentials of civil liberty."[41]

Congress had closed the mails to obscene materials and lotteries with its Comstock law of 1873. During the early 1900s there were sporadic Post Office rulings against dissident journals such as the atheist-socialist *Appeal to Reason, The Challenge,* and even William Jennings Bryan's *Commoner.* But when the Postmaster General held that a correspondence course offered by the American School of Magnetic Healing was fraudulent, the Supreme Court decided that this was a matter of opinion not subject to decision by an administrative officer.[42]

Controversy over the exclusionary powers of the Post Office came to a head in Lewis Publishing Company v. Morgan (1913). Congress had required that a publication with second-class mail privileges list the names of its editor, publisher, and stockholders, and identify subsidized text as advertising. Postal authorities went after several journals of the Lewis company, charging fraud. Though this action was due in part to the publications' radical editorials, the decidedly unradical American Newspaper Publishers' Association challenged the constitutionality of the law. Chief Justice Edward D. White upheld the government, though he warned: "We do not wish even by the remotest implication to be regarded as assenting to the broad contentions concerning the existence of arbitrary power through the classification of the mails."[43]

The most substantial restraint on freedom of the press in the prewar years stemmed not from radical politics but from a turf war between judges who held journalists in summary contempt for stories that in their view interfered with the legal process, and reporters and publishers who held that this violated their First Amendment rights. Connecticut's supreme court argued: "There is no constitutional right to publish every fact or statement that may be true. Even the right to publish accurate statements of judicial proceedings is limited."[44]

Some encounters in the ongoing war between courts and newspapers:

The Missouri Supreme Court held a paper in contempt for criticizing one of its decisions as pro-railroad.

Minnesota's court upheld a conviction for a newspaper account of an execution on the ground that it violated an 1889 statute that banned such reportage in order "to avoid exciting an unwholesome effect on the public mind."[45]

The Idaho Supreme Court imprisoned the editor of the *Boise Capi-*

tal News. His crime: he published Theodore Roosevelt's denunciation of a court ruling that kept the names of Progressive party electors on the November 1912 ballot.

Justice Holmes in Patterson v. Colorado (1907) upheld a contempt proceeding against a newspaper for lampooning the Colorado Supreme Court while a lawsuit was under way.

In 1915 the Supreme Court reviewed a Washington state law penalizing publications that advocated crime or disrespect for law. The article at issue, "The Nudes and the Prudes," criticized arrests in a nudist colony. This was held to encourage breaches of the law forbidding indecent exposure. Holmes upheld the statute, observing that laws such as this one were "not unfamiliar."[46]

The conflict between freedom of the press and the right to a fair trial came to a head in Toledo Newspaper Company v. U.S. (1918). It involved a typically Progressive issue, the rights and powers of a public utility. The franchise of the bankrupt Toledo Railways and Light Company had expired, and the *Toledo News-Bee* implied that the federal district judge presiding over the receivership was in the utility's pocket. The outraged jurist issued an injunction against the paper, which nevertheless continued its attack. He then cited the editor and publisher for contempt.

Chief Justice White's majority opinion held that a judge had the right to punish for contempt when his ability to do his job was threatened. Freedom of the press did not include "the right virtually to destroy such institutions" as the courts: "However complete is the right of the press to state public things and discuss them, that right, as every other right enjoyed in human society, is subject to the restraints which separate right from wrong-doing." Holmes dissented—not on First Amendment grounds, but because he could find no state law at stake nor evidence of obstruction of justice. It is not surprising that the *Nation* concluded in 1915: "For some time past there has been a distinct trend towards regulation of the American press."[47]

Other aspects of modern life made freedom of speech more of a public issue. The early 1900s saw the beginning of the distinctive modern linkage of sexual and cultural radicalism with free expression in literature and the arts. Attorney Theodore Schroeder's Free Speech League pioneered in this cause, as did a 1909 National Free Speech Convention of writers and sculptors. (The advocacy and the practice of free expression did not always coexist on the wilder shores of cultural radicalism. The anarchist–Single Tax community of Arden, Delaware, expelled the novelist Upton Sinclair for being too talkative, and had him jailed for disturbing the peace—and for breaking the state's Sunday law by playing baseball and tennis.)[48]

Communities with strong Puritan or Catholic influences, such as Boston, continued to censor books and plays on the grounds of public and religious morality (thus providing rich meat for the satirist H. L. Mencken). And courts were not loath to play the role of guardians of public purity. But the general trend was away from such controls, in pace with the growing diversification of American culture.[49]

In the 1920s Prohibition, the use of the automobile as a carrier of illicit liquor and bootleggers, and the introduction of wiretapping to gather evidence created new contexts for search and seizure cases involving the Fourth and Fifth Amendments. One observer equated enforcement of the Volstead Act with wartime constraints on civil liberties.[50]

Olmstead v. United States (1928) directly confronted the problem of adapting old conceptions of civil liberty to the conditions imposed by new technology. Chief Justice William Howard Taft held that evidence obtained by the secret wiretapping of telephone conversations did not violate either the Fourth Amendment search and seizure rule or the Fifth Amendment ban on self-incrimination. Holmes and Brandeis dissented, the former on public policy grounds, arguing that wiretapping was a "dirty business" and that it was more important for the government to be law-abiding than to prevent a few criminals from escaping, Brandeis because the new technology posed a serious threat to the right to privacy.[51]

The *Olmstead* decision hardly gave a blank check to wiretapping. Taft justified it in part by the scale of the Seattle bootlegging operation that it helped to uncover, and went out of his way to point out that if it wished to, Congress could make telephone conversations inadmissible in the federal courts. The telephone industry filed an amicus brief in *Olmstead* attacking wiretapping, in which it argued that telephone conversations should be as privileged as letters. The practice soon was outlawed in twenty-eight states.[52]

In terms of the number of people affected, the most significant new source of controversy over free expression was that new and suddenly pervasive mass medium, the movies. The complexity of films' production and distribution, the size of their audiences, and their impact on viewers led to a fresh look at the age-old question of the relationship between public authority and the dissemination of facts and ideas.[53]

The British solution to the problem of movie regulation, after parliamentary hearings in 1909, was to establish a Board of Film Censors, a compromise between Home Secretary Herbert Samuel's desire for state censorship and the Cinematographic Exhibitors' Association's desire to be let alone. The board was supposed to enforce a list of sixty-seven "exceptions," running from "Materialization of the Conventional Figure of Christ" to "Suggestion of Incest." But about half the country's movie exhibitors were not members of the association, and thus not under the board's purview. A number of films excluded from the United States were shown in Britain.[54]

The American response was more varied and complex. Two incidents underscored the explosive social potential of the new medium. Showings of a film of the July 4, 1910, Reno prizefight in which the black boxer Jack Johnson knocked out the white James Jeffries, led to race riots in a number of communities. New York's Mayor William Gaynor promised to ban the film if he could find legal justification; the 4 million–member Society of Christian Endeavor worked to stop its distribution. Taking aim at the forthcoming Johnson–Jess Willard bout in Havana, Congress banned fight films from interstate commerce, an action upheld by the Supreme Court.[55]

Even more disturbing was the impact of D. W. Griffith's powerful epic *The Birth of a Nation.* The NAACP and supportive white Progressives such as Frederic C. Howe and Jane Addams sought to block showings of the movie on the grounds that it was inflammatory and unfair. After public protests by blacks in Boston, a state law was passed allowing city officials to suspend movie theater licenses. The film was banned in Chicago and St. Louis.[56]

What was to be done about so potent a medium? Various models were at hand: the common law principle of no prior restraint but legal vulnerability thereafter; censorship; the regulatory commission licensing system used to regulate other new technologies; industry self-regulation. Local and state censorship was the first response. Corrupt municipal license bureaus offered little hope of effective control. A police censorship board was set up in Chicago in November 1907, charged with banning "immoral and obscene films." San Francisco followed in 1908. State boards were established in Pennsylvania, Kansas, Ohio, and Massachusetts, and proposed in New York and elsewhere.[57]

The trade responded. The Association of Motion Picture Exhibitors asked the People's Institute, a typical Progressive reform organization fostering good citizenship among New York City's immigrants, to set up a voluntary censorship system. The Motion Picture Patents Company, producers of two thirds of American movies, agreed to accept the decisions of this nonpublic New York—soon to be National—Board of Censorship of Motion Pictures. By 1910 the thirty or more local censorship boards that had sprung up in earlier years had been reduced to two: in Chicago and Worcester, Massachusetts. The bulk of movie censorship now was in the hands of the Board of Censorship. Movie companies voluntarily submitted their products to the board and gave it financial support. John Collier (who later would be a leading advocate of Indian rights) was its general secretary and the Progressive urban reformer Frederic C. Howe its chairman. Its members were drawn from organizations such as the YMCA, the Charity Organization Society, the Children's Aid Society, the City Vigilance League, the League for Political Education, the Federation of Churches, and the New York Federation of Women's Clubs.

The board soon passed on almost every film shown in the United States. During its first five years it reviewed some twenty thousand films, rejecting 20 percent on grounds of obscenity, explicit depiction of crime, morbidity, blasphemy, libel, or scenes which in its judgment would have a bad effect on basic morality or erode social standards. Howe defended the board as preferable to state censorship, which he feared would be "more . . . censorious . . . when it reviewed the treatment of subjects such as socialism, the IWW, and labor conflict."[58]

The triumph of privatized regulation did not entirely eliminate the pressure for government oversight. New York's Mayor Gaynor appointed a Committee on Moving Pictures in 1911. This body proposed an ordinance for "moral regulation through administrative action rather than through minute statutory requirements enforced through the courts." The mayor would have the power to revoke or suspend exhibitors' licenses; the courts could review the reasonableness of his actions.[59]

A political alliance composed of the Vanderbilt real estate interests, legitimate theaters, small exhibitors, and supporters of pre-exhibition censorship objected. Tammany pols insisted on adding a censorship provision to the ordinance; Gaynor then vetoed it on the ground that this was unconstitutional prior restraint. (Rumor had it that the Tammany amendment was designed to bring about the bill's defeat.)

Finally, in 1913 an ordinance was passed regulating the size, lighting, ventilation, and other safety and comfort conditions of movie theaters—but not the content of the films they showed.[60]

Chicago's police censors continued to do their work, prohibiting sixty-eight films (ten of them for violations of wartime neutrality) in late 1914 and early 1915 alone. The Ohio state board was particularly active, earning John Collier's contempt for its ineptitude—and for its conservatism, as when it banned a mildly pro-labor film, *The Strike of Coaldale.*

In 1915 the United States Supreme Court upheld the Ohio and Kansas movie censorship laws. According to Justice Joseph McKenna, "The exhibition of moving pictures is a business pure and simple, originated and conducted for profit, like other spectacles, not to be regarded . . . as part of the press of the country or as organs of public opinion." The First and Fourteenth Amendments did not apply: "We immediately feel that the argument is wrong or strained which extends the guaranties of free opinion and speech to the multitudinous shows which are advertised on the bill-boards of our cities and towns."[61]

John Collier of the Board of Censorship criticized this refusal to extend the protection of the Bill of Rights to the movies. But other Progressive-minded observers differed. One argued: "We would have to shut our eyes to the facts of this world to regard the precaution unreasonable or the legislation to effect it a mere wanton interference with personal liberty"; another found the decision an example of the Court's Progressive tendency "to construe constitutional provisions liberally rather than to invalidate state legislation which is directly connected with the interests of public safety and morals."[62]

The post–World War I Red Scare temporarily injected new life into movie censorship. State Senator Clayton R. Lusk, the author of New York's postwar antiradical laws, proposed to set up a three-member review commission. Senate minority leader (and later New York City mayor) James J. Walker condemned the measure as "the most un-American bill ever introduced into this Senate," and the movie industry vigorously opposed it. But it became law. From August 21, 1921, to December 31, 1922, New York's censors eliminated 79 films and 4,690 scenes. Under pressure from organizations such as B'nai B'rith's Anti-Defamation League, the commission went after hostile references to religious and racial groups. Three times its decisions were appealed to the courts, and in each case it was upheld.[63]

Censorship boards still existed in seven states (they had been tried in thirty) and over thirty cities in 1928. And a number of state laws forbade particular scenes: attacks on social groups, prizefights, fighting between men and animals. A New York judge concluded that since motion pictures had a far greater attraction than books or newspapers for children, illiterates, and the ignorant, state regulation was necessary.

But the growing clout of the movie industry, and the general American hostility to public censorship except in time of national emergency, prevailed over state surveillance. A Massachusetts referendum overwhelmingly defeated a proposal that the Department of Public Welfare censor movies, a result ascribed to massive industry spending and a popular postwar revulsion against government controls. Governor Alfred E. Smith of New York closed down his state's censorship commission when he regained office in 1923. Meanwhile, the Republican politico Will Hays was put in charge of the industry's trade association, the Motion Picture Producers' and Distributors' Association. From this post he issued and enforced standards which effectively countered public censorship.[64]

Then another turn of the technological wheel injected a new element: films with sound tracks were more difficult to amend or alter than the silents. But the Pennsylvania Supreme Court held that the state's censorship law applied to them as well. The advent of talkies, along with growing criticism of the movies as a big (and Jewish-dominated) business, and the influence of Catholic laymen and the church hierarchy in matters of public morals, led to the Motion Picture Production Code of 1930. This was the movies' primary regulatory instrument until the 1960s. The result was the distinctive blandness (and, perhaps in consequence, the universal appeal) of American movies during the 1930s, 1940s, and 1950s. If you have a message, went a Hollywood maxim, send it by Western Union.[65]

Radio broadcasting was as widespread in its impact as the movies. Radio's sudden and sweeping entry onto the American scene in the 1920s was a replay of the appearance of motion pictures over a decade before. Yet the new medium met with no public censorship. Instead, federal licensing, and the implicit threat of a government crackdown if accepted standards were transgressed, were the only external checks on the content of radio shows.

This was due in good part to the technology of the new medium. One distinctive feature was the sheer number of its outlets. Thirty stations reached sixty thousand households with radio receivers in 1922; by 1930 there were 618 stations and 13,750,000 sets. Different, too, was the near-impossibility of prior restraint, given the continuous flow of programming over the airwaves. Radio was to newspapers and the movies as automobiles were to trains: more pervasive and free-flowing, and hence less subject to supervision, except as a public utility.[66]

The Radio Act of 1927 provided for the licensing of stations according to the "public interest, convenience or necessity," just as the Interstate Commerce Commission licensed trucking and bus companies, or state public utilities commissions licensed gas, electricity, and telephone companies. The act specifically forbade its regulatory agency, the Federal Radio Commission (FRC), to censor the content of radio communication.

Yet censorship, of a sort, there was. The standards used for licensing—technical adequacy, financial responsibility, regularity of service, comparative popularity—weighed heavily against stations with selective audiences and messages. Inevitably this affected program content. Thus, the Chicago Federation of Labor was denied an exclusive channel on the ground that its appeal was too narrow.

In 1932 the District of Columbia Court of Appeals reviewed the FRC's denial of a license renewal to a Los Angeles evangelical station that consistently attacked Jews and Catholics. The court upheld the commission on public interest grounds. Radio, like the movies, could not claim immunity under the First Amendment, even though it was a more appropriate medium for the expression of opinion on matters of public concern. As long as FRC program reviews kept the channels of communication open and uncluttered, minor abridgments of speech were acceptable.[67]

The rapidly changing character of the medium brought still other issues of free expression to prominence. The consolidation of large numbers of stations into a few national networks led to accusations of monopoly, and to charges that the networks were applying pressure to keep controversial speakers off the air. The major networks fought hard and successfully to retain control over what they broadcast. The Federal Communications Commission of 1934, like its predecessor the Federal Radio Commission, was denied the power to oversee program content. And the networks in the 1930s began to draw about them the cloak of First Amendment immunity that they claim today.

Meanwhile, another major technological innovation came into

view: television. David Sarnoff expected in 1931 that within five years TV reception would be up to radio's standard. And what might be transmitted by the new wonder? Well, prizefights for one thing—but under the present law it appeared that such transmissions would not be legal. *Plus ça change . . .*[68]

The Passions of Politics and War

Radicalism and war were the most conspicuous civil liberties testing grounds of the early twentieth century. The story is a familiar one: state and local clampdowns on anarchists, syndicalists, and socialists before 1917; federal repression of pro-German, neutral, and other dissenters after the United States entered World War I; an assault on radicals of every stripe during the postwar Red Scare. At the same time, these assaults contributed to the rise of a new civil liberties consciousness that reinvigorated the old American commitment to free expression.

The politics of free speech came to the fore in dramatic fashion when Leon Czolgosz killed President William McKinley in September 1901. The anti-McKinley Hearst newspapers had printed an Ambrose Bierce poem forecasting the president's death just before this, which led to much discussion of the proper limits to freedom of the press. New York and a few other states passed criminal anarchy laws, and a federal law in 1903 excluded anarchists from the United States, the first restriction of immigrants on political grounds since the Alien Act of 1798. The Naturalization Act of 1906 was even tougher. An applicant for citizenship had to swear that he or she was "not a disbeliever in or opposed to organized government" or a member of a group with such beliefs.[69]

Still, given the enormity of the crime, the reaction to McKinley's murder was relatively muted. While the *Independent* wanted "a law providing restraint for life for all who preach or glory in assassination, whether they plead insanity or not," it also warned: "We must keep the distinction in mind between doctrine and action. It is of no use to try to suppress thinking by violence. Thinking must be conquered by thinking; liberty must make liberty safe . . . There are other greater evils than even the occasional murder of a President." The *Nation* pointed out that McKinley's American-born assassin Czolgosz would not have been reached by the 1903 anarchist exclusion act, and concluded: "The root of the trouble is that you cannot legislate against a state of mind." Massachusetts Senator George Frisbie Hoar thought that "there are governments in the world that ought to be overthrown by force and violence," and Governor Joseph W. Folk of Missouri observed: "No one should be allowed to teach anarchy, it is said; but who is to judge what is anarchy?"[70]

Only thirty-eight people were kept from entering the United States under the 1903 law between 1903 and 1921, and only fourteen were deported for anarchist beliefs between 1911 and 1919. Theodore Roosevelt did order Attorney General Charles Bonaparte to exclude an anarchist publication, *La Question Sociale,* from the mails, and before he left office told Congress that "when compared with the suppression of anarchy, every other question sinks into insignificance." But no other restrictive legislation was enacted until the Espionage Act of 1917. Only at a time of special emotional intensity, as in the wake of the McKinley assassination or when the nation was at war, was Congress inclined to act.[71]

The appearance in 1905 of the Industrial Workers of the World (IWW), the first syndicalist-Marxist revolutionary organization in America, the rise of a substantial Socialist party, and growing labor-capital conflict led to considerable antiradical activity before the First World War. One example: in order to restrict IWW activity in San Diego, the city council in 1912 designated a downtown area long used for political, commercial, and religious meetings at night "a congested district" and banned all meetings there. IWW members, Single Taxers, and AFL men formed a Free Speech League, and forty-one speakers in succession were arrested. Hydrants were turned on full force to break up the gatherings; the police set up checkpoints outside of town where suspected Free Speech League adherents were turned back; vigilantes ran others out of town, with much brutality. President William Howard Taft wanted to restrain the local authorities, but his Justice Department saw no way to do so.[72]

Efforts to suppress radicals faced a variety of legal constraints. A Dayton, Ohio, city ordinance gave autocratic powers to the city's chief of police, and a socialist speaker was arrested; but a municipal judge held the ordinance unconstitutional. A similar Los Angeles edict forbidding public assemblages to discuss "the doctrines of any economic or social system," enacted after a riot on Christmas Day 1913, also failed to survive a legal test. Schenectady, New York's socialist mayor, George Lunn, was arrested for speaking without a permit to textile strikers near Utica during the 1912 campaign. But the state attorney general denied the right of a municipality to interfere in this way with free speech. And after a federal judge in Washington state canceled the naturalization papers of a Socialist party member, the national press unanimously criticized his action.[73]

When the socialist editor Alex Scott criticized the behavior of the police during the 1913 Paterson, New Jersey, textile strike, a local court sentenced him to one to fifteen years at hard labor under the state's antianarchist law. He appealed, amid much sympathy from the *Kansas City Star*, New York's *Tribune, Globe,* and *World,* and the *Boston Transcript.* The *Outlook* (for which Theodore Roosevelt was a contributing editor) observed that Scott had only echoed what leading New York newspapers were saying about the brutality of the police. The *Los Angeles Times* and the *New York Times* criticized what they called an anarchistic response to anarchists: "There is safety in freedom . . . The radical suppressed becomes more radical; the radical enlarged becomes conservative." New York City Police Commissioner Arthur Woods agreed: he kept the police out of sight and allowed protesters of every shade of opinion to speak unhindered in Union Square.[74]

America's involvement in the First World War, and the social unrest that followed in its wake, fostered an assault on freedom of speech and of the press unmatched since the Civil War. It had obvious conservative sources, but the wartime pressure for conformity was also a projection of the Progressives' desire for a more coherent, unified society. Many of them, both inside and out of Woodrow Wilson's administration, saw American entry into the war as a logical extension of the domestic reform impulse. Attitudes toward state and society that had been gathering strength during the prewar years strongly shaped this ultimate application of public power. Thus, in the fashion of domestic social reform organizations, a Congress of Constructive Patriotism sponsored by the National Security League gathered in Washington in January 1917, its delegates appointed by bar associations, aeronautics and auto clubs, women's organizations, and the like. The prevailing rhetoric was familiar, too: "It was a Congress interested, first of all, in the future great problem of the world— how to combine efficiency with liberty and gentleness."[75]

The desire for cultural cohesion and the reality of cultural pluralism came now to their most forceful confrontation. It was during the years from 1915 to 1918 that the *Readers' Guide to Periodical Literature* replaced its more traditional subject designations "Liberty of Speech" and "Liberty of the Press" with the more modern "Free Speech" and "Freedom of the Press," and the term "civil liberties" itself came into widespread use.[76]

According to Frank Cobb, editor of the *New York World*, Woodrow Wilson foresaw the consequences of America's joining the conflict: "Once lead this people into war, and they'll forget there ever was such a thing as tolerance." Cobb added: "He thought the Constitution would not survive it; that free speech and the right of assembly would go." There is some reason to doubt that Wilson in fact said this to Cobb, given his attitude toward those opposed to his war policies. In 1915 he attacked foreign-born critics for "pouring the poison of disloyalty into the very arteries of our national life," and in 1917 he warned: "Woe to the man, or group of men, that stands in our way in this day of high resolution." Frederick Lewis Allen warned that what had happened in wartime Europe could happen in the United States as well: "We may have our own Liebknechts thrown into prison, our own Haldanes scorned by public and press, our own conscientious objectors punished, our own Bertrand Russells expelled from our university faculties." With much foresight he predicted that if there was censorship, it would be stupidly managed.[77]

The Committee on Public Information (CPI) embodied the mix of reform and insistence on cultural unity that characterized Progressivism gone to war. The muckraking journalist Arthur Ballard, who wrote for the radical *Call* and *Masses*, was most responsible for the creation of the CPI. He hoped that it would enable the United States to avoid the censorship indulged in by the other warring powers. The CPI's director, George Creel, was a Progressive journalist, no supporter of government censorship. (A. Mitchell Palmer, who as attorney general presided over the postwar Red Scare, also had strongly progressive domestic policy credentials.) Much of the CPI's output stressed themes congenial to Progressives: that this was a war for democracy, for social justice, for the self-determination of peoples. But increasingly, perhaps inevitably, the CPI espoused a more narrowly defined, nationalistic war patriotism.[78]

The wartime control of expression in the United States should be seen against the backdrop of the English response. Britain's Boer War experience gave some warning of what was to come. Mobs frequently broke up antiwar meetings; dissidents were threatened with prosecution for seditious libel. The political theorist Albert V. Dicey spoke out for free expression in terms that reflected the elite character of nineteenth-century liberalism (in contrast to its American counterpart): "The hint that the right to advocate the stopping of the war ought to be qualified by deference to popular sentiment means nothing less than that legal freedom is at an end, and that instead of rights secured by the law of the land, we must accept the capricious dictates of popular sentiment enforced by the sanction of popular violence."[79]

The Defense of the Realm Act (DORA) was the basis of Britain's control of dissent in World War I. Prowar British Liberals, like their American Progressive counterparts, rationalized the need for wartime constraints. The Fabian Sidney Webb accepted the sacred right of rebellion—and the equally sacred right to suppress rebellion. He thought that while the state should not unduly persecute conscientious objectors, it might test their sincerity by raising the cost to them of living up to their principles. Home Secretary Herbert Samuel held that there was no general policy "of suppressing opposition to the war or to the enactment of conscription." And it is true that Prime Minister David Lloyd George (in need of Labour party support) protected pacifist Labour papers such as the *Herald* and the *Labour Leader*.[80]

Still, DORA was strict enough. It empowered the government to imprison without charge or trial those whom the Home Secretary thought should be interned "by reason of their hostile origin or associations." Aliens were forbidden to change their names to more acceptably English ones. They needed permission to travel more than five miles from their registered addresses, or to own guns, cars, cameras, maps, or pigeons. Any pamphlet intended as war or peace propaganda had to be submitted to the authorities before publication (though there was no censorship of newspapers). DORA's broader powers were tested in the courts, which readily endorsed them.[81]

A British law journal dolefully observed in February 1915: "At the present moment, the Common Law lies under the iron heel of militarism." Lord Chancellor Halsbury called DORA "the most unconstitutional thing that has ever happened in this country." In response to criticism, Parliament restored the constitutional right to a jury trial, but DORA defined British policy toward dissent for the duration of the war.[82]

American policy was shaped by a more complex set of competing values: the Progressive pursuit of social unity; conservative xenophobic nationalism, inflamed by war feeling; the tradition of free speech and a free press. An Espionage Act was introduced in Congress on April 2, 1917, just before the declaration of war. The administration sought to suppress action—and words—that might impede the war effort. At the same time it had to avoid the accusation that it wanted to limit or restrain partisan criticism of government policies.

The Espionage Act levied heavy fines and prison terms on those convicted of interfering with the enlistment of troops or industrial production. In its initial form it gave the Postmaster General broad powers of prior censorship. The *New York Times*, antiwar Progressive Republican Senator William Borah, and prowar conservative Republican Senator Henry Cabot Lodge were among those objecting to this "Censorship Section." The House rejected it, and instead a system of voluntary censorship, overseen by a censorship board appointed by the president, was agreed upon. Postmaster General Albert S. Burleson tried to be reassuring:

> We shall take great care not to let criticism which is personally or politically offensive to the Administration affect our action. But if newspapers go so far as to impugn the motives of the Government and thus encourage insubordination, they will be dealt with severely . . . For instance, papers may not say that the Government is controlled by Wall Street or munition manufacturers, or any other special interests . . . We will not tolerate campaigns against conscription, enlistments, sale of securities, or revenue collections. We will not permit the publication or circulation of anything hampering the war's prosecution or attacking improperly our allies.

He warned, too, that newspapers would be judged by their past utterances, not by newly announced intentions. Although socialist journals would not be banned unless they contained treasonable or seditious matter, "the trouble is that most Socialist papers do contain this matter."[83]

Even in wartime this was too much for many journals. "Must We Go to Jail?" asked the conservative *North American Review*. The pro-Wilson *World* condemned Burleson's "intellectual reign of terror," and the fervidly prowar Theodore Roosevelt complained in May 1918 that the actions of the Post Office made it dangerous for anyone, especially newspapers, to tell the truth if it annoyed government authorities. When New York City's postmaster excluded *The Masses* from the mails, prominent attorney Dudley Field Malone and CPI chief George Creel protested. The magazine ceased publication, but it immediately reappeared as *The Liberator*.[84]

At the same time there was substantial voluntary cooperation by the major news outlets, which were under heavy government pressure to conform. War Industries Board chairman Bernard Baruch announced: "In the eyes of the Board there is no distinction between a newspaper and a factory." The Associated Press and the United Press sent to their clients only material conforming with government requirements. In this way a Senate report detailing the flaws in American aircraft production got little notice. Those who did pay attention to it suffered for their temerity: mail circulation of the *Christian Science Monitor* was stopped for three days, the *Detroit News* was barred from circulation in Canada, and a foreign edition of the *New York Times* that ran the report was suppressed.[85]

By the war's end, amendments to the Espionage Act had significantly extended the reach of the government. Some seventy-five newspapers (forty-five of them socialist) came under Post Office constraints. Two score of them lost their second-class mail privileges; the others agreed not to print discussions of the war. More than two thousand persons were arrested, and over a thousand imprisoned, for Espionage or Sedition Act offenses, but only ten for acts of sabotage. Of 3.5 million enemy aliens in the country, 6,300 were arrested and 2,300 interned. There were 135 loyalty investigations of federal employees in 1917, 2,537 in 1918.[86]

Semi- and nonoffficial speech control was even more pervasive. A phalanx of patriotic organizations—the National Security League, the American Rights League, the American Defense Society—and a host of lesser, shadowy groups such as the Terrible Threateners, the Sedition Slammers, the American Anti-Anarchy Association, the Knights of Liberty, the Yale Legion, the Traveling Salesmen's Liberty League, the Anti-Sedition League, and the Minute Men of America fed prowar fervor and rooted out disloyalty. The American Protective League, an organization with more than 350,000 members in 1,400 local units, was charged by the Department of Justice with investigating and uncovering "subversion." By the end of the war this ever more explicitly antiradical and antiliberal organization had conducted over 3 million loyalty investigations. State Councils of Defense—groups of community leaders organized to spur the war effort—often acted as well to suppress dissent.[87]

A number of states passed laws penalizing idleness. Georgia's governor announced his readiness to take the lead in a movement to gather up the state's vagrants and put them to work. Such a roundup did occur in New Jersey after a gubernatorial proclamation; a thousand men hurriedly applied for jobs at the Newark Employment Bureau. Delaware's statute required every male aged eighteen to fifty-five to be engaged in a lawful occupation. Otherwise they could be assigned to useful work by the state's Council of National Defense, their wages to be agreed upon by the council and their employers. The state supreme court upheld this law on the grounds that it was necessary to produce food and supplies in wartime and that, given the state's reduced capacity to prevent crime during the war, this was an acceptable way of preserving civil order.[88]

The judiciary contributed to the prevailing hysteria by indulging in expansively illiberal interpretations of the Espionage Act. Federal district judge Walker Burns of Houston charged a grand jury in October 1917: "I have a conviction as strong as life, that this country should stand . . . [the defendants] up against an adobe wall tomorrow and give them what they deserve . . . I wish that I could pay for the ammunition. I would like to attend the execution and if I were in the firing squad I would not want to be the marksman who had the blank shell." Judge Kenesaw Mountain Landis, who before the war had levied a $29 million fine on Standard Oil, instructed an American Protective League audience: "What we need is a new definition of treason. Then we can use the side of a barn for those who would destroy our government." A California judge ordered the seizure of *The Spirit of '76*, a film depicting the Wyoming Massacre and Paul Revere's Ride, on the ground that these scenes of the American Revolution might turn viewers against the nation's British ally.[89]

The sheer exorbitance of this assault fed a growing reaction. A civil liberties establishment, with organizational and ideological expertise inherited from the domestic battles of the Progressive era, began to resist the wartime and especially the postwar assault on civil liberties. That defense drew both on a new formulation of the role of civil liberty in a modern society, and on venerable American traditions of hostility to government and freedom of speech and of the press.

Secretary of Labor William B. Wilson and his assistant secretary Louis F. Post (considerably so), unlike Attorney General Thomas Gregory, were sensitive to civil liberties issues. A *Harvard Law Review* note accepted the constitutionality of the original Espionage Act, but took issue with the readiness of the courts to regard declarations such as "this is a capitalists' war," "the government is for profiteers," and "the Selective Service Act is unconstitutional" as statements of fact, and thus potentially seditious, rather than mere expressions of opinion.[90]

Hyperbolic patriotism ran the risk of spilling over into buffoonery or manifest unconstitutionality. When the wealthy socialist Rose Pastor Stokes was sentenced to ten years in prison for a speech critical of the war, the *Literary Digest* delicately observed: "There are many regrets that the first notable victim [of the Espionage Act] should not have been a more dangerous enemy of the commonwealth." And when the Mount Vernon, New York, board of aldermen tried to bar Hearst's *New York Journal* and *American*—notoriously lukewarm toward the war—from circulation or sale in their city, a New York court had no trouble in finding this a violation of freedom of the press.[91]

Some federal judges, such as Charles F. Amidon in North Dakota and Albert B. Anderson in Indiana, refused to succumb to wartime hysteria. The most noteworthy instance was Learned Hand's reversal (not sustained by the circuit court of appeals) of the decision to deny the mails to *The Masses*.[92]

Although the war fostered repressive organizations, it saw as well the rise of an institutionalized defense of civil liberties. The Civil Liberties Bureau of the American Union against Militarism, the American counterpart of the left-wing antiwar British Union of Democratic Control, soon became the American Civil Liberties Union (ACLU). The wartime acts and their enforcement led also to the first substantial modern debate over the place of civil liberties in the American system of government. As the legal scholar Ernst Freund noted in 1921: "The suspicion of disloyalty during the war, and the dread of radical attacks upon the established economic system raised an issue that for decades had been dormant." Out of this came a civil liberties sensibility, vocabulary, and body of legal concepts that set the terms of discussion for decades to come.[93]

It was generally agreed that government could put some restraints on civil liberties in time of war. The question was instead one of standards, bounds, limits—and how to set them. The Progressive-minded constitutional authority Edward S. Corwin defended the Espionage Act on the grounds that the American people were not "a moral unit," that there were "irreconcilables in our midst." Many who now wanted to limit congressional power over the press, he observed, had been "distinctly opposed to the curtailment of legislative discretion by definite, unbending constitutional limitations" when it came to the social and economic legislation of the prewar years. Freedom of speech and of the press, Corwin concluded, were in the custody of legislative majorities and juries, which was where the Founders intended them to be.[94]

Catholic social reformer John A. Ryan took another tack. He argued that there was no moral privilege to make false statements or advocate wrong doctrine. Government had the unquestioned right to restrict freedom of speech for the more efficient prosecution of the war. Nor was there a right to speak against the war itself, or against those measures that were necessary for its successful prosecution.[95]

The conservative Yale law professor William R. Vance relied more on the distinction between criticism of and opposition to the government and its laws. He pointed to the historical precedents of seditious libel and blasphemy, and the variety of court-approved prewar laws against speech of various kinds. It was, he thought, within the power of Congress and the state legislatures to declare almost any sort of utterance seditious that would have been so regarded under common law in 1787.[96]

In the long run, however, it was Oliver Wendell Holmes and Zechariah Chafee who set the tone for the twentieth-century American understanding of civil liberties. Holmes made the strongest defense of the wartime restrictive legislation in his *Schenck* decision (1919). Here appeared his enormously influential "clear and present danger" rule, and his vivid admonition that there was no right to shout "Fire!" in a crowded theater. (But, asked Chafee, what about the man who gets up between acts and informs the audience honestly, but perhaps wrongly, that there are not enough fire exits, or that they are locked?) Holmes argued that the common law rule of no prior restraint was not a realistic way of dealing with freedom of speech and press in wartime. Rather, the law of seditious libel should apply, thus opening the door to restrictive legislation.[97]

Chafee was the major proponent of a broader view of freedom of speech, and ultimately Holmes moved in his direction. He warned that the Court slighted society's interest in free speech by treating it as an individual concern which must give way to the larger stake in national safety. And he took issue with Vance's attempt to preserve civil liberties in the amber of 1787: "The First Amendment was written by men . . . who intended to wipe out the common law of sedition, and make further prosecution for criticism of the government, without any incitement to law-breaking, forever impossible in the United States of America."[98]

The postwar Red Scare brought civil liberties even more fully into the mainstream of American public discourse. The Bolshevik Revolution and the economic dislocation following the war led to radical challenges, labor unrest, and government crackdowns everywhere in the Western world. Even relatively tolerant Britain was not immune. The Aliens Order of 1919 preserved the worst features of the wartime Defense of the Realm Act, empowering the government to arrest or deport aliens without showing cause or being subject to judicial review. The Home Secretary established a Home Intelligence Department with DORA powers as a separate branch of Scotland Yard—very close in time and spirit to the creation of the Bureau of Investigation, the precursor of the FBI, in the United States.[99]

A *Columbia Law Review* contributor observed in 1920: "We Americans are beginning to hear much of political crime in our domestic affairs." Wilson's administration responded to the postwar fear of radicalism much as it did to the wartime fear of disloyalty. Attorney General A. Mitchell Palmer organized January 2, 1920, raids on alien radicals which netted over five thousand suspects. Compared to the crushing of the Spartacist revolt in Germany or the rise of fascism in Italy, the American reaction to postwar radicalism was relatively mild. But coming as it did in the wake of a war which had already upset many accepted notions as to the proper (that is, properly distant) relationship between the state and the individual, the American Red Scare had a resonance that went beyond its actual scale.[100]

In many respects the Red Scare relied on wartime attitudes and techniques. Organizations such as the National Security League honed their antiradicalism on wartime hunts for disloyalty. Palmer tasted the uses of government power when, as Alien Property Custodian, he seized German-held assets and companies. Warlike too were his "Palmer raids" by droves of agents with batches of blank arrest warrants. There was much harshness in the roundup and jailing of those seized. The Justice Department's Bureau of Investigation, established in 1919 to ferret out domestic radicalism, was another inheritance from the warfare state.[101]

The Red Scare played itself out as well on the state and local levels. By 1920 thirty-four states had sedition and criminal syndicalism laws, with penalties averaging ten years in prison. Montana took aim at "any language calculated to incite or inflame resistance to any duly constituted State authority"; West Virginia sought to prevent the inculcation of "ideals hostile to those now or henceforth existing under the laws and constitution of this State." More than a thousand people were prosecuted under these laws.[102]

The fact of the Red Scare is no mystery, given the immediate postwar mood. That it so quickly subsided, and left so small a mark on American civil liberties policy, needs more explaining. As the assault on free speech grew, so did a civil liberties lobby. A September 1919 meeting of British liberals and like-minded Americans in New York focused on the issue of free speech. So too did increasing numbers of moderates and conservatives and a self-interested press. A number of editors were asked in early 1920 what a satisfactory antisedition act should include. About a third thought that no new legislation was required; another third were uncertain; the rest wanted stiffer punishment and the deportation of alien anarchists. The most common attitude was that it was necessary to distinguish between advocates of peaceful change in the form of government and advocates of change by force.[103]

A poll of union leaders found that 305 favored the deportation of "'red' agitators," 176 were opposed, twenty-two were divided, six were indifferent—and sixteen asked what a "'red' agitator" was. Nevertheless, Samuel Gompers, who strongly supported the war and opposed Bolshevism, called for a blanket proclamation freeing those imprisoned under the Espionage Act.[104]

The Palmer raids drew wide criticism. In a formulation common at the time, *Outlook* did not agree "that such arrests will be supported either by public opinion or by the courts, except for cases of those aliens who by their agitation have abused the hospitality of the Nation. We detest the anti-American theories of these radicals, and the more we detest them the more earnestly we hope that they will be combatted by American methods." Lawyers and judges, often of unimpeachable conservatism, also spoke out against the hysteria of the time. An attorney chastised the Missouri Bar Association for supporting peacetime seditious libel laws: "Talking may be the safety-valve after all that will prevent social explosion." George W. Anderson, a federal district judge in Boston, said of the Palmer raids and the treatment of the detainees: "It may . . . fitly be observed that a mob is a mob, whether made up of government officials, acting under the instructions of the Department of Justice, or of criminals, loafers and the vicious classes."[105]

The Red Scare crested in 1919. The failure of a new antisedition bill to get out of the House Rules Committee in 1920 was revealing. Those speaking against it included the AFL, the National Popular Government League, the Friends of Irish Freedom (reacting against the bill's ban on mailings that made "an appeal to racial prejudice" or tended to cause "rioting"), civil rights expert Zechariah Chafee, many journalists—and Attorney General Palmer himself, who disliked the measure because of the power it gave his rival in repression, Postmaster General Burleson.

Palmer's alternative was the Davey Act, proposed in the wake of a Justice Department claim that there were sixty thousand revolutionary agitators in the country. It allowed indictments for sedition without evidence of conspiracy: engaging in propaganda was enough. The bill's manifest threat to free speech and press evoked widespread concern. The AFL's Samuel Gompers and Maryland's conservative Senator Joseph I. France were among its critics, as were leading Episcopal bishops and a flock of newspaper editorialists, many comparing it to the Alien and Sedition Acts of 1798. It, too, failed.[106]

Hoping to ride antiradical hysteria to the Democratic presidential nomination, Palmer predicted a May Day 1920 wave of attacks on government leaders; the police (and the press) were mobilized; when nothing happened, "the Fighting Quaker" became "the Quaking Fighter." On the day before he left office in March 1921, Woodrow Wilson approved a congressional resolution repealing most of the wartime internal security laws.

The New York State Assembly's Lusk Committee, charged with investigating subversion, issued an enormous report documenting the pervasiveness of "revolutionary radicalism." It wanted the legislature to create a bureau of secret police under the state attorney general; to authorize the Board of Regents to investigate the loyalty of teachers before granting them licenses, extending its authority to private schools and other institutions; and to ban the Socialist party from elections. These Lusk bills were passed by the legislature, but lame duck governor Al Smith vetoed them in 1920, and they were not seen again.[107]

The most dramatic reaction to rogue antiradicalism came when the New York Assembly denied its Socialist members their seats, pending a judicial hearing on their eligibility. The five ran again in a special election held to fill their vacant places, and were returned with increased majorities. Three were ousted once again; the other two resigned in protest. These actions set off a firestorm of criticism. Newspapers, regardless of party, almost unanimously condemned the legislature. Charles Evans Hughes, the 1916 Republican candidate for president, soon to return to the Supreme Court as Chief Justice, led a protest joined by numerous other respectables. *Outlook* took note of "the rather strange phenomenon . . . of vigorous anti-Socialist Americans whose loyalty and patriotism no one can question, coming to the defense of these five Socialists."[108]

Legislated conformity, whatever its ephemeral popularity, did not sit well with a society that normally relied on a mix of popularly enforced mores and a live-and-let-live individualism. When Connecticut passed an anti–red flag law banning the display of banners of that color "as a symbol calculated to, or which may, incite people to disorder or breaches of the law," the *Yale Law Journal* balefully warned: "And the Harvard game approaches in New Haven—if not this year, then next!" (And indeed the pioneering Massachusetts red flag law of 1913 had been repealed in 1915 because it appeared to render illegal the display of the Harvard crimson.)[109]

The incoming Harding administration was no more noted for its dedication to civil liberty than for its dedication to civic virtue. But in their corrupt and easygoing way the Harding crowd had little taste for enforcing conformity or repressing dissent. An American Civil Liberties Union official found Harding's attorney general Harry M. Daugherty a welcome change from the fanatical Palmer: "A nice fat man with a big cigar in his face and instead of getting excited as Palmer used to do he grins when somebody talks about revolution and says, well, he thinks it probably best 'not to agitate the agitator' too much." On Christmas Day 1921 Harding pardoned Socialist party leader Eugene V. Debs, who had been given a ten-year jail sentence in 1918 for violating the Espionage Act—something Wilson had resolutely refused to do.[110]

Although the Red Scare petered out, the civil liberties issue did not readily fade. State and local constraints persisted. Judges continued to uphold ordinances requiring official permission to hold street meetings. New Jersey's court found nothing wrong when the mayor of Rahway had the fire department wash a Socialist speaker off his platform at an unauthorized public meeting. Even a dissenter found this amusing: the plaintiff "possessed an inflexible purpose and, as the event proved, a flexible platform."[111]

In general, though, the 1920s saw not only the lifting of the war-era pall of repression, but (despite Prohibition, the Klan, and immigration restriction) the emergence of a more open-minded civic culture. Discussing "civil liberty" in 1921, Charles and Mary Beard took note of "the new spirit of liberty for all persons." When the mayor of Johnstown, Pennsylvania, ordered all blacks who had not been in residence for at least seven years to leave the city, and permitted only pro-fascist speakers to hold public meetings, there was a nationwide protest. Both actions were quickly revoked, and he was denied reelection.[112]

The American Civil Liberties Union took on a role comparable to that of the NAACP in racial issues, and civil liberties lawyers—Clarence Darrow, Dudley Field Malone, Arthur Garfield Hays—became familiar figures on the legal stage. ACLU director Roger Baldwin participated in a Paterson, New Jersey, strikers' rally and was sent to jail for six months in 1924 for "unlawful assembly" under a hitherto inert 1796 New Jersey law. A group of Baldwin's supporters convinced themselves that he was the victim of unspeakable brutality in the county jail in which he was confined. They descended on the jail one Saturday night, demanding to see the martyr. His embarrassed jailer confessed that for some time Baldwin had been let out to spend his weekends in New York.[113]

The ACLU reported in 1929 that there had been fewer lynchings than at any time in the previous fifty years; that intellectual freedom in schools and colleges was increasing; that the deportation of aliens because of their political or economic views had declined (though so too had the pool of deportable aliens, what with immigration restriction); that there had been only one case of mob violence, compared to hundreds when the Klan flourished; and that in 1928 the last inmate incarcerated under state criminal syndicalism laws had been released.[114]

The major expression of the new standing of civil liberties law was the Supreme Court's incorporation of the First into the Fourteenth Amendment. Decades before it was ready to do this in the realm of civil rights, the Court defined a national law of civil liberties transcending the authority of the states. Dissenting opinions by John M. Harlan in Paterson v. Colorado (1907) and Louis D. Brandeis in Gilbert v. Minnesota (1920) were pioneering attempts to apply Fourteenth Amendment due process to First Amendment cases. Then in Gitlow

v. New York (1925), Holmes upheld the wartime conviction (under New York's criminal anarchy act of 1902) of a newspaper publisher who had printed a manifesto of the left wing of the Socialist party, but in doing so he brought into a majority decision the view that the First Amendment was incorporated in the Fourteenth. One alarmed observer feared that the entire Bill of Rights would come under the rubric of Fourteenth Amendment–protected "liberty" if *Gitlow* was extended to its logical conclusion: "The 'liberty' of the states is being unduly sacrificed to this new conception of the 'liberty' of the individual."[115]

Fiske v. Kansas (1927) was the first case in which the Fourteenth Amendment was used to protect the right to freedom of speech. An IWW organizer was found guilty of violating the Kansas criminal syndicalism law. In part because the IWW was in its last days and could not by any stretch of the radical-fearing imagination be considered a threat to the Republic, a unanimous Court held the conviction to be a violation of the free speech provisions in both the Kansas and the federal constitutions.[116]

The *Fiske* decision rejected not the Kansas syndicalism law but only its application in that one case. In Whitney v. California (1927) the Court sustained the 1925 conviction and one-to-fourteen-year jail term meted out to the socially well connected Charlotte Anita Whitney under California's 1919 criminal syndicalism statute. But the spectacular impropriety of the case did more to weaken than to bolster the standing of state restraints on opinion. Even William J. Locke, the legislator most responsible for the act, objected that "the law was never intended to halt free speech nor to punish persons for their thoughts." More important, the Court's decision explicitly brought freedom of speech under the "liberty" protected by the Fourteenth Amendment. Constraints on free expression now had to meet the standard tests of due process: the restriction must be within the police power; the means employed must be reasonably related to the end; the statute must not be unreasonable, oppressive, or arbitrary. A commentator thought it "exceedingly questionable" whether the Kansas and California criminal syndicalism laws, passed as emergency measures, had any further utility.[117]

Newspapers had come to be enmeshed in a web of government restrictions: limits on access to the mails; wartime censorship; legislative prohibitions on blasphemy, obscenity, and defamation. Judges continued to impose summary contempt citations on journalists who in their view interfered with the work of the courts. An Anti-Saloon League editor went to jail for accusing the Indiana Supreme Court of undermining Prohibition; a New Mexico judge imprisoned an offending editor for six months with the admonition: "You are a low-down skunk—a measly yellow cur." The North Carolina newspaper editor (and Wilson's wartime secretary of the navy) Josephus Daniels was sentenced to a $1,000 fine or sixty days in jail for condemning a court's handling of a railroad receivership in 1925. Daniels refused to pay his fine; his friends in the courtroom surged forward to pay it; the angry judge sent the editor to prison.[118]

When the *Saturday Press*, a Minneapolis scandal sheet, linked the city's mayor and chief of police with Jewish gangsters, it was brought to book under a 1925 Minnesota law aimed at defamatory journals. In 1928 the state supreme court upheld the law—and this particular application—as a valid exercise of the police power: "The distribution of scandalous matter is detrimental to the public morals and to the general welfare . . . The constitutional rights of the individual are as sacred as the liberty of the press."[119]

The United States Supreme Court held otherwise. It struck down the law in Near v. Minnesota (1931), holding that the First Amendment rights of the defendants were protected from state interference by the Fourteenth Amendment. In doing so, the Court extended to freedom of the press the same federal protection that it was crafting for freedom of speech. Pierce Butler complained in dissent: "It gives to freedom of the press a meaning and scope not heretofore recognized and construes 'liberty' in the due process clause of the Fourteenth Amendment to put upon the States a federal restriction that is without precedent."[120]

The advent of the Great Depression imposed new strains on civil liberties. Local authorities—Mayor Frank Hague in Jersey City, the police in many localities—clamped down on labor organizers and radicals, and state courts continued to be more inclined than their federal counterparts to uphold local restrictions on speech.

The conflict between judges concerned that the accused get a fair trial and journalists out to get all the information they could without divulging their sources remained unresolved (as it is today). When confronted with academic freedom cases, the courts found it difficult to deal with them as civil liberties issues rather than as conflicts involving the contractual relationship between teachers and their institutions. And of course World War II and the cold war resurrected federal restraints on free expression and belief in substantial and unsettling ways.[121]

Nevertheless, it is evident that the conditions of early twentieth-century life—new social and economic tensions, technological change, the stresses of war—gave civil liberties a fresh form and content as a public issue. By the early 1930s the First Amendment had a place in American law and public discourse far closer to the current understanding than to the one that prevailed in 1900.

4 · Private Vices, Public Mores

Modern America nourished both a burgeoning variety of forms of social behavior and a rising reaction against that diversity. Old American conflicts—between individual freedom and social control, between contrariety and conformity—were reshaped, intensified, and
fought out in the context of a new society.

Traditional laissez-faire beliefs weighed against social as they did
against economic regulation. Legal theorist Christopher G. Tiedeman,
who wanted to limit the states' police power, observed in 1900 that
immorality was largely a self-inflicted wound, whose social effect was
"secondary and remote, and does not connote a trespass upon any
one's legal rights." He did not believe that "repressive legislation"
could "elevate or improve the moral character of a people" any more
than regulation could purify a market economy.[1]

Public figures politically dependent on or ideologically attuned to
urban America also opposed the regulation of mores. New York
Mayor Seth Low reassured a German-American audience in an October 1901 campaign speech: "Now it is not expected that, if we are
elected, the laws will be administered in a narrow and provincial
spirit." Progressive Governor Joseph Folk of Missouri thought that the
banning of Sunday baseball might be acceptable in small towns, but
not in big cities. He opposed the censorship of plays deemed to be
immoral and the use of the law to stop small-time gambling.[2]

Nevertheless, there was a substantial effort in the early twentieth
century to control social behavior. The prevailing assumption was
that the role of government must grow in pace with the increasing
density and variety of society. What gave this moral crusade its considerable power—most notably in its assaults on prostitution and the
liquor trade—was the variety of the interests that coalesced behind it.
The conservative desire for social control, the religious quest for

moral conformity, and the reformist search for social uplift joined to turn private vices into threats to public mores.[3]

Frailties of the Flesh

Government lightly regulated morals in the nineteenth century. The only significant national law, the Comstock Act of 1873, barred the use of the mails for obscene or pornographic purposes. Anthony Comstock, the activist clergyman chiefly responsible for this legislation, has long been an object of ridicule: Comstockery has gained a place in the language as the embodiment of prudery. But John Collier, who later was a major figure in movie censorship and in the reform of Indian policy, praised Comstock as a pioneer in the Progressive assault on social ills: "He warred against the organized, commercialized promotion of obscenity among the young . . . He did in the field of sexual concern what other representatives of the middle class were doing, are doing, and will do in many other fields."[4]

The 1920s were a time when the more liberated artistic and cultural values that took form in the prewar period trickled down into middlebrow culture, and when, through the movies, the racier values of working-class immigrant culture spread into society at large. The journalist Frank Kent took note in 1925 of a great rise in the number of smutty magazines on newsstands, particularly in the smaller cities and towns where most Americans still lived. Of 110 periodicals on sale in Steubenville, Ohio, he found 60 of them libidinous. The spread of pornography, of a national consumer culture, and of political indifference all went, he thought, hand in hand: "You will find in one section exactly what you find in another. From coast to coast, the radio, movies, golf, bobbed hair, business, short skirts, trashy literature, automobiles, lip sticks, bad manners, rotten liquor, absorption in money making, almost complete political inertia, and an unparalleled muddy-mindedness about public matters—that's the country today."[5]

The courts often were hostile to these new currents in American life. The Supreme Court in 1932 held that the Comstock law applied to "filthy" as well as to (presumably even more objectionable) "obscene" reading material. A New York judge attempted to deal with the new freedom on the stage: "A pantomime symbolical of the retirement of a husband and wife upon their wedding night, although unattended by improper language or actual exposure of the person, may be indictable as a public nuisance where it suggests, induces, excites impure imaginations and is calculated to corrupt public morals." Another jurist in 1917 thought it proper that a birth control pamphlet, "What Every Girl Should Know," be banned: "This contains matters which should not only not be known by every girl, but which perhaps, should not be known by any." Why? To remove the fear of pregnancy, he thought, would be to increase the risk of immorality.[6]

A few judges were ready to give a place to new cultural values. John M. Woolsey of the New York Federal District Court did not find Marie Stopes's birth control manual "Married Love" obscene. Augustus Hand of the New York Federal Circuit Court of Appeals refused to convict Mary Ware Dennett for sending *The Sex Side of Life* through the mails. It was, he held, wise public policy to so instruct the young. And in the landmark case of U.S. v. One Book Entitled *Ulysses* (1934), Hand overrode the government ban on that novel's publication in the United States. But in general, law and legislation regarding pornography did not significantly change for another quarter of a century.[7]

Laws restricting Sunday activities—"blue laws"—were perhaps the most common pre-1900 regulation of social behavior. They had both a religious and a social welfare base: they sanctified the Sabbath while guaranteeing workers a day of rest. (Similar statutes served similar ends in Britain and France.) But new forms of entertainment and recreation were spreading, and ever-larger numbers of people had divergent views as to the proper way to spend their Sundays.[8]

The result was intensified conflict over Sabbatarian policy. When in 1907 a Kansas City judge enforced Missouri's Sunday law against the city's theaters, cigar stores, barber shops, and soda fountains, their owners combined and fought back, despite hundreds of indictments and numerous convictions. An often intense politics of Sunday closing, involving shopkeepers, organized religious groups, and other segments of public opinion, would be a persistent part of twentieth-century American state and local public life.[9]

Sunday baseball heightened the conflict between old and new ways of spending the Sabbath. In 1914 the Maryland Supreme Court held that a Baltimore antibaseball ordinance applied even if the game were played only for recreation. Most decisions, however, cleared the way for the great American pastime. Kansas and Missouri courts held that baseball was not a game but a sport or athletic exercise, and that it was not "labor" to play on Sunday. Judge (later Mayor) William J. Gaynor of New York City argued: "Fathers and mothers would much rather know that their grown sons are at a ball or golf game on Sunday afternoon, than not know where they are."[10]

Those aspects of American life that made Sunday restraints obsolete—the automobile, movies, mass sporting events—reached flood stage in the 1920s. An effort was made to enact a federal law enforcing strict restraints on Sunday activities. The proposed statute made it illegal for federal employees to work on Sunday; no trains would be allowed to cross state lines; mail would not be moved. But powerful opposition readily overwhelmed this hopeless enterprise. Tens of thousands of ex-servicemen and many American Legion posts objected; the Catholic Knights of Columbus condemned the imposition of a Puritan Sunday. Restraints of the sort proposed were linked to Bolshevism: "uniting the anti-red drive with the anti-blue drive," as one journal put it.[11]

The courts constantly reviewed Sunday laws. A Minnesota act that set a six-day maximum work week in hospitals, telephone and telegraph offices, garages, and places of public amusement was held to make distinctions that violated the equal protection clause of the Fourteenth Amendment. In defining "necessary" activities, courts reflected the changing life-style of an urban consumer society. Exemptions from Sunday bans by 1927 included the sale and delivery of food; agricultural work; mail, telephone, and telegraph services; highway repair; work by lawyers and public officials; publishing and delivering newspapers; operating garages, filling stations, hotels, and restaurants; and showing movies. Because so many activities were approved as work of necessity or charity, Massachusetts, New York, California, and other states began to pass "one day in seven" laws designed to protect the welfare of workers without forcing a Sunday closedown.[12]

Gambling was among the oldest (and least effectively) regulated forms of social behavior. Its ubiquity and private, one-on-one character made it all but impossible to control. Commercial gambling was well ensconced in American cities: more than sixty of them licensed gambling of various sorts in 1909. When San Francisco's Board of Supervisors sought to outlaw slot machines, eight of the city's leading banks joined in opposition.

But as social and technological change made gambling an increasingly commercialized activity, public opinion and law and legislation responded. Religious and middle-class moralists pointed to its erosive moral and economic consequences. So did socialists, who criticized the ubiquitous "nickel slots" in St. Louis drugstores and barrooms in the 1890s. The constitutions of the new states of Arizona and New Mexico outlawed wagering.[13]

This was not a uniquely American attitude. Britain's House of Lords created a Commission on Betting to look into that practice in 1902, and a Joint Commission on Lotteries and Indecent Advertisement met in 1908. Regulation, however, was problematical. Both commissions opposed giving the Postmaster General the power to control lotteries by opening or refusing to deliver suspect mail. In 1913 the British Cabinet deplored the spread of bookmakers and lottery promoters operating from the Continent, but saw no way to stop it.[14]

American public policy was more hostile to gaming. The courts generally refused to lend aid or give relief to aggrieved parties in gambling transactions. In 1903 the Supreme Court upheld a law forbidding the use of the mails by lotteries, a major new application of the Constitution's commerce clause. Two years later the Court found San Francisco's antigambling ordinance "a proper exercise of governmental authority," despite the fact that it was manifestly aimed at the city's Chinese population. In 1912 Justice Lucius Lamar upheld a South Pasadena, California, ordinance restricting pool halls, noting *en passant:* "That the keeping of a billiard hall has a harmful tendency is a fact requiring no proof." Nebraska's supreme court was more specific: "Such a room is not, we concede, per se a nuisance, but without regulation and supervision it is likely to become so anywhere, and in a village it is apt to degenerate into a trysting place for idlers and a nidus for vice."[15]

Prizefighting and horse racing were drenched in gambling. And they had ethnic and economic characteristics similar to organized prostitution and the liquor traffic. Not surprisingly they became objects of substantial concern around the turn of the century. Injunctions prohibiting prizefights increased in number. Arkansas blocked a contest between "Gentleman Jim" Corbett and Bob Fitzsimmons in 1896 on the ground that it was a public nuisance. The Indiana Supreme Court in 1895 approved an injunction against a corporation that put on fights and appointed a receiver to take over the company's affairs. When a 1901 Cincinnati fight was advertised as a "sparring contest"— but with tickets sold—the governor of Ohio used the National Guard to stop it.[16]

Meanwhile, new technology was making heavily promoted

prizefights an increasingly lucrative form of mass entertainment. A 1912 federal act forbade sending fight movies through the mails. To circumvent this law, a projector was set up in Canada to show the film of the April 1915 Havana bout between Jack Johnson and Jess Willard to an audience gathered on the American side of the border. A federal judge denied that it was legal to exhibit the fight "by the use of air, sunlight, electric light and otherwise." And he concluded that the congressional obligation to serve the general welfare made the 1912 act constitutional: "The brutalizing and pernicious effects, especially on the young, of looking on physical encounters between human beings in the shape of actual fights . . . are well known and recognized almost everywhere."[17]

Horse racing raised more difficult problems, for this was a widely popular, respectable sport. Track and racehorse owners, telephone and telegraph companies enriched by offtrack betting, railroad and streetcar companies serving the tracks, and wealthy gamblers constituted a powerful set of supporting interests. Legislation against racetrack gambling nevertheless became an important issue in a number of states around the turn of the century. Louisiana and the District of Columbia prohibited betting at the track; a New Jersey law sought to abolish racetracks except as part of state or county fairs; an Illinois statute that made bookmaking illegal practically eliminated horse racing in that state by the time of the First World War.[18]

New York's 1894 state constitution forbade lotteries, bookmaking, and other forms of gambling. The Percy-Gray law of 1895, ostensibly enforcing that prohibition, in fact made it possible for ontrack betting to flourish. Complaints mounted, and in 1908 Governor Charles Evans Hughes led a campaign for a corrective bill. This quickly became a classic Progressive battle. Those with (so to speak) a stake in racetrack betting included the State Racing Commission, headed by the banker August Belmont, the eight licensed tracks, and the agricultural county fair associations that shared in the profits. But clergymen and other reform spokesmen joined in the crusade, and after months of intricate political maneuvering and appeals to public opinion, Hughes had his way.[19]

California's most active track, in Emoryville, saw $38 million bet during the 1907–8 season alone. Machine politicians made sure that the state senate's Committee on Public Morals did not interfere with the Sport of Kings. But in 1911 reform elements took control of the legislature and passed a law abolishing racetrack gambling. The issue came before the electorate in a hard-fought 1912 referendum, and a majority of more than 200,000 voters supported the new act.[20]

Gambling attracted less attention from a Prohibition-fixated public during the 1920s. New York, Illinois, and Kentucky were the only states to have ontrack betting. Antigambling sentiment, fueled by old-time religion and social reformism, appeared to be declining. John C. W. Beckham, a former governor, won the Kentucky Democratic primary in 1927 by promising to make racetrack parimutuel betting illegal. This became an important political issue, pitting the Louisiana Churchmen's Federation against the racetrack owners' Kentucky Jockey Club. The Klan, the Anti-Saloon League, the Southern Baptist Convention, the Episcopal church, and the evangelist Billy Sunday joined in the fight against racetrack gambling, blending the rhetoric of the prohibition and antitrust movements. Yet the Republican gubernatorial candidate, who resolutely ignored the issue, crushed Beckham in the election—although the rest of the Democratic ticket was elected.[21]

Most states banned lotteries in the 1920s. But the new consumer economy bred variants that called for regulation. Large retailers frequently offered trading stamps, a marketing device dating from the late nineteenth century. The protests of small merchandisers and shopkeepers led a number of states to bar their use on the ground that they were essentially lotteries. The courts struck down almost all of these attempts as beyond the police power: trading stamps did not have the element of chance essential to a lottery. Other marketing gimmicks such as guessing contests in newspapers, where awards were in fact determined by chance, did not fare as well.[22]

Tobacco and drugs, like horse racing and boxing relatively free from oversight during the nineteenth century, now also became public issues, in part because of new moral, physical, and social anxieties, in part because of changes in the frequency and extent of their use.

An anticigarette movement of some size appeared around the turn of the century, along with a takeoff in smoking. Lucy Page Gaston (who, it was said, traded on her resemblance to Abraham Lincoln) was the doyenne of the anticigarette crusade. Kansas City's streetcar company held a week-long referendum on its 1910 no smoking rule in 1912; women and children were among the 80 percent of patrons participating. By a three-to-one margin the rule was sustained. A Los Angeles police official darkly reported in 1916 that 90 percent of male juveniles who were arrested, and almost as many females, were cigarette smokers: "Surely there must be some conclusion to be drawn from such figures." Convinced that crime was "more or less closely associated with cigarette smoking among juveniles," the city set up anticigarette clinics. By 1914 ten states—among them Iowa, Tennessee, New Hampshire, Wisconsin, and Indiana—forbade sales of "the Little White Slaver." The Supreme Court upheld Tennessee's ban, but (as in the case of liquor) did not allow the state to block residents from importing cigarettes for their own use.[23]

Estimates (guesses, really) as to the number of drug addicts in turn-of-the-century America went as high as 250,000. A number of states passed laws against morphine and cocaine in the 1890s. But they often exempted the use of cocaine in patent medicines; indeed, the drug was sanctioned as a remedy by the Hay Fever Association.

After 1900 addiction came to be viewed more as an attribute of urban immigrant lower-class life than of individual moral frailty. In short, it became a social issue. Instances were cited "where groups of schoolchildren have been taught to use" cocaine, and the Pure Food and Drug Act of 1906 required that patent medicines containing cocaine so indicate on their labels. The registration of addicts and free prescription of drugs was tried in Jacksonville, Florida, and in Tennessee. New York sought to prohibit or at least regulate the prescription of addictive drugs, in the face of substantial opposition from doctors. The state's Boylan Act of 1914 provided for the commitment of habitual users; yet its Whitney Act of 1917 allowed physicians to prescribe drugs to addicts in the course of treating them.[24]

American narcotics policy, strongly colored by considerations of race, class, ethnicity, and social control, was inclined (then as now) more to prohibition and prosecution than to prevention and treatment. The response in tone and timing resembled the contemporaneous campaigns against prostitution and liquor. This was evident in the federal response to the drug problem, the Harrison Anti-Narcotics Act of 1914. That law restricted the sale and use of drugs, relied on the tax power to prohibit the importation of narcotics for four years, and in effect made a doctor's prescription necessary for opium or cocaine. Its passage owed much to social and racial fears, which overrode traditional American hostility to federal control of behavior. It drew as well on the belief that social and medical science had the know-how to deal with drug addiction.[25]

The constraints of federalism and the intractability of the drug problem limited the effectiveness of the Harrison Act. Complaints rose that it offered no way of distinguishing between drug addicts and occasional users, no uniform accounting procedure to oversee the sale and use of drugs, no medical treatment for addicts. Court decisions narrowed its writ until Doremus v. U.S. (1919) reinforced the broad power of the national government to regulate drugs.[26]

By 1918 it appeared that the number of addicts with daily access to morphine, heroin, and cocaine had increased enormously. A New York legislative investigation estimated that there were 200,000 of them in New York City alone. Drugs were smuggled in from Canada and Mexico, and then sold by doctors and "bootleggers." And it was feared that the exposure of American soldiers to the opium and morphine widely used in the French army increased the likelihood of a postwar drug epidemic. The Narcotics Division of the Treasury Department was established in 1919, and the manufacture of heroin was prohibited in 1924.[27]

Most notably in New York and New Orleans, there were continued attempts to deal with the problem by dispensing drugs to addicts in public clinics. This approach failed either to cure addiction or to stem its spread. An observer remarked that if the prohibition of liquor followed the course of drug prevention, "we may expect to see a great increase in the number of drunkards when it goes into full effect." Yet it appears that the use of drugs tailed off during the 1920s and 1930s. By one estimate, one in three thousand Americans was an addict in 1936, compared to one in four hundred in 1900. The World War II rejection rate of draftees for drug addiction was one in ten thousand, in World War I one in one thousand. What had happened? Two things, probably: a natural rise and fall in the use of particular drugs, and the impact of a high level of social, political, and legal disapproval of the practice.[28]

Prostitution, a far more visible problem than drug addiction, spawned a commensurately more substantial campaign of suppression. Commercialized sex had a powerful effect on the Progressive social imagination. Walter Lippmann speculated that "it would be interesting to know how much of the social conscience of our times had as its first insight the prostitute on the city pavement."[29]

The assault on prostitution, like its close companion the crusade against drink, drew on the same values that fueled the movements to conserve the natural environment, control trusts, and improve the lot of the poor. It was easy to speak of the need to conserve human and social as well as natural and economic resources; to equate vice lords and beer barons with other plutocrats of the time; to see prostitutes and drunkards as victims of "the interests." Like the boss-run machine and the big business trust, commercialized vice and the liquor trade stirred fears of frightening new interlocked organizations that preyed not only on fallible individuals but on the health of the nation, on society itself.[30]

The antiprostitution movement, like its antiliquor counterpart, moved from an emphasis on individual moral fault to a mix of moral, political, economic, scientific, and gender-related concerns. As with Prohibition, interest in the issue rose and fell: the "Prostitution" entry in the *Readers' Guide to Periodical Literature* listed 36 items between 1890 and 1908, 156 from 1910 to 1914, 41 from 1915 to 1924. As was so often the case with Progressive social policy, broad-gauged support ensured some reform; but it also imposed limits on the scale and depth of change.[31]

The social forces that made prostitution a public issue were not unique to the United States. A National Vigilance Association was active in late nineteenth-century Britain; Morality Associations held mass meetings in Hamburg during the 1890s to protest police-regulated prostitution. Eugene Brieux's *Damaged Goods* (1901), a play about a middle-class French family destroyed by syphilis, thrilled and chilled middle-class audiences in Europe and America, much as Upton Sinclair's novel *The Jungle*, with its vivid description of conditions in the meat-packing industry, led to frissons of gustatory anxiety a few years later.[32]

The British movement against prostitution drew on social democratic sentiments and eugenicist beliefs. The Cabinet inclined toward regulation in 1906: "Some people might think it desirable that these women should be quartered in blocks of flats. Otherwise they might be spread over the town and find their way into respectable streets, creating scandal there and depreciating the value of the property." But the National Council of Public Morals issued a manifesto in 1911 that pointed to prostitution, obscene literature, and a low birthrate as symptoms of national degeneration. Its signers included Christian leaders, prominent doctors, the Fabian Beatrice Webb, and the Labour party's Ramsay MacDonald. The Criminal Law Amendment Act of 1912—Britain's counterpart to the American Mann Act—struck at the white slave traffic by giving constables the power to take suspects

into custody without a warrant and permitting the flogging of convicted procurers.[33]

The variety of the sources of public anxiety over prostitution,
stretching from traditional moral-religious qualms to new concerns
over class, race, ethnicity, and public health, made its regulation an
important public issue. Harvard president Charles W. Eliot (who included among "the recognized safeguards against sex and perversions"
such practices as "bodily exercises, moderation in eating, abstinency
in youth from alcohol, tobacco, hot spices, and all other drugs which
impair self-control") tried to enlist support for an assault on "the social evil" by yoking the new science of eugenics to traditional social
moralism: "The family life of the white race is at stake in its purity,
in its healthfulness and in its fertility." So too did the head of the
Southern Baptist Mission in 1914, who claimed to have talked to
more than fifteen thousand prostitutes. His conclusion: their moral
depravity was the chief cause of their situation; their life reflected
their sexual desires. This man of the cloth was also a man of science.
He made a careful study of his subjects' appearance and expression,
and found them to be a "separate and distinct class of people," physically as well as morally.[34]

The assault on commercialized vice took two major forms: the
elimination of urban red light districts, and a campaign against the
white slave traffic culminating in the passage of the Mann Act of
1910. The well-publicized results of New York's Raines law of 1896
strengthened critics of regulated prostitution. That act forbade Sunday liquor sales except in hotel dining rooms. But hundreds of saloons
quickly became "hotels," with rooms used by prostitutes. Opponents
put pressure on the brewers supplying them, and on the surety companies underwriting the bonds that owners had to post; a 1905 law made
them illegal.[35]

Public concern was fostered by a stream of investigations typical of
the period. Some forty-three city and three state investigations of
prostitution took place between 1910 and 1917. *The Social Evil,* a
1902 report by New York's Committee of Fifteen, criticized regulated
prostitution in Paris, Berlin, and other foreign cities. This was not a
peculiarly American view: a special French commission recommended an end to regulated prostitution, and during the early years of
the century 48 of 162 German cities stopped the practice.[36]

Particularly influential was *The Social Evil in Chicago,* the 1911
report of the Chicago Vice Commission (which the Chicago post of-

fice banned from the mails). It treated professional prostitution as a big business—the average prostitute, it found, had a capitalized value four times that of an industrial worker—whose work force was pushed into the trade by low wages for women in industrial employment.[37]

By 1909 openly regulated prostitution existed in only three of fifty-five large American cities. New York City police commissioner Theodore A. Bingham's was a lonely voice when he called for dividing the city into four areas, with a regulated red light district in each. Equally isolated was the attempt of Mayor Samuel ("Golden Rule") Jones to segregate prostitution in Toledo, but to make it cheerless by banning pianos, music, and revelry from brothels.[38]

The decline of tolerance for red light districts is reflected in two judicial decisions dealing with prostitution in New Orleans. The United States Supreme Court in L'Hote v. New Orleans (1900) accepted a city ordinance that restricted the area in which prostitutes could live and work. It saw no assault on the constitutional rights of adjacent property owners or of prostitutes, but only a proper exercise of state power: "One of the difficult social problems of the day is what shall be done in respect to those vocations which minister to and feed upon human weakness, appetites, and passions . . . The management of those vocations comes directly within the scope of what is known as the police power." In 1917 the Louisiana Supreme Court reviewed a New Orleans ordinance prescribing segregated districts for black and white prostitutes. Even the acceptable racial policy implicit in the move did not condone the legalization of what had come to be so unacceptable a social practice. The court rejected the ordinance as *ultra vires:* beyond the power of the municipal corporation.[39]

The assault on red light districts had palpable results. By 1918 they were prohibited in about two hundred American cities; by the beginning of the 1920s almost every state had laws against pandering, and thirty-eight of them had "red light" injunction and abatement acts that enabled citizens as well as authorities to secure injunctions against brothels. New regulatory bodies joined in the assault. The Chicago Morals Court, established in 1913, employed female probation officers and doctors, and sought to deal with prostitutes in a humane and scientific manner. New York's Bureau of Social Hygiene sponsored an influential study (paid for by John D. Rockefeller, Jr.) which strengthened the view that the business should be eliminated, not regulated. Between 1911 and 1913 Pittsburgh's Morals Efficiency

Commission reduced the number of brothels in the city from 247 to 65, their inmates from 1,000 to 342. That city's license court also helped by refusing scores of permits to saloon-hotels. A Morals Bureau closed every open house in the city; the campaign then shifted to more clandestine traffic.[40]

New York's experience showed the diversity and power of the anti-prostitution crusade. The city's reformers found an unexpected ally during the 1890s in Tammany boss Richard Croker. His rival, Big Tim Sullivan, was building a separate machine based on police-protected gambling and prostitution. In an anti-Sullivan ploy, Croker appointed a Tammany-dominated Committee of Five to investigate morals in New York City. But the issue quickly got out of his control. The breakup of the red light districts became a major theme of anti-Tammany reform, and the criminal code was amended in 1900 to include pimps and brothel owners. Adultery became a criminal offense in 1907.[41]

It took years to put together a compound of law and mobilized public opinion sufficient to make a difference. But from 1912 on, police semitoleration tailed off. The Bureau of Social Hygiene estimated in 1916 that since 1912 the number of New York's brothels had been reduced from 142 to 23, their inmates from 1,686 to about 50; establishments in tenement houses were pared from 1,172 to 482, assignation hotels from 90 to 56.[42]

A nine-block red light district in Chicago was suddenly closed down by a combination of police action and court injunctions. Cleveland tolerated 396 known houses of prostitution with about 4,000 inmates in 1906; in 1911 the count was 44 houses with 350 inmates; by 1915 the city's red light district was gone. Baltimore, too, was reported to be brothel-free in that year. Portland, Oregon's vice commission recommended that a "tin-plate ordinance" be passed requiring that every multitenant building post a plate by the front door with the name and address of the owner. Atlanta's antivice movement had a strong religious tone: it was led by the Men & Religion Forward Movement, which mixed businesslike organization and sales techniques with evangelical fervor. In Buffalo the Federation of Churches took the lead in bringing injunctions against houses of prostitution, and by 1916 the old Tenderloin was full of vacant houses.[43]

Seattle was a classically wide-open frontier town, and Hiram Gill won the mayoralty in 1910 on a platform promising to keep it that way. But he was recalled in a special election decided by women, who had just gotten the vote. George F. Cotterill, his successor, sent anti-fornication squads into downtown hotels. Gill ran again in 1912 but lost. He then underwent a (public) change of heart of considerable dimension, and in 1914 was elected on a platform promising to abolish prostitution in the city. He made the choice of the Ministers' Association his chief of police, and soon boasted that Seattle was the cleanest city in the United States.[44]

Prostitution was a solidly ensconced, respectable part of San Francisco's life. A leading house of assignation, with four floors of supper-bedrooms, was financed by one of the largest trust companies in the West. The Board of Health in 1911 adopted the recommendation of Dr. Julius Rosenstirn of Mt. Zion Hospital that a European style of regulation be adopted, and set up a municipal clinic giving compulsory physical examinations twice weekly to licensed, card-carrying prostitutes. The city administration apparently used the clinic to extract payoffs from these women.

Public sentiment against prostitution grew, and in 1913 a Red Light Law was passed by the same coalition that ended racetrack gambling in California. Business and political interests allied with the trade launched a well-financed referendum campaign to suspend the law, and managed to reduce substantially the statewide majority for it from fifty thousand to twenty thousand votes. But that majority carried the day. Popular opinion and powerful int .ests such as the San Francisco real estate board opposed the relegauzaton of prostitution. By 1917 San Francisco's segregated district was gone.[45]

As brothels were equated with saloons, so was the traffic in prostitutes—white slavery—with the liquor trade. They had similar qualities: control by foreigners, backing by powerful business interests, illicit ties to political machines. And just as it became more and more evident that the interstate sale of liquor called for national control, so—indeed, sooner—did that perception take hold with regard to the traffic in women.

The white slave scare is a choice example of the rapid rise and fall of issues typical of modern American public life. From the turn of the century on, newspapers and magazines, public figures, and professional groups paid increasing attention to the existence of an international traffic in young women. The titillation inherent in the story made it a natural for popular journalism.[46]

Indeed there *was* an international traffic in prostitutes; and it was true that foreigners, including Jews, were prominent in the trade. Industrialism and urbanization added to the numbers of unattached males and vulnerable young women; the greater ease of travel and communication produced networks that sent prostitutes to South America and other places of high demand. But the organized recruitment of prostitutes in itself was not new. And the extent of the white slave traffic was grossly exaggerated.

British and American laws passed in 1907 forbade the importation of alien prostitutes. But the Supreme Court decided in 1909 that the American law was invalid if the defendant did not know that the woman was an alien. In that event vice itself rather than the traffic in vice was being punished, and this came under the state police power rather than federal authority. The decision spurred Congress to pass the Mann Act in 1910, which relied on the congressional power over interstate commerce to proscribe the transportation of women across state lines for immoral purposes. (A comparable English law, the product also of aroused public opinion, was passed in 1912.) When the Supreme Court upheld the Mann Act in 1913, it equated it with federal regulation of food and drugs, lotteries, obscene literature, and diseased cattle or people. Between June 1910 and January 1915, more than a thousand people were convicted under the law.[47]

After the United States entered the First World War in April 1917, the campaign against prostitution had a new object of concern: the physical and moral purity of a vastly expanded army. A government Commission on Training Camp Activities took the view that continence was the best policy, and criticized the British system of regulated brothels in France. State authorities and the United States Public Health Service (which created a Division of Venereal Diseases in 1917) sought to instruct young men and women on the dangers of venereal disease with a massive sex education campaign called the American Plan. Sixteen states passed laws in 1918 and 1919 providing for the examination, reporting, and treatment of venereal disease.

Controls far beyond anything attempted in prewar cities were imposed on the areas surrounding military training camps. Prostitution and the sale of liquor were banned in "pure zones" five miles wide. Prostitutes within those areas could be arrested, given compulsory medical examinations and administrative hearings before health boards, and, if held to be "diseased," they could be sent to detention camps for indeterminate periods of time until they were "cured." Thirty-five thousand women (and no men) were arrested under these provisions; more than fifteen thousand were detained.[48]

But far from being the next stage of an expanding national anti-prostitution policy, the wartime experience turned out to be quite atypical. It already was clear that with red light districts and white slavery banned, the assault on vice had lost its force. In the autumn of 1914 journalist George Creel detected a sudden falloff in the crusade against prostitution. As red light districts (in theory) closed down, the fervor went out of the fight, and the next step in so decentralized a system of government was far from obvious. No one seriously proposed a national law—much less a constitutional amendment—outlawing prostitution. And after the passage of the Mann Act, fear of white slavery ebbed. The *New York World* in 1914 denounced the "White Slavery Hysteria" as a modern version of the witchcraft mania.[49]

There were as well new impediments to the enforcement of anti-prostitution laws. The courts' practice of applying the Mann Act to cases of private as distinct from commercial vice came under attack: "It may be inquired," wrote one critic, "what and whose code of morals denounces sexual intercourse between unmarried persons." The Pennsylvania Supreme Court held that the Pittsburgh Morals Bureau was an unconstitutional government body, and the city's mayor announced that the bureau's duties would be taken over by the police. New Jersey's high court in 1919 voided the state's injunction and abatement act because it did not allow for a jury trial to determine whether there was in fact a public nuisance that could be enjoined.[50]

The red light districts of American cities, broken up by the time of the First World War, rarely returned in the 1920s. A United States Public Health Service poll found among mayors, chiefs of police, businessmen, and labor leaders overwhelming sentiment against regulated prostitution. When a red light district reappeared in Atlantic City, real estate interests and the press vigorously attacked it as a threat to the tourist business.[51]

Needless to say, prostitution continued, fostered by automobiles, dance halls, and speakeasies. Pimp-controlled streetwalkers increased in numbers as madam-run brothels faded, an instance (dressmaking was another) of the displacement of female entrepreneurs by males. The depression added to the economic pressures pushing women into prostitution; and the end of Prohibition fostered mob control of the trade. There appeared to be a large increase in prostitution in 1932–33, as compared to 1927–28.[52]

Regulation failed to keep pace—indeed, it faded away—as prostitution became a more shadowy and elusive presence. During the early 1920s all fines for prostitutes were abolished in New York City; only four women were fined for sex offenses in Philadelphia in 1921. But venereal disease now came more fully under public surveillance. By the early 1920s every state had regulatory legislation.[53]

It was clear that the double standard still flourished, even if the conspiracy of silence had been breached. Only thirteen states even pretended to hold both parties liable for an act of prostitution; in twelve others a man could be charged with frequenting a brothel. Fifteen states and the District of Columbia held the woman alone chargeable for prostitution; and the courts of California, New York, and Iowa upheld that distinction. A number of states prescribed the compulsory medical examination of an arrested prostitute; if she had VD, that became part of the evidence against her. Sex between unmarried persons was a crime in seventeen states, including New York, in 1931. But enforcement was practically nil—save for unsavory exceptions such as the revelation that members of New York City's Vice Squad were arresting and blackmailing women on prostitution charges.[54]

The Crusade against Drink

National Prohibition was the crowning achievement of the early twentieth-century effort to shape the social behavior of the American people. Indeed, it still stands as the nation's most sweeping experiment in social engineering.

But it was by no means evident at the turn of the century that this would happen. During the last half of the nineteenth century fifteen states tried prohibition; all except Maine, Kansas, and North Dakota had abandoned the effort by 1900. And even where prohibition was enacted into law, the prevailing view was that it could not be enforced. After ten years of state prohibition marked by widespread violation and nonenforcement, Iowa in 1894 passed a licensing act. Maine's pioneering state law leaked like a sieve by the early 1900s. Federal officers routinely collected their $25 license tax from liquor sellers, who also paid a weekly fine to state authorities. The courts, with discretionary sentencing power, turned laxity into a fine art.

Illegal distribution flourished also in New Hampshire, where by 1900 prohibition had been on the books for fifty years. Manchester's "Hall system" of periodic fines was a form of regulation (and a source of income). When the state supreme court ordered that New

Hampshire's illicit saloons be closed by January 1, 1902, the consequence was a small majority vote for repeal of the prohibition act. Vermont, too, voted narrowly (29,711–28,982) for repeal in February 1903.[55]

Otherwise the regulation of drink rested on local option laws (in thirty-nine states by 1905), and on high license acts whose popular name—mulct laws—betrayed their primary intent. The 1890s were a time of codification, extending and elaborating on local option rules while looking to the national government to manage the interstate liquor traffic. State liquor legislation tapered off around the turn of the century. Federal laws were skimpy and specific: bans on the sale of liquor, beer, or wine in army canteens (1901) and in the District of Columbia (1903); a 1905 order by the Commissioner of Internal Revenue that sellers of patent medicines whose chief component was alcohol be licensed as retail liquor dealers.[56]

Outlook argued that local option was the best policy: "The most that law can do is to make vice difficult and virtue easy." But local option and high license fees were no more satisfactory than prohibition. New Hampshire's State Board of License Commissioners wallowed in corruption. While federal tax data suggested that more people sold liquor under prohibition than under the state's new license system, convictions for drunkenness increased. The *Atlantic Monthly* concluded in 1905: "The old system worked well, but the new system is not working well."[57]

The lesson of experience seemed to be that prohibition was of doubtful efficacy, that the problem of drink "cannot be dealt with by general enactments or at long range." In any event, it appeared that American liquor consumption was declining. And demographic and cultural trends—the growth of large, polyglot cities; the diverse and cosmopolitan life of a mass urban industrial society—were likely to consign prohibition to the dustbin of outdated lost causes.[58] Instead, it became one of the most successful reform movements of the early twentieth century. How and why did this happen?

The crusade against liquor displayed in full measure the diversity of sources that made for successful social policy in early twentieth-century America. The old, strongly religious belief in the evil of drink continued to flourish. Indeed, the identification of alcohol with immigration, big cities, and cultural modernism gave new edge and vigor to the Protestant fundamentalist wing of the prohibition movement.[59]

The cause also had a place in corporate capitalism's endless search for social and workplace order. By fostering a more sober and harder-working labor force, it would allow "the corporation to solidify its position at the expense of labor." Prohibition appealed as well to Progressive social reformers who had neither hay in their hair nor corporate contracts in their pockets. They were moved by the manifest, and ever more vividly reported, physical and social harms wrought by drink; and they were intellectually convinced by the scientific and sociological case against liquor. In this sense the prohibition movement, like political reform and trust-busting, was fueled by a "Revolt of Decent Citizens."[60]

Prohibition's political success lay in its capacity to appeal to elements spread across the spectrum of American social thought, from the most traditional to the most modern. Because as a public policy it was so many things to so many people, it became the law of the land. And because in practice it came to alienate or disappoint so many of its supporters, it was repealed.

That prohibition was an attractive response to the strains of modern society is evident in the fact that it took on new life in a number of other nations at the turn of the century. Discussion of *die Alkohol Frage* (the liquor question) burgeoned in Germany; French concerns focused on alcohol's adverse impact on the quality of the army and the size of the population. The *Nation* observed: "Abroad it is not the older prohibition movement that counts, but an awakening of the masses to the destructive effect of alcoholism on national efficiency."[61]

It is instructive to compare the American and British approaches to liquor control. Like its American counterpart, the nineteenth-century English temperance movement had a strongly evangelical base, stressing individual reformation. Thereafter the two nations' campaigns against alcohol diverged. The impetus for British temperance reform lay mainly in the Liberal party, in America among Republicans. If the alliance of liquor interests with Democratic city bosses was a common theme in American politics, the English equivalent was an increasingly close linkage of "the trade" with the Conservative party. The British case differed, too, in that the issue centered not on prohibition and local option but on the less politically explosive questions of regulation and compensation of owners of delicensed public houses.[62]

In a 1903 manifesto a number of leading social reformers called for a large reduction in licenses, with limited compensation from the profits of the trade and wide local government powers of initiative and control. Beatrice and Sidney Webb's *History of Liquor Licensing* (with an appendix titled "The Movement for the Regulation of Manners") provided a historical underpinning for this effort. The labor movement, with evangelical strands not shared by its more ethnically diverse American counterpart, jumped into the fray as well. Philip Snowden's *Socialism and the Drink Question* (1908) made the necessary linkage; most Labour MPs were total abstainers; union leader John Burns assured an American correspondent: "Tell the people of America that England's face is toward the light."[63]

After regaining power, the Liberals in 1908 proposed a Licensing Act that called for closing a third of the nation's public houses over a fourteen-year period, after which there would be no compensation for license nonrenewal. Brewers and distillers strongly opposed this, backed by widespread popular support for free access to drink. A Conservative journal warned of local option: "The application of popular control to social habits is a principle to be watched very narrowly, as it may easily develop into the grossest tyranny." The House of Lords, many of whose members held investments in breweries and public houses, rejected the act. But the movement to reform drink by reducing the infrastructure of the trade went on, securing higher taxes in the 1909 budget and restricted opening hours during the First World War.[64]

The American crusade against drink had an altogether more broad-gauged and complex character. In the late nineteenth century its primary voices were the Prohibition party and the Women's Christian Temperance Union (WCTU), both firmly rooted in Midwestern, small-town Protestantism, and as peripheral to political power as their third party and female character suggest. But the movement underwent a sea change around the turn of the century. The Prohibition party faded into obscurity, and the antidrink crusade turned to new devices: the initiative and the referendum, the Anti-Saloon League. The result was a growing body of restrictive local, state, and national legislation, culminating in the Eighteenth Amendment.

New techniques did not in and of themselves create the conditions for success. That came from a growing public sense that the problem was real, large, and important, and that existing policies were inadequate. Prohibition benefited from the same perception of a new—and troubled—urban industrial immigrant America that fed the movements to reduce child labor, set maximum hours laws, improve tenement housing, and restrict immigration. The WCTU, the paradigmatic voice of prohibition as religious moralism, linked the restriction of drink to support for the eight-hour working day, peace through arbitration, juvenile courts, and industrial education.[65]

The waxing belief that drink was a social problem took a variety of forms. Regulation came to be seen as "part of the question of public sanitation and social control." There was greater awareness of liquor's physiological dangers: "It is no more a sumptuary law to restrict the sale of alcohol than to restrict the sale of cocaine, opium, bad milk, gunpowder, or dynamite," argued one partisan. An 1893 Connecticut law required that the medical consequences of drinking be taught to students. Textbooks enlightened their readers with arresting medical axioms: "The majority of beer drinkers die from dropsy"; "Tobacco has done more to cure insanity than spirituous liquors."[66]

Exploring "the social basis of prohibition," economist Simon Patten contrasted the popular taste for alcohol with scientists' informed hostility to drinking, and suggested that changes in the character of the food supply might provide alternatives to drink. He warned that prohibition "cannot now be made a national issue without disrupting social bonds that are necessary to unity and peace." But he expected that "prohibition will grow as national unity grows. When we all become Americans we will all be abstainers."[67]

Another sign of the times was the appearance of business regulations against drinking, fed by the new interest of employers in workplace efficiency and of reformers in workplace safety. The Department of Labor asked a number of the nation's larger employers how they handled the drinking problem. About 1,800 of them prohibited or restricted the use of alcohol by their employees; more than 5,000 said that they tried to regulate the drinking habits of the men they employed. This was not a class issue. The American Federation of Labor supported restrictions on alcohol in the workplace, while H. A. Chadwick, editor of the *Seattle Argus*, was one of many conservatives opposed to so manifest an interference with personal liberty.[68]

The ever-broader coalition of interests that more than anything else explains national prohibition may be seen at play in two contexts: regional (the spread of prohibition sentiment in the South) and organizational (the rise of the Anti-Saloon League as a new kind of political pressure group).

Fundamentalist Protestantism was at least as important to southern as to northern and western prohibitionism. And southern Progressives were as attracted to the medical, efficiency, and social control arguments for prohibition as their northern counterparts. Nevertheless, it seems clear that it was the heightened racism so evident in early twentieth-century southern public life that invigorated the prohibitionist cause there.

The 1906 Atlanta race riot set off a wave of prohibitionist voting in Georgia and elsewhere. A 1908 *Collier's* article conjoined negrophobia and anti-Semitism by attributing the rape of a fourteen-year-old white girl in Louisiana to obscene labels on whiskey bottled and sold by the Lee Levy Company of St. Louis. Southern prohibitionism in this context became "a popular uprising against a known cause of bestial crime," to be equated with the federal government's efforts to keep liquor from Indians, "that other weaker race." It was widely believed that "the negro problem and the whiskey problem are very intimately connected," that "it was necessary to remove the saloon from the negro to save Southern industry and civilization."[69]

Southern advocates of prohibition argued as well that it would eliminate a major cause of lynchings and interracial violence. Booker T. Washington was one of them: "The abolition of the bar-room is a blessing to the negro second only to the abolition of slavery. Two-thirds of the mobs, lynchings, and burnings at the stake are the result of bad whiskey drunk by bad black men and bad white men." He thought that the issue cut across racial lines. A white contemporary agreed. The traditional goal of temperance—"an attempt to make men good by law"—was not the main purpose of the new movement. Its concern, rather, was with the drinker as husband, father, voter, worker, and citizen. Prohibition was not merely temperance reform but an act of statesmanship, a public policy with implications for religion, education, industry—and race, for liquor led both blacks and poor whites to violence.[70]

Southern prohibition emerged from the bottom up. The fact that the most significant voting unit in the region was the county, rather than smaller (and hence more diverse) wards or towns, fostered the spread of dry areas through local option. And each state's political culture gave its own cast to the crusade against drink.

South Carolina's Dispensary, the first state-run liquor outlet system, was abolished in 1907 because of the well-founded popular belief that it was permeated by political corruption. (This was not solely a prohibitionist victory: Vincent Chicco, who ran Charleston's "blind tigers" (speakeasies), played an important part in the fight against his public competitor.) Alabama also had a dispensary system, with similar corruption among its managers and of little benefit to rural areas. A 1907 local option law encouraged county prohibition, and by the beginning of 1908 only seventeen of sixty-seven counties allowed the sale of liquor. In 1908 the dispensary was closed, and a fiercely contested election was held over a prohibition amendment to the state constitution. But the most influential newspapers and Alabama's senators opposed this threat to personal liberty and state revenues, and it was defeated by a seven-to-five margin.[71]

Prohibition traditionally attracted little support from Democrats and less from Republicans in late nineteenth-century Tennessee. But there was much local sentiment in favor. By 1903 fifty-five of the state's ninety-six counties had banned saloons. During the early 1900s the issue became important in state politics. Fierce political-electoral contests erupted over attempts to end the sale of liquor in cities and towns; a 1907 act restricted Nashville saloons to the downtown area. In 1908 the state's Republicans opportunistically allied with prohibitionist Democrats to get control of the legislature, and passed a 1909 statewide prohibition law over the governor's veto.[72]

The dry cause in North Carolina readily fit into the larger context of Progressive reform. Josiah W. Bailey, a future senator who chaired the state Anti-Saloon League, called drink the major cause of crime and poverty. But he opposed national prohibition as a threat to states' rights, and doubted the efficacy of a statewide ban on liquor. Local option, he thought, was the best way to handle the problem. The Watts Act of 1903 excluded saloons and (often Republican-owned) distilleries from rural districts, and the prohibitionists comfortably won a 1908 state referendum. The dry position was supported by cotton and textile manufacturers, railroad companies, and reform-minded public men such as former governor Charles B. Aycock.[73]

Governor James S. Hogg of Texas favored prohibition along with woman's suffrage and business regulation as early as the 1890s, and after 1910 the Texas Democratic party's Progressive wing tended to be prohibitionist. Racism was inextricably entwined with the more general social-reformist context of the crusade against drink. Thomas B. Love, a prominent Texas Progressive, observed: "The Negro ought not to be permitted to vote on the question of whether or not liquor shall be sold in Texas any more than the Indian should be permitted to vote on the question of whether or not liquor shall be sold in the Indian country."[74]

Given this rich conjunction of interests, it is not surprising that by 1908, except for a few wet tendrils—southern Florida, New Orleans, the North Carolina Piedmont region, and a number of southern cities—the South was dry. This was true of seven eighths of the region's land, according to one estimate; the remainder had fewer saloons than New York City.[75]

As distinctively new as southern prohibitionism was the Anti-Saloon League (ASL), one of the most effective lobbying groups in American history. Like prohibition itself, the ASL had no single, simple character. It was the instrument of rural and small-town evangelicals lashing out at the saloon and through it the city and the immigrant; it was a classic middle-class Progressive reform organization, drawing on well-educated clergymen and other professionals and running public relations and political lobbying campaigns with up-to-the-minute efficiency. And it served the purposes of businessmen seeking a docile and hardworking labor force.[76]

The ASL began in 1893 as an alliance of denominational temperance societies. It gained its first footholds in Ohio, Pennsylvania, Illinois, Nebraska, and West Virginia, tapping a distinct American subculture. The most successful organized pressure group in the early twentieth century was Protestant fundamentalist at its core. A sample of 641 ASL activists revealed that even though they came predominantly from the Northeast and from the cities, four out of five were fundamentalist in their religion and Republican in their politics. The League quickly became national, in the pattern of Progressive reform organizations. It cooperated with the WCTU, the Sons of Temperance, the Catholic Abstinence League, and the Scientific Temperance Association: testimony to the diversity of interests concerned with drink by the turn of the century.[77]

The ASL quickly displaced the Prohibition party as the major voice of the movement. John D. Rockefeller, Jr., gave the League $350,000 between 1900 and 1919, but its success stemmed primarily from the fact that it tapped a reform impulse transcending particular interest groups. It spoke to the prevailing Progressive belief that people "must be forced to take a certain action because it is best for their own welfare." And it purveyed its "pro bono publico, semireligious platform" through a highly effective reward-your-friends, punish-your-enemies politics.[78]

Ohio's Republican governor, Myron Herrick, alienated the ASL when he failed to support the 1905 Beal Law, which required a local option election when 40 percent of the voters in a city or town so petitioned. The League threw its support to Herrick's Democratic opponent, Union Central Life Insurance Company president John M. Pattison, a prominent Methodist and prohibitionist. Herrick lost by 44,000 votes; the rest of the state Republican ticket was elected. In Newark, New Jersey, eleven candidates for the state legislature, all pro-saloon, were defeated by an ASL-supported slate of independents. The result was that the Democrats took control of the state legislature, and John F. Dryden, the Republican president of the Prudential Insurance Company, failed to be reelected to the United States Senate.[79]

The ASL took credit for closing thousands of saloons by local option in Indiana, Illinois, and other midwestern states. In fact it was capitalizing on a "temperance tidal wave" evident in Europe as well as the United States. But the League's importance grew as the anti-drink movement moved from local to county option and then to state and finally national Prohibition.[80]

That triumph, customarily regarded as a victory of the old America over the new, was also the product of a distinctively Progressive mobilization of public opinion to impose a particular social policy on a pluralistic American culture. It relied not on party politics but on the pressure of Protestant churches and their instrument, the ASL, reinforced by the reformist mind-set of high Progressivism and the impact of America's entry into World War I.

Those quintessentially Progressive devices the initiative and referendum were made to order for the cause. Antidrink sentiment in hundreds of communities now had direct, unmediated outlets of expression. Illinois voters closed down 1,500 saloons in April 1908; the same fate befell 500 more on a single day in Michigan, Colorado, and Nebraska. A coral-like structure of restrictive legislation inexorably grew. By 1908 it affected some 33 million Americans; by 1911 a dozen states, primarily in the South and West, had prohibition, and local option was available almost everywhere.[81]

As the crusade against drink turned to statewide and national Prohibition, resistance increased. Beer and liquor interests mobilized in opposition. *Beverages*, the official journal of the Liquor Dealers' Association, argued for self-reform of the saloon as the only way to avoid prohibition. The oxymoronically named United Nevada Industries kept the drys in that state at bay until November 1918.

Even in so new and lightly populated a state as Arizona, alignments on the issue were complex. Druggists, the Orthodox church, and the state Federation of Labor joined liquor interests in opposing the drys; mine owners who wanted less drunkenness among their Mexican workers and blacks who were barred from white saloons backed the prohibitionists. When the drys won a narrow victory in 1914 (helped mightily by the movie version of Ten Nights in a Barroom), it was, as the New Republic observed, the product of a combination of specific factors more than of broad public sentiment.[82]

Eight states rejected statewide prohibition in referenda between 1909 and 1913. Ohio, which had a marvelously ambiguous provision in its 1851 Constitution ("No license to traffic in intoxicating liquors shall hereafter be granted in this state; but the General Assembly may, by law, provide against evils resulting therefrom"), adopted county local option in 1908, and by mid-1909 sixty-three of the state's eighty-eight counties were dry. But the urban centers remained wet, and a counteroffensive sparked by the Brewers' Association from 1910 on induced eighteen counties to hold second elections which restored saloons. The liquor interests won another victory at the 1912 Ohio constitutional convention, which adopted a restricted licensing provision. The state's voters rejected prohibition (along with woman's suffrage) by a margin of almost 85,000 votes in 1914, and by 55,000 in 1915.[83]

The politics of prohibition heated up in cities as well. A 1911 Tennessee law made the sale of liquor a public nuisance and prohibited shipments into the state. But the Memphis political machine relied heavily on liquor revenue, and enforcement was nil. In 1915 the state legislature provided for the unseating of city officials who failed to perform the duties of their office. Mayor Hilary Hewse of Nashville and Memphis boss William Crump were removed, and the courts upheld their ousters.

When the bars were closed in Kansas City, Missouri, its Kansas namesake across the river became a mecca for the trade. Saloons paid what was in effect a $50 monthly license fee in the form of forfeited police court bonds, giving the town a hefty annual revenue of about $80,000. City and county officials refused to interfere; the state attorney general opened court proceedings to annul the city's charter; its mayor was deposed from office twice, and finally resigned in the face of contempt proceedings.[84]

A general "abatement of the prohibition movement" appeared to be under way by 1916. A decisive majority in Vermont turned down statewide prohibition in that year; fifteen wet townships in Illinois banned liquor, but ten dry ones returned to licensing. An ASL attempt to get the New York legislature to pass a local option law failed, as did a campaign for statewide prohibition in Maryland. The victorious candidate for governor in Kentucky won on an antiprohibition ticket. Neither the Democratic, the Republican, nor the Progressive party platforms of 1916 so much as mentioned the issue.[85]

But the First World War gave new legitimacy everywhere to the cause, fostering what the French economist Yves Guyot called "le delirium anti-alcoolique." Russia's government monopoly on vodka was abolished. There was considerable discussion of the need to limit drink in Great Britain, and in 1916 a Strength of Britain Movement with much business support sought the withdrawal of pub licenses for the duration. Then-munitions minister David Lloyd George declared that the sale of alcoholic beverages impeded war production. He secured a Central Control Board which prohibited whiskey in the west of Scotland, the Orkneys, and the Shetlands, took over the trade in the Carlisle area, and closed the pubs during working hours.[86]

It is hard to imagine that the Eighteenth Amendment would have been enacted without American entry into the war. But that action added crucial strength to a crusade which was well developed before April 1917. Prohibition, said an advocate, was "one of the accepted progressive issues of our politics," which "emphasizes in its arguments possibilities of better living conditions, better standards of home life and of workmanship and of morality, and in general proclaims . . . the invigoration and uplift of the rank and file of our Commonwealth."[87]

Prohibition had burst the bounds of its rural-fundamentalist origins. Urban, native-born middle-class support rapidly grew as the new immigration burgeoned. Between 1914 and 1916 states with a combined population of 12 million adopted Prohibition. Michigan, which attracted rural southern and midwestern whites as well as immigrants to its new industrial economy, was the first of the large industrial states to vote for it, in 1916. By then over half the states had declared for or adopted Prohibition. If local option areas were included, over 60 percent of the population and 85 percent of the land area of the United States had gone dry.[88]

National Prohibition was fostered as well by the enforcement difficulties of state and local control. Local option made regulation of a national industry difficult; licensing was in the hands of everything from courts of common pleas (in New Jersey) to city councils or excise boards. Worcester, Massachusetts, made a statement of sorts in 1910 by electing a prohibitionist mayor while voting to restore saloons.[89]

The Supreme Court in Leisy v. Hardin (1890) denied on interstate commerce grounds the power of a state to prohibit the shipment of liquor into its territory. Republicans in Congress responded with the Wilson Act, which affirmed the right of the states to control the flow of goods within their borders. But in 1905 the Court, ever sensitive to impediments to a national economy, said that states could not forbid liquor consignments from being paid for on delivery because that would invalidate contracts made between the seller and the buyer. This decision further stimulated an already booming mail order liquor business. The large express companies became "veritable distributaries" of the liquor dealers. One prohibitionist spoke of "a direct offensive warfare by the Federal Government, in alliance with certain States, against the domestic social and economic policies of other States."[90]

Congress responded in 1913 with the Webb-Kenyon Act, which prohibited the interstate shipment of liquor when it violated the law of the receiving state. The bill was passed over Taft's veto, and in 1917 the Supreme Court upheld its constitutionality in a case stage-managed by ASL director Wayne Wheeler. But while it revitalized state prohibition, Webb-Kenyon ran the risk of fostering an "abatement of the prohibition movement" on the national level.[91]

These developments whetted the desire of the dry forces for a constitutional amendment which would impose prohibition on the resistant urban immigrant industrial states. At a 1913 Columbus, Ohio, convention, a coalition of organizations led by the ASL formally launched a campaign for a saloonless nation by 1920. And in December 1914 (the same month in which Congress passed the anti–drug traffic Harrison Act) Alabama Congressman Richmond T. Hobson, supported by a 150-foot-long petition bearing 6 million names, introduced a constitutional amendment banning the sale and distribution (but not the manufacture and use) of alcoholic beverages.[92]

Major obstacles stood in the way. A majority of Hobson's Alabama colleagues opposed the amendment on the ground that it threatened states' rights. Josiah W. Bailey of North Carolina wildly warned that if Prohibition were enacted, "there will not be a square foot of territory in the United States where it will be unlawful for negroes and white people to intermarry." Others argued that the loss of liquor excise revenue would lead to a higher income tax and to excise taxes on necessities. And what about compensation for the substantial property losses that the liquor industry would suffer if it were outlawed?[93]

Even in 1914 there were warnings that national Prohibition would have a corrupting influence on law and politics; that the demand for drink would be met by the lowest level of traffickers; that bootleggers, speakeasies ("blind pigs" in the jargon of the time), and impure and dangerous blends would appear; that Prohibition without substantial federal enforcement would suffer the same fate that befell the Civil Rights Act of the 1870s and the Fifteenth Amendment.[94]

But the war played into the hands of the prohibitionists. They tied their cause to the nation's military readiness and to the doctrine of social efficiency. Frank A. Vanderlip, president of the National City Bank, endorsed Prohibition in 1917, declaring: "I believe that we are facing a serious threat to our National character and efficiency." Another observer thought that "perhaps the most important new support that has come to the prohibition movement in recent years has come through its assimilation of the great American doctrine of mental and physical efficiency." The American Medical Association gave its imprimatur in 1917 to a declaration on the harmfulness of alcohol.[95]

Business, medical, scientific, and social scientific thought came together to support the ban on drink. Boston social worker Robert A. Woods favored national Prohibition because it held out greater promise of success against liquor manufacturers, and would make enforcement easier by separating liquor from politics. America's entry into the war decisively strengthened that appeal. The need to conserve grain for food and to increase the nation's productive capacity and the fighting ability of its armed forces were powerful new incentives. In March 1917, on the eve of war, Congress excluded all journals with liquor ads from dry areas of the country; in November 1918 it enacted a War Prohibition Act.[96]

Outlook hoped that this would be strictly a wartime expedient, and proposed that a small commission of experts inquire into and report on the character and desirability of a permanent national Prohibition law. But the movement had gone far beyond this. In December 1917 Congress adopted a new and more sweeping constitutional amendment prohibiting the manufacture, sale, or transportation of alcoholic beverages, and sent it to the states for ratification. The ASL had pushed hard for passage before forty new urban congressmen appeared as a result of reapportionment after the 1920 Census. Between January

1918 and February 1919 every state legislature but those of New Jersey, Connecticut, and Rhode Island voted for Prohibition, in almost every case overwhelmingly. The total vote of the forty-five state senates was 1,297 to 336 in favor; of the assemblies 2,942 to 999. (Even more than normal disorder erupted in the Louisiana legislature when, after its ratification vote, an embittered wet legislator said: "Now, Mr. Speaker, I move that this House take a recess in order to give the prohibitionists time in which to 'get tight' and celebrate their victory.")[97]

The experience of antiprohibitionist Massachusetts is revealing. Both United States senators and a majority of the congressional delegation opposed the Eighteenth Amendment, and it was not expected that the state legislature would ratify. But it became clear that support for Prohibition went far beyond the evangelical element commonly associated with the ASL. A Council for National Prohibition included prominent businessmen, doctors, and academics. Although organized labor in general was opposed, three hundred manufacturers polled by the Allied Industries of Massachusetts supported Prohibition by a ten-to-one margin.

State legislators were bombarded by pro-amendment letters and petitions from their constituents. Political leaders of both parties, fearful lest the issue enter into the next state election, pushed for legislative ratification without a referendum. The Massachusetts House did so by a vote of 145 to 91, the Senate by 27 to 12. Massachusetts became the first major industrial state to ratify the Prohibition amendment.[98]

Advocates celebrated the triumph: "perhaps the most far-reaching movement for economic and moral well-being ever carried through by the deliberate action of a free people"; "perhaps the most remarkable social and political development of the time . . . the direct product of evangelical activity" in an age of supposedly declining religious faith. The British *New Statesman* was impressed by the variety of contributing factors: public health and medical professionals concerned over alcoholism, buttressed by a flood of statistics on crime, pauperism, and insanity; reformers and child welfare agencies; civic and good government associations; employers and the business efficiency movement; the popular appeal of making army camps pure; the growing political power of the western states.[99]

The heart of the successful crusade against drink was a coalition of evangelicalism, native middle-class reformism, and efficiency-minded business. But the movement caught up too many strands of social policy, served too many otherwise conflicting interests, to be defined primarily in class or ethnocultural terms. The scale of the forces behind Prohibition was proportionate to the audacity of this sweeping attempt at social engineering.[100]

Jerusalem Lost

Until the civil rights era of the late twentieth century, Prohibition was the nation's most sustained attempt at large-scale social regulation. The enabling Volstead Act, which came into effect in January 1920, defined—many thought it overstretched—the Eighteenth Amendment's ban on "intoxicating liquors" to include any beverage with an alcoholic content of more than half of 1 percent. The law exempted the hard cider and home beer favored by Protestant rural America, which heightened its sectarian tone.

The conservative lawyers Elihu Root and William D. Guthrie challenged the Eighteenth Amendment as an unconstitutional invasion of states' rights, but the Supreme Court brushed aside that argument in 1920. Rhode Island tried to set its acceptable alcohol content level higher than the Volstead standard. This, too, the Court rejected, as it did the casuistical argument of a number of state attorneys general that the lack of popular referenda voided their state legislatures' ratifications of the amendment.[101]

The real battleground was not Prohibition's legality but its implementation and enforcement. By 1923 seven of the eight English-speaking Canadian provinces also were dry; and here, too, the primary concern was with evasion of the law. Meanwhile, American prohibitionists flushed with victory turned their attention to the British Isles. W. E. ("Pussyfoot") Johnson went over in 1920 to proselytize for the cause, predicting a dry Britain in a decade. But Prohibition there had a limited and declining appeal. The terms of debate were different. *Nineteenth Century* observed in 1927: "While in Great Britain Prohibition is chiefly advocated on social or medical grounds, in the United States the driving force behind the Prohibition movement is religious sentiment." The primary British policy concerns, as before the war, were whether or not to nationalize the trade and how sharply to reduce the number of pub licenses.[102]

When Herbert Hoover in 1929 called Prohibition "a great social and economic experiment, noble in motive and far-reaching in purpose," he echoed the view, widely shared when it first came into force, that

this was "the boldest and most momentous experiment in social reform which the world has known." The Anti-Saloon League's Wayne
Wheeler equated Prohibition with the campaign for a national child
labor law. Almost two thirds of 526 labor leaders polled in 1920 expected workers to benefit from Prohibition. A number of mayors of
medium-sized cities, asked in 1922 to comment on its effects, widely
agreed that it had reduced drunkenness, crime, unemployment, and
the use of drugs. *American City* concluded that Prohibition enforcement was as onerous—and as necessary—as the regulation of traffic.[103]

But the ethnocultural and socially restrictive aspects of Prohibition
assumed increasing importance as the decade wore on. Many dry
labor unions were what their leaders called "100% American." The
predominantly white, native-born, Protestant Railroad Brotherhoods
were the most actively prohibitionist labor group. A spokesman for
the World League against Alcoholism called Prohibition "an adventure in social democracy," but warned that newer immigrants did not
have the experience in self-government or social responsibility that
was part of the heritage of the older stock. He concluded that "the
answer to 'the great American experiment' to-day . . . lies with the
influential old American groups of the East, and especially in those
sections where the sharpest contrasts in 'new' and 'old,' wealth and
poverty, 'class' and 'mass,' privilege and lack of opportunity, are most
often and most closely associated."[104]

Public opinion and ultimately public policy shifted from overwhelming endorsement to overwhelming rejection of Prohibition.
The change was analogous to the experience of an occupied country:
at first guerrilla opposition; then the rise of a diverse and legitimate
resistance; then the final sweep to victory.

Substantial numbers of Americans never did acquiesce in Prohibition. A *Literary Digest* map on the eve of enforcement showed where
they were: in California, Minnesota, Wisconsin, southern Louisiana,
New Jersey, Pennsylvania, and in large cities with substantial numbers of immigrants. Ohio held the first state referendum on Prohibition after the passage of the Eighteenth Amendment in November
1919; by a minute margin—500,450 to 499,971—it was rejected. New
Jersey Governor Edward I. Edmunds entered office in 1920 pledged to
keep the state as wet as possible, and soon signed into law a bill legitimating 3.5 percent beer. By a large margin Massachusetts voters
backed a referendum resolution to the effect that beer with a 4 percent
alcoholic content was not prohibited.

Judges in Rhode Island, Kentucky, Louisiana, Missouri, and New York granted injunctions restraining federal officials from enforcing the Prohibition law. And when an Ohio court decision in early 1919 temporarily allowed liquor stores to reopen, a constant flow of inter-urban trolleys, trains, express wagons, trucks, and cars created a sixty-mile-long "Avenue de Booze" between Detroit and Toledo.[105]

Immigrants and capitalists, for their own very different reasons, were conspicuous early critics. The New York Italian newspaper *Il Cittadino* condemned Prohibition as an attack on "human liberty" which deprived 3 million Italian workers of their wine, "a beverage of daily habit of a quasi-absolute necessity." While many corporate leaders welcomed the prospect of a more sober work force, New York hotel owners and real estate men joined with former navy captain Will H. Stayton and AFL president Samuel Gompers to form the Association Opposed to National Prohibition, soon to become the Association against the Prohibition Amendment (AAPA), an after-the-fact riposte to the Anti-Saloon League.[106]

As the decade progressed, both the moral and the practical rationales for Prohibition were steadily undermined. Enforcement quickly ran into the Fourth Amendment's search and seizure constraints, nourishing the view that to make Prohibition work was not worth its cost in individual rights. Many who were sympathetic to the need "to return to a moral view of the relation of government to life" were disturbed by the threat to "the spirit of liberty and individuality"—and the increase in crime—that enforcement seemed to foster. The *New Republic* observed in 1926: "There is a grave discrepancy between the moralistic socialism of prohibition and the easy-going individualism of American personal conduct and manners." It became increasingly clear that "the soul of American prohibition is belief, belief in a religion, a philosophy, an attitude towards life which the more educated and thoughtful citizens of the modern world have long since rejected."[107]

As Prohibition became ever more closely identified with its fundamentalist backers, it began to lose the support of American social and political elites. A conservative critic warned: "The cause of Prohibition has owed its rapid success in no small measure to the support of great capitalists and industrialists bent upon the absorbing object of productive efficiency; but they have paid a price they little realize . . . To undermine the foundations of liberty is to open the way to Socialism." Another found it "natural that the same person who is so zealous to deprive millions of his fellow-citizens of innocent enjoyment should be so keen in advocating the so-called Child Labor Amendment." Just as the ASL's Wayne Wheeler saw the Prohibition and child labor amendments as parts of a single reformist impulse, so did his opposite number, Will Stayton of the AAPA, link the two as instances of undesirable government activism.[108]

The success of the crusade against drink was due to the range of interests supporting it; a comparably broad coalition brought it down. Support for repeal spread across the ideological spectrum. By the late 1920s many of the institutions that shaped (or at least spoke for) public opinion—the press, political parties, unions, intellectuals, big business, "society," the Catholic and Episcopal churches—had turned against the Noble Experiment.[109]

This change in opinion went hand in hand with an expanding evasion of the law. It was estimated in 1925 that 15 million gallons of wine, four gallons per person, were made annually in Chicago's homes. Many Americans were legally licensed to dispense alcohol: druggists, doctors, vinegar manufacturers and transportation companies, priests and rabbis. As Prohibition came in, the demand for sacramental wine grew by over 800,000 gallons, and a government report indignantly concluded: "Not more than one quarter of this wine is sacramental—the rest is sacrilegious." By the mid-1920s a vast network of rumrunners, beer barons, and speakeasies had replaced the old system of distillers, distributors, and saloons.[110]

The initial impression that Prohibition reduced drunkenness and crime was eroded by a flood of statistics to the contrary. Cincinnati was thought to be relatively dry; yet disorderly conduct arrests increased from 32,352 in 1920 to 90,852 in 1924. Arrests for drunkenness in New Orleans climbed from 2,399 in 1920 to 12,511 in 1922; they rose as well in western Massachusetts, though not to pre-war levels.[111]

The growth of an illegal supply system brought with it gang warfare and jurisdictional fights that made the practices of old-time brewers and distillers seem tame. A rumrunners' war in Detroit led to scores of casualties and the disappearance of hundreds. There as elsewhere, juries refused to convict bootleggers; the courts were paralyzed. The police estimated that there were 100,000 speakeasies in the city. Nevada was plagued by lax enforcement; Denver could not cope; the lack of public support crippled efforts to cut down on smuggling into Florida.[112]

By the late 1920s America was awash with disbelief in the Noble Experiment. A massive subculture of jokes, slang, stories, and expertise about bootleg scotch, bathtub gin, and speakeasies gave evasion an aura of cultural acceptance. Grape juice distributors fixed labels to their product "warning" that if it was permitted to sit for sixty days it would turn into wine. When Will Rogers observed in 1928, "If you think this country ain't dry, you just watch 'em vote; and if you think this country ain't wet, you just watch 'em drink," his audience was not outraged, or rueful, but only amused.[113]

Feeding this mood were enforcement abuses ranging from the government's inserting poison into industrial alcohol to Prohibition agents' raids and seizures. H. L. Mencken compared the harassment of Prohibition violators by federal judges to the treatment of antiwar protesters under the Espionage Act, and observed that judges were widely thought to punish only those who failed to bribe enforcement officers.[114]

Public relations embarrassments and scandals steadily grew. Mabel Walker Willebrandt, who as assistant attorney general was a conspicuous advocate of Prohibition, resigned to join the company producing Vine-Glo grape jelly, a product whose appeal lay in the fact that it could be turned into "wine" by adding water. Harold D. Wilson, the chief enforcement officer in Massachusetts, was fired by the Commissioner of Internal Revenue for being indiscreet and temperamentally unfit. Wilson claimed that he had angered Senator Henry Cabot Lodge and other leading Bay State Republicans by raiding a vinous banquet attended by the party leaders. A crackdown on corruption in Prohibition enforcement in Gary, Indiana, led to the indictment and conviction of fifty-five people, including the mayor, the present and former sheriffs, the county prosecutor, a judge, deputy sheriffs, and policemen.[115]

Mounting charges of corruption shook confidence in the Treasury Department's Prohibition Bureau. John F. Kramer, its first commissioner, became an Anti-Saloon League lecturer after he left office; and indeed the ASL acted as an unofficial branch of the bureau, receiving over $13 million in federal funds between 1920 and 1925. General Lincoln C. Andrews was put in charge of the bureau to clean it up. He abolished the old districts and divided the country into twenty-four new ones, each to be headed by a supposedly apolitical administrator. But this threatened an established patronage system, closely linked to Republican senators, congressmen, and state leaders. The ASL, which had its own men firmly ensconced in the old system, rose in protest, and acceptable adjustments were hurriedly made. Andrews and Roy C. Haynes of the ASL brought a messianic zeal to Prohibition enforcement; but by 1927 they were gone, replaced by colorless bureaucrats. As the *New Republic* observed: "The fire and brimstone method . . . has spent itself."[116]

The ASL steadily lost its prestige and power. Fred L. Crabbe, the Kansas ASL superintendent (one of his brothers held the same position in Maryland; another was the attorney general of Ohio), bribed state officials; he was ousted from his position and faced disbarment. Edmund E. Shumaker, a Methodist minister and for twenty years superintendent of the Indiana ASL, was a political power in his state. He secured a law from the legislature that made the mere possession of whiskey a crime. But the state supreme court found it unconstitutional. Shumaker spoke of changing the makeup of the court in the next election. Arthur L. Gillion, the state's Republican attorney general, a Swiss-American from northern Indiana opposed to the Klan and the ASL, indicted him for contempt of court. In 1927 Shumaker was sentenced to a $250 fine and sixty days in jail. The *Nation* was uneasy over this action—"To crush Shumaker's dictatorship the court has gone far to setting up one of its own"—but it was evident that even in Indiana the public mood was changing.[117]

The Ohio Prohibition enforcement law permitted state and local authorities to divide the fines levied by justices of the peace on Prohibition (and auto speed law) violators, a fertile source of corruption. The United States Supreme Court in 1927 held that the law violated the defendants' right to trial by an impartial tribunal. An ASL-sponsored referendum seeking to reestablish these local judicial powers was condemned by the state's automobile clubs and a Constitutional Law Enforcement League as "commercialized justice," and lost by a two-to-one margin.[118]

The structure of political support for Prohibition also eroded. When Warren Harding convened a conference of governors to discuss enforcement, only fourteen of the forty-eight attended. Acceptance was paper-thin at best in states with large cities and many immigrants. Maryland's chief executive flatly declared that the law could not be enforced. In 1923 the New York legislature repealed the Mullen-Gage Prohibition enforcement act, and though the upstate press and *Outlook* urged Governor Al Smith to veto the bill, he signed it into law.[119]

Antiprohibitionists at first aimed to modify the Volstead Act rather than repeal the Eighteenth Amendment. The journalist Frank Kent told an English audience in 1923 that it was a waste of time to talk of repeal: Prohibition, he noted regretfully (and with unconscious irony), was as solidly ensconced in the Constitution as black suffrage. Constitutional law expert Howard McBain estimated that 5 percent of the population in thirteen states could block repeal. He thought that nullification by nonenforcement on the state level, as in the case of the post–Civil War civil rights amendments, was more probable.[120]

But in November 1926 voters in five states—Montana, Nevada, Wisconsin, Illinois, and New York—supported proposals to repeal or modify Prohibition. Progressive and liberal prohibitionist sentiment rapidly waned. The National Conference of Social Work avoided the subject in its meetings, and the *New Republic* argued that Prohibition hurt the cause of active government. The AFL, the American Legion and trade, bar, and medical associations joined in the attack. While the National Council of Churches' Research and Education Division continued to defend the Noble Experiment, the *Christian Century* tempered its support with criticism of the ASL's ties to unsavory politicos and the strongly Methodist-Baptist flavor of its 1928 convention. The liberal theologian Reinhold Niebuhr argued that if Prohibition had to rest on the compulsion that appeared to be necessary for its enforcement, it was better repealed.[121]

The end of national Prohibition, like its beginning, came to rest on that ultimate American political test, the passage of a constitutional amendment. The major parties, internally divided into wet and dry wings, still were reluctant to inject themselves into the controversy. But by 1928 it was obvious, in the words of one observer, that "prohibition is the largest political issue the American people have grappled with since the Civil War." And the Democrats' nomination of the wet Catholic governor of New York, Al Smith—"Alcohol Al"—meant that avoidance was no longer possible. Smith went down to defeat, but more because of his Catholicism than his wetness, and the repeal movement continued to gather strength.[122]

The rush to repeal between 1929 and 1932 resembled nothing so much as the triumph of Prohibition a decade earlier. The Great Depression administered the coup de grace to the Eighteenth Amendment, as America's entry into World War I had ensured its victory. And just as that earlier success built on a well-developed structure of local and state Prohibition, so did repeal gain credence from the advanced decay of enforcement. Forty-two states had enforcement laws in 1929, but only twenty appropriated funds for that purpose; of these, only six assigned more than $50,000, none as much as $150,000. The states together spent only one eighth as much enforcing Prohibition as they did enforcing their fish and game laws.[123]

The ASL and other dry spokesmen became more openly anti-Catholic after Wayne Wheeler died in 1927 and Al Smith was nominated in 1928. Clarence True Wilson of the Methodist Board of Temperance warned: "From Rome, from Italy, and from France, through a vast international organization the word has gone out to 'wipe out' Prohibition as a means of wiping out American Protestantism." Wilson tried to defeat the new apportionment of Congress required by the growth of the urban industrial states; it appeared that twenty-one agrarian states would lose twenty-seven seats as a result of the 1930 Census. He proposed that the estimated 7.5 millon foreign-born who were not citizens be excluded from the population count on which apportionment was based. But northern threats to seek a similar exclusion of disenfranchised blacks in the South scotched this effort.[124]

The 1930 Wickersham Commission on Law Enforcement, charged in effect with supporting Prohibition, nevertheless had to discuss—and thus to publicize—the links between enforcement and organized crime. The commission proposed to improve matters by concentrating enforcement in the Department of Justice and speeding up the administration of justice through codified Prohibition laws. But such palliatives now had little appeal.

The onset of the depression dealt a body blow to one of the great rationales for Prohibition: that it was a mainstay of economic prosperity. One advocate guessed that $15 to $30 billion had been diverted from the purchase of liquor to the consumption of goods, and concluded that Prohibition was an "unqualified economic success," that "involuntary poverty has been eliminated in the United States." Unfortunately his findings, published as *Prohibition and Prosperity*, appeared in 1930.[125]

Public opinion measurably shifted. A *Literary Digest* poll in early 1930 reported that 30.5 percent of 4.8 million respondents still supported Prohibition (8 percent fewer than in 1922), while 40.6 percent (twice the 1922 total) favored repeal. The Association against the Prohibition Amendment now came into its own. As the ASL once drew sustenance from the ideology and the rhetorical style of Progressive reform, so did the AAPA reflect the conservative ideology of individual freedom and laissez-faire so widespread in the twenties. It was no accident that AAPA leaders Pierre du Pont and Jouett Shouse, and the content and even the format of the association's propaganda, re-emerged in a few years in the anti–New Deal American Liberty League.[126]

The great debate over Prohibition that figured so largely in the 1928 presidential campaign was all but over by 1932. Most Republican leaders pushed for a national referendum on repeal, and got their way in the platform; the Democrats came out flatly for repeal. The *New Statesman and Nation* observed: "There is . . . no longer any doubt that repeal of prohibition is in the field of practical politics."[127]

After the Democrats' sweeping 1932 election victory, the rush to get rid of Prohibition became a stampede. In early 1933 a repeal amendment passed the Senate by a 63–23 vote, the House by 289–121. Forty-three state repeal conventions met in 1933; only Georgia, Kansas, Louisiana, Mississippi, and North Dakota failed to ratify. In the thirty-seven elections for delegates to these conventions, 73 percent of the voters supported repeal; proratification votes ranged from 78 percent to 89 percent. It was of some symbolic significance that in the same week in December 1933, the Twenty-First Amendment went into effect and a federal court allowed *Ulysses* to enter the country.[128]

Like its rise, the fall of Prohibition was the product of a broad, pluralistic coalition. And diverse attitudes and interests shaped the regulatory structure that emerged after repeal. Three states—Georgia, Alabama, and Kansas—remained dry. Twelve southern and western states allowed the sale of beer only; twenty-nine others provided for the sale of liquor, but with a bewildering variety of restrictions. Most created special governing authorities, usually liquor control commissions. Eleven commonwealths—including Pennsylvania, Michigan, and Ohio—set up state monopolies for the distribution and sale of alcoholic beverages; a few provided for state manufacture of liquor. Kentucky's constitution forbade intoxicating liquors, but the legislature in effect allowed every citizen to be his own physician, able to prescribe alcoholic "medicines" for himself.

A mass of (often conflicting) regulations governed the conditions of sale. Liquor advertising and alcoholic content were closely restricted. Private clubs would, it was hoped, foster temperate drinking; and some states sought to confine public drinking to food-selling establishments in order to prevent the return of the saloon. Sunday sales generally were prohibited, as were "tied house" contracts linking liquor manufacturers to retail outlets. But there was no attempt to close bars during the day as in England. Numerous rules set limits on who could buy alcoholic beverages, based on age, state of inebriation, economic condition (Massachusetts and a few other states barred welfare recipients), race (Indians), mental condition (insanity), and gender (women in Massachusetts taverns).

Conflicting views abounded also on the relationship of taxation to liquor. State commissioners and others with a stake in larger sales, and those wishing to prevent the return of bootlegging, favored lower taxes; prohibitionists and taxing authorities favored higher taxes. Under the umbrella of repeal—as under the umbrella of Prohibition—diversity prevailed.[129]

The fate of this most ambitious—and most restrictive—of early twentieth-century social reforms dramatically defined the extent to which state power could subordinate private vices to public mores. Sweeping rules might, under special conditions, be enacted into law. But broad social agreement was necessary for this to happen; and in so large, diverse, and dynamic a society, even a constitutional amendment was an insufficient guarantee of its permanence.

Once it was carved back down to the bedrock of state and local option, Prohibition, ironically, had more of a life after repeal than might have been expected. The policy lesson, in the realm of mores, was clear: if the constraints sought were limited and in accord with local and immediate attitudes and interests, then they might survive, even flourish. But if they went national, and relied more on the authority of the state than on the weight of prevailing public opinion, the likelihood of successful implementation was low and of popular hostility high.

5 · Crime and Punishment

We have seen how the desire for social order and cultural cohesion fueled public policies designed to regulate the mores of a diverse, rapidly changing society. Those considerations had substantial policy consequences as well in the realm of crime, a public issue gravid with significance for the stability and good order of American life.

The basic concerns of American criminal justice were old and familiar ones: What was the scale and character of crime? Was it increasing or decreasing? And what about its causes? Was it due primarily to nature and heredity, and thus to individual character, or to nurture and environment, and thus to society? And what should be the chief goal of criminal justice: to punish or to rehabilitate criminals?

The policy debate over crime during the early twentieth century did not stray from, add to, or resolve these questions. What did occur was a substantial change in the scale of public concern and the responses of government. An ever-broader configuration of ideas and interests, issues and institutions, meant that the response to crime, as in other areas of social policy, was notable not for its divergence from the past, or its singleness of purpose, but for the range of its concerns and the diversity of its responses.[1]

The Face of Crime

When Americans thought about crime in the early twentieth century, they often turned to Europe for comparisons. Then as now, the New World fared poorly when set against the Old. The American murder rate was variously estimated to be ten to twenty times as high as those of European nations. Chicago's total of 187 murders in 1905 was half that of England and Wales combined, which had sixteen times its

149

population. The elevated American rates frequently were ascribed to particular groups (blacks freed from slavery, the new immigrants), less so to a general national predilection toward violence.[2]

Blame often was placed on the laxness of American law enforcement. According to one study the conviction rate for murderers in Germany was 95 percent, in the United States 1.3 percent. Germany, like other European countries, had a national police system, could expel undesirables, and had a better grasp of what was going on: "The German police have wonderfully intimate knowledge of the movements of the people," one admirer observed. In 1907 Berlin had 5,303 policemen for its two million people; Chicago, with about the same population, had 2,688. And violent crime was handled with severity: of thirteen London murderers apprehended in 1903, eleven were hanged. One judge estimated that new trials were granted in only 3.5 percent of appealed cases in England; in the United States the figure was 46 percent.[3]

The American Institute of Criminal Law and Criminology sent a commission in 1909 to look into the criminal law systems of other countries. What most struck the American observers was the greater certainty and speed of English procedure. Infrequent bail, the relative unimportance of defects in an indictment, far more interventionist judges: these were features of the British (and Continental) systems sadly lacking in the United States. The British Criminal Appeals Act of 1907, which empowered a judge to dismiss an appeal if he was convinced that "no substantial miscarriage of justice has actually occurred," further enabled the judiciary to secure swift justice.[4]

These differences were evident in a comparison of the trials of Harry K. Thaw in New York for killing his wife's lover, the architect Stanford White, and the British case of Horace G. Rayner, who murdered a well-known London merchant. In both instances the defendant pled insanity. Within two months after the crime Rayner had been tried, convicted, and sentenced; his trial took a single day. A year and a half and two trials after Thaw killed White, he was found to be not guilty because of insanity.

The relatively homogeneous character of the British population—especially within each class—made swift justice more feasible. The bar was close-knit and cohesive. Jurors, overwhelmingly lower middle class, were speedily empaneled and quick to agree. Indeed, so efficient was the British criminal law system that the thrust of reform there was not to tighten but to ease it. This was the intent of measures such as the Criminal Appeals Act of 1907. Meanwhile, the Americans—a heterogeneous people with conflicting values and interests, hobbled by a complex and unwieldy federalism and a politicized, often corrupt judiciary, and afflicted by a widespread popular disrespect for law and a public opinion too often given to sentimentality—could do little to staunch the rising flood of criminality. So went the conventional wisdom of the time.[5]

In fact, rising crime rates were a source of growing anxiety in early twentieth-century Europe. Experts agreed that serious crime was on the upswing in Britain, France, and Germany. French Minister of Justice Aristide Briand expressed alarm in 1912 over the nation's crime statistics, blamed lenient judges, and called on local officials to suggest remedies. British concern over the rise of juvenile crime, as well as the desire for more humane treatment of young offenders, lay behind the creation of the Borstal detention system by the 1908 Prevention of Crime Act.[6]

The features of British criminal justice that so won the admiration of Americans persisted in the 1920s. The number of prisoners in British jails steadily declined: by 1923 only 8,000 were in local prisons and 1,600 in state institutions, compared to 20,000 and 10,000 a half century before. Almost 70,000 defendants were charged with indictable offenses in 1926, but only 7,924 were committed for jury trials. The Criminal Justice Act of 1925 eliminated a number of obsolete rules; the Children and Younger Persons Act of 1933 set up a system of juvenile courts.[7]

The role of juries continued to decline, while courts of summary jurisdiction gained importance. "The modern tendency of Parliament to increase the number of indictable offenses which may . . . be disposed of summarily, is the most significant development in English criminal law administration during the last half-century," concluded one expert in 1930. Indictment procedure was simplified, and grand juries (temporarily suspended during the war) were abolished in 1930. There were few appeals; and when one did occur, on average it took less than five weeks for a judgment to be rendered. Criminal law, said a 1935 review, had become the most lucid and certain branch of British law.[8]

Whatever insights (or anxieties) were engendered by comparisons abroad, the sources of the causes and character of American crime were to be found at home. The growing attention paid to the subject fed both hereditarian and environmental theories. Belief in the inheritability of criminal tendencies, popularized in the late nineteenth century by the Italian criminologist Cesare Lombroso, was reinforced after 1900 by the rise of eugenics and racial theories of social behavior. For many this was little more than a scientific rationale for traditional hostility toward blacks, immigrants, drunkards, and the poor.

But hereditarian assumptions could take a more sophisticated form. One study of a thousand young multiple offenders traced what it thought was the indirect influence of inheritance through ailments such as epilepsy and feeblemindedness. At the same time it stressed the interrelatedness of heredity and environment: "We may regard the idea of bare criminalistic traits, especially in their hereditary aspects, as an unsubstantiated metaphysical hypothesis." The straightforward prewar assumption that criminality was related to mental deficiency came under question. When the army's World War I intelligence test was administered to a large sample of criminals, their scores were above the norm. A 1918 review of the previous decade's developments in criminology found it benefiting from the insights not only of biology but of psychology and other social sciences as well. The result was a "more cautious and catholic" approach than emphasis on a single cause: "It is inaccurate to speak of a criminal instinct, or of an instinctive type of criminal."[9]

Simple correlations, like simple solutions, gave way as the complexities of criminological inquiry grew in pace with the complexities of modern society. True, the straightforward identification of crime with cities and immigrants, a familiar theme in nineteenth-century America, continued during the peak years of the new immigration and after. Hearings in the House of Representatives in 1922 pointed to the high crime rates of immigrant children, and concluded that their inferior germ plasm made them worse than their immigrant parents. But more layered, multifaceted explanations also made headway. Interpretations of the post–World War I crime wave dwelt on the heterogeneity of the population and the consequent lack of social solidarity, and on the breakdown of criminal law administration. More particular sources of social malaise also were noted: unemployment, the ease with which autos could be stolen, the lack of education. Los Angeles officials blamed their city's crime wave on drug users: one police officer maintained that if 2,500 addicts were removed, crime would decline by 90 percent.[10]

By the end of the 1920s an ever-richer collection of environmental explanations had gone far to erode the earlier stress on hereditary causes. Both the uniqueness of the scale of postwar crime and the role that the foreign-born and their children played in it came under question. A massive review of millions of criminal cases concluded that in proportion to their numbers, the foreign-born committed far fewer crimes than did the native-born. And the Wickersham Committee Report of 1931 openly questioned the linkage of foreigners with crime. The war, the automobile, Prohibition, yellow journalism, the disintegration of parental authority, the waning of school discipline, the exaggeration of sex, sports fetishism, inebriety and drug addiction, political corruption, the coddling of criminals, growing disrespect for law: the whole modern liturgy detailing the causes of crime was in place by 1930.[11]

Was crime in fact on the rise in post-1900 America? The consensus among historians is that the overall rate of violent crime declined over the course of the nineteenth and early twentieth centuries. But burgeoning immigrant cities and an ever more racially tense South appeared to generate if not more then at least more visible violence. And social and economic change led to new forms of criminal activity. A greater flow of data (about half the states collected relatively detailed crime statistics during the early twentieth century, and a 1904 federal crime census attracted much attention) and the flowering of sensational journalism also did much to foster the public sense that crime was a significant social problem.[12]

The most evident growth was in crimes against order and property. Their potential increased in modern society, and the law took due notice of that fact. The particularization of crime—as of so many other aspects of modern life—steadily grew. A discussion of "Modern Crimes and Penalties" dwelt on the secular changes of modern life: electricity (leading in Connecticut to "an act to prevent the stealing of electricity"); modern transportation (resulting in laws against stealing rides on railroads or getting on or off trains while they were in motion); laws defining misdeeds and imposing penalties regarding bicycles, petroleum, explosives, anaesthetics, medicines, sanitation, food adulteration, fraud, gambling, liquor, game, child labor, corporations and trusts. Of 100,000 Chicago criminal arrests in 1912, more than half were for violations which had not existed twenty-five years before.[13]

Around the turn of the century "crimes of mobility"—offenses such as bigamy and swindling, made easier by the scale and looseness of the new American society—were on the increase. And now there appeared the greatest of all technological contributions to the modern annals of crime: the automobile. A study of 120,000 arrests in Detroit from 1913 to 1919 found that the two great causes were the automobile and Prohibition.[14]

Gangs and gambling, and alliances of criminals with politicians and saloonkeepers, had long been part of the urban scene. Josiah Flynt's *World of Graft* (1901) described a demimonde of colorful criminals and local gangs, and offered a topology of cities: Chicago, he thought, was honest, New York dishonest. But the turn-of-the-century urban underworld took on new dimensions. Awareness of the Mafia as an international conspiracy now emerged, spurred by the 1890 slaying of New Orleans's police chief and the consequent lynching of eleven Italian immigrants, a Sicilian immigrant's murder of a Denver priest while he was administering communion, and the killing in Palermo of a New York City detective, Joseph Petrosino.[15]

Jewish and Italian pimps, thieves, and pickpockets rose to challenge the Irish, who had traditionally dominated New York City's underworld. Police Commissioner Theodore A. Bingham took public note in 1908 of the high rates of Jewish crime against property and Italian crimes of violence, and estimated that half of New York City's criminals were Jewish. He came under severe criticism for this. But it was evident that crime's ethnic dimension was a source of growing public concern.[16]

Chicago was . . . Chicago, well before the days of Al Capone and Prohibition. The city's traditional underworld was made up primarily of lifelong professional criminals, whose rare court appearances usually occurred when their payoff-for-protection arrangements with the police broke down. This happened when their loot turned out to be the property of a powerful corporation; or when the press became interested; or when the politicians controlling criminal prosecutions sought to make some political capital, as in the conflict between the Democrats' Roger Sullivan and Carter Harrison factions between 1910 and 1913.

The big change in early twentieth-century Chicago was the rise of criminal syndicates less subject to shifts in political power. One organization operated a gambling ship three miles offshore on Lake Michigan, complete with pioneering use of radio to secure racetrack results. But they brought with them, too, more of the spectacular crimes of violence that earned the city its distinctive reputation. Rival groups of gamblers engaged in mutual bombings even before Prohibition days. A judge observed in 1908: "Human life is the cheapest thing in Chicago."[17]

The new face of crime fully emerged in the 1920s. Because of technological and cultural change, remarked one observer, "criminal law is being forced into fields which are essentially non-criminal." Newly defined crimes such as driving recklessly or violating drug and liquor laws led another observer to ask: "Does the Modern Conception of Criminality, which seems to be shifting from a basis of individual guilt to one of social danger, presage the abandonment of the classic requirement of a *mens rea* [criminal intent] as an essential of criminality?" President Herbert Hoover's Committee on Social Trends concluded in 1932: "The prevalent conception of a crime now is an act declared by the state to be an offense against it," in contrast with the traditional definition of offenses against persons or property.[18]

One measure of the expanding realm of crime is that the federal government's penal code had 264 sections in 1900 and 383 in 1930; state penal code sections increased from 7,156 to 9,609. Newly minted federal crimes included First World War draft violations (almost 18,000 such cases were finally dropped in 1925), violations of the Harrison Anti-Narcotics Act (over 42,000 charges outstanding in 1923), and of course violations of the federal Prohibition law (the basis of 7,291 of 55,587 federal criminal prosecutions in 1920; 50,743 of 76,136 in 1925; and 56,992 of 87,305 in 1930).[19]

The Illinois Crime Survey of 1927–28 reviewed the state's impressive record in that field of human endeavor: labor violence and family feuds in the mining areas and hills of Williamson County, bootleg wars, bank robberies in small towns (some $600,000 was stolen during a fifteen-month period). This activity was blamed in part on "the finest hard road system in the country," and on two crime cultures: rural Appalachia and the cities.[20]

The popular perception of crime in the 1920s focused on large cities. Clarence Darrow, writing from Chicago in 1926, concluded that while the automobile and Prohibition had made new forms of crime more visible, the overall crime rate was most likely stable, or even declining. But Prohibition and the mass media fixed the image of the crime-drenched metropolis. Patterns evident for decades before—crime as a form of upward mobility for immigrants and second-generation Americans; gangs and rackets; close alliances between criminals, politicians, judges, and the police—now were widely seen as paradigmatic expressions of what was representative of (and worrisome about) American civilization.[21]

These perceptions fed on more than fantasy. The 1929 homicide rates of thirty-one major American cities were almost twenty times as large as that of England and Wales, a ratio unchanged since the turn of the century. In a few dramatic instances the gap widened dramatically: the Chicago robbery rate in 1924, adjusted for population, was one hundred times greater than London's. The highest murder rates were not in the major northern cities but in southern towns with large black populations and long traditions of violence. Homicide was the second major cause of death (after tuberculosis) for Birmingham, Alabama, blacks aged twenty to thirty-four. And the detention and delinquency rates of black children in New York City had already attracted attention.[22]

New social realities and media-fed perceptions came together in that recurrent (im)morality play, the spectacular murder trial. Courtroom dramas in which sex and/or money figured prominently reached new heights of notoriety during the 1920s, as corporate and political wrongdoing had before the war. To some degree these spectacles were simply the products of yellow journalism responding to the need to compete with other newspapers and the movies. But they contributed to the popular inclination to regard crime as a major public concern.[23]

Legal commentators criticized "trial by newspaper." Most serious was the publication of details before a trial, a practice that obstructed the detection and apprehension of criminals and jury objectivity and selection. The belief that antisocial news had antisocial consequences led to (unsuccessful) attempts at state licensing of journalists in Illinois, Oklahoma, and Connecticut. Yet a long-term study of sensational news in over a hundred papers concluded that the space devoted to crime in 1928 was proportionately less than fifty years earlier. The trouble was with the tone and color of the reporting. An American Society of Newspaper Editors' code of ethics in 1923 proposed that newspapers approach crime news in the spirit of "social sanitation." The New York State Crime Commission noted that "waves of news" were mistaken for "waves of crime" and fostered the belief that criminals escaped justice.[24]

The doings of organized crime—gangsters, racketeers, and mobs—jousted for space and attention with prominent murder trials. "Racketeering" as a synonym for organized crime first appeared (where else?) in Chicago during the early 1920s, supposedly in reference to the underworld "racketers" (noisemakers) who congregated around Twelfth and Halstead streets. Just as "the trusts" became a convenient term for the new big businesses that evoked widespread anxiety during the prewar years, so did "the rackets"—numbers gambling; extortion of employers, unions, retail stores, and small businessmen— become in the 1920s and 1930s a worrisome aspect of urban life.[25]

Particularly disturbing was a development not unlike the growth of big business at the turn of the century: the growing presence of organized gangs ("mobs") controlling whole realms of illegality: gambling, prostitution, and above all the distribution and sale of alcohol. Prohibition raised urban criminal organizations to new heights of scale, system, and violence. Chicago now became the "crime capital of the world." The linkage of crime with politics, always close, was particularly so for bootlegging, which depended on widespread connivance with the authorities. The 1929 report of the Illinois Crime Commission observed: "We had the best opportunity ever provided for a study at first hand of the multiplied ways by which a city can be misgoverned."[26]

The public reaction to the new urban underworld was shaped also by its ethnic makeup. According to one estimate 30 percent of the one hundred leading Chicago criminals in 1930 were Italians, 29 percent were Irish, 20 percent Jews, and 12 percent blacks. The bloody competition between gangland leaders that led to Al Capone's ascendancy in 1927, in which more than five hundred "competitors" were killed, may be viewed as a gruesome mimicry of the processes by which Rockefeller's Standard Oil emerged a generation before, or by which city bosses secured their political supremacy.[27]

By 1929 it was reasonable to conclude that "crime is the nation's biggest business." Estimates of its value ranged from $3 billion to $13 billion a year, compared to $5 billion for the auto industry and $4.5 billion for the cost of the national government. About 400,000 criminals were in jail; an estimated million more were not. Some 12,000 murders were recorded in 1928, and it was feared that a major economic depression might well create "a veritable reign of anarchy and bloodshed."[28]

The depression indeed came, but it did not significantly alter the prevailing configuration of crime in America. The economy collapsed and unemployment soared, yet there was no evident increase in crime rates. The inmates of America's prisons increased by 33 percent between 1926 and 1930, but only by 8 percent between 1930 and 1934.[29]

In the mid-1930s, no less than a decade before, it was clear that "modern crime has gone big business." Its cost to the American people each year was conservatively estimated at $15 billion. "The rackets"—the forcible imposition of price, labor, and other standards on businessmen and retailers—replaced rum-running as the favored work of organized crime. This "method for control of business competition, and commodity price regulation, otherwise illegal by the provisions of the Sherman Anti-Trust Law and the Clayton Act," became an organized conspiracy of criminals, lawyers, businessmen, labor leaders, and politicians comparable to bootlegging in its prime. [30]

Gambling, drug, and prostitution syndicates—arrangements among gangsters in various cities, that avoided interstate activity and the attention of the feds—grew in number. Organized crime in the mid-1930s by one count was involved in sixteen major areas of activity: pinball, policy (numbers), racetracks, prostitution, loan-sharking, nightclubs, union and industrial shakedowns, real estate, stolen jewelry, stocks and bonds, gambling (dice, cards, numbers and other lotteries), produce and other foods, garages and autos, abortions, gunrunning and counterfeiting, and narcotics. Still, it appeared by the mid-1930s that crime had declined from its mid-1920s peak; and, given the decrease in opportunity with the passing of both prosperity and Prohibition, this may well have been the case.[31]

Criminal Justice

As crime assumed a larger place in the public consciousness, so too did the question of what to do about it. A complex tension existed between conscience and convenience, between the desire to make the system more rehabilitative, more humane and responsive to due process, and the desire to make it a more efficient and economical instrument of social control. As the number and diversity of crimes expanded, so did the range of policy responses: "The scope of penalties is . . . greatly widened by being made to cover all violations of the amended law . . . In such thickets of legislation one can hardly move without being scratched by a prohibition."[32]

New forms of social regulation, new views of the sources of crime and the nature of criminals, led to new public policy expectations. But old fears of social disorder, and traditional views of crime and punishment, also had stronger appeal in a time of rapid social change. The by-now familiar result: heightened pressures both for change and for preservation, producing a more lively and diverse public policy agenda.

Take, for example, those venerable American rites of violence, vigilantism and lynching. A strong movement against the propensity of Americans to take the law into their own hands emerged in the early 1900s. Did this stem from the desire to substitute due process for lynch-law justice, or from the desire to strike down a form of lawlessness that posed a threat to social order? Surely from both—and in a complex intermixture of motives. So it was with the criminal justice system at large.[33]

Another revealing development was the declining significance of criminal motivation. The dominant nineteenth-century view was that intent did much to determine the criminality of an act. But modern life and thought reduced its significance. One legal journal predicted: "The criminal law of the future will be greatly concerned with cases in which a particular state of mind is unimportant."[34]

This increasingly nuanced view left its mark on the vexing question of the relationship between crime and insanity. The 1843 McNaghten legal test—Was the accused aware of the moral rightness or wrongness of his act?—had come to be regarded by most psychiatric opinion as too simple and restrictive. Massachusetts's Briggs law of 1921 required the pretrial psychiatric examination of a defendant accused of a capital offense or previously convicted of a felony. This would be carried out by the state's Department of Mental Diseases; the result could be admitted as evidence in the trial. By 1934, 4,392 defendants had been examined. The number found to be mentally incapable of standing trial declined from one in four during the mid-1920s to one in ten in the early 1930s, a reflection, perhaps, of social anxieties stirred by the depression. For the most part courts continued to leave the determination of the accused's mental state to juries, and to prefer a direct choice between sanity or insanity. Still, when state laws in Washington, Louisiana, and Mississippi sought to exclude the insanity plea from criminal trials, the courts struck them down as unconstitutional.[35]

The question of how to deal with crime and criminals had an important place in early twentieth-century social policy-making. Solutions proliferated in pace with the expanding perception of crime's character and causes. These included broad social programs (immigration restriction, the sterilization of mental and moral defectives, birth control) and structural innovations (expanded probation, parole, indeterminate sentencing, and juvenile courts; an appointed judiciary and restricted juries; a national crime bureau). Another new idea was gun control. Former New York police commissioner Charles M. McAdoo saw no reason why homeowners needed to keep guns for self-defense; and the *Chicago Tribune* announced in 1921 that it would no longer accept revolver ads. By the mid-1920s a number of states had laws regulating the ownership and use of pistols. The National Firearms Act of the early 1930s imposed a federal license tax on guns, copying the same enforcement inadequacies as the Harrison Narcotics Act of 1914.[36]

A major theme in Progressive thinking about crime was the belief that the system too readily allowed the guilty to avoid punishment. Oliver Wendell Holmes concluded in 1904: "At the present time in this country there is more danger that criminals will escape justice than that they will be subjected to tyranny." William Howard Taft was a prominent critic of the delays that plagued the justice system, primarily because he feared that they lessened respect for law and encouraged anarchic acts such as lynchings. He observed that in 1885 there had been 1,808 recorded homicides and 108 executions of convicted murderers; in 1904 there were 8,482 murders but only 116 executions. Taft admired (as did so many others) the British system of justice, in which strong-minded judges had greater control over juries, appeals, and other time-consuming obstructions to the swift execution of the law.[37]

Closely related was the belief that the courts' procedural rules made it too easy to subvert justice through technical niceties. One observer thought that "the two great evils of our criminal law to-day are sentimentality and technicality." Federal court judge Charles Amidon argued in 1906 that the criminal justice system was breaking down because of the high percentage of appeals granted in criminal courts on the basis of technical points of pleading and practice.[38]

This complaint had a questionable basis in fact. A review of early twentieth-century state reports found that few appeals for new criminal trials were granted, and almost none on grounds of pleadings or practice. Of fifty-three appeals of Pennsylvania homicide decisions from 1905 to 1910, forty-three were affirmed and ten were reversed. The average length of the trials in these cases was four days; in only one did it exceed eight days. But the legal scholar John T. Wigmore noted the importance to the public of notorious instances of reversals, not just percentages. And Roscoe Pound found that over 40 percent of state court reviews of criminal cases led to the granting of new trials. In any event, the turn of the century saw the rise of concerted campaigns against new trials granted because of minor technicalities, suggesting once again that it was heightened awareness as much as new realities that gave early twentieth-century crime policy its special tone.[39]

These efforts reflected as well the Progressive urge to fix uniform norms on a diverse society. A 1902 Commission to Revise and Codify Criminal Laws found "a strange provinciality and a ragged incompleteness" in federal criminal law, the result of long neglect by Congress. Federal law had little impact except in the territories; most criminal law was defined by state and local authorities. The list of federal capital crimes had not been expanded since 1790; indeed, Congress in 1897 restricted capital punishment to murder, rape, and treason. What was needed, some thought, was a national common law of crime.[40]

After the First World War there was a "renewed quest for certainty" in the pursuit of criminal justice. Prewar crime commissions dwelt on the causes of crime; those after, most notably in Cleveland, concentrated on the criminal justice system: how to strip it of politics, how to make it more efficient. The American Institute of Criminal Law and Criminology devoted itself to the scientific study of crime; the National Committee for Mental Hygiene to the clinical study of criminals' mental makeup. Studies correlated personal characteristics with recidivism, on the model of insurance life expectancy tables. The ultimate goal: "a scientific management of the problem of crime by courts and administrative agencies," indeed, to make the court "an agency for the scientific determination of guilt."[41]

The search for system was evident on every level of criminal justice. More and more sheriffs received salaries rather than fees, though glaring instances of abusive fee practices persisted in a number of rural areas. Offenses and penalties were increasingly defined by statute. At the same time, the definition of crime kept expanding to reflect new social values and new technology: "Life and property assume new aspects, and, in the opinion of legislators, require new protection," said one authority. Later experts were more caustic: "The criminal law is the formal cause of crime." State and local courts enjoined unions, saloons, and brothels in ways that came close to, or overlapped with, criminal jurisdiction. After the Supreme Court's 1927 decision that illegally acquired income was taxable, the new federal crime of income tax evasion became the instrument of choice against elusive mobsters such as Al Capone and white-collar criminals on Wall Street.[42]

The distinction between criminal and noncriminal jurisdiction was further clouded by the expanded enforcement powers granted to private charities: to Legal Aid Societies in caring for needy families in homes; to the Society for the Prevention of Cruelty to Children in dealing with neglected children (the New York SPCC secured 53,620 convictions for abuse or neglect in a twenty-eight-year period); to the New York County Medical Society in dealing with quacks and abortionists; to anti-vice organizations in enforcing public morality.[43]

These changes did not lessen the widespread belief that crime had outstripped the capacity of the system to handle it. In 1922 the American Bar Association's Committee on Law Enforcement took note of a rising tide of lawlessness since the turn of the century and recommended a number of crime-busting steps—a ban on the private manufacture and sale of firearms, an antilynching law, the creation of a federal bureau of criminal records and statistics, and procedural changes favoring the prosecution—to counter the effects of "mollycoddling and sympathy by misinformed and ill-advised meddlers."[44]

As so often was the case, substantial inertial forces blunted the reform impulse. When the Missouri Society for Criminal Justice recommended about fifty bills designed to make the system simpler and more effective, resistance in the legislature killed them all. While the number of acts defined as crimes steadily increased, police, prosecutors, courts, and jurors appeared to be less inclined to enforce them. Public sentiment was strong and growing against the strict enforcement not only of Prohibition but of laws aimed at cigarettes, prostitution, and driving infractions as well.[45]

The great majority of criminal cases never came to a jury trial or to sentencing. The desire of prosecutors to avoid weak cases was an important factor; so too was shaky evidence and the chance of a slipup on the tortuous road of the criminal justice system. Most urban felony cases first came before magistrates, who dismissed charges in the mid-twenties at rates ranging from 28 percent in St. Louis to 58 percent in New York and 63 percent in Chicago. The proportion of convictions to homicides remained small: 14 of 221 reported murders in

New York in 1917, 44 of 336 in Chicago in 1919. Confusion, haste, incompetence, and machine politics, as well as a lack of incriminating evidence, helped to account for these figures. Dismissals in rural jurisdictions ran much lower—around 10 to 11 percent—in part because a case bound over was more profitable to the justice of the peace who handled it.[46]

Bail was widespread, and widely varied in its scale and terms. In England it still came primarily from friends and relatives, but American cities now had a substantial infrastructure of surety companies and professional bondsmen. Plea bargaining, perhaps the most notable aspect of modern criminal justice, came into widespread use during the early 1920s. And when sentencing did occur, it often was ritualized: multiples of five years were common.[47]

At the beginning of the 1920s, the legal scholar Roscoe Pound, who regarded "the legal order as a piece of social engineering," nevertheless found a need for more individualized criminal justice. He feared that a heavily bureaucratized system tended to "overcallousness, to violation of the constitutional rights of accused persons in the supposed interest of efficient enforcement of the penal laws . . . American prosecutions today are coming to be conducted with a ferocity without parallel in common-law trials since the Stuarts." Yet at the end of the decade he criticized the lack of coordination among criminal justice agencies, and stressed the need for administrative consolidation.[48]

Pound's was an ambiguity that pervaded the criminal justice system—and, indeed, American thinking about crime. Walter Lippmann speculated in 1931 on the paradoxical inclination of Americans to be uniquely inclined to impose social restrictions yet uniquely tolerant of lawbreaking: "By their moral convictions they prohibit all sin, and by their liberal conviction they have kept the prohibitions from being enforced." Early twentieth-century policy toward the primary instruments of criminal justice—the police, the courts, sentencing, prisons—amply testifies to the depth and persistence of this ambivalence, an ambivalence not lessened but intensified by the conditions of modern life.[49]

Nineteenth-century American police forces had a distinctive character. They were local, intimately linked to politics and politicians, with little of the statist tone of their European counterparts and usually smaller in relative size. The central government bore much of the cost of the police in large European cities: 80 percent in Berlin, a third in London and Paris. But not in the United States, where even the few state-appointed metropolitan police boards of the mid-nineteenth century had given way to home rule by 1900.[50]

Police responsibilities changed in step with the expanding definition of crime and widening social and economic regulation. The New York City charter of 1897 included a long list of police duties, among them to preserve public order, supervise traffic and the fighting of fires, assist immigrants, and inspect public places. The 1910 police regulations of the District of Columbia covered a rich body of urban ordinances which the police were supposed to enforce, in addition to their traditional crime-fighting role. These included regulating pawnbrokers, junk dealers, and secondhand clothing sellers; checking on the storage of inflammable substances; licensing street vendors; and regulating vehicles, animals, street litter, and noise.[51]

It is not surprising that the close interconnection of the police with politics, and with the interests that they were expected to oversee, became a source of constant concern. The incompetence and corruption of policemen, judges, sheriffs, deputies, and jailkeepers took on a special importance in American public life after 1900, not only because of the growing public awareness of crime but also because of the Progressive view that it was a treatable social disease.[52]

One solution was to try to make police departments a branch of the municipal civil service, and to turn policemen into professionals. European police forces came to be seen as model civil servants to be emulated rather than instruments of state power to be avoided. August Vollmer, Berkeley's police chief from 1905 to 1932, embodied the new view of policing as a mix of social work and crime prevention carried out by trained professionals.[53]

Specialization came hand in hand with the professional ideal. The use of policewomen spread rapidly in the years before World War I. Ten were appointed in Chicago in 1913, eight of them widows. Their primary role was to protect urban women and children, though the *New York World* was skeptical of their ability to deal with dangerous criminals, particularly in the white slave traffic.[54]

Still more notable was the rise of the state police. In their modern form they date from the establishment of the Pennsylvania State Constabulary in 1905. Fierce labor conflicts in that state's coal and iron industries led to the rise of brutal company-hired coal and iron police, and the use of inexperienced and heavy-handed National Guardsmen. The Pennsylvania law creating the new constabulary declared that "as far as possible" they were "to take the place of the police now appointed at the request of the various corporations." The *Nation* praised the efficiency and honesty of the constabulary in tracking down those responsible for the Coatesville lynchings of blacks. And soon they had a whole new range of law enforcement responsibilities, with the rise of automobile-assisted crime and the consequent breakdown of local sheriff-imposed law and order in rural districts.[55]

As so often was the case with Progressive social policy, new responses to new conditions supplemented rather than superseded the existing order of things. The intensely local, political character of America's police was modified but hardly supplanted by the new professionalism. Thus, when the state legislature at the behest of New York City's Mayor William J. Gaynor attempted to restrict the "third degree" and other forms of police severity, the response of the police and public opinion led Governor John A. Dix to veto the bill. Newton D. Baker recognized in 1915 that although the police had complicated new duties to perform, Americans' ambivalence toward the competing claims of social order and individual freedom was undiminished: "It will never be easy for us to give up the internal elasticity of our system in exchange for a rigid regimentation of society in which our daily lives will run by rules."[56]

The 1920s saw no significant change in this complex interplay. The evolution of the American police from a politically controlled branch of local government to a modern, scientific, relatively apolitical institution has been slow and gradual, and is far from completed today. The police in some towns—Kansas City for one—still were political appointees, and the police chiefs of New York, Detroit, Seattle, and other cities remained subject to political removal. Four police commissioners followed one another in rapid succession in Mayor Jimmy Walker's New York.

Yet the sheer scale of modern crime, and the high mobility of criminals, dictated that if the American police could not literally be nationalized, they could be subject to national standards of professionalism, and could have at hand uniform instrumentalities such as the registration and fingerprinting of criminals. Complex record keeping, sophisticated crime prevention methods, and civil service–based appointment procedures spread widely.[57]

Not surprisingly, the state police became ever more important in the age of the auto, filling the gap between that will-o'-the-wisp a national police force and the inherent localism of city and county law enforcement. By 1921 fifteen commonwealths had small state police forces. They patrolled the highways, those new ganglia of the American population, and to some degree they met the growing need of rural and suburban dwellers for protection from an increasingly mobile criminal class.

They took on yet another role in response to the postwar explosion of strikes and radical activity. The state police of Alabama, Tennessee, Connecticut, Michigan, West Virginia, Pennsylvania, and Texas were reorganized in the Red Scare year of 1919. Pennsylvania's state police quelled a November 1920 riot in Carlisle, and in the wake of the 1919 Boston police strike the Massachusetts legislature contemplated replacing the district police with a state system. Colorado's wartime Department of Safety was reorganized in 1921 as the military-structured Colorado Rangers. Governor Oliver Shoup credited them with reducing "industrial uneasiness" in the state.[58]

The First World War military experience also left its mark on urban policing. The 1920 *Official Manual* of the St. Louis police was very military in its detailed instructions. Marine Brigadier General Smedley Butler attained some fame in the late 1920s by leading the Philadelphia police in a vigorous (and quite unsuccessful) campaign of Prohibition enforcement. He called with no greater success for an expanded state police composed of young, unmarried, well-trained men, enlisted for four-year terms. And by the early 1930s that postwar creation the Federal Bureau of Investigation, in effect a national police force, had won its unique reputation for crime-fighting prowess.[59]

Yet old American suspicions of national body of law enforcers, and indeed of police in general, remained strong. Far from becoming paramilitary forces, the state police concentrated more and more on problems engendered by the automobile. In Colorado, Governor Shoup's successor, William Sweet, argued that the state's Rangers deprived the people of their right to self-government, and that public safety was best handled by the local police and the National Guard.

For all their utility, the state police were constrained by their cost, their threat to local government (and local police forces), and the disquieting air of militarism emanating from a statewide uniformed force. The growing hostility to Prohibition did not help. By 1924 only New Jersey had added a state police force since the war; and Governor Edward Edwards, whose successful campaign included the pledge that he would make "New Jersey as wet as the Atlantic Ocean," called for its abolition. (The more rural-minded legislature instead increased the force's appropriation.) Only twelve states had police forces with general policing powers by the mid-1930s.[60]

As Prohibition's popularity waned, criticism of strong-arm police tactics grew. Police brutality attracted attention comparable to earlier concerns over police corruption. A 1931 exposé, "Our Lawless Police," concluded: "In no previous period of our national life has a general popular antagonism toward public authority, and distrust of it, been more prevalent throughout the United States." Borrowed from the argot of Freemasonry, the "third degree" became a common term for brutal police interrogatory methods. Seven states passed laws making it a criminal offense between 1908 and 1912; appellate courts heard 106 "third degree" cases from 1920 to 1930. One of these revealed that New York's chief of police used a boxing glove to avoid incriminating marks; a rubber hose frequently served the same purpose in other jurisdictions. One suspect was taken to the morgue at three in the morning and forced to examine the wounds of the deceased for forty-five minutes; another accused of murder was chained overnight in a mosquito-infested cell, and was questioned the following day with the scalp of the dead woman at his feet.[61]

The courts, like the police, were a prime target of criminal law reformers. And like the police they varied greatly in their settings, functions, and constituencies. Thus, the appellate courts of California's Alameda County were of necessity most concerned with due process and formal procedure; trial courts concentrated on criminal cases; police and municipal courts had a more general mandate to enforce social regulation.

Courtroom cultures ranged from the very old to the very new. Premodern violence erupted at times. In 1912 a Hillsville, Virginia, judge sentenced Floyd Allen to a year in jail for attacking a law officer; Allen and two relatives opened fire in the courtroom, killing the judge, the prosecuting attorney, and the sheriff, and wounding the clerk of court and several jurors.

The urban criminal justice system was more closely attuned to modern times. New social types appeared, such as Manuel Levine, a twenty-eight-year-old Jewish immigrant who became an assistant police prosecutor in New York in 1907 and worked for greater fairness in the treatment of the poor by the criminal courts. Thomas Woolwine of Los Angeles, in what would be a recurring twentieth-century pattern, portrayed himself as a crusading district attorney, at war with the mayor and the police commissioner, determined to enforce all the laws on the books. He raided bucket shops (social clubs that sold liquor without permits) and brothels. But the courts dismissed his suits against patrons; the state supreme court overruled him on the clubs, which reopened; and (by his account) machine politicians prevented him from serving out his term.[62]

The criminal courts of New York City—Magistrates' and Special Sessions—were processing half a million people a year by 1920. Many immigrants had their first postdebarkation contact with American government in them; the Magistrates' Court was called the "supreme court of the poor." During the early years of the century these tribunals were notably crowded and inefficient. Immigrants had to cope with their own ignorance, inept attorneys, conviction-hungry prosecutors and judges, and anti-immigrant juries. Overworked and incompetent magistrates frequently bound over minor cases for Special Sessions review. Defendants, unable to make bail, stayed in jail, often at great cost to their families and almost always for more than the maximum term of the crime for which they stood accused. The Inferior Criminal Courts Act of 1910 brought more centralized control under the chief judge of Special Sessions, and civic reformers fended off attempts to politicize that position.[63]

Chicago's Municipal Court was a model of adaptation to the new demands of urban criminal justice. Its 1909 docket groaned under the weight of 125,000 cases, forcing it to make its own rules of practice and procedure. The chief justice handled its administrative work, and sitting judges were given wide discretion in framing rules of practice and procedure. Here was an illustration of what a court "organized on business principles" and common sense could do. Records were kept of the physical and moral status and the hereditary and environmental conditions of delinquents and persistent offenders. Crime was punished with greater certainty and swiftness than anywhere else; all but 9,358 of the 128,861 civil and criminal cases pending in 1909 were expeditiously handled.[64]

Nevertheless, the court found it heavy going in the face of entrenched interests. Aldermen frequently secured the release of constituents imprisoned for violating a city ordinance: more than a tenth of all convictions in the first year of Mayor Fred Busse's 1907–1911 term. When Municipal Court judge McKenzie Cleland worked out probationary measures and other practices designed to make justice for the poor swifter, cheaper, and more humane, threatened courthouse and clubhouse interests saw to it that he was restricted to civil cases.[65]

The most notable innovation of the time was the creation of juvenile courts to deal with delinquents of too tender an age to be exposed to the rigors of the regular judicial process. The first "Children's Court" appeared in Chicago in 1899; by 1904 eight states and eleven large cities had them, and by 1916 they existed in forty-six states. They were supposed to be corrective and reformatory rather than punitive, and to be free to vary substantially from regular court procedure.[66]

Recent examinations of these courts focus on their role as agents of social control. The treatment of immigrant children and their families by Milwaukee's Juvenile Court was hardly a model of compassion and understanding. And a photograph of one of these courts in operation (see illustration) suggests that it may well have been a fearsome place for a young defendant.

But for its time, and in the minds of its proponents, children's courts were instruments of social betterment. One advocate declared in 1910: "The child . . . henceforth shall be viewed as the ward of the state, to be cared for by it, and not as an enemy of the state, to be punished by it." There is reason to think that working-class families welcomed these courts, and Judge Ben Lindsey's Children's Court in Denver won a generally well deserved reputation for compassion and effectiveness.[67]

American courts did not undergo significant alteration during the 1920s, though there continued to be much obeisance to the great god Procedural Reform. Trial juries were all but abandoned in misdemeanor cases, and more and more states allowed defendants to waive a jury trial. Injunctions flourished as a judicial instrument for ordering that saloons be closed, liquor be seized, and Prohibition lawbreakers be arrested.[68]

The old American suspicion of judicial authority and a taste for "lawless enforcement of law" lived on alongside the new passion for law and order. Juvenile courts came under attack for abandoning traditional procedural safeguards. Appellate courts subjected criminal convictions to close scrutiny: fourteen southern state supreme courts reversed 91 of 342 criminal appeals in 1922, 21 northern courts reversed 28 of 94. And most states continued to limit the prosecution's power to appeal criminal decisions.[69]

Adherence to procedure could even lead an occasional court to go against the prevailing racial and religious prejudices of the time. Mississippi's supreme court in 1916 set aside a guilty verdict in a trial because the prosecutor said of the accused: "She is a negro—look at her skin; if she is not a negro, I don't want you to convict her." Equally unacceptable was the argument in another trial that "the testimony of one soldier boy, perhaps of one person who was not a Jew, was . . . of greater weight than that of all Jews, however upright, intelligent or numerous, who had knowledge of the facts."[70]

The effort to establish a more uniform and "modern" criminal justice policy appears to have left its most substantial mark on the sentencing of criminals. Greater specificity in the definition of crimes, the desire of the reform-minded to reward the good behavior of prisoners and of the economy-minded to lower the costs of incarceration, encouraged major changes in pardoning and probation, indeterminate sentencing, and parole.

Granting pardons, traditionally a prerogative of the executive, had become common (and complicated) enough by 1915 to call for a mini-treatise on the subject. Probation, too, which like pardoning reflected the strong American belief in a second chance, was far more extensive and highly developed than in Europe. Massachusetts set up a state probation system in 1891, and many other commonwealths followed suit. Of twenty thousand Boston probation cases in one year, more than half involved convictions for drunkenness. Juvenile offenders, and first offenders in property cases, also were beneficiaries in New York and elsewhere.[71]

By the early 1930s thirty-two states had probation provisions; those without clustered in the South. Massachusetts had 13,084 adults on probation in 1911 and 30,518 in 1931; New York had 10,726 in 1913 and 19,817 in 1932. Fewer male youths were in prison in 1923 than in 1910, primarily because of the growth of probation.[72]

A federal system was slower to develop. In 1916 the Supreme Court held that probation had to be authorized by Congress. But an enabling statute did not become law until 1925, and adequate appropriations and judicial implementation were not provided until the 1930s. In general, the costs and complexities of oversight kept federal probation from having the impact that its proponents hoped for (and its enemies feared).[73]

According to a 1911 English review of American criminal justice, indeterminate sentencing represented "a new mental attitude towards the conception of punishment on the part of a large section of the English-speaking race . . . The idea of recreating criminal man to honest citizenship—this, rather than his conversion into a religious man—lies at the root of the modern doctrine of reformation as the primary object of punishment." But British indeterminate sentencing was limited to juvenile delinquents and preventive detention of "moral defectives." There was no equivalent to the American policy of reducing the sentences of adult criminals for good behavior. A number of states also authorized suspended sentences, and the idea of "the reformatory sentence"—one that prepared prisoners for freedom—attracted much attention. Although the Michigan Supreme Court struck down that state's indeterminate sentencing law in 1891, a constitutional amendment to allow it won by a seventy thousand–vote majority in 1902.[74]

By 1911 three quarters of the states had parole laws, as did a number of foreign nations. Like pardoning and indeterminate sentencing, paroling accorded well with the prevailing belief in social reform through procedural change. A federal parole law was adopted in 1920.[75]

Indiana's indeterminate sentencing and parole law of 1897 attracted much attention. It prescribed maximum and minimum terms for various crimes, but within those limits allowed considerable leeway for variance in sentencing. In its first two decades of operation only about one out of four prisoners violated their parole. Prison commitments declined between 1890 and 1910, and the earnings of the parolees more than met the costs of the system.[76]

Reports dwelt on paroling's national success. A 1915 survey concluded that recidivism occurred in only 3 to 7 percent of the cases. In the first two years of Tom Johnson's first term as governor of Ohio, 1,160 prisoners were pardoned and paroled, as compared to 84 in the previous administration; 173 returned to prison. Of the 1,461 California convicts paroled between 1893 and 1912, 214—about 15 percent—violated their paroles, primarily by drinking or leaving their place of employment without permission. Few returned to crime.[77]

These sentence-reducing devices did much to ease the persistent overload of the criminal justice system. Nevertheless, the widespread belief in the 1920s that crime was a growing social problem overrode earlier optimism. There were frequent outbursts of public anger over abuses and failures. Criticism often focused on the arbitrary way in which paroles were granted, and on the inadequacy of supervision.

Judges often clashed with boards over particular parole decisions; police chiefs tended to oppose the practice, district attorneys to favor it. Pennsylvania judges sometimes preempted parole by imposing maximum-minimum sentences such as "from 20 years to 19 years, 11 months, and 29 days."[78]

Pardoning, too, fell into some disfavor. Refusals by Indiana's Board of Pardons doubled from 407 in 1923–24 to 811 in 1925–26. The most notable expression of the new taste for severity in sentencing was New York's influential Baumes law of 1926, which mandated life sentences for four-time felony offenders and increased the portion of a sentence that had to be served before release.[79]

Punishment—imprisonment, execution—is the final stage in the criminal process. It, too, had a prominent place in the response to crime as a social problem susceptible to new controls, new solutions. Rehabilitation, which "deals with the offender rather than with the offense," was hailed as a significant new development in American penology (although in fact it had strong nineteenth-century precedents). Like indeterminate sentencing, prison reform melded an old American belief in individual regeneration with the promise held out by the new science of penology.[80]

American prisons at the turn of the century ranged from the relatively enlightened reformatories of New York, Massachusetts, and other northern states to malodorous county prisons, corruption-ridden urban jails such as New York City's Tombs, and the unspeakable convict labor camps and chain gangs of the South. Unlike their Jacksonian predecessors, reformers bent on improving these institutions wanted them to be not remote from society but as close to everyday life as possible.[81]

Instances of change abounded. New York's Bedford Reformatory pioneered a new approach to women prisoners which stressed rehabilitation over correction. Katharine Bement Davis, Bedford's innovative superintendent, became New York City Commissioner of Corrections in 1914. Organized labor told the New York Commission on New Prisons of its desire to see Sing Sing rebuilt as a scientifically designed clearinghouse for convicts, who then would be distributed to institutions appropriate to their crime, previous record, and disposition. While opposing prison labor, the unions endorsed industrial training for first-time offenders.[82]

State employment of convict labor grew, spurred by both financial and rehabilitative incentives. Between 1885 and 1905, convicts working under publicly controlled systems increased from under a third to more than half of employed prisoners. Exposés of the conditions of southern convict labor as a new form of peonage became more frequent. Under the leadership of Governor Hoke Smith, the Georgia legislature after a bitter fight ended the state convict lease system, instead apportioning prisoners to the counties—perhaps easing consciences but hardly lessening the horrors of black convicts' lives.[83]

Opposition to the prison as reformatory came from a number of sources: from those who wanted less money spent and prisoners not "coddled," of course, but also from organized labor, which usually looked on prisoners doing productive work (the high road to regeneration for most reformers) as unfair competition. Before 1900 labor unions sought state laws (with some success in New York, Massachusetts, and Pennsylvania) limiting or forbidding contract and other forms of prison labor. Manufacturers, too, such as those making furniture, shoes, wagons, and stoves, worked against this competitive threat. By 1905 twenty-eight states forbade contract labor by convicts. Most of them did marginal tasks such as farming and rural road work—although eight years after the passage of a 1907 Pennsylvania law allowing prisoners to be employed on county roads, only three of the state's sixty-seven counties had availed themselves of it. The Hawes-Cooper Act of 1929 prohibited the interstate shipment of prison-made goods, part of an AFL-led drive to restrict prison labor to products designed exclusively for state use.[84]

Local and state prison systems were highly resistant to change. New Jersey's twenty-one state sheriffs, who made profits of $30,000 to $60,000 from state per diem payments for their prisoners, were the chief obstacles to reform of that state's county jails. Fifteen years later a state prison inquiry found widespread abuses in the prison labor system (although a 1911 New Jersey law abolished prison contract labor) and criticized discipline in the jails as too severe.[85]

The factors that shaped prison policy did not straightforwardly divide along the lines of humanitarianism and social control, of conscience and convenience. Many convicts were said to prefer traditional prisons to reformatories: discipline was less harsh, the uncertainties of indeterminate sentencing were absent. And then as now the irreducible realities of prison life prevailed. In Nebraska's state penitentiary in 1912 there were five murders in forty-eight days, with subsequent revelations of widespread drug and liquor traffic, abuse by the guards, and sodomy among the prisoners. The impressive new Washington State Reformatory turned out in practice to be hobbled by political patronage, inadequate programs, and repressive prison discipline.[86]

By 1930 the American prison system was notable for its size and variety. Federal prisons had increased since 1904 from four to six, state prisons from fifty-nine to sixty-four, reformatories from fourteen to thirty-four, county and local jails from 1,260 to almost 15,000. The federal prison population had grown from 1,641 to 12,181, that of the states from 59,000 to 124,000. A new society had brought with it not less but more crime: new opportunities, new definitions. Modern urban life—and national Prohibition—added to the prison population, despite the end of immigration during the 1920s. The federal government, swamped by Prohibition's convict-generating capacity, boarded out thousands of prisoners and accused persons awaiting trial in city and county jails, paying a per diem allowance that was an invitation to further cost- and corner-cutting by prison authorities.

Yet a look back in the mid-1930s led to the conclusion that "very few new techniques" had done much to improve the state of the prisons or the character of their inmates. The United States lagged behind Europe in the professionalization of prison personnel and social services for released prisoners. For all the talk (and a little implementation) of prisoner classification and segregation, new housing arrangements, training, and education, it appeared that "for the vast majority of prisons in the United States between 1900 and 1934 . . . working conditions have actually grown worse."[87]

This perception found confirmation in the case of the Norfolk, Massachusetts, penitentiary, the site of some of the brightest of Progressive reform aspirations. It was designed around 1930 to be a model custodial-rehabilitative institution, cultivating the atmosphere of a hospital or a community (it was initially called the Norfolk Prison Colony) rather than a penitentiary. But within a few years Norfolk was not by any stretch of the imagination a community or a hospital whose inhabitants happened to be felons. Instead it was that all too recognizable institution, *a prison*, which offered some treatment, some recreation, some minor rehabilitation. Staff shortages; conflicts among house officers, guards, and social workers; manipulation and resistance by the inmates; pervasive coercion, brutality, punishment: these were the everyday realities of Norfolk.[88]

Prison riots are another measure of the resistance to change perhaps inherent in penal institutions. Overcrowding and idleness set off the Joliet, Illinois, riot of June 1917. A number of outbursts occurred in 1929: in Cañon City, Colorado, where seven guards, taken as hostages, were killed by "Danny" Daniels, who then shot four other prisoners and himself; in New York's Dannemora, Auburn, and Clinton; and at the federal prison in Leavenworth, Kansas. President Herbert Hoover requested emergency funds to enlarge the two federal penitentiaries at Leavenworth and Atlanta—their respective capacities were 1,452 and 1,560, their actual inmate populations were 3,800 and 3,900—and to add a new prison in the northeast. New York's response was an expanded parole system and a new maximum security prison, Attica—destined in 1971 to be the site of America's bloodiest prison riot.[89]

A final measure of the constraints that worked on the criminal justice system was the experience of the movement against the death penalty. The optimism of the early 1900s as to the capacity of public policy to rehabilitate criminals, and the more general humanitarianism of the time, gave new life to opposition to capital punishment. This was not a uniquely American issue. The utility (and the class basis) of capital punishment was a source of public controversy in early twentieth-century France. Paris in July 1910 experienced bloody riots against executions, which were seen as assaults on the proletariat.[90]

By 1900 capital punishment had been ended in eight American states (and restored in two). Under the leadership of Congressman (and former general) Newton M. Curtis, the number of capital offenses in the federal criminal code had been reduced from seventeen to three in 1897. And the number of public executions, a not uncommon practice in the nineteenth century, sharply declined as (especially in 1903) a number of states abolished them.

As was the case with Prohibition, an old cause took on new life after 1900 with a broadening spectrum of support. The new "science" of penology added the greater likelihood of rehabilitation to the dictates of Christian charity and the general national belief in a second chance as arguments against capital punishment. The prospect of a higher conviction rate also appealed: it appeared that Michigan, Wisconsin, Rhode Island, Maine, and Colorado—states with no death penalty in the early 1900s—had above-average records of criminal convictions.[91]

Between 1907 and 1917, nine midwestern and western states ended the death penalty. State legislatures and constitutional conventions

(as in New York, with Theodore Roosevelt a leading advocate of retention) debated the issue. Public figures continued to speak out against
executions, and a number of states adopted the electric chair because
it supposedly did its job quickly and painlessly. Juries tended increasingly to avoid execution by finding defendants guilty of second- rather
than first-degree murder. By the mid-1920s twenty-two states allowed
juries to avoid the death penalty even in first-degree sentences.[92]

Ultimately, though, a mix of old values and new conditions worked
against the abolition of capital punishment. While humanitarian objections to the death penalty increased, so too did public concern over
a reported rise in capital crimes. Lax administration of the law, delays
and untried cases, the jury system, and an overuse of the appeals process were all blamed for the fact that relatively few murderers were
put to death.

Indeed, a number of states around the turn of the century passed
laws imposing the death penalty for crimes not previously so punished, a product in particular of the rising southern hysteria over
blacks assaulting white women, but also a consequence of the rapid
spread of mass-circulation newspapers. Sensational press coverage of
a particularly brutal crime led to an Illinois law making kidnapping
punishable by death. Colorado, which had already ended the death
penalty, repealed life imprisonment for crimes in 1901; but several
brutal and well-publicized lynchings aroused public opinion against
the leniency of the state law.[93]

Even before the United States entered the First World War in 1917,
anti–death penalty sentiment was ebbing. Arizona Governor George
W. P. Hunt, a prominent advocate of the "new criminology," proposed the abolition of capital punishment, but the new state's voters
turned it down. A major reason was the widespread belief that Mexicans—75 percent of the jail population—were not deterred by prison
terms alone. There was much popular disapproval of Hunt's prison
reforms, in particular his liberal pardoning practices, and his Democratic opponent appealed to new women voters to support the retention of capital punishment.[94]

In April 1917 the Pennsylvania legislature defeated a law to abolish
capital punishment. The bill was the product of a popular outcry over
the sentencing to death of two youths, aged sixteen and seventeen, for
the murder of the father of one of them: one of the young men was
mentally impaired, and the guilt of the other was in doubt. The vote
to keep the death penalty came in the wake of American entry into

the war. More immediately still, an explosion in a Philadelphia munitions factory, supposedly caused by saboteurs, killed 150 (mostly women) workers and hardened public opinion. Indeed, the war substantially strengthened antiabolition sentiment. By 1920 the death penalty had been restored in Arizona, New Mexico, Washington state, Missouri, and Oregon; attempts to end or modify it were defeated in Connecticut, Massachusetts, New York, Utah, Vermont, and Indiana. No state abandoned executions during the next two decades.[95]

The 1931 report of the Wickersham Commission—President Herbert Hoover's National Commission on Law Observance and Enforcement—summed up the ideas and accomplishments of early twentieth-century criminal justice policy. It stands as a monument of sorts to the eclectic, fact-saturated, conflicted, and ambiguous thinking about crime that characterized the period. It was thoroughly grounded in scientific criminology and an environmentalist approach; it freely criticized police brutality and found no special correlation linking the foreign-born with crime. At the same time, the report had little that was new to recommend, took no notice of the depression, and reaffirmed (on the eve of repeal) the need to enforce the Eighteenth Amendment.[96]

And yet the Wickersham Report in its way was a forward-looking document. For in the years—indeed, the decades—to come, American thinking about crime underwent no great sea change. Attitudes toward criminals would continue to be a kaleidoscopic mix of leniency and severity; approaches to punishment continued to range from utopian rehabilitation to biblical vengeance. The policy circle of criminal justice remained—remains—stubbornly unsquared.

6 ▪ Social Welfare

Social welfare assumed an increasingly important place in the public policy agendas of the major European nations during the late nineteenth and early twentieth centuries. In no way is this surprising. The family, the village, the church, charitable institutions—traditional sources of succor for those in need—seemed ever more inadequate to the demands of urban industrialized life. And ever more obviously the state was the only viable alternative.

Comparative Perspectives

But public welfare had a much harder time of it in the United States. True, it is notoriously difficult to compare the levels of welfare among vastly different national societies. Nevertheless, by the time of World War I, every major west European country had some form of occupational injury, health, and pension insurance, and many offered unemployment insurance. American states made some progress along these lines (most notably in workmen's compensation), but far below the European level. The federal government had even less to show.[1]

Bismarck's Germany was the first modern nation to pass significant welfare legislation, primarily to check worker unrest but also to strengthen the nation-state. Large groups of workers were left uncovered: shop employees, apprentices, miners, seamen, railroad workers, agricultural laborers, domestic servants. And the authoritarian taint of the Bismarckian benefits made them of doubtful relevance to Western democracies. France had free medical aid and old age assistance legislation by 1905; 644,000 people (of a population of 38.5 million) were receiving some help by 1912.[2]

Concern over labor unrest and the threat of socialism fueled Britain's extensive post-1900 plunge into welfare legislation. Board of

178

Trade president Winston Churchill wanted to "thrust a big slice of Bismarckianism over the whole underside of our industrial system." Important, too, was sympathetic public opinion, buttressed by an increasing working-class vote. Newspaper and magazine revelations, exhaustive government commission reports, and the leadership of Liberal politicians such as Churchill and Chancellor of the Exchequer David Lloyd George, created what the historian Asa Briggs has called a "social service state," an advance over the minimal "night-watchman state" of the nineteenth century but less than the "welfare state" of the mid- and late twentieth century.[3]

Britain's major achievements included a clutch of laws designed to improve working conditions, a workmen's compensation law in 1897, unemployment compensation in 1905, the Old Age Pensions Act of 1908, and the National Insurance Act of 1911. As in the German case, major occupational groups such as agricultural laborers and domestic servants were excluded; coverage and benefits were limited. And little more was done in the 1920s beyond the creation of a weak Ministry of Health in 1920 and some extension of unemployment compensation. The modern British welfare state had to await the Beveridge Report of 1942 and the creation of the National Health Service in 1948.[4]

Welfare legislation may appear to have had at least as promising a future in the United States. The social needs created by rapid industrial and urban growth were great; and nowhere did workers have such access to the vote, and to the political power that in theory flowed from it. Organized labor and organized socialism were expanding. So were the numbers of socially concerned academics and intellectuals, and massive revelations of social and economic need in periodicals and by public investigations: the public opinion fuel of the modern welfare state. American Progressivism, like British liberalism, seemed to offer an appropriate intellectual context for a wave of welfare legislation.[5]

But differences in society and culture, economics and population, and politics and government made early twentieth-century American social welfare in effect a dog that did not bark. European social services could, and did, feed on old traditions of noblesse oblige and corporatism and new realities of class conflict, which had no close American equivalent. American ethnic and regional diversity also militated against strong national welfare policies, as did cultural traditions of individualism and self-help, hostile economic and religious interests, the lack of a strong bureaucratic tradition, and a government controlled by an often corrupt party politics. There was no labor party; organized labor had no social welfare program; the major parties relied primarily on ethnocultural appeals, whose programmatic content had more to do with economic development and the protection of particular group interests than with a welfare agenda. No less influential was the tradition of American federalism, the assumption that social policy was primarily the responsibility of the states. And the conservative predisposition of the courts put a damper on social legislation.

These conditions were reinforced by the massive inflow of immigrants, of diverse strains and peasant backgrounds, who did not readily respond to the seductions of state welfare policies. And the prevailing view was that on the whole, the American standard of living was uniquely high: certainly so for the relatively skilled native American workers whose counterparts formed the cutting edge of labor-socialist politics in the Old World. It is not surprising that reform-minded professional elites, and not broad popular movements, were responsible for what American social welfare policy there was.[6]

The American welfare record should also be viewed in the general context of early twentieth-century public policy. That context included a new stress on efficiency and social order; an accompanying (but often antithetical) rise in the number of issues, interests, and ideas clamoring for recognition; and the persistence of established values, mores, and institutions. Progressive America featured a panoply of legislative and private investigations, journalistic exposés, concerned experts, and pressure groups second to none. Yet the most sustained welfare efforts—almost entirely on the state and local levels—were designed to protect women and children and to compensate for industrial accidents, areas of concern where sentiment ran strong, costs ran low, and ideological conflict was minimal.

American involvement in the First World War produced a temporary growth of federal power, and heady postwar welfare policy expectations. The National Conference for Social Work was chaired in 1919 for the first time by a federal official: Julia Lathrop, chief of the Department of Labor's Children's Bureau. President Warren G. Harding endorsed the 1921 Kenyon bill for a Department of Public Welfare to oversee education, public health, industrial working conditions, child welfare, and other social concerns.

But vested interests and traditional views of government were not so readily overborne. The AFL opposed the new department as a threat to the Department of Labor (with which it had a cozy relationship). The head of the Pennsylvania Department of Labor warned against the Kenyon bill's Americanization provisions and the danger of centralized government; the General Federation of Women's Clubs was afraid that education issues would be submerged; the League of Women Voters preferred to concentrate on the Sheppard-Towner maternity bill and a separate department of education, and feared for the fate of Lathrop and her Children's Bureau in the new department. "Thus," an observer noted, "from all quarters—health, education, social service and veterans service; from spokesmen of labor and from spokesmen for women—came doubts, misgivings and indignant protests." The bill went nowhere.[7]

Another revealing episode was the short, unhappy life of Cincinnati's "Social Unit" experiment. This idea, put forward in 1914 by social worker Wilbur C. Phillips, gained favor in the wake of the war. The National Social Unit Organization chose Cincinnati's immigrant-populated Mohawk-Brighton area of thirty-one square blocks, with a population of about fifteen thousand people, to organize into "blocks" of about one hundred families, each of which would elect a Council of Nine, which in turn would elect representatives to a neighborhood Citizen's Council. There would be as well an Occupational Council composed of representatives chosen from among doctors, nurses, social workers, teachers, recreational workers, ministers, and trade unions. "The Social Unit," said one of its proponents, "aims to restore some of the attributes of village life to city dwellers."[8]

Former American Medical Association president Charles Reed called it an experiment in practical democracy; Gifford Pinchot and Interior Secretary Franklin K. Lane were active in the national organization; Mrs. J. Borden Harriman and Mrs. Charles L. Tiffany were among its supporters. The experiment considerably improved public health reporting and record keeping, and 4,034 of 4,153 residents voted for its continuation beyond the initial three-year experimental period.

But problems internal and external plagued the enterprise from the start. The elected block representatives soon were dominated by the occupational councils of physicians, nurses, and social workers. Cincinnati's Mayor John Galvin attacked the scheme in March 1919, at the height of the Red Scare, as radical, un-American, and a spur to worker discontent. The city's health officer turned against it out of fear that it would undercut the Department of Health. And so the Social Unit idea slipped into history's dustbin.[9]

American welfare was notable not only for its paucity but for the diversity of its organization. The New York State Reconstruction Commission found five types of state welfare administration in the nation: uncoordinated, with each institution under its own board; functional groupings (departments of charities, correction, and the like); single state boards of control, with lay and business rather than professional management; unpaid boards of charities and corrections; and single directors of public welfare. This luxuriant variety whetted the reorganizing appetite of welfare experts: starved for substance, they focused on structure.[10]

Statistics gathering was relatively noncontroversial and found much favor. There was talk (but little more) of a National Dependency Index; a 1920 guide to New York social welfare statistics stretched from "Abortion" to "Workmen's Compensation"; reports multiplied: 527 on New York City welfare problems alone between 1915 and 1925. Herbert Hoover took on the presidency of the American Child Health Association, firm in his belief in data gathering and private philanthropy. But the poverty and unemployment brought on by the Great Depression overwhelmed what social welfare there was.[11]

Why did a country with so powerful an economy, so strong a sense of national élan, so (relatively) open and participatory a system of government perform so meagerly in the realm of social welfare? The search for an answer will cover three major policy areas: *poverty* (charity, welfare, and old age pensions); *public health* (pure food and drugs, mothers' pensions, and national health insurance); and *labor legislation* (industrial accidents and workmen's compensation, child labor, maximum hours and minimum wages, and unemployment).

Poverty and Pensions

Poverty was one of the oldest objects of social welfare, and similar systems of poor relief prevailed in nineteenth-century Britain and America. Each had poorhouses, workhouses, and "outdoor" (direct) relief supplemented by private charities and Charity Organization Societies. Poverty law in both countries was infused with the distinction between the worthy and the unworthy poor, and the need to subject the latter to stringent workhouse and other requirements. The American magazine *Charities* agreed with its British counterparts that no relief should be given on easy terms, and that "private spontaneous relief" was preferable to public welfare.[12]

Stirrings of discontent with traditional policy appeared in both countries around 1900. Britain's Conservatives set up a Royal Commission on the Poor Laws in 1906. Its majority report vividly described the plight of the poor and the inadequacy of the system but relied on voluntary agencies such as the Charity Organization Society to meet the problem. The commission's minority report (written and—characteristically—copyrighted by H. G. Wells) sought a greater role for the state.[13]

Reform was slow, impeded by the influential Boards of Poor Law Guardians and by the sheer inertial weight of the existing system. On the eve of World War I, British Poor Law administration rested on 350 to 400 statutes, some 5,000 judicial decisions, and more than 2,500 pages of Poor Law and Local Government Board orders. One critic thought that "for hopeless confusion in the matter of law, administration, and finance, the domain of Public Assistance takes the first place." Until the coming of the post–World War II welfare state, British poverty policy changed only marginally, as with the gradual growth of unemployment compensation.[14]

Around the turn of the century, American charities policy appeared to be evolving rapidly from its traditional religious-moral basis into the social science of "philanthropology," with social workers, a new class of professionals, operating "the machinery of benevolence." Their leaders were second to none in their dedication to efficiency and system: "Men study the aims, the methods, the expenditures, the results of a charitable organization with as little emotion as they study those of a railroad or a box factory," remarked one of them. If asked how much of the organization's money was spent on administration, said an American Charity Organization Society spokesperson, the ideal answer was "all."[15]

Statements such as these lend credence to the view that thinking about poverty was fueled by the conservative goals of social control and economy in spending evident in much turn-of-the-century American social policy. But to dwell on these strands alone is to miss the larger point: this stress on efficiency developed hand in hand with the growth of a larger-minded sense of poverty's social causes, one that gave new meaning to an old humanitarianism. The chairman of the 1899 National Conference of Charities and Corrections did some program relabeling: from "Misconduct and Misfortune" to "Causes Within and Outside the Family." Charity Organization Society spokesman Edward T. Devine held the "surplus misery" of the time to be a social and not merely an individual problem, and grandly announced: "We may quite safely throw overboard, once and for all, the idea that the dependent poor are our moral inferiors, that there is any necessary connection between wealth and virtue, or between poverty and guilt."[16]

The new shibboleths of charity and social work—prevention rather than relief, environmental over personal causes, an awareness of the pernicious social effects of poverty, reliance on research and surveys—were characteristically Progressive in spirit. As a survey of the time put it: "The charity organization movement . . . 'Americanized' itself, ceased to look at poverty through the spectacles of a particular class movement as in England, and began to deal with it in a more courageous spirit, by methods more harmonious with American resources, and American traditions."[17]

This is not to say that older attitudes and conditions—moral judgments as to the worthy and the unworthy poor, a reluctance to allocate public funds on a large scale, the strength of localism and suspicion both of politicized and of bureaucratized welfare—faded away; quite the contrary. It was this interplay of surging new attitudes and reinvigorated old ones that gave early twentieth-century American charity policy its distinctive—and distinctively limited—character.

The existing welfare infrastructure was ill adapted to the goals of the Progressives. Privatism and localism, the poorhouse and direct relief, were the keystones of the old order. Most of New York City's welfare burden in 1900 was handled by four private organizations: the Charity Organization Society, the Association for Improving the Condition of the Poor, United Hebrew Charities, and Catholic Charities. "Farming out" the poor—paying for their temporary upkeep, often in private homes—was a common American practice, buttressed by a structure of town and county almshouses. Paupers were disfranchised in eight states, including Massachusetts, New Jersey, and New Hampshire. In a number of states laws forbade pauper immigration.[18]

Tramps and vagrants came under close scrutiny on both sides of the Atlantic. An English Vagrancy Commission in 1906 recommended compulsory labor colonies; such places already existed in Belgium,

Germany, and Switzerland. An estimated half million tramps, mostly young men aged sixteen to twenty-one, were on the roads in America, in large part because of the lack of winter employment in the country-side. American policy came under criticism for insufficient harshness toward permanent tramps and vagrants and inadequate care for casual ones. One count had it that between 1901 and 1905, 23,964 casuals were killed on the railroads and 25,236 were injured: more deaths than among passengers or railroad employees. Extensive local legislation sought to regulate the movement and behavior of these ubiquitous migrants. Many communities prohibited begging and vagrancy; New York required the registration and identification of beggars. Boston had a much-admired system of lodging house supervision by building, health, and police officials, compulsory bathing rules, and the com-mitment of habitual vagrants to the state farm.[19]

The most notable aspect of the new approach was its tendency to focus on the structure instead of the substance of the problem: how to manage the poor rather than how to do something about poverty. One object of Progressive assault was the dense institutional undergrowth of existing private, local, and state establishments. The desire for economy, a distrust of machine-ridden state government, the fear that state aid would promote lobbying and influence peddling and weaken private benevolence, and anti-Catholicism fed opposition to public support of private charitable agencies. Pennsylvania distributed about $7 million in local welfare aid in 1900, and its dependence on local almshouses, county insane asylums, and grants to private institutions came under growing criticism. The bishop of Hartford, Connecticut, and the state Board of Charities had a damaging fight over the board's policy of denying Catholic religious instruction to children in the publicly supported orphanage.[20]

Patronage suffused the staffing of public institutions. A state sena-tor had his daughter, a nephew, three nieces, and numerous friends appointed to Indiana's Hospital for the Insane. California's Board of Charities was plagued by intricate infighting between philanthropists dedicated to scientific charity and politicians and businessmen inter-ested in economy and efficiency.[21]

By 1916 almost every state had a board overseeing its charitable in-stitutions. The major concern of the Indiana Board of Charities, organ-ized in 1889, was with waste, particularly in direct relief. Institutional care was held to be more economical, though (not coincidentally) it was shunned by its recipients. An 1899 law required stricter investigation of each charity case and set spending limits. The result was a sharp reduction in spending on the poor: from $321,000 in 1899 to $210,000 in 1900. By the early 1900s the number of persons aided was half of what it had been in the 1890s; the tax rate for poor relief had been lowered and the population of county asylums reduced.[22]

Turf conflicts between established institutions and the new centralizers flourished in New York. The state court of appeals held in 1900 that since the Society for the Prevention of Cruelty to Children (SPCC) did not come under the purview of the State Board of Charities, it was not a charitable institution. Bills were introduced into the legislature to subject the SPCC, and indeed all private charities, to board supervision. The charities fiercely and successfully resisted.[23]

Illinois reorganized its State Board of Charities in 1906. *Re*-reorganization of the board became a major political issue two years later. Its head appointed twenty-three leaders from business, medicine, law, and "applied philanthropy" to advise on a plan for concentrated management of the state's welfare institutions. Local treasurers and small merchants reacted against the threat to their interests posed by the centralization of finances and purchasing. Finally, in 1909 a compromise reorganization bill was passed.[24]

State welfare expenditures rose from $37 million in 1902 to $52 million in 1913: little or no gain when adjusted for inflation. Yet by one count new state welfare laws increased from 133 in 1900–1901 to 229 in 1906–7. Growing awareness that a variety of human needs had to be addressed in a new society uneasily coexisted with the desire to trim the welfare system to the winds of efficiency, economy, and centralized control.[25]

The rhetoric of the new philanthropy—the metaphorical identification of poverty with crime and disease, and the belief that, like these, it could be cured—dominated Progressive discourse. The Reverend John Haynes Holmes told the readers of *Bankers' Magazine:* "Now we learn that the poor shall cease to-morrow if we so will. With this discovery of our modern social science, the world enters into a new era of progress and enlightenment." Louis Brandeis took note in 1911 of the shift from "sporadic, emotional charity to organized charities, and from mere relief to preventive measures." Dayton, Ohio's, director of public welfare declared that "public welfare work has come to be extended beyond the fondest dreams of social workers a generation ago." But his office did not exist in many other cities. And the limited scale of state and local welfare expenditures, coupled with the dearth of national programs, suggests how wide a gulf existed between Progressive rhetoric and American reality.[26]

The prevalent social values of the 1920s hardly strengthened the view that poverty was a remediable social problem and not a sign of individual inadequacy. Professional social workers, in the more individualistic spirit of the 1920s, spoke less of "cases" and more of "clients," and boasted: "This is the day of individualism in treatment. We are outgrowing the old practice of massing and classing humanity for purposes of identification, of relief, of correction."[27]

The demands of an expanding society led to a rise in state welfare spending, from $52 million in 1913 to $151 million in 1927, a 290 percent increase, while the cost of living rose about 180 percent. And the First World War left an important legacy to philanthropy. War bond drives increased the expertise of community fund-raising, and after the war Community Funds and Peace Chests—the prototypes of today's United Way—proliferated.[28]

Politics and ideology as usual kept the response to poverty stuck in its traditional ways. In 1925 the Pennsylvania Poor Law Commission wanted to close down a state poorhouse system that would have been at home in the England of Henry VIII. It lumbered under the weight of a thousand overseers of the poor and 458 township and borough districts, seven in each county, whether it was Cameron (pop. 6,000) or Philadelphia (pop. 1,823,000). Philadelphia's Republican boss Ed Vare endorsed the proposal that poor districts be run by county commissioners, and the legislature agreed. But the Grundy-Mellon state Republican machine, at war with Vare, joined with the state's local interests to induce Governor Gifford Pinchot to veto the bill.[29]

Public aid to nonpublic institutions also persisted. In 1929, twenty-four state legislatures appropriated over $7 million to private charities; all but five states allowed local authorities to make payments to private associations. The largest subsidies, to hospitals, were in Connecticut, Delaware, Maine, Maryland, and Pennsylvania.[30]

A three-year campaign in New York secured the repeal of that state's century-old poor law in 1929 and its replacement by what was trumpeted as a modern public welfare law. Designed to make relief for the poor an act of public welfare rather than of charity, the statute in fact reflected the bureaucratic urges of social work professionals.

Mandatory provisions such as appointing rather than electing the town welfare officer proved to be of little significance when the depression arrived.[31]

The massive impoverishment wrought by the Great Depression overwhelmed the deeply inbred assumption that poor relief was needed by only a small and distinct class. The private charity and public welfare systems of cities, counties, and states could not begin to cope with the demands cascading over them. Yet the beliefs underlying the existing system did not readily give way, and opposition to the dole was widespread. Not until the advent of Franklin Roosevelt and the New Deal did large-scale public welfare programs come into being. Even then, and since, the American response to poverty continued to reflect the classic tensions of the past: political and cultural constraints on public spending; the desire to alleviate suffering versus the fear of fostering dependency; the ongoing conflict between the view of the poor as a distinct and outcast breed and the view that there but for the grace of God go we.

Old age pensions were one of the most widely discussed new approaches to poverty in the early twentieth century. When life expectancy rarely stretched beyond the normal working years, elderly indigents were rare enough to be dealt with by their families or the established system of poor relief. But as people began to live longer, some more systematic form of welfare was called for. Pension plans—the first attempt to lessen poverty through state aid without regard to social status—began to appear in late nineteenth-century Europe, led by Germany in 1889. Questions of funding arose immediately. Short-term financial questions determined the final shape of Britain's 1908 pension bill. The Treasury opposed a contributory system because no administrative machinery existed for the collection of a pension tax. For their own differing reasons, the Trades Union Congress and private friendly (insurance) societies also opposed a contributory approach, favoring instead universal, noncontributory pensions.

A French old age pension act in 1910 followed on the heels of the 1908 British law. After much controversy, the plan came to rest on compulsory contributions by both employee and employer. It provided insurance for practically the entire working population with salaries of less than three thousand francs a year, an estimated 17 million people. Small farmers, tenant farmers, artisans, and small employers were included. But the plan assumed the regular payment of premiums for thirty years. And existing interests had to be accommodated; great care was taken not to interfere with friendly and mutual aid societies.[32]

The United States in fact already had a massive pension plan that far outstripped its European counterparts—for Civil War veterans and their dependents. By the 1890s the Pension Office was the largest government office in the world; by 1900 it was distributing annual benefits of nearly $140 million to about a million veterans and their dependents. But the extension of this practice to other groups in the population proved to be impossible. The Civil War pensions were designed primarily to ensure Republican political supremacy in the North. And the politics and corruption that so often attended its administration hardly made it a model for architects of an American welfare state.[33]

Nevertheless the problem of retired workers mounted with the post-1900 increase in life expectancy. By 1929 an estimated 25 percent of the population sixty-five and over had an annual income of under $300 a year, below the subsistence level. Almshouses remained the predominant form of state poor relief, housing about fifty thousand inmates over sixty-five. The American Association for Labor Legislation, the leading advocate of workingmen's health and old age insurance, sought an alliance with organized labor for a federal pension plan. But AFL president Samuel Gompers's hostility to experts and his distrust of a political and legal system controlled, as he saw it, by class enemies precluded any concerted effort. One authority thought that only pension plans conditioned on poverty could be funded from general taxation; otherwise the revision of state constitutions would be necessary.[34]

State and private charity and employer, union, and fraternal pension plans remained the only sources of nonfamily support. Union pensions were few in number—about fifteen in all—and poorly funded, giving some 11,500 pensioners $4 million a year. By 1927 there were close to five hundred industrial pension plans, covering 4 million employees, almost half of them railroad workers, 17 percent in public utilities and another 17 percent in metal products industries. These plans paid about eighty thousand pensioners $50 million a year. While contributory schemes had risen from 10 percent of the total in 1911–15 to over 60 percent in 1926–1928, for the most part pensions were paid out of the companies' current income, were increasingly regarded as a competitive burden (even before the depression struck), and usually required long periods of service before the employee qualified.[35]

The growing numbers of the elderly and the manifest inadequacy of existing devices spurred labor unions, fraternal societies, and welfare advocates to seek statewide old age pension plans. Enabling acts were introduced in twenty-four legislatures in 1923 alone, with Pennsylvania setting the pace. By 1929 some three hundred state old age pension acts had been introduced since the first one appeared in Massachusetts in 1903; sixteen states had appointed twenty-six investigating committees on the subject. Yet only six laws, in practice providing almost no pensions, were on the books. Montana and Wisconsin together had fewer than a thousand pensioners; Alaska boasted a grand total of 287 in 1927. It was reasonable to conclude in 1929 that "pensions systems are as yet in the experimental stage and will be for some time to come."[36]

The movement picked up with the depression: thirteen more state legislatures passed pension acts by 1933. But even this modest performance ran into trouble. The governors of California, Washington, and Wyoming vetoed their state bills; the supreme courts of Arizona, Pennsylvania, and Colorado found them unconstitutional; an Ohio constitutional amendment designed to permit old age pensions was defeated in a referendum.

The political earthquake wrought by the Great Depression and the New Deal made viable (indeed inevitable) what only a few years before had seemed to be well beyond the reach of the political order. The Social Security Act of 1935 created a federal old age pension plan and a system of unemployment insurance. Yet in its initial form the most lasting and important achievement of the New Deal was "an astonishingly inept and conservative piece of legislation," suggesting how potent were the attitudes and interests of the past.[37]

The Public's Health

Concern over public health provided a far stronger spur to public policy than did the desire to alleviate poverty. The science of public health was manifestly more successful than the "science" of social work. And the objective of a healthier population had universal appeal, cutting across class and ideological divisions.

Nevertheless, there was no American equivalent to Britain's Public

Health Acts of 1872 and 1875 and, most notably, the National Insurance Act of 1911. The mix of Tory paternalism and Liberal-Labor welfare statism that produced British national health insurance had no American counterpart. Nor did the inclination (as in France) to see deficiencies in public health as a sign of "national degeneracy," a concern heightened by the tensions of prewar Europe.[38]

The United States was the only major industrialized nation with no health insurance program by the time of the First World War. True, desultory attempts to expand the federal government's role in public health cropped up around the turn of the century. The Marine Hospital Service was renamed the Public Health Service in 1903, in recognition of its responsibility for checking on the health of the flood of immigrants. The economist Irving Fisher argued for a Department of Public Health: by his reckoning the life of each American was worth $2,900; 600,000 of the annual total of 1.5 million deaths could be avoided by more effective public health measures, thus eliminating enormously expensive waste of life. The 1910 Owen Act proposing such a department had the support of the American Medical Association, the Metropolitan Life Insurance Company, and the American Association for the Advancement of Science. But those with a stake in the manufacture and sale of drugs and patent medicines opposed it, as did a doctors' National League for Medical Freedom. They, abetted by general public indifference and hostility to federal activism, defeated the bill.[39]

There was one major exception to this languor: the Pure Food and Drug and Meat Inspection Acts of 1906. Regulation of so essential a commodity as food made increasing sense as distribution and marketing became more national. A similar sentiment took root in Britain, where a series of food and drug acts between 1875 and 1907 supplanted a system of local regulation which left "the people's food . . . partly in the care of the justice of the peace." Interest group politics swirled around British food and drug regulation as it did around its American counterpart. Opponents of a Poisons and Pharmacy bill, drafted in 1906 and passed in 1908, included the Pharmaceutical Society and the Royal College of Surgeons, fearful that the act overly benefited chemists (druggists), agricultural societies opposed to the inclusion of cattle medicines, and Home Office experts critical of the act's administrative inadequacies.[40]

The traditional view of the American Pure Food and Drug and Meat Inspection Acts of 1906 is that they were the products of two new forces: the growing influence of food hygienicists, led by government chemist Harvey Wiley, who campaigned doggedly for higher standards of purity in canning and packaging; and urban middle-class anxiety, brought to a head by Upton Sinclair's gory portrait of meat packaging practices in his novel *The Jungle*. Another factor has been much emphasized in recent years: the interests of large food, drug, and meat companies, which expected that more rigorous standards would drive out smaller competitors. As in the case of Prohibition and other major social policies of the time, the larger truth is that all of these considerations—in short, the range of ideas and interests that defined public policy in the Progressive years—entered into the story.[41]

The politics of food regulation in the states was no less complex. A Public Health Society lobbied (and bribed) a pure food bill through the Missouri legislature in 1899. This law banned the use of alum in the preparation of baking powder. Backing it were four large baking powder firms whose product was made from cream of tartar, the supply of which the companies controlled; their competitors relied on alum.[42]

The career of Lucius Polk Brown, Tennessee's pure food and drugs inspector from 1908 to 1915, tells us much about the play of politics in public health regulation. Every one of his successful convictions under the state's Sanitary Food Law of 1909 was of blacks or people with foreign names. He had to struggle constantly to avoid entanglement in the politics of Prohibition. When a Republican governor gained office in 1912, Brown fought hard for reappointment against business opposition, with the support of consumer and women's groups. Finally, in 1915 he went off to head the Bureau of Food and Drugs in New York City's Department of Public Health. But he soon clashed with Tammany mayor John Hylan over patronage versus professionalism in department appointments, and in 1920 a disillusioned and defeated Brown resigned.[43]

As canned and packaged products increased, labels came to be the only way for consumers to know their contents. The politics of product labeling turned out to be as contentious as the politics of product content. During the 1920s the Corn Products Refining Company and the American Farm Bureau Federation sought to amend the Pure Food and Drug Act to permit the use of corn sugar without so indicating on product labels. The National Canners' Association, joined by the Agriculture Department, opposed this, claiming it would weaken consumer confidence in the canning industry.[44]

"Misbranding" and "adulteration" came to be defined in the courts not as terms of scientific accuracy but according to the commonly understood relationship between the product and its label. In consequence, judges began to relax the traditional rule of caveat emptor. The leading Iowa case of Davis v. Van Camp Packing Company (1920) held that a consumer could argue that the manufacturer had breached an implied warranty as to the purity of his food product. Other courts relied on negligence or fraud. The result was that courts held food producers to a higher standard than was yet applied to manufacturers.

Yet government enforcement was beset by difficulties. The Department of Agriculture's enforcement budget was less than $1 million in 1932, while the value of the food and drug products it supposedly supervised was $15 to $20 billion. True, producers were cited over eighteen thousand times from 1906 to 1932, and the government secured more than sixteen thousand convictions. But the very large number of guilty pleas stemmed from the fact that many firms "regard the system of confiscation, suspensions of sentence, and light fines as a very moderate license charge for plying their trade." And not until 1938 did the Food, Drug, and Cosmetic (Wheeler-Lea) Act extend regulation to labels and advertising.[45]

Because of the obvious public stake in pure food and drugs, and the equally obvious interstate character of their distribution, the courts had no trouble with the constitutionality of federal regulation. Indeed, they encouraged control: Holmes in 1911 invited Congress to prohibit false therapeutic claims on drug labels, and it obliged in 1912. Yet the Supreme Court could not avoid the constraints of federalism. It held in 1913 that foodstuffs packaged in accordance with federal law did not have to be relabeled when shipped to a state whose law was more stringent. That decision gave a marked advantage to manufacturers in states with milder regulation.[46]

In fact, there was no real system of federal supervision. The states initially enforced the Pure Food and Drug Act, as they and the cities did with public health regulation in general. Growing concern over the quality of food, the safety of drinking water, and the danger of inadequate sanitation made public health an important issue. New York in 1913 created a Public Health Council composed of three doctors and three laymen, empowered to divide the state (outside New York City) into sanitary districts subject to a uniform sanitary code. State health officers and urban health departments burgeoned, as did their capacity to investigate, enjoin, subpoena, and arrest. A number of states authorized boards of health to license physicians.

The new public health infrastructure of the states and cities reflected the growing conviction, fed by science and experience as well as by ideology, that illness and death, like other social ills, could be ameliorated by proper public policy. Statistics indicated that deaths from communicable diseases such as tuberculosis, diphtheria, typhoid, and scarlet fever were declining. At the same time, deaths from industrial accidents and degenerative diseases were on the rise— which suggested to one observer that public health "will serve the community quite as much by guiding social legislation as by combating communicable disease."[47]

The growth of cities made the urban environment a subject of special concern. "Rat days" in California (1909) and Indiana (1913) aimed at the extermination of rats, flies, and mosquitoes, and school instruction on communicable diseases was substantially increased. A 1906 New York City ordinance banning the burning of bituminous coal produced air quality superior to that in any English city. British legislation did not face the black smoke problem until the Public Health Act of 1926; and that law did not forbid the domestic use of bituminous coal, by far the greatest source of contamination.[48]

Tuberculosis attracted particular attention, in part because it was common among black laundresses, cooks, and other service people who came into close contact with middle-class whites. But turn-of-the-century public health policy cannot be attributed solely to particular interests and biases. The sharp reduction of infant mortality in large cities around the turn of the century through vaccination, the regulation of milk, public baths, garbage removal, and the like had broad public support.[49]

The public's interest in the wholesomeness of the products that it consumed increased during the 1920s. State legislatures in 1923 considered over eight hundred public health bills, and enacted a quarter of them; food regulation was the leading topic. A network of cooperation grew among city, state, and federal agencies, and by the early 1920s it was evident that government inspection had substantially reduced the incidence of food contamination. Over an eighteen-year period during which 26,102 food samples were inspected in Connecticut, the proportion free from adulteration increased from 59 percent to 90 percent.[50]

Compulsory vaccination was another burgeoning public health issue. Popular opposition led to riots in the immigrant city of Milwaukee during the 1890s, and to the impeachment of the health commissioner. The Illinois Supreme Court did not allow the Chicago board of education to exclude an unvaccinated child in 1908, and a federal circuit court struck down a San Francisco ordinance requiring that the city's Chinese residents be inoculated with antiplague serum. Nevertheless, almost every state had a vaccination law by the turn of the century, though most were limited to schoolchildren. And the Supreme Court in 1905 sustained a Cambridge, Massachusetts, requirement for the vaccination of the population at large.[51]

Treatment of the mentally ill also became more prominent as a public concern. The states' assumption of fiscal responsibility for mental institutions opened the door to a large increase in state hospital admissions: from 24,651 in 1890 to 41,165 in 1900; 61,182 in 1922; and 78,452 in 1930. The variety as well as the size of the inmate population took off. As life expectancy increased, so did the number of senile elderly in mental hospitals. Victims of paresis, the terminal stage of syphilis, made up almost a fifth of all male admissions to New York's mental hospitals between 1911 and 1919. Immigrant-flooded big cities were another growing source of patients. Government was called on to provide the ever larger state hospitals in which a predominantly untreatable patient population was warehoused.[52]

Although state and local hospital expenditures rose substantially—from $43 million in 1902 to $200 million in 1922 and $349 million in 1932—American hospitals remained far more often private than public. Voluntary, not-for-profit community hospitals provided the great majority of beds; and the institutional history of American hospitals before the 1930s was determined more by the dynamics of their relations with doctors and the fee-paying capacity of patients than by public policy.[53]

The character, and the limitations, of early twentieth-century American social welfare emerge with particular clarity in the unhappy history of mothers' pensions designed to ensure better care for infants, and the all but nonexistent history of public health insurance. Paternalist sentimentality toward mothers and children merged with a new concern for the health of the national population and the increasing influence of women's organizations to fuel the movement for mothers' pension laws. The cause elicited coy comments on the need to foster an "infant industry," or that as the Agricultural Department's Bureau of Animal and Plant Industry dealt with food-stuffs, so must the "child crop" be fostered by a Children's Bureau in the Department of Commerce and Labor. A government pamphlet on prenatal care was welcomed as "a beginning of doing for the children of the country what it has done superbly for the country's crops and herds."[54]

In the wake of a prototypically Progressive 1909 White House conference on the care of dependent children, Missouri and Illinois allocated funds for this purpose. By the 1920s more than forty states had authorized mothers' pensions of varying (though always modest) amounts, some with work requirements, administered locally. The Sheppard-Towner Act of 1921 provided federal grants in aid for maternity benefits to the states. Its chief sponsors were Julia Lathrop of the Children's Bureau and a number of women's organizations; the primary reason for its passage was congressional awareness that women now had the vote. The fact that in 1918 the United States had only the eighteenth lowest maternal death rate and the eleventh lowest infant mortality rate among the nations of the world also left its mark. So too did the emotive tug of this jointure of maternity and infancy.

Yet even this seemingly unexceptionable form of social welfare wilted in the hostile climate of the 1920s. The bill was enacted in the face of strong opposition from the American Medical Association, which attacked it as the entering wedge of state medicine. "Shall the children of America become the property of the state?" asked one critic, a danger much on the minds of conservatives and Catholics. Minimal appropriations (an average of $1.25 million a year), along with voluntary state participation and required matching grants, limited Sheppard-Towner's impact. When the time for reappropriation arrived in 1926–27, Congress grudgingly allowed the program to continue only until 1929, a dramatic illustration of the powerful political, economic, and cultural resistance to federal welfare in the early twentieth-century United States.[55]

Health insurance won widespread acceptance in Europe but ran into a stone wall in the United States. Business and labor leaders alike spoke out against compulsory health insurance even before the First World War: the former for obvious economic and ideological reasons, the latter because of the widespread suspicion of the active state among AFL leaders. Advocates such as the American Association for Labor Legislation and I. M. Rubinow vainly tried to overcome the opposition of private industrial insurance companies.[56]

As in the case of Britain, where data generated by the Boer War on the (ill) health of the population stimulated public concern, statistics on draft exemptions for health reasons in 1917 and 1918 affected opinion in the United States. The success of the workmen's compensation movement led to considerable expectation that health insurance would be "the next step in social progress." A number of state commissions looked into the subject, and fifteen state legislatures entertained proposals in 1917. The American Federation of Labor, previously opposed to compulsory state-run health insurance, changed its stand in 1918, as did New York's state labor federation. Yet none of this led to legislation. The only popular vote on health insurance—a California referendum over an enabling amendment to the state constitution—decisively defeated it. State and national health insurance schemes would have a marginal place on the American welfare agenda for decades to come.[57]

The Condition of Labor

Poverty and public health were traditional subjects of social welfare. The condition of labor—who might work, under what conditions, and on what terms—was the most conspicuous early twentieth-century addition. The burgeoning industrial work force raised a host of new concerns involving health and safety, age, sex, wages, working conditions, unemployment, and retirement. Once again the American record conspicuously lagged behind those of its major Western counterparts, constrained by the persistence of established rules, practices, and values; by the policy stasis created by a pluralistic welter of conflicting interests; and by the limits imposed by federalism and judicial review.

As in the case of other welfare programs, there was much reason to expect a different outcome. Heightened public awareness of working conditions spurred by legislative investigations and organized interest groups, a greater readiness on the part of the courts to accept legislative activism, and more responsive political leadership fostered a wave of activity during the early years of the twentieth century. By one count labor laws passed by the states averaged fifty-one a year from 1890 to 1899, and ninety-one a year from 1900 to 1908; by another about four hundred such statutes, notable for their variety and specificity, were enacted in 1909 alone. Many more were proposed but failed, such as a Massachusetts bill to "provide wages for the maintenance of the supernumerary members of the industrial army of the commonwealth." Increasingly varied work environments led to particular, detailed regulation: of tunnel and subway workers in New York; of dust-generating factories; for the special needs of women and children.[58]

Twenty states created industrial departments for information gathering and oversight between 1907 and 1916. By 1913, forty-two states had bureaus of labor statistics, and a number had state industrial commissions; twenty-two passed child labor laws between 1909 and 1916, twenty states in the same period enacted mothers' pension bills; thirteen ended the defenses of assumption of risk and fellow-servant negligence in industrial accident cases; eleven between 1911 and 1916 passed workmen's compensation acts, modeled on the 1906 English law.[59]

But the number and strength of conflicting interests, and the constraints inherent in the American system of government, severely limited the regulation of labor. A Wisconsin attempt to pass an industrial disputes act like Canada's was plagued by disagreement among economists, union leaders, socialists, and manufacturers. The Texas legislature authorized the state board of health to inspect factories; but it allocated no funds for the purpose, and loaded the law with unenforceably vague references to "sufficiently" protected elevators, "reasonable" temperatures, the elimination of fines on workers "as far as possible," and accident safeguards for power machinery "where practicable." Special interests and considerations of political patronage led New York's relatively progressive legislature in 1915 to try to weaken the labor, safety, and health laws of the state and abolish the New York City Tenement House Department.[60]

Supervision filtered through a web of laws, agencies, and courts. The Pennsylvania Industrial Board issued orders, rules, and regulations much like a public utilities commission, and the courts almost always accepted them. But in so industry-minded a state, this body trod warily. And in general the courts weakened the effect of legislation: suspended sentences for convicted violators of labor laws rose from 26–40 percent in the early 1920s to 60–75 percent during the depression years of 1933 and 1934. By the end of the 1920s, American workplace regulation was spare, static, underfunded, and underenforced. Only with the political and policy transformation brought on by the Great Depression and the New Deal did federal supervision over entry, wages and hours, working conditions, and compensation for those out of work begin to take on new forms.[61]

The physical well-being of workers was an area of concern where the states' police power unequivocally applied: the courts had few problems with health and safety regulation. Here the old humanitarianism and the new stress on industrial efficiency came together. But the power of received values, and the limited amount of room for the concept of social welfare in early twentieth-century American political culture, were evident even in this least contentious form of workplace regulation.

A number of factory safety laws were on the books by 1900, but the need for greater coverage grew steadily. More than seventy thousand railroad workers (5 percent of the total) were killed or injured in 1905, half a million workers of all sorts in 1906. Only 10 to 15 percent of injured employees were entitled to compensation from their employers.[62]

Coal miners, like dependent mothers, were particularly appealing subjects for the protective oversight of the state. A cluster of mine disasters (two of them, killing 361 and 239, respectively, in December 1907; over 300 deaths in a November 1909 fire) induced Congress to establish a federal Bureau of Mines. Leading coal mine owners appear to have been more influential than scientists, engineers, the United Mine Workers, or humanitarian Progressives in securing this act. Like the Pure Food and Drugs statute, it better served the interests of large than of small operators. But while much new state mine safety legislation came on the books between 1905 and 1915, enforcement remained inadequate. It is true that fatalities per million tons of coal fell between 1907 and 1920; but the respective contribution of regulation and of technology to this trend is difficult to determine. The regulation of safety in America's mines, as in its factories, remained decentralized, disorganized, piecemeal.[63]

Nineteenth-century courts often determined the level of compensation for industrial accidents. But neither injured workmen and their dependents (for whom this was a slow and chancy business likely to enrich their lawyers as much as themselves) nor employers (who complained of the pro-victim attitude of juries and of the uncertainties inherent in the process of legal adjudication) were content with this system. A leading treatise on negligence concluded in 1898: "The law of master and servant in its relation to the law of negligence affords perhaps the most striking example in the last half century of gross injustice done by this disposition to restrict responsibility and suppress litigation." Appellate courts appear to have been increasingly inclined to reverse jury awards to the injured. Trial judges took cases from juries or found that certain acts as a matter of law constituted negligence by the injured party, and instructed juries to find accordingly. The contrast with Britain, where several new injury compensation acts had been passed, was striking.[64]

The manifest inappropriateness of the old negligence rules to the large industrial workplace led legislatures to limit their application. Publicly administered workmen's compensation insurance was an attractive alternative. Germany in the 1880s established a typically paternalistic, detailed system of collective liability and government-supervised insurance. Most other European nations followed suit around the turn of the century. England's 1897 act, extended in 1900 and 1906 to agricultural workers, linked compensation to a private insurance system. Perhaps because of this it produced more litigation than other British social legislation. Arguments over whether or not an accident had arisen out of or merely in the course of employment often led to findings against compensation.[65]

At first the going was harder in the United States. Maryland passed a pioneering law in 1902. But it was rarely applied, and in short order an injured workman, who sought greater compensation than the act allowed, successfully challenged its constitutionality. The first federal Employers' Liability Law (1906) sought to protect railroad workers. The Supreme Court held it unconstitutional, but a second law in 1908, limited to injuries received while engaged in interstate commerce, won its approval.[66]

New York's 1910 law was unusual in that it made employer participation compulsory. The state court of appeals in the *Ives* case (1911) called the act "plainly revolutionary" when "judged by our common law standards," and struck it down as an unconstitutional deprivation of employers' property without due process. But other state courts accepted voluntary systems, and Washington's tribunal upheld a compulsory act. The constitutional law expert Ernst Freund summed up the resulting situation: "If at the beginning of the year 1911 the constitutional status of workmen's compensation was one of uncertainty, at the end of the year it could hardly be characterized otherwise than as one of confusion."[67]

The New York decision turned out to be more notable for the oppo-

sition it evoked than for its precedential force. "The court has chosen
... the path of legal formalism," *Survey* concluded, and predicted that
businessmen would be more sensible. *Outlook* warned that the decision was "not in accordance with the best legal authorities in the
United States," and prominent legal scholars Freund, Frank J.
Goodnow, Roscoe Pound, and W. W. Willoughby argued for the law's
constitutionality. Even conservatives such as Francis Lynde Stetson,
P. Tecumseh Sherman, and William J. Moran of the National Civic
Federation objected to the decision, and Theodore Roosevelt pounced
on it as a prime instance of judicial obduracy.[68]

New York's legislature hurriedly enacted a constitutional amendment (ratified by a heavy popular majority) enabling it to pass a new
law, which a unanimous court of appeals accepted in 1915. "The court
has changed its attitude," a commentator sardonically noted. "One
[decision] is devoted largely to stating standards which it does not
specifically apply, and the other to applying standards which it does
not specifically state." The United States Supreme Court rejected a
challenge to the law without dissent in 1917. Justice Mahlon Pitney's
opinion relied on a broad definition of the police power and on the
sociological and economic arguments for workmen's compensation.
Edward Corwin overoptimistically proclaimed: "Constitutional
'rigorism' is at an end."[69]

The anthropologist William F. Ogburn thought that the appearance
of workmen's compensation half a century after the rise of the conditions that made it necessary was a fine example of his theory of cultural lag. But after its rocky start, workmen's compensation won a
degree of acceptance unique among early twentieth-century American social welfare policies. It appealed across the ideological spectrum: a classic instance of an idea whose time had come. Corporations
and business groups seeking to temper social discontent, and also to
avoid both state insurance and the vagaries of juries and judges, made
common cause with labor unions and humanitarian reformers—and
with casualty insurance companies, which saw the prospect of much
new business.[70]

By 1917, thirty-seven states had compensation laws. One estimate
was that about a quarter of the industrial work force came under
them, although agricultural, casual, domestic, mercantile, clerical,
and intrastate railroad workers did not. The courts generally con-
strued these acts in a liberal manner. But they were more cautious
than their British equivalents in defining what constituted a com-

pensable accident. Thus, the Michigan tribunal held that lead poisoning was not an accidental injury. Nor did the judges match the ingenuity of their European counterparts in developing new theories of responsibility, relaxing the rules of proof, and imputing fault to employers. "It is by humane fictions that the tribunals manage ingeniously to discover faults, or rather to invent them, where there are none, just in order to give the victims the right to indemnity," a French jurist observed.[71]

State workmen's compensation appeared to be a moderate success by the 1920s. Death payments averaged between $2,500 and $3,000. Jury verdicts probably would have provided more, but costs were lower, and the system did seem to foster greater workplace safety and a reduced accident rate. Still, protection was spotty. Coverage in a number of states was limited to hazardous occupations, and domestics and farm workers generally were excluded. Attempts in New York (1918–1924), Minnesota (1917–1921) and Wisconsin (1929–1933) to establish systems run by the state rather than private companies ran afoul of private insurance interests and popular suspicion of government.[72]

There was a manifest need for simpler, briefer procedural and evidentiary rules to govern the work of compensation commissions. The courts imposed annoying restrictions, which often led to long, costly legal battles. Wisconsin's commission was notable—and unusual—for the degree to which its decisions rested on its own and other boards' experiences rather than on the decisions of the courts.[73]

It was also necessary to square the several state compensation systems with one another. Could a right of compensation granted in one jurisdiction be enforced in another one?—a far from negligible question, given national corporations and a mobile work force. Traditional contract law did not readily apply to a system of compensation, and the courts had to do some imaginative analogizing to make it work across state lines. The 1908 federal compensation law for railroad workers generated incessant litigation—172 cases had come before the Supreme Court by 1934—primarily because it differentiated between railroad employees working in interstate commerce (which it covered) and those who did not. One study concluded that the law was negated by the costs of litigation, and that the engagement in interstate commerce required by a federal system was so difficult to define that workmen's compensation was best left to the states.[74]

Attempts to limit the hours of work fared less well, despite the close and obvious relationship of a long workday to industrial accidents. The problem lay in the constitutionality of the state's regulating an essential element in the labor contract. During the late nineteenth century, various trades—plumbers, railroad employees, brickmakers, stonecutters, bakers, barbers, horseshoers, engineers, drug clerks—secured state-mandated eight-hour laws. The response of the courts was spotty. Craft-oriented restrictions in the 1880s stood; industrywide laws faced more opposition. Attorney Frederick L. Stimson observed: "These decisions have undoubtedly given the quietus in the United States to any attempt to limit generally the time that a grown man may labor."[75]

But in Holden v. Hardy (1898) the Supreme Court upheld a Utah law limiting miners' hours on the ground that the dangerous nature of the work justified this application of the state's police power to preserve public health. The labor reformer Florence Kelley thought that the *Holden* decision "checks that blighting tendency of the state supreme courts" to strike down labor legislation.[76]

Encouraging, too, was the fact that the courts generally upheld laws and ordinances limiting the working hours of municipal employees. When the New York Court of Appeals decided in 1903 that an eight-hour regulation applied to city contractors' employees (as distinct from workers hired by the city itself) was unconstitutional, an enabling amendment to the state constitution quickly put things right. And Sunday restrictions on labor stood up as health regulations. It appeared to one observer that the courts were upholding hours regulation laws that were more protective than in Europe: "The growing liberality of American courts in the scope they concede to the legislative police power should be ground for general satisfaction."[77]

This optimism was dampened by the *Lochner* decision of 1905. An 1895 New York law that set an eight-hour maximum workday for bakers narrowly passed muster in the New York Court of Appeals, hardly a fount of receptivity to labor legislation. Nevertheless, the United States Supreme Court by a five to four vote found the statute unconstitutional: the first (and almost the last) time that it used liberty of contract to limit the states' police power. Justice Rufus Peckham's majority opinion was very much a policy statement: "This interference on the part of the legislatures of the several states with the ordinary trades and occupations of the people seems to be on the increase." He argued that the New York act ran aground on the antipathy of American law to restraints on competition and trade. His was the quite subjective view that the bakery trade did not endanger the health or safety of its workers. (Justifying his concurrence, Justice David Brewer told an audience: "I think I may safely appeal to all of the gentler sex before me, and ask them if making and baking bread is a specially hurtful and unhealthy labor.")[78]

The New York Court of Appeals annulled an hours law for women in 1907 with reasoning similar to that in *Lochner:* "The tendency of legislatures, in the form of regulatory measures, to interfere with the lawful pursuits of citizens, is becoming a marked one in this country, and it behooves the courts, firmly and fearlessly, to interpose the barriers of their judgments." But in general *Lochner* met with little approval. Criticism of the decision was widespread in legal and popular journals; it came to be seen as an extreme instance of "the growing assertion of the judicial prerogative to declare laws unconstitutional, because a particular legislative measure does not meet the view of the court as to what is reasonable or necessary legislation."[79]

Legal battle soon was joined in a different and more appealing context: hours laws that protected the safety and morality of female workers. In Muller v. Oregon (1908), Brewer—without citing *Lochner*—spoke for a unanimous Court in upholding a state law that limited the working hours of women. As he later explained, he did so "in the firm belief that there was something in [a woman's] place and work in life which justified the legislature in forbidding her to contract for factory work beyond a limited time . . . The race needs her; her children need her; her friends need her, in a way that they do not need the other sex."[80]

This musty paternalism was buttressed by the plaintiff's brief in the *Muller* case submitted by Louis D. Brandeis (but prepared primarily by his sister-in-law Josephine Goldmark of the National Consumers' League), which relied far more on women's working conditions than on judicial precedents: "In patent cases counsel are apt to open the argument with a discussion of the state of the art. It may not be amiss, in the present case, before examining the constitutional question, to notice the course of legislation as well as expressions of opinion from other than judicial sources." At the same time, Brandeis adhered to a Brewer-like view of gender difference: "Long hours of labor are dangerous for women primarily because of their special physical organization . . . Physicians are agreed that women are fundamentally weaker than men in all that makes for endurance: in muscular strength, in nervous energy, in the powers of persistent attention and application."[81]

This compelling merger of Progressive fact gathering and Victorian sentiment continued to win judicial acceptance. In 1910 the Illinois court, responding to a massive brief (again based on Goldmark's research), reversed an 1895 decision and upheld a ten-hour law for women. The New York Court of Appeals made a similar about-face in 1915. And in Bunting v. Oregon (1917), Goldmark and Felix Frankfurter won the Supreme Court's approval of an Oregon law with a brief that devoted 54 pages to legal argument, 76 to the contested statute, and 647 to the work experience of women. By the First World War it appeared that, at least for women, maximum hours legislation had become accepted regulatory policy.[82]

No form of workplace regulation should have been more attractive than restricting child labor. Its appeal was manifest: preserving the innocence of childhood and the sanctity of the home; safeguarding the health of the nation's future citizens; eliminating a threat to the American wage standard. Once again, traditional humanitarianism and the new desire for an efficient social order came together. stunted factory children were no more acceptable than widespread drunkenness, maimed workers, or exploited women. And indeed Congress twice passed acts to deal with this problem. But the Supreme Court found them unconstitutional, and it proved to be impossible to enact an enabling constitutional amendment. What happened to child labor regulation says much about the pressures for and the constraints against social welfare in the early twentieth century.

The campaign against child labor had deep roots. The first societies for the prevention of cruelty to children appeared in mid–nineteenth-century America, and then by direct imitation in Britain. Child welfare there attracted labor leaders Tom Mann and Ben Tillett, as well as the usual clutch of middle-class reformers. In the early years of the twentieth century, several British laws—the Factory and Workshop Consolidation Act of 1901, the Employment of Children Act of 1903, the Children's Act of 1908—set down rudimentary child labor regulations.[83]

The American movement faced a very different political and social environment. Business interests, federalism, and ethnocultural diversity worked against it, as did a social ethic that found nothing wrong with—indeed, romanticized—children toiling on farms, or on city streets as newsboys. At the same time, mainstream opinion was repelled by the images (literally, in the work of the photographer Lewis Hine) of children slaving in mills and factories and sweatshops. Certainly the issue was a real one: by 1900 an estimated one in six children aged ten to fifteen, a total of 1.75 million, worked. In a southern mill town in that year, only about 150 of 1,300 school-age children were attending school. In what was taken to be an act of unusual civic-mindedness (and in that context perhaps it was), the mill owner offered to build two schoolhouses if the town's school committee agreed to maintain all of three grades of schooling.[84]

By 1900, twenty-eight states had put some limits on child labor in factories, and a dozen or so in mines. But the major southern textile states (Alabama, Georgia, the Carolinas), where child labor was widespread, had little or no regulation. They became the initial target of the child labor movement. For southern Progressives such as Edgar Gardner Murphy (who founded the Alabama Child Labor Commission in 1901), the juxtaposition of white children with the new southern reality of large textile mills had a special emotional resonance.

The exploitation of children in northern factories and sweatshops also began to attract more attention. A New York Child Labor Committee was organized in 1902 by the social workers Florence Kelley, Lillian Wald, and Robert Hunter. The National Child Labor Committee (formed in 1904) brought the issue onto the national scene. In 1910 child labor reform won the classic imprimatur of a Progressive cause: a nineteen-volume Department of Labor report, *The Condition of Woman and Child Wage-Earners in the United States.*[85]

A number of industrial states—Massachusetts, New York, and Illinois among them—passed child labor laws during the early 1900s. But enforcement was difficult. For example, the glass industry in Pennsylvania, Illinois, and New Jersey supposedly was subject to factory inspection, but industry influence made regulation a farce. Illinois's chief inspector from 1897 to 1903 had spent the previous twenty-seven years with the Illinois Glass Company; James Campbell, a long-time officer of the Pittsburgh Glass Workers' Union, blocked the enforcement of Pennsylvania's weak law against child labor in the industry until he was removed by the governor in 1903.[86]

The Pennsylvania legislature was particularly obdurate; in 1907 it killed all child labor proposals. Reflecting the political clout of merchant tailors and clothing manufacturers, the state's chief inspector of factories argued against an anti-sweatshop bill on the ground that he was not empowered to inspect homes. The courts also did their part: in 1905 a Pennsylvania judge struck down a law restricting child labor in mines on the ground that its employment certificate requirement violated the Fourteenth Amendment. Why? Allowing the child's school record to be used as proof of age was discriminatory, given the lack of a state compulsory education law.[87]

Gradually, enforcement became more effective, the courts more supportive. Almost all of twenty state court decisions interpreting child labor laws between 1915 and 1917 found for the child against the employer. But the capacity of competing states to attract industry by allowing child labor led most reformers to seek a national law. The National Child Labor Committee proposed such an act in 1906, and Indiana's Senator Albert Beveridge made the cause his own.[88]

Opposition to federal regulation was strong and diverse. Southern-ers viscerally protective of states' rights—including state child labor law advocate Edgar Gardner Murphy—were hostile, as of course were spokesmen for affected industries. Other sources of opposition were the old Puritan view of work as morally beneficial, Catholic hostility to state interference with the family, and the need of working-class (and particularly immigrant) households for the income that child labor contributed. Despite these counterforces, the appeal of the cause led Congress in 1916 to enact the Keating-Owen Child Labor Act. This was a limited measure, directed only at industries clearly en-gaged in interstate commerce, likely to affect 100,000 to 150,000 of the nation's 1.85 million working children.[89]

Unique to—and characteristic of—the United States was the fact that the politics of national child labor regulation came to center on its constitutionality. A defender pointed out that other products or activities of doubtful morality—lottery tickets, liquor, wild game killed in contravention of state laws, women transported for illicit purposes—had been denied the channels of interstate commerce. Why not the products of child labor? Surely that practice no less directly affected the health, vigor, and morals of the nation's future citizens.

Opponents argued that even this modest measure went beyond the reach of congressional authority over interstate commerce, and that no federal police power existed under which Congress might inter-vene. One suggested imaginatively that by the same token Congress could prohibit the transportation of cotton produced in a state that had laws against black suffrage or woman's suffrage or that had not adopted a uniform marriage and divorce law. This states' rights argument had more than southern appeal. The liberal *Nation* opposed a federal state in 1914, arguing that many state laws already were effective, that the workmen's compensation system was an appropriate model, and that a national act would strain the Constitution and create a whole new scale of federal interference.[90]

Five lower federal courts upheld the 1916 law, and its constitutionality seemed secure. But the Supreme Court in Hammer v. Dagenhart (1918) found it unconstitutional, distinguishing between the production of goods and their movement in interstate commerce. This decision came after American entry into the First World War had greatly increased the demand for child labor, resulting in a substantial decline in school attendance. The federal commissioner of education estimated that four to five times more children were leaving school than was normally the case. Violations of compulsory education and state child labor laws were widespread; and with the war's end, the need for a federal law seemed greater than ever.[91]

Congress enacted a second child labor law as an amendment to the Revenue Bill of 1918, basing it this time on the taxing power. But the Supreme Court in Bailey v. Drexel Furniture (1922) once again said no. Taft's majority opinion (with the concurrence of Holmes and Brandeis) repeated the *Hammer* view that the law unconstitutionally extended the power of the central government.[92]

The only answer appeared to be a child labor amendment to the Constitution. On June 2, 1924, Congress sent the Twentieth Amendment to the states for ratification. The Anti-Saloon League's Wayne Wheeler endorsed it, identifying the cause with Prohibition. Catholic social reformer John A. Ryan spoke out often and strongly in its favor, denying that a federal law would interfere with the family or give Congress the power to control education. But only four state legislatures ratified the amendment; thirty-six rejected it or refused to ratify.[93]

This was the first constitutional amendment approved by Congress to fail since 1861. In the South, states' rights opposition neatly conjoined with that region's stake in child labor in its textile mills. But the amendment fared little better in the North; and here elements revealing in their range and diversity led to its downfall. The key defeat came in a November 1924 Massachusetts referendum. This was a major industrial state, whose textile industry had been harmed by the draw of cheap labor to the South. Calvin Coolidge favored the amend-ment; so did Senators Henry Cabot Lodge and Thomas Walsh. Yet the voters turned it down by a margin of almost 2.5 to 1.

Why? In part because of the prevailing economic and social conser-vatism of the 1920s. The National Association of Manufacturers, the American Farm Bureau Federation, and the Grange set themselves against the amendment; the Associated Industries of Massachusetts, the Sentinels of the Republic, and Harvard president A. Lawrence Lowell claimed that it smacked of Bolshevism. One supporter warned: "Child labor regulation goes hand in hand with school expansion; school expansion means federal taxes; and federal taxation is a night-mare to the great corporations whose business bestrides state bound-aries." The constitutional law authority Thomas Reed Powell acidly observed: "The holy name of states' rights is easily forgotten when employers wish their laborers sober and unctuously invoked when they wish their laborers young."[94]

But there were more popular sources as well. One was the general postwar reaction against active government: "War time interference with business and private affairs has left many people cold to any extension of national control, wrote one observer." And many voters were convinced that this restriction amounted to undue state interfer-ence with the rights of parents: lay and clerical Catholic leaders strongly opposed it on that ground. So child labor regulation remained in the province of the states until the labor legislation of the New Deal in the 1930s, and more particularly the Supreme Court's U.S. v. Darby Lumber decision of 1941, reversed the legacy of *Hammer* and *Bailey*.[95]

The constraints that worked on early twentieth-century American so-cial welfare are even more evident when we move from the relatively attractive realm of workplace safety and health regulation to more distributive (or even redistributive) policies such as unemployment insurance and minimum wage laws. The boldest act of the early twen-tieth-century British social welfare program was the institution of compulsory health and unemployment insurance. Concern over un-employment was much greater in England than in America, in part because the problem there appeared more extensive and intractable. Reformist intellectuals such as the Webbs, whose statist inclinations were wedded to a Protestant-Victorian morality, wanted "conditional relief" and compulsory labor exchanges; Winston Churchill, ever mindful of individual freedom, wanted voluntary labor exchanges and nonconditional social insurance. As he put it, he did not wish to mix morality and mathematics.[96]

An "Insurance Scheme" designed to provide some coverage of for working class against "sickness and breakdown" was enacted in 1911. Coverage for sickness, invalidism, and unemployment now was supplied (though in a limited way) to perhaps a third of the population. This National Insurance Act, building on previous workmen's compensation and old age pension laws, met little opposition. Said an observer: "For some reason the nation had lost fear, by 1911, that such an act as this, based on alien principles and proposing large changes, could really bring hurt." With the passage of a similar law in Germany, "a new social epoch appears to have been thus suddenly introduced in both countries."[97]

The United States had nothing comparable until the 1930s, though proponents of social insurance were active in the early 1900s. The American Association for Labor Legislation, formed in 1906, interested itself in the issue; substantial proposals by Henry R. Seager and Isaac M. Rubinow appeared in 1910 and 1913. But the constraints evident in other realms of social welfare operated with even greater force here: the opposition of employers; the obstacles of federalism and constitutionality; the widespread belief that unemployment and destitution were less severe in America than elsewhere; the identification of the industrial working class with those alien outsiders, the immigrants.

It had long been an article of American faith that unemployment was peripheral, best handled by providing more information on job prospects. But from the 1890s on, the perception took root that unemployment was a structural problem, not limited to marginals such as tramps and hoboes. Major American magazines published eight articles on the subject between 1900 and 1904, sixty-four between 1905 and 1909. When the number of those without jobs skyrocketed during the 1914–15 recession, big city mayors responded with emergency blue ribbon committees. New York's John Purroy Mitchel appointed Elbert Gary of United States Steel to head a group which talked of scientific management, set up municipal workshops—and resisted direct relief.[98]

The abuses of private employment agencies, the growth of unemployment in industrial centers, and a shortage of farm labor in agricultural states led to the establishment of state employment offices. By 1914 there were over sixty of them in eighteen states. A National Employment Exchange was set up in New York with a $100,000 endowment. "It was found," a student of the movement reassuringly observed, "that it is not at all necessary that the office force [of a labor exchange] should be made up of economists or sociologists. This work, like any other business, can be learned by people of ordinary intelligence." But the exchanges remained unintegrated and marginal. Samuel Gompers of the AFL saw no need for them, and most employers continued to hire at their plants.[99]

Public employment agencies based on the wartime United States Employment Service were the major response of state government to the postwar rise in joblessness. Otherwise, aside from scattered public works assistance (such as a $50,000 emergency public works fund in Pennsylvania), unemployment policy stagnated in the arid realm of commissions, investigations, and reports. Advocates of unemployment insurance looked enviously at Britain, whose 1911 act was extended in 1920 to all workers except those in agriculture or domestic service.[100]

The Great Depression thrust unemployment onto center stage in American welfare policy. But the weight of the past hung heavy. Local and state authorities continued to bear the burden of public works, relief (such as it was), and employment information. No American state had an unemployment insurance system until Wisconsin's Unemployment Compensation Act created one in 1931. Given the manifest emergency of the depression, it was thought, this modest, noncompulsory, noncontributory plan might survive judicial scrutiny.[101]

The major response to the flood of joblessness was emergency relief commissions perpetuating the hoary traditions of the poor laws and the dole. This meant constant worrying over whether recipients were sufficiently "destitute and in necessitous circumstances" to be entitled to relief. Thirteen state constitutions prohibited state aid to individuals, and some confined aid to particular classes of persons. Courts varied in their readiness to hold that the emergency allowed states to transcend these limitations. Not until the construction projects and work relief programs of the New Deal was there a clear shift of emphasis from the cold calculus of charity to employing the unemployed.[102]

For all the boldness of its departure from existing practice, the un-employment insurance provision of the 1935 Social Security Act was steeped in the special constraints imposed by the American polity: federalism, judicial review, the power of special interests, hostility to the welfare state. The federal government would tax employers and employees; the states were expected to create their own insurance funds. Linking compensation with wages, limiting benefits to strikers and denying them to agricultural workers, domestic servants, and merchant seamen, the Social Security Act underlined the fact that while the problems of modern America heightened the need for na-tional solutions, the structure of the American state and the scale and diversity of American society made those solutions peculiarly diffi-cult to attain.[103]

Minimum wage laws posed perhaps the greatest challenge to pre-vailing beliefs as to the proper scope of labor legislation. Britain passed wage regulation act in 1909, and an American movement appeared at about the same time. In both cases support stemmed not so much from workers as from reformers with a mixed bag of motives. They were concerned that large numbers of workers could not maintain an "efficient standard of living"; they worried about the sweated labor of immigrants, or wished to secure industrial peace by siphoning off worker discontent.[104]

But no uniform legislation seemed possible in America, where reg-ulation of this sort was widely held to reside (if anywhere) in the states. The New York Court of Appeals accepted a minimum wage statute for public employees in 1904. But Louisiana's 1898 constitu-tion forbade the legal regulation of wages. The familiar question of constitutionality hung heavy over the issue. At a time when even something so manifestly related to workers' health and safety as reg-ulating the hours of work made heavy going against the strictures of liberty of contract and Fourteenth Amendment due process, the pros-pect for minimum wage laws was bleak indeed.[105]

Eleven states had instituted some sort of minimum wage legislation for women and children by 1917. Conservatives inveighed against this interference with the laws of the market; one linked the minimum wage with syndicalism as "akin in being phases of the same spirit of unrest and discontent now sweeping over the world." But in practice these scattered acts were innocuousness itself.[106]

Massachusetts set up the first state minimum wage board for women in 1912, in response to the prodding of state commerce secretary Mary Dewson, Wellesley professor Emily Balch, and various women's organizations. (The Lawrence textile strike also concentrated the legislators' minds.) A Minimum Wage Commission was to decide where to recommend a minimum wage, based on the "necessary cost of living." The state supreme court approved of the law in 1918. But soon the commission was abolished, and its duties shifted to the Department of Labor and Industry; thereafter, no women served on the regulating body. Between 1914 and 1928 the law was applied to nineteen industries with ninety thousand employees, a fifth of the female work force. Its findings were advisory, not compulsory; enforcement rested on publicity. And when the *Boston Transcript* refused to report that certain stores were not paying minimum wages, despite a legal requirement that newspapers publish the findings of the commission at regular advertising rates, the court found that obligation to be unconstitutional. A legislative committee in 1923 recommended that the act continue in force only for another five years.[107]

State by state the politics of minimum wage legislation played itself out. Oregon's law authorized a commission to set compulsory minimums for women and children. The state supreme court upheld it, and average weekly earnings for women rose about 10 percent by 1914, with no evident ill effects on Oregon's economy. A relatively effective minimum wage law in California was sustained by employers' fear of public opinion and the inertial force of habit in obeying the state wage commission's orders. Washington state's act had the support of trade unionists, and the acquiescence of business (presumably because it did not apply to the agricultural and canning industries, where the bulk of women and children worked). When the law's coverage was expanded in the 1920s, conservative state governments reduced it to ineffectiveness. In New York, Florence Kelley, the Consumers' League, and the National Women's Trade Union League, spurred by the horror of the Triangle Shirtwaist fire, sought a minimum wage act. But immigrant and native-born unions split over the issue; the AFL's Samuel Gompers opposed it, as did the National Civic Federation and the Associated Industries.[108]

Judicial hostility in the 1920s deprived the minimum wage movement of what headway it had left. The Supreme Court in Adkins v. Children's Hospital (1923) invalidated a District of Columbia law that empowered a wage board to set minimum wages. It relied on a *Lochner*-like liberty of contract argument, plus the "sociological" observation that access to the vote ended women's need for special protection in the workplace. Oliver Wendell Holmes vigorously dissented: "It will need more than the Nineteenth Amendment to convince me that there are no differences between men and women, or that legislation cannot take those differences into account."[109]

Only the impotent Massachusetts type of voluntary law appeared to be legal. Even a state law pegging the wages of public employees to the prevailing wage rate, which the Supreme Court had upheld in 1903, was invalidated in 1926 on the ground that the standard was too indefinite, a decision, said the *Harvard Law Review*, which "brings out all the more clearly the lengths to which the Court will go in its recent attitude toward social legislation."[110]

The initial effect of the Great Depression and its massive increase in unemployment was to weaken still further (if this was possible) the base of support for minimum wage laws. But the view began to take hold that a minimum wage, like price-fixing and crop reduction, was a way of putting a floor under the shrinkage of purchasing power, and might spur economic recovery. A New York law created a board empowered to determine reasonable wages for women, much as public utilities commissions did with rates. The Supreme Court in Morehead v. Tipaldo (1936) struck it down on freedom of contract grounds, thereby endangering seventeen similar state laws and stirring a storm of protest. Even Herbert Hoover condemned the decision as an assault on the powers reserved to the states.

Now the Court responded. An important part of its famous "switch in time that saved nine" was its West Coast Hotel v. Parrish decision of 1937, in which Chief Justice Hughes for a five-to-four majority upheld a Washington minimum wage law not discernibly different from the New York statute. Meanwhile, the minimum wage movement had moved from the state to the national level, leading to the Fair Labor Standards Act of 1938, which established the first (though exemption-plagued) national minimum wage. The Court unanimously accepted its constitutionality in 1941. And so the minimum wage, like so much else in the welfare state, entered a realm where politics and resources rather than federalism and constitutionality shaped its contours.[111]

As a social issue, early twentieth-century social welfare had a character much like civil liberties, the regulation of mores, and the response to crime. The conditions of life in the new society—a growing body of interests, issues, and ideas, and a denser infrastructure of media-stirred public opinion, politics, law, and government—invested each of these issues with a richer and more varied tone, making it a significantly larger item on the agenda of American public life. At the same time, it became clear over the decades from 1900 to the early 1930s that a greater public interest in social welfare did not necessarily have sweeping policy consequences. New social conditions fostered new proposals; but they also strengthened old fears—of the poor, of spending, of the state. The sheer scale and diversity of a pluralist modern society led to stasis and gridlock as often as it led to innovation and change.

MODERN TIMES:
IMAGES

Privacy and other issues of personal identity took on new meaning in a world of urban crowding, physically shaped by the congruence of tall buildings, mass retailing and transit, and motor vehicles.

City streets had long been crowded; now they were congested in a recognizably modern way. From *Geographical Review*, 3 (1917), 282–283.

Even more widespread, and no less distinctively modern, was the social experience of mass entertainment. By far the most dramatic expansion of that experience came with the introduction, and rapid spread, of moving pictures. The immigrant masses of New York shared that first universal medium with the rest of the nation. From *Survey*, 34 (1915), 314.

Club Cocktails

When others are offered, it's for the purpose of larger profits. Refuse substitutes. All varieties.

Simply strain through cracked ice and serve.

G. F. HEUBLEIN & BRO.
Sole Proprietors
Hartford   New York   London

"In or about December, 1910," Virginia Woolf observed in *Mrs. Bennett and Mrs. Brown* (1924), "human nature changed." Certainly it appears that around that time advertising began to take a new tack in its treatment of some of the social values to which it pandered, or sought to mold. A new conception of women as social actors (and consumers) rather abruptly appeared: in 1911, just after Woolf's divide, a short-haired young woman quaffing a cocktail was a suitable subject for a liquor ad in a national magazine. From *Harper's Weekly*, 55 (Oct. 14, 1911), 23.

This is Al. Jennings

He says: "Jiminy! It's the Hottest, Fastest Gun I ever Saw!"

SAVAGE
AUTOMATIC PISTOL
"Aims Easy As Pointing Your Finger"

Crime, too, could be domesticated into fodder fit for the dialogue of advertisers with a growing mass market. From *Literary Digest*, 48 (April 11, 1914), 837.

The Progressive conscience, reflecting the modern conception of the special status of the child, led to institutional reforms such as children's courts. But a carefully staged courtroom scene suggests that this new social awareness hardly displaced a more traditional conception of adult authority. From *Charities*, 11 (1903), 419.

Education also entered a more modern phase, its policymakers drawn to new schemes such as the Gary system, which was designed to make urban schooling more efficient and practical. Then as now, educational social engineering ran into much resistance from those subject to the plans of the planners. This photo shows New York City police responding to an anti–Gary system riot in the Bronx. From *Literary Digest*, 55 (Nov. 3, 1917), 28.

Drugs—long available, but before 1900 a subterranean, repressed social problem—now came to public attention in a recognizably modern way. The policy response was an all too familiar one: treatment programs (ineffective) and drug busts (inconclusive). The photos at left show lines of men (top) and women (bottom) awaiting drugs and treatment at the New York Municipal Bureau in the summer of 1919; the photo above shows agents of the Federal narcotics squad with confiscated opium derivatives, "which," says its caption, "but for the timely arrival of the agents would have been peddled to addicts all over the country." Facing page: From *Literary Digest*, 64 (March 6, 1920), 27–28. Above: From *Literary Digest*, 76 (Feb. 24, 1923), 34.

Even that pervasive phenomenon of recent times, the passion of the *jeunesse dorée* for blue jeans, had an early twentieth-century provenance. In protest against the high cost of clothing after the end of World War I, overalls for a season became the dress *de rigueur* of the caring classes: "Overalls are now correct for all occasions; . . . students do their profoundest thinking in the garb formerly thought suitable for the horny-handed son of toil, and even the younger Rockefeller and other millionaires have declared that they will don blue jeans if need be." Above: The overalls movement strikes the University of North Carolina. Facing page: "The Standard of Revolt." From *Literary Digest,* 65 (May 1, 1920), 24.

Finally, the social categories of race and gender began to take on a more modern aspect. Relations between blacks and whites both improved and worsened under the impact of new conditions of life. Sports spectacles and new forms of organized protest challenged old stereotypes. But new social science and race war (moved to Northern urban settings such as Chicago) reinforced racism. Facing page, top: The end of "The Fight of the Century"— Jack Johnson defeats Jim Jeffries, Reno, Nevada, 1910. From *Harper's Weekly*, 54 (July 16, 1910), 9. Facing page, bottom: Black women marched in New York in the summer of 1917 to protest racial violence. From *Outlook*, 116 (1917), 586. Above: Testing the mental ability of a World War I recruit. From *Outlook*, 118 (1916), 488. Below: A crowd of Chicago rioters surrounds a house into which a fleeing black has taken refuge. From *The World's Work*, 45 (1922–1923), 132.

Asians, too, faced severe discrimination—and began their long and patient use of American institutions to transform their lives. The photo above pictures the first move in a suit brought by the Federal government against the San Francisco school board, testing the constitutionality of that city's attempt (ended after some arm-twisting by Theodore Roosevelt) to exclude the Japanese from the public schools. From *Harper's Weekly*, 51 (Feb. 9, 1907), 205.

Women—half the nation—attained what was arguably the major social policy gain of the new century: they secured the right to vote. Above, Jeannette Rankin, America's first congresswoman, addresses her colleagues in the House. But the old politics adapted to woman's suffrage by using prostitutes as "repeaters" (below). Here, as elsewhere, the past persisted in stubborn and complex coexistence with modernity. Photo above from *Outlook*, 116 (1917), 619; below, from *Outlook*, 82 (1906), 117.

III · GROUPS

We turn now to the last of the congeries of social concerns that engaged the early twentieth-century American polity, the status of immigrants, aliens, blacks, Indians, and women. This book began by looking at intimate, individual relationships and rights: of husbands and wives and parents and children; of privacy and free expression. It concludes with the largest, most collective, in a sense the most public, of identities: nationality and citizenship, race and gender.

The result is a by now familiar story. The expanded public consciousness that arose with a new society gave these matters fresh importance in American public life. Nationality-defined immigration restriction, an increasingly detailed and restrictive conception of citizenship, the heightened legitimacy (and the first intimations of limits) of racial segregation, a growing ambiguity in attitudes toward Indians, and a major increase in the civil rights of women constitute the rich, conflicted record of early twentieth-century social policy regarding ethnicity, race, and gender.

7 ▪ Immigrants and Aliens

What to do about immigration in the early twentieth century was a social issue with powerful cultural resonance. A general receptivity to immigrants and the relative ease with which they could become citizens were defining characteristics of nineteenth-century America. Immigration restriction and racial and other constraints on the status of aliens were revealing policy responses to the strains of a new society.

Restriction

Public concern over immigrants and aliens rose in Europe as well around the turn of the century. Which, and how many, immigrants should be admitted, and the pace, character, and extent of naturalization, became weighty issues on both sides of the Atlantic.

In nineteenth-century Britain, as in the United States, the trend was to liberalize immigrant entry and citizenship. A Royal Commission on Naturalization and Allegiance in 1869 observed in typically equivocal liberal fashion that letting place of birth determine nationality "has the effect of obliterating speedily and effectually, disabilities of race, the existence of which within any community is generally an evil, though to some extent a necessary evil." It upheld the common law rule that everyone born in a Crown dominion was a British subject, and the Naturalization Act of 1870 guaranteed a naturalized subject all of the rights and privileges of one native-born.[1]

Imperial diplomacy sought to avoid racial restrictions that might antagonize China and Japan and interfere with trade: then-Colonial Secretary Joseph Chamberlain in 1897 persuaded the Australian prime minister not to exclude immigrants on the basis of race or color. But

Australian public opinion dictated otherwise, and the new Australian Commonwealth of 1901 enacted an Immigration Restriction Act designed to secure "a white Australia."[2]

East European Jewish immigration into England became a significant public issue around the turn of the century. Liberal attitudes still had currency in the Cabinet: "Though undesirable in many ways owing to differences of race, language, sanitary habits, and ideas of life, which make them alien to English people, [Jewish immigrants] have yet certain good qualities of thrift, intelligence, orderliness, and industry, which help to mitigate the evils of their settlement among us." An 1894 Board of Trade report found that Jewish agencies handled the social needs of the immigrants and that their children rapidly assimilated to English ways.[3]

The immigrant flow was hardly torrential. About 3 percent of London's inhabitants in 1890 were foreign-born; a decade later only about ten thousand had been added to the city's alien population. Many Jewish immigrants eventually moved on to the United States, a process fostered by Jewish agencies. But the concentration of Jews in London's East End caused concern. The 1892 Trades Union Congress called for restriction, and in 1901 the secretary of the Shoemakers' Union declared: "I do not know a Jew in London that makes good work." Fabians Sidney and Beatrice Webb, the Liberal J. A. Hobson, Conservative Unionist Joseph Chamberlain, and the right-wing British Brothers' League worried about the Jewish influx. In 1902 the Conservative Balfour government set up an Aliens Commission to suggest legislation. Its 1903 report came up with drastic recommendations, including alien registration and declaring certain areas of the country off-limits to alien settlement.[4]

The Aliens Act of 1905 expanded the power of immigration officers to decide who was an undesirable alien and thus subject to deportation; and it paid much attention to data gathering and the machinery of regulation. Many Liberals were uneasy with the law and its anti-Semitic sources (according to one observer, "The Alien question in England, as elsewhere, is mainly the Jewish question"). A contributor to the *Nation* thought that "the constant reference to the evil of admitting to England Polish and German Jews has an ugly sound." The political scientist Sir Alfred Zimmern called the law "one of the most immoral and hypocritical, as well as one of the most foolish measures which have been passed during the memory of the present generation." It combined a maximum of provocation with a minimum of real effect; it was bad in its anti-Semitism, and in establishing one standard of duty for Englishmen and another for foreigners.[5]

After the Liberals came to power in 1906, they let enforcement lapse. Home Secretary Herbert Gladstone wanted to give the benefit of the doubt to immigrants who claimed that they were escaping religious or political persecution. There was much evasion of the rule that vessels with more than twenty steerage passengers were to be classified as immigrant ships and thus subject to inspection. In any event, economic and other forces dictated that the great body of Jewish migrants went to America.[6]

The Aliens Restriction Bill of August 5, 1914, enacted when the First World War began, required aliens to register with the police and empowered the Home Secretary to issue deportation orders. Yet a new Imperial Law of Nationality two days later codified recent decades' changes in naturalization law, established an imperial as well as a local British nationality, and removed remaining disabilities against voting and officeholding (many of them inactive) that still applied to foreign-born citizens. The tension between the liberal nineteenth-century attitude toward immigration (reinforced by emigration and a falling birth rate) and xenophobia given new life by racism, anti-Semitism, and war made the status of aliens a continuing (if largely symbolic) issue in British public life.[7]

Comparable developments—a sharp increase in the flow of southern and eastern European immigrants (including many Jews); their concentration in cities (so that the East Side of New York had some superficial resemblance to the East End of London); hostile reactions from trade unionists, conservatives, and Progressive reformers—made immigration a significant issue in America as well. But in social scale and policy consequences American immigration policy was very different from the British experience, as different, indeed, as immigrants are from aliens.

Immigration to America was very much larger and more diverse, and of substantially greater national importance. The eventual response—severe restrictions on the numbers and national origin of those allowed into the country—denoted a xenophobia like that of other nations. But the triumph of immigration restriction, like the triumph of Prohibition, was the product of a uniquely American mix of traditionalism, reform, and social control.

Defenders of immigration often saw the issue in terms of the past.

Review of Reviews editor Albert Shaw recalled that "from the beginning the Americans have been a composite European race, and we must reconcile ourselves to the idea that the earlier stock is to be superseded by the later . . . Through it all, American life seems to have more, rather than less, of its old power to assimilate the newcomer." The chief clerk of the United States Census Office conceded in 1908 that "in the years to come, the increasing effect of immigration will doubtless appear in changed customs, realignment of religious beliefs, and some variation in national and political ideals—in fact, in the establishment of a new and composite civilization." He noted also that the states with large foreign populations were the most prosperous in the Union, and concluded that there was little to fear and much to gain from the influx. New voices also were heard. The National Association of Manufacturers, interested in cheap labor, joined with liberals such as president Charles Eliot of Harvard and spokesmen of nationality groups to organize the Immigration Protective League. William James defended cultural pluralism on the grounds that diversity was a social necessity, and that harmony rather than unity was an essential condition of justice. This view was shared by the black intellectual W. E. B. Du Bois, the philosopher Horace Kallen (who later popularized the idea of cultural pluralism), and the urban sociologist Robert Park.[8]

Opponents of immigration were no less diverse. Organized labor was an increasingly vocal advocate of restriction. Terence V. Powderly, former head of the Knights of Labor and commissioner of immigration from 1897 to 1902, called for the expulsion of Chinese aliens and spoke of the threat that new immigrants posed to public health. The AFL's Samuel Gompers—an immigrant himself—was far readier to advocate restriction than his English counterpart Keir Hardie. Progressives John R. Commons and Edward A. Ross and scientific racists Madison Grant and the writer Jack London identified immigration restriction with social reform and race purification. Southern conservatives, the Daughters of the American Revolution, and the New England Brahmins Henry Cabot Lodge and Prescott F. Hall of the Immigration Restriction League identified it with the preservation of the American past.[9]

The impact of immigration on politics became more important in this time of national political reform. The head of the Department of Commerce and Labor's Bureau of Statistics noted that the states with the largest numbers of foreign-born residents most strongly backed

William McKinley against William Jennings Bryan in 1896, and concluded that the present immigrants were assimilable, a safe and valuable addition to the country—if only they would vote! Another observer claimed that new citizens were least chained to party loyalty, and hence most likely to take an independent path in voting. Thus, many supported the third party candidate William Randolph Hearst in New York City's 1905 mayoralty election.[10]

The restrictionist Edward A. Ross admitted that intelligent naturalized foreigners—Britons, Germans, Scandinavians, and Jews—were more likely than most native Americans to pursue an independent course in politics. The South had the fewest naturalized voters—and the most prejudiced politics, blocking efficient, progressive government. But he dwelt on the corrupting influence of foreign voters in politics and government, particularly in the big cities. The large, floating, nonvoting body of foreign-born laborers detracted from labor's political strength and added to the social vices afflicting America's cities. Urban political machines most feared those forces "that bore from within—social settlements, social centers, the quick intelligence of the immigrant Hebrew, stricter naturalization, and restriction of immigration." Meanwhile, the core society decayed: "While we Americans wrangle over old issues of clericalism, separate schools, and 'personal liberty,' the little homogeneous peoples are forging ahead of us in rational politics and learning to look pityingly upon us as a chaos rather than a people."[11]

The immigration issue battened on economic as well as political and social concerns. A strong argument could be—and was—made for immigration's positive effect on economic growth and national prosperity. The labor economist Isaac A. Hourwich, with financial support from Louis Marshall and the American Jewish Committee, sought to demonstrate that the new immigration pushed up the wage rates of native workers. But the general view was that the numbers and bargaining weakness of the newcomers perpetuated low wages. For the first time a substantial body of public opinion looked on immigrants as a detriment rather than a spur to the economic health of the nation.[12]

Immigration restriction in many respects was a paradigmatic Progressive cause. It spoke directly to the widespread desire to preserve a core national identity in the face of social change; it touched on a multitude of political, social, and economic problems; and it called for massive fact gathering and complex regulation.

Boston social worker Robert Hunter observed that the same selfish forces who opposed Prohibition promoted immigration, with similarly adverse social consequences. Analogies to other Progressive causes came readily to mind: "The plan for a proper restriction of immigration rests upon an even higher plane than the [Pure] Food Law; it is to benefit not alone our bodies but to insure the welfare of our homes, our States and our nation"; "The problem of immigration is but a part of the great conservation movement. It has to do with the conservation of the American people, all that it stands for."[13]

Americans were divided in deep and complex ways over this issue. Elite Yankees, backwood xenophobes, instrumentalist Progressives, and organized labor were no more (or less) incongruous an alliance for restriction than were the nationality groups, cosmopolitan liberals, steamship companies, and large corporate employers who favored immigration. But on balance, the felt need to eliminate those aspects of American life that made for disharmony, conflict, and diversity, and the belief that regulatory mechanisms lay at hand to do just that, operated as forcefully in the realm of immigration policy as in Prohibition or antitrust. By 1910 a substantial body of legislation defined unfit newcomers mentally, physically, morally, and economically. And large-scale restriction—like national Prohibition—was an increasing possibility.[14]

Early restrictionist legislation was generally aimed at particular social qualities, not at national or ethnic groups. Criminals, paupers, and the insane (in 1882), contract laborers (in 1885), and anarchists and prostitutes (in 1903) were among the classes excluded. Congress by large margins enacted a literacy test in 1896, but Grover Cleveland vetoed a bill so tainted with social inegalitarianism.

The Chinese were the only national group explicitly excluded before 1900. They were barred from admission for a ten-year period in 1882 and again in 1892; in 1902 their status had to be reconsidered. Some traditionalists—the *Nation* and *Arena* magazines, Massachusetts Senator George Frisbie Hoar, Illinois Senator Shelby Cullom—wanted the ban lifted. The Chinese, argued one supporter, were conservative, docile, and well-behaved; through citizenship, qualified suffrage, and the education of their children they could be readily assimilated. In any event, "not homogeneity but heterogeneity has been the law of our national life."[15]

But the prevailing view—supported by organized labor and most professional politicians—was for exclusion. Pennsylvania Senator

Boies Penrose, chairman of the Committee on Immigration, reported that fifty thousand of his constituents demanded that Chinese exclusion be retained. When his colleague Matthew Quay proposed that Chinese who embraced Christianity or had aided Catholics in Peking during the Boxer Rebellion should be admitted, Penrose found this "both picturesque and poetically just" but impractical. The Geary Law of 1902 renewed exclusion and made no provision for the entry of merchants, students, or professionals. Only Hoar of Massachusetts, an old school Republican, opposed the bill in the Senate.[16]

Immigration and Progressivism flourished together, and together they fed restrictionist sentiment. A 1907 act codified existing immigration laws, and in typical Progressive fashion created a commission to study the issue. Headed by Vermont Republican Senator William P. Dillingham, it gathered massive testimony and documentation, and in a 1910 report backed by forty-two volumes of evidence powerfully reinforced the view that here was an American social problem of the first magnitude.[17]

The Dillingham Commission earned retrospective notoriety for legitimating racial theories of social behavior. It strongly (and often spuriously) endorsed the view that the new immigrants threatened the American social and economic fabric. Yet its policy recommendations, chief among them a literacy test to control the number and character of entrants, hardly matched the scale of the problem as the commission perceived it. More striking was the course of events from the Dillingham report of 1910 to the adoption of the quota system in the 1920s, a major instance of early twentieth-century social policy-making at work.

Liberal antirestrictionists vigorously criticized the idea of a literacy test. This is a big country, argued the *Independent;* it can readily support a population of 300 to 400 million. The Dillingham bill under consideration in 1912 was "a curious inversion of our plain destiny and desire in that it shuts out immigrants and restricts population and development." Jane Addams criticized the racist assumptions behind the literacy test, which did not really measure character or ability. She had seen many highly educated immigrants deteriorate after their arrival, many illiterate ones rise to success.[18]

But an ever-stronger restrictionist sentiment had the support of the AFL, the Grange and other agrarian organizations, and widespread popular belief that the new immigration posed a threat to American society. Only through restriction, went the argument, could wages be raised and American democracy be preserved. Congress responded by repassing the literacy test. But William Howard Taft in February 1913 vetoed it, as Cleveland had in 1896. The traditional commitment to free entry (bolstered by the work force needs of big business) still— just—prevailed.[19]

After the outbreak of the First World War, immigration restriction— like Prohibition and woman's suffrage—came into its own. One sees here with special clarity the shift in American political culture from the structural concerns of the Progressive years to the ethnocultural concerns of the 1920s. As the philosopher Horace Kallen observed: "What this war did was to turn the anxiety about property into one about people." The debate over immigration policy centered on the question: What is an American?[20]

The war led to what *Scientific American* called "an unintentional experiment in restriction" by cutting the immigrant intake from 1.2 million in 1914 to under 300,000 in 1916. The *New Republic* welcomed this falloff, but feared that the flow would resume after the war, "when we shall be working upon urgent problems of national reorganization . . . Restriction in the interest of assimilation is the policy clearly indicated by the times." The magazine called for federal supervision over immigrants both before they came and after they arrived, "the same sort of benevolent guardianship that the state now exercises over the legal infant."[21]

Other voices, spread across the ideological spectrum, continued to insist on the immigrants' value and assimilability. Americanization advocate Frances Kellor worried lest ill-treatment induce them to return to their homelands. Former House Speaker Joseph Cannon, noting that a third of the membership of the House had names that did not appear in the First Census, caustically declared: "I am willing to put down with the aliens of this House." The cultural critic Randolph Bourne concluded that the war had made clear how strong was Americans' identification with their countries of origin. This was as true of the older Anglo-Saxon stock as of the new immigrants. There was, Bourne thought, no distinctive "native" American culture. He expected younger Americans to accept a new cosmopolitanism, to create a new American nationality with a closer relationship to Europe and a more receptive attitude toward social reform. But the war's stimulus to xenophobia was the greater social reality. The pace of legislation quickened. When Wilson in January 1917 vetoed a literacy test, this time Congress overrode him. And when the war ended, both public opinion and a new restrictionist device—nationality quotas—ended a policy of receptivity to immigrants as old as the Republic.[22]

The United States was hardly alone in this regard. The relatively free movement of people across national boundaries was one of the elements of nineteenth-century European life obliterated by the cordite of the western front. Though Britain faced little immigrant pressure after the war—its chief demographic concern, rather, was with the increasing outflow of its people to other parts of the globe—anti-foreignism (often laced with anti-Semitism) was a conspicuous element in postwar English political life. One Conservative called the Liberals "the Foreigners' Party," and warned that the old English stock was threatened by "Germans, Poles, Hungarians, Greeks, Levantines, Russians and all the jetsam of Europe, thus sapping national character and strength."[23]

The Restriction Act of 1919 tightened government control over immigration, and Parliament passed three Nationality and Status of Aliens Acts between 1917 and 1927. Canada, too, began to worry more about aliens. A sixth to a seventh of the population was foreign-born; worse, said one observer, "a disturbingly large proportion of our total population dilutes our citizenship, adds nothing to the spiritual meaning of Canadian life, resists incorporation, and yet is necessary in the mechanical work of production." Canadian Jews in particular were "an element which for the time being shows little sign of heartily adopting our institutions and points of view."[24]

France had a war-ravaged population whose birth rate was declining even before 1914. So the more than 2 million immigrants who entered the country during the 1920s, and made up 11 percent of its industrial work force by 1931, filled a manifest need. The parties of the right and center, sensitive to employers' interests, tended to oppose tighter immigration laws. A liberal new French nationality law in 1927 was designed "to render it easier for aliens to acquire French nationality." But public concern grew over the presence of foreigners, and so did pressure for restrictive policies confining them to the secondary labor market and discouraging their participation in the nation's social and political life. Communists, the Radical party, and health and police officials pushed for more stringent controls. Popular hostility to immigrants would become a significant part of the polarized French politics of the 1930s.[25]

It became apparent soon after the war that the 1917 literacy test provision did not substantially affect the immigrant flow to the United States. Sidney L. Gulick, a Protestant churchman long involved in missionary work in Japan, advocated immigration quotas based on the numbers of each national group already in the country. While severely limiting Asian immigration, at least a quota system did so on the same basis as for other groups. Gulick also called for federal bureaus to register, distribute, and educate immigrants, and for congressional legislation to protect the newcomers. "The final success of our democracy," he warned, "depends on just and equal law applied justly and equally to every individual in the United States regardless of race."[26]

Much irony attends the ultimate fate of his proposal. The superheated postwar political atmosphere, fueled by widespread fear of social unrest, was made to order for immigration restriction. The *New Republic* called for "a truce to immigration," arguing: "We cannot accept the laissez-faire view, that it is no concern of the American people what kind of immigrants come, what influences are at work to draw them to this country, what happens to them after they get here, how their coming bears upon our own current social and economic problems."[27]

Fearful that a renewed flood of immigrants would make it difficult for returning veterans to find jobs and that many aliens were radicals and revolutionaries, the House Immigration Committee in 1919 proposed the Burnett bill, which in effect suspended immigration for the next four years. To bolster its case it released a report by the State Department's Wilbur J. Carr that warned of the unassimilability of Polish Jews. No less anti-Semitic was Harry McBride, chief of the State Department's Visa Bureau, which after the war replaced the Labor Department's Immigration Bureau as the chief administrative overseer of the immigrant flow.

There still were factors blunting the edge of restriction. Canada, Mexico, and Ireland would not be affected by the ban; exceptions would be made for victims of religious persecution. But mainstream opinion was clear—as clear as it was for Prohibition. Most newspapers favored the bill; the old interest in a continuing labor supply gave way to fears of radicalism. Only the foreign language press strongly supported the existing system.[28]

Although the Burnett bill did not become law, Warren G. Harding's landslide victory in the 1920 election made it clear that a more inner-directed nationalism was in the air and that something would be done about immigration. Proposals included immigration holidays of up to five years, and more intensive examination of emigrants before they left the Old World. The new president sent a special mission of inquiry (headed by the actress Lillian Russell) to Europe. It concluded that desirable emigrants, needed in their home countries for postwar reconstruction, were not coming to America, and endorsed a ban on immigration.[29]

Instead, the Immigration Act of 1921 established a quota system of 3 percent of the foreign-born of each nationality in the United States as recorded in the 1910 Census, with an annual maximum of 355,000 entrants. This meant that 55 percent of the immigrant intake would come from Northern Europe, 45 percent from the south and east. Initially introduced by Senator Dillingham, a champion of quotas since 1912, the bill came to be identified most closely with House Immigration Committee chairman Albert Johnson, from Washington state. This former member of the Asiatic Exclusion League and the Dillingham Commission now emerged as the chief congressional advocate of quota-based restriction.[30]

The restrictionists attracted broad and varied support, as had the proponents of national Prohibition a few years before. The AFL and the American Legion lobbied for the bill; Scandinavian newspapers and the liberal *New Republic* favored it; one commentator welcomed restriction for the widened opportunity it offered to native blacks. Even *American Industries*, the voice of the National Association of Manufacturers, came out against unregulated immigration. The act breezed through both houses (the Senate vote was seventy-eight to one), and Harding signed it on May 29, 1921.[31]

The law took effect fifteen days later, and its southern and eastern European quotas were quickly consumed. Great confusion (and much hardship: seventeen Armenian women and children were among those turned back, later to be massacred by the Turks) attended the new policy. And, as in the case of Prohibition, large-scale evasion quickly emerged. Estimates of illegal entrants ranged from 100,000 a year to 1,000 a day.[32]

The new policy was administered in the xenophobic spirit that had led to its creation. Henry H. Curran, a newspaperman and former New York City mayoral candidate, became commissioner of immigration for the Port of New York in July 1923. He provided accommodations at Ellis Island appropriate to the different classes of immigrants: mattresses, sheets, and pillows for first- and second-class passengers; steel beds with wire springs for those who came in steerage. In 1924 he reflected that the longer he ran Ellis Island, "the stronger is my wish that fewer would go by—a smaller quantity and better quality—or, with certain exceptions, none at all for a while."[33]

Unlike Prohibition, which was set in the amber of the Eighteenth Amendment and the Volstead Act, the quota act of 1921 was to be in force only until June 30, 1922. The AFL, worried by persistent unemployment, called for continued restriction; but its influence on a Republican Congress and administration was limited. Meanwhile, industrialists initially acquiescent because of their fear of Bolshevism and the large number of unemployed began to worry again about a labor shortage. Complaints arose that recent immigrants avoided work in steel mills and smelters or on the railroads. The *New Jersey Journal of Commerce* lamented: "A certain class of worker is necessary to the progress of our industries, and the present immigration law has practically eliminated this class." The *New Republic* took note of the fact that captains of industry were beginning to clamor again for cheap alien labor. But it maintained that "the common sense of the great majority of Americans, who live by the labor of their hands, will oppose the abrogation of the quota law until an equally effective restrictionist measure has been devised to take its place."[34]

To finesse the economic counterargument, advocates emphasized the cultural and racial grounds of restriction. Madison Grant's racist philippic *The Passing of the Great Race*, written in 1916, had wide influence during the early 1920s. Harvard president A. Lawrence Lowell argued: "It is . . . largely a perception of . . . homogeneity, as a basis for popular government and the public opinion on which it rests, that justifies democracies in resisting the influx in great numbers of a widely different race."[35]

President Harding tried to satisfy both camps: "If we keep out undesirable immigration we shall soon have an abundant immigration that is in every way desirable." Manufacturers such as Elbert Gary of United States Steel, who wished to maintain "the pool of normal unemployed," and the American Farm Bureau Federation, fearful lest the supply of Mexican farm workers be threatened, sought to ease restrictionist policy. But few congressmen served these interests. The Grange and other Midwest and Plains farm spokesmen opposed the importation of farm workers of the "Latin type." The department store owner Edward A. Filene, contending that it was "important to business that we produce more consumers rather than produce more commodities," believed that half a century of restriction would create a better-educated, more efficient, more prosperous, and hence more highly consuming population.[36]

Overwhelming House and Senate majorities extended the 1921 quota act to 1923 and then to 1924, to a drumbeat of press comment on the success of the new policy in reducing the size and altering the shape of immigration. The *New Republic* concluded in 1924 that the law had worked reasonably well to prevent "a deluge of inassimilable peoples. We accept the restriction of immigration as a social and political necessity in the present condition of the United States." But the journal took issue with a new proposal now welling up in Congress that the quota base year be set back from 1910 to 1890, thus substantially reducing the potential immigrant draw from southern and eastern Europe. It preferred legislation designed "to make us a more homogeneous nation, instead of splitting us into a collection of mutually hostile racial stocks."[37]

Calvin Coolidge was a more full-throated advocate of restriction than his predecessor Harding. He supported moving the quota base to an earlier date than 1910, limiting admission to those capable of assimilation, and registering aliens. On May 26, 1924, a few days before the expiration of the existing law, the Johnson Immigration Act swept through Congress, opposed by only half a dozen senators and about seventy congressmen from states with large immigrant populations. The political columnist Mark Sullivan thought that "the sentiment in Congress is more nearly unanimous on immigration than perhaps on any one subject," and thought that if restriction had come earlier, the Ku Klux Klan might not have reemerged.[38]

The Johnson Act more than halved the annual immigrant intake to 170,000 a year, and dictated that it shrink still further, to 150,000 in 1927. It gave preference to skilled farmers and the relatives of citizens, and set quotas based on each nationality's share of the more "normal" 1890 census rather than that of 1910. Despite President Coolidge's desire for a nominal Japanese quota, the act flatly excluded immigrants ineligible for citizenship, that is, Chinese and Japanese. Sidney Gulick, the father of the quota idea, regretted this: "If we allow any immigration by quotas, such quotas should . . . include all peoples." The law also provided that after July 1, 1927, quotas would be based not on the proportion of the foreign-born in a past census year but on the "national origins" of the current American population. This provision was the work primarily of Pennsylvania Senator David A. Reed, who was advised by eugenics-minded anthropologists and sociologists from the University of Pittsburgh.[39]

Because the Johnson Act provided for the admission of family members, and required certificates granted by consulates abroad (thus eliminating the trauma of rejection in America), the State Department's Philip C. Jessup called it "one of the most humanitarian systems of restricted immigration ever devised." It offered as well "the pleasing possibility of Nordic supremacy." The nation, said journalist Mark Sullivan, "has set its steps firmly, and, almost certainly, irrevocably toward becoming a homogeneous nation." Another celebrant declared: "It is based on bedrock principles. It marks a turning point in American civilization."[40]

This expedient mix of numerical restriction and group selection took its place beside Prohibition as a major expression of the urge to restore a more unified, less fractured society, the postwar extension into social policy of the Progressive effort to secure similar ends in economic and political reform. Quota restriction, like Prohibition, was Progressivism gone to ethnocultural war.

During the first ten months after the enactment of the 1924 law, about seventeen thousand more common laborers left the United States than entered. The National Association of Manufacturers worried about the shrinking supply of unskilled labor, although the more au courant National Industrial Conference Board stressed that the real wages of American workers were likely to rise. In a 1925 speech to the American Legion, President Coolidge proposed that the new policy would reduce intolerance. Americanism, he declared, does not depend on the length of time spent in the United States; now "we are all . . . in the same boat." Meanwhile, the attitudes that gave birth to the Johnson Act remained, and soon the depression would decisively strengthen the economic argument for restriction.[41]

The need to recalculate quotas based on national origins posed a statistical problem comparable in its complexity (and ultimately its impossibility) to Congress's charge to the Interstate Commerce Commission to come up with a valuation of America's railroads. Under the 1924 act the secretaries of commerce, labor, and state were to work out revised quotas under the national origins provision. They delegated the task to a Quota Board of six statistical experts, chaired by a Census Bureau official. The board's approach was to determine the size of each nationality group in 1790, and then trace additions to it since. Working from incomplete pre-1890 data on the foreign-born population, the experts assumed that the composition of the native stock had changed little if at all since 1790. But of course there were millions (how many, no one knew) of "mixed" stock. The Cabinet secretaries reported to the president in 1927 that they had grave doubts as to the accuracy of the data they were collecting.

The Carnegie Endowment for International Peace commissioned a study which concluded that under a national origins system Great Britain and Northern Ireland would have substantially larger shares of places, the German quota would drop from 50,000 to 20,000, and the Irish Free State and Scandinavian shares would be sharply reduced. Most southern and eastern European countries would be cut back to the minimum quota of 100 a year; Italy's alone would rise slightly to 5,716. "It seems like going back to Plymouth Rock and Jamestown for a basis of restricting immigration to this great country, much of whose greatness has been wrought by immigrants since 1885," *Outlook* dourly observed.[42]

German, Northern Irish, and Scandinavian spokesmen predictably demanded that the 1890 baseline for determining quotas be maintained, and the Senate yielded to the pressure of "these hyphenate groups." Connoisseurs of historical irony will savor the fact that Albert Johnson, the author of the 1924 law, along with a majority of his Immigration Committee, favored the repeal of the national origins clause. His was a heavily Scandinavian district, and he was up for reelection in 1926. He and Senator David Reed of Pennsylvania, the author of the national origins provision, clashed in Senate debate in 1927. The United States Chamber of Commerce and the AFL joined in opposing the provision "because of its flimsy historical basis, and the static, unrealistic conception of American life reflected by it." Herbert Hoover was against the provision as well, citing the impossibility of determining national origin quotas "accurately and without hardship." The Senate voted in 1927 to defer them for a year, and did so again in 1928.[43]

But a strongly restrictionist public opinion could not be indefinitely ignored. After Attorney General William D. Mitchell advised him that he was legally obligated to do so, President Hoover issued a proclamation on March 22, 1929, establishing national origin as the basis of immigration quotas (adding the hope that Congress soon would repeal the provision). Its effect was to reduce further (by 11,000) the annual number of immigrants allowed in; to almost double the quotas for Britain and Northern Ireland, from 34,007 to 65,721 (65 percent of the total); and to reduce the Irish Free State quota by 38 percent, Germany's by almost half, and the Scandinavians' by two thirds. "It is the first law of the kind," said Britain's *New Statesman*, "to be founded upon a social theory." Columbia University president Nicholas Murray Butler saw in it the same "pharisaical nationalism" that lay behind Prohibition and the Smoot-Hawley Tariff.[44]

The depression soon made criticism of the national origins quota system supererogatory. Immigration fell to less than 100,000 (two thirds of the legal maximum) in 1930, and to only 23,000 in 1933, when for the first time in American history more people left the country than entered it. Only 22 percent of available quota slots were used in October 1930, 13 percent in December, 10 percent in February 1931: a 90 percent reduction in five months. Meanwhile, the Hoover administration vigorously enforced the provision barring those "likely to become a public charge," applying it to all but prosperous Europeans. Almost every European country also restricted immigration, and the Latin American nations and Canada were reluctant to admit aliens to permanent residence. Everywhere, the *New Republic* noted, "the older dogma of freedom of movement has given way to a carefully supervised and discriminating selection of those seeking admittance."[45]

Discussion now focused on immigration from countries outside the quota system; in particular, Mexico. Restrictionists, organized labor, social and public health workers, and some Mexican-American leaders who wanted a breathing spell favored a quota on Mexican migrants. Ranchers, farmers, and railroad, lumber, and mining interests in the Southwest stood opposed, as did those who feared its effect on Mexican-American diplomatic relations, or thought the frontier unpoliceable, or expected that the flow would adjust itself naturally. In short, the issue raised an alignment of forces of a character and complexity similar to that evoked by European immigration. And as in the European case, economic realities made the issue moot: about 340 Mexicans entered in 1932, compared to 25,000 in 1929. Like other major ethnocultural issues of the early twentieth century, immigration restriction subsided (save for the question of European refugees) as a public issue until the post–World War II years.[46]

Aliens, Citizenship, and Race

One side of the coin of immigration policy was who, and how many, to let in. The other was how to deal with the newcomers once they arrived. Should they be hurried into citizenship, and into cultural assimilation, as quickly as possible? Or was it better to be more selective as to who among the newcomers would be allowed to stay, to become citizens, to be regarded as Americans?

The Constitution gave Congress the power "to establish a uniform rule of naturalization" for aliens. Laws in the 1790s fixed the residence requirement for citizenship first at two and then at five years. The tensions engendered by the French Revolution and political warfare between Federalists and Jeffersonian Republicans led to a fourteen-year residence requirement in the Naturalization Act of 1798, which the Jeffersonians repealed in 1802. For the remainder of the nineteenth century (except for the Know-Nothing interlude of the early 1850s), citizenship for aliens after a relatively brief residence was all but unquestioned. The Fourteenth Amendment made citizenship a birthright of black Americans; the Dawes Act of 1887 began the process (not completed until 1924) of extending it to Indians as well; Puerto Ricans became citizens in 1917.[47]

The mass immigration of the late nineteenth and early twentieth centuries, and the acquisition of noncontiguous territories (Puerto Rico, the Philippines) in the wake of the Spanish-American War, raised new questions as to the status of aliens. Among these were their eligibility for citizenship; expatriation and deportation; the reentry of aliens who had returned home; and divided nationality between husbands and wives.

One sign of the changing temper of the time was the rise of complaints that immigrants too freely adopted new "American" names. The list of private bills authorizing name changes appended to New York's annual volumes of legislative acts "reveals the fact that a widespread racial metamorphosis in this respect is under way," wrote Frederick Dwight. He held that this was unfair to the original bearers of those names: "One may doubt the wisdom, as a practical matter, of permitting a destruction of the evidence of race origin . . . As data for the study of criminology are collected with greater and greater care, it becomes increasingly important that such lines of research should be kept open and not obliterated." What to do? Legislation forbidding the adoption of existing surnames would help; and the state might usefully publish a table of acceptable artificial names.[48]

Anxieties such as these, and the Progressive desire for honest and efficient government, led to the tightening up of the nation's naturalization laws. President Theodore Roosevelt set up a Commission on Naturalization in 1905. That body vividly portrayed the corruption, fraud, and disarray of a process run by more than 5,000 state and 157 federal courts. A new Naturalization Act in 1906 allowed only federal courts and state courts of record to grant citizenship, forbade naturalization three months before a federal election, and created a Bureau of Immigration and Naturalization under the Department of Commerce and Labor.[49]

A year later Congress ended the tradition that American citizenship was permanent no matter how long one resided abroad, and prohibited naturalized American citizens from reassuming the nationality of their homeland in time of war. Jurisdiction over immigrants and immigration, exclusively federal since 1891, moved from Treasury (1891–1903) to Commerce (1903–1913) to Labor (after March 1913). "By amendment and interpretation," observed Bureau of Immigration head Louis F. Post in 1916, "the immigration laws have become alien laws, alienage rather than migration being the major fact in administrative decisions under them."[50]

While naturalization became harder, deportation became easier. For almost a century after the Alien and Sedition Acts of 1798, the federal government had little or no power to expel aliens. But an 1891 statute allowed it to deport illegal immigrants within a year after their entry. And the 1892 law renewing the exclusion of Chinese gave the commissioner of Internal Revenue the power to deport Chinese laborers without a residence certificate. That capacity was extended to anarchists in 1903 and to prostitutes in 1910. And the October 1918 amendment to the Espionage Act lifted all time limits on the power to expel.[51]

Deportation became less subject to legal rules and judicial oversight. Traditionally the courts held that aliens resident in the United States could return from a temporary visit abroad without passing again through the immigration process. But revisions of the naturalization law made this less certain, and much litigation followed. The

Supreme Court in 1914 decided that public health and immigration inspectors could exclude returning aliens, subject to pro forma approval by a review board.

What did this mean in human terms? A skilled workman who had lived in the United States for fifteen years, and had six children, visited Italy to see his mother; on his return he was ordered deported as likely to become a public charge. A federal court uneasily upheld that decision. Louis Post was greatly distressed by the policy change: "Nothing in my official experience in the Department of Labor has impressed me more deeply than the conviction that fundamental personal rights should be more scrupulously guarded in immigration cases than is possible through administrative decisions made in the course of executive routine." In 1915 the Supreme Court set aside a decision by immigration authorities to deport an immigrant merely because of a labor oversupply at his ultimate destination. But the 1917 immigration law gave the "likely to become a public charge" ground for refusal of entry much more general meaning than it had before, thus adding substantially to administrative discretion.[52]

A number of activities previously open to aliens now were closed. Voting by holders of first papers was a common practice in the nineteenth century. For example, around election time the Lancaster County, Nebraska, district court clerk published reminders that foreigners needed their first papers to vote. Party committees paid the naturalization fee for batches of aliens; no one was ever denied his first papers. But growing popular disapproval led to the end of alien suffrage in a number of western states in the early twentieth century. The 1928 election was the first in which no alien could vote for anyone, anywhere.[53]

A large popular majority approved a 1914 Arizona initiative proposal that at least 80 percent of the work force of any company employing more than five workers had to be made up of native-born citizens. The British and Italian ambassadors protested, and the State Department asked the governor of Arizona not to enforce the law, since it conflicted with treaty obligations. Italian and Asian residents filed suit in federal court, and in Truax v. Raich (1915) the United States Supreme Court unanimously found the Arizona law unconstitutional under the equal protection clause of the Fourteenth Amendment: the state could not block an alien's right to engage in a legal occupation. This was the first time since Reconstruction that the amendment was interpreted in a way that echoed its original purpose of protecting individual civil rights. But the *Nation* reflected a common sentiment when it argued that the statute had used a bad method for a good purpose.[54]

At the same time the Court in Heim v. McCall upheld a New York law forbidding employers on public works projects from hiring alien workers, a statute that the *New Republic* regarded as a proper labor regulation. The Bricklayers' and Masons' Union brought the suit against contractors building the city's new subway system: nearly all of the workers engaged in the dirty and dangerous job of excavation were foreign-born noncitizens. In a related state case Justice Benjamin Cardozo sustained the statute on the ground that it had a justifiable relationship to the public welfare: "The state in determining what use shall be made of its own moneys, may legitimately consult the welfare of its own citizens rather than that of aliens."[55]

Constitutional law expert Thomas Reed Powell could not accept the view that the state might discriminate as it pleased. Aliens were not public welfare recipients; they were exchanging their labor for wages. In fact, the *Heim* decision's potentially crippling effect on subway construction spurred a strong reaction. Contractor, real estate, and immigrant interests urged the legislature to change the law, and it was quickly amended to permit the employment of aliens if citizens were unavailable.[56]

The First World War and the postwar Red Scare stoked a popular inclination to identify the foreign-born with disloyalty and radicalism. The courts made no distinction between philosophical anarchists and anarchists of the deed when it came to their exclusion from the United States: "mere personal abstention from violence" was not enough. Thirty-six aliens were deported as anarchists from Seattle in 1919, shipped out on what the press called "the Red Ark." Included in their ranks were an American citizen and twenty-seven natives of England, Scotland, Ireland, Denmark, Norway, and Finland; the average residence in the United States of these deportees was more than twelve years. Nebraska, Tennessee, and Washington disqualified aliens from teaching in the public schools. American Fascists tried to take advantage of the prevailing attitude with the claim that by working to rid Italian immigrants of their radical tendencies, they were Americanizing them.[57]

Despite the presumably mollifying effects of immigration restriction, the place of aliens in American life during the 1920s remained contentious and uncertain. New licensing laws required citizenship for at least thirty-three occupations, from running a pool hall to driving a bus. Noncitizens could not hold a municipal job in most cities. Chester, Pennsylvania, touted the slogan: "No aliens in Chester after 1926." Prohibition enforcement also eroded the position of aliens: the courts held violations of the Volstead Act to be "crimes involving moral turpitude," thus subjecting them to deportation.[58]

There were limits on the constraints to which aliens could be subjected. An act calling for their compulsory registration was introduced into Congress in December 1925. Its goals were to curb illegal entry, hasten assimilation, and further the prosecution of criminals and anarchists. The AFL disapproved of the measure as likely to further industrial espionage and strikebreaking, and Walter Lippmann spoke out against it at a January 1926 protest meeting. The bill failed to pass, as did a 1929 attempt to exclude aliens from the count in the (long-delayed) reapportionment of Congress required by the 1920 Census.[59]

No serious obstacles prevented resident aliens from becoming citizens. Between 1929 and 1934 Bureau of Naturalization examiners recommended that 542,996 petitions be granted; the courts accepted 541,868 (99.8 percent). Of 26,402 recommendations for denial, the courts acceded to 20,568 (78 percent). The author of a treatise on aliens' legal disabilities thought it appropriate to describe these as limitations on a status otherwise comparable to that of citizens.[60]

The courts continued to exercise some oversight over expulsion proceedings: resident aliens were entitled to the protections of the First Amendment, and the Fourth Amendment was partially applicable in deportation cases. In 1915 the Supreme Court held that the commissioner of immigration could not exclude an immigrant on the ground that he might become a public charge because of the depressed state of the labor market at his point of debarkation. "It would be an amazing claim of power," said Holmes, "if commissioners decided not to admit aliens because the labor market of the United States was overstocked."[61]

But aliens who entered illegally could be held without a warrant; they were not entitled to counsel in expulsion or exclusion hearings; there were no legal rules of evidence or statutory requirement for counsel. Congress in 1917 empowered the secretary of labor to issue deportation warrants and make final decisions. Out of this came the Labor Department's Board of Review, a quasi-judicial administrative body which in 1927–28 heard 38,258 cases involving 71,698 aliens.[62]

The Immigration Service served in effect as detective, policeman, prosecutor, and judge, and was not reluctant to act on the basis of prevailing racial, political, and personality stereotypes. Deportations rose from 2,762 in 1920 to 19,426 in 1932, at times occurring ten to twenty-five years after entry. Officials directed their attention to those "likely to become a public charge," or with "criminal tendencies" or a "weak moral nature"—"words," as one observer said, "of indefinite meaning and still more indefinite application."[63]

Hostility to aliens picked up again with the depression, stimulated by the competition for work. Proposals for their registration reappeared in Congress. The American Civil Liberties Union opposed this, though it proposed that border patrols be strengthened to keep illegal immigrants out. Hoover's secretary of labor William N. Doak conducted a few Palmer-like raids on alien radicals, and justified a campaign against "illegal invaders" as a form of unemployment relief. When it was pointed out to him that the United States traditionally had been a haven for political refugees, he replied: "Yes, and we've been reaping the harvest ever since."[64]

It became common for the auto industry, railroads, and public utilities to refuse to hire aliens. About thirty-five unions with half a million members did not require citizenship in 1931, but fifteen unions with 1.5 million members did. A Detroit Common Council resolution in February 1930 ordered the firing of all noncitizens who held city jobs. Some businesses also adopted this practice: employees got slips telling them that they had been "discharged to make jobs for American citizens." The Detroit Federation of Labor was thought to be behind this move, which led to a large increase in naturalization applications. Michigan's Spolansky Act of 1931 called for the registration, photographing, and fingerprinting of aliens and the deportation of "undesirables." Despite massive protests from organizations representing the foreign-born, and the state attorney general's view that the law was unconstitutional, Governor Wilber M. Brucker signed it.[65]

The ambiguous place that the foreign-born occupied in early twentieth-century American public life figured in two new—and antipodal—social policies: Americanization, an effort to assimilate newcomers to the dominant culture; and a continuing attempt to set Asian immigrant aliens apart on grounds of race.

The Americanization movement was strongly rooted in the social reform impulse of the Progressive years. *Outlook* in 1901 pointed to the appearance of two autobiographies, Jacob Riis's *Making of an*

American and Booker T. Washington's *Up from Slavery*, as expressions of a highly desirable process of cultural assimilation to an American norm; and in the same year the *Independent* welcomed the inflow of immigrants into the anthracite miners' union as "A Factor of Americanization."[66]

Reformers worried about the distribution, protection, and education of immigrants. The Dillingham Commission was criticized for failing to discuss the assimilation of immigrants after they arrived in the United States. The YMCA instituted a program of Americanization which combined instruction in English with an ideological mix of patriotism, industrial efficiency, and Christian manhood. Los Angeles Americanization teachers and naturalization officers agreed in 1914 on a "diploma method of naturalization," in which a diploma earned for courses in English and citizenship qualified an alien for citizenship.[67]

World War I strengthened the case for Americanization. "Preparedness" took on a civic as well as a military meaning: educating new immigrants in American values was as pressing a need as mobilizing the nation's armed forces. The lesson of the war was that a homogeneous population made for a strong state, a heterogeneous population made for a weak one. But citizenship alone was not enough: "Naturalization should be the outward and visible sign of an inward and spiritual transformation—not merely a vaccination-mark to be carried by the wearer as proof of his immunity from foreign military service," wrote one observer. The *North American Review* thought it "high time for us to require that aliens coming hither to live shall become Americans," and suggested that new immigration from a country be based on the percentage of earlier arrivals who became citizens.[68]

But defining an "American" was by no means easy. In 1916 the *American Journal of Sociology* asked 250 prominent citizens "What Is Americanism?" The answers, thought the conservative novelist Agnes Repplier, showed how little cohesion or solidarity existed in the nation's polyglot population. W. E. B. Du Bois, she indignantly observed, defined Americanism as the abolition of the color line, Eugene V. Debs as the elimination of privately owned industry.[69]

A febrile mix of patriotism and socioeconomic conservatism fueled the wartime Americanization movement. Programs (soon vigorously at war with one another) were set up in the federal government's Bureaus of Naturalization and Education. More than thirty states undertook Americanization efforts, as did hundreds of companies, thousands of school boards, unions, YMCAs, the DAR, and the American Legion—some fifty thousand organizations in all, by one estimate.[70]

In 1917 the Providence, Rhode Island, firm of Browne and Sharpe found that 1,312 of its 6,000 workers were not citizens. Classes in English and civics were offered, and a letter from the company asking the noncitizens why they had not taken out their first papers induced all but 206 of them to do so. The public schools of Rochester, New York, became an "Americanization factory," dedicated to turning immigrants into English-speaking citizens. A government-created National Americanization Committee, dominated by business interests, sought (with no evident success) to coordinate this massive national effort.[71]

This was quite different from the wartime repression of aliens in Europe. The British sought not to lessen but to deepen the gulf separating enemy aliens from the rest of the population. When the Allies protested the use of German-Americans for Red Cross and other volunteer work at the front before America's entry into the war, Theodore Roosevelt and the Department of State defended the policy. Revealing, too, was a May 1918 amendment of the Naturalization Law, which provided for the automatic naturalization of aliens serving in the armed forces.[72]

Cultural pluralism, like the quest for conformity, was an ineluctable American social reality. The philosopher Horace Kallen popularized the term just when the Americanization movement came into its own; and the two ideas had a not always adversarial relationship. Progressive advocates regarded Americanization as a humane, reformist cause. Frances Kellor, the most prominent of them, resisted the movement's more oppressive tendencies: "Americanization is the science of race relations in America, dealing with the assimilation and amalgamation of diverse races in equity into an integral part of its national life." Race fusion, the elimination of ghettoes, fair wages and leisure time for workers: these were among her objectives. The Progressive journalist George Creel, who would head the wartime Committee on Public Information, criticized government policy toward the foreign-born for being too harsh and unfeeling.[73]

It was after the war ended that Americanization took on its most ideologically rigid form. A social psychologist of the time thought that "the war lasted long enough to make America painfully conscious of her peculiar problem of nationalism, but was not of long

enough duration to fuse the divergent ethnic elements permanently."
It turned Americanization into an effort to impose conformity in language, custom, and thought; the policy handmaiden of immigration restriction.[74]

And just as immigration restriction became more explicitly race-minded after the war, so too did Americanization. "We need an American race, an American breed, if we are to have fundamental Americanization," ran a typical plea. At the same time, corporate interest in Americanization declined—in part because as restriction took hold there were fewer and fewer immigrants to Americanize, in part because corporations were more interested in expanding than acculturating the work force. So while Americanization triumphed as an attitude, a mood, it faded as a public policy. Its final stronghold was the public schools, where dull but patriotic civics texts and schoolroom flag salutes held sway.[75]

When it came to considerations of race, policy toward aliens took on its most sinister hue. The American empire—including the Philippines and Puerto Rico—produced by the Spanish-American War energized that concern. Annexation, said one observer, "demands a more searching examination of the powers, the duties, the purposes of our republic as marked by the Constitution than has any question arising since the Civil War." What was the status of the inhabitants of the new territories? Were they citizens? Potential citizens? Wards? Colonial subjects? Traditionalists such as ex-President Benjamin Harrison and Supreme Court Justices Fuller, Harlan, Brewer, and Peckham held to the view that full citizenship followed the flag. Anything less, said Fuller, "substitutes for the present system of republican government, a system of domination over distant provinces in the exercise of unrestricted power." Harlan warned that "a radical and mischievous change in our system of government would be the result. We will . . . pass from the era of constitutional liberty guarded and protected by a written constitution into an era of legislative absolutism."[76]

But a narrow Court majority—Modernists, they were called—thought otherwise. In its Insular Cases decision of 1901, the Supreme Court decided that the people of the newly acquired territories did indeed have, and could be kept in, less than full citizenship. They put forth a new doctrine of "incorporation," in which territories need not be states or its inhabitants full-fledged citizens (although other "fundamental" rights would be guaranteed). This view, associated particularly with Chief Justice Edward D. White (who was "much preoccupied by the danger of racial and social questions of a very perplexing character"), in effect legitimated the position that giving full citizenship to alien races was bad public policy. In ensuing cases a growing Supreme Court majority accepted the incorporation doctrine, making it "sufficiently elastic to permit of a government which, while maintaining the essentials of modern civil liberty, has not attempted to impose upon the new peoples certain ancient Anglo-Saxon institutions [such as voting and jury trials] for which their history had not adapted them."[77]

Asian immigration raised the issue of race and citizenship in an even more direct and sustained manner. Chinese migrants had been excluded since 1882. But a significant illegal flow continued; those already here raised families; and the Japanese continued to immigrate. The effort to restrict the citizenship and other rights of Asian residents was part of the same social policy impulse that endorsed Prohibition and immigration restriction. The same gamy brew of old prejudices and new social science was evident; present, too, was the countering influence of interests and attitudes that supported Asian-Americans, and of legal rules and constitutional constraints.

Anti-Asian sentiment was strongest on the West Coast, but it had become national as well. In the wake of the Geary Law of 1902, which extended Chinese exclusion and tightened the regulation of those already here, large numbers of Chinese in Jacksonville, Philadelphia, and Denver were arrested on suspicion of being illegal aliens. Nearly all of Boston's 250 or so Chinese were taken into custody— and soon discharged, but not without suffering hardship and injuries. The Chinese government responded with a boycott of American goods. *Outlook* criticized "the present harsh, unjust, and unintelligent administration" of the exclusion law; exporters pressured the government to afford greater protection to the Chinese; the Portland, Oregon, chamber of commerce welcomed them as workers. But popular hostility to Asians was very strong; and the general trend of opinion favored constraints on citizenship as well as immigration.[78]

The issue was aggravated by increasing Japanese immigration. About eighty-five thousand Japanese migrants came between 1899 and 1903, 80 percent of them to the mainland, the rest to Hawaii. A demand arose that the Chinese exclusion law be extended to the Japanese. San Francisco's Mayor (and later California Senator) James

D. Phelan and Stanford sociologist Edward A. Ross were strong advocates, as was the state Federation of Labor. Those interested in trade with or missionary work in Japan, organized in the American Asiatic Association, opposed exclusion. So did presidents David Starr Jordan of Stanford and Benjamin Ide Wheeler of the University of California, Harvard's Charles W. Eliot, various chambers of commerce, San Joaquin and Santa Clara Valley fruit growers, and the occasional traditional liberal.[79]

The Russo-Japanese War of 1904 heightened fears of "the yellow peril," and in 1905 the *San Francisco Chronicle* launched a vitriolic campaign against Japanese residents. In October 1906—just before a local election—the San Francisco school board stirred up an international issue by excluding Asian students from white schools. An 1885 state law permitted this; but the action conflicted with an American treaty with Japan, and only a handful of San Francisco's twenty-five thousand schoolchildren were Japanese. Theodore Roosevelt roundly condemned the move in his December 1906 message to Congress, and had a chilly confrontation with the school board. Pressured by the federal government, the board finally backed down. But the flow of Japanese—and the politically attractive cause of restriction—continued. A March 1907 presidential proclamation, conjoined with a "gentlemen's agreement" in which Japan agreed to discourage emigration, effectively stopped the flow of Japanese laborers. And, like the Chinese, those already in the United States were barred from citizenship.

The status of Asians resident in the country remained a contentious issue. Race-based restrictions kept cropping up—and frequently ran into legal or political difficulties. A federal court in 1900 invalidated an attempt by San Francisco's Board of Health, responding to the threat of bubonic plague, to prohibit Chinese and other Asians from leaving the city unless they were inoculated. A proposed Municipal Segregation Bill in 1909, authorizing California municipalities to confine "undesirable, improper and unhealthy persons" to prescribed school districts, was dropped under pressure from President Roosevelt and the governor. Ordinances seeking to restrict or ban the operation of laundries in particular areas of a city—manifestly aimed at Asians—often were struck down by the courts. But not always: the California court in 1909 accepted a Los Angeles ordinance banning laundries from all but seven "industrial districts," unless motorized devices—rarely used by Asians—were employed.[80]

Federal courts often reviewed immigration hearings involving Asian migrants. There was a manifest tension between prevalent racist and restrictionist attitudes on the one hand and race-blind legal rules and the judges' desire to assert their prerogatives against the immigration bureaucracy on the other. When the Supreme Court in U.S. v. Tu Joy (1905) refused to reverse the decision of immigration officers to deny admission to a Japanese immigrant, it was criticized for implicitly favoring illiterate blacks over educated Japanese. A federal judge wryly observed: "It may be that a highly educated and cultured Japanese or Chinese or Malay or Siamese is better calculated to make a useful and desirable citizen than a savage from the Guinea coast, but it is not for the courts to give effect to sound reasoning." In 1908 the Court reserved to itself the power to decide whether or not a hearing was unfair.[81]

The most substantial controversy over the rights of Asians concerned land ownership in the West. Here two well-defined jurisdictions clashed sharply: the states' police power over the public welfare and federal authority in international affairs. But the issue also took on an edge because it pitted a well-established legal commitment to the sanctity of property and freedom of contract against a newly legitimized racism.[82]

California struck out against Japanese land ownership. It was widely believed that resident Japanese were buying up large amounts of choice farmland. Although a 1911 treaty gave equal residency, trading, manufacturing, and land-leasing rights to citizens of the two nations, anti-Japanese sentiment grew, vigorously stoked by Progressive Governor Hiram Johnson. In 1913 the state legislature considered the Webb-Heney Alien Land Law, which prohibited aliens who were not (or could not be) citizens from owning land. Representatives from California districts where foreign capital was invested (a British syndicate linked with the Union Oil Company, for example) opposed the bill. So did the organizers of the Panama-Pacific Exposition, and even the Asiatic Exclusion League, which feared that the law would sidetrack its campaign for full exclusion of Japanese immigrants.[83]

The Japanese government protested, pleading the 1911 treaty, and the federal government sought to intervene as it had over the San Francisco school exclusion. President Wilson opposed the bill; former President Taft warned against so direct an insult to the Japanese and assault on the national treaty power; Secretary of State William Jennings Bryan implóred the legislature to restrain itself. Undeterred, the legislature passed the bill and Governor Johnson (after some hesitation) signed it.[84]

Like the literacy test for immigrants, the law failed to achieve its purpose. California Japanese owned outright only 26,707 acres of farmland in 1913 and 29,105 in 1918; but they leased another third of a million acres, and frequently sequestered holdings in land corporations with American citizens (often their native-born children) holding the majority of the stock. This and the generally heightened racial consciousness and anti-immigration sentiment in the wake of the First World War ignited demands for more restrictive legislation. Congress's Committee on Immigration and Naturalization held Pacific Coast hearings in the summer of 1920, and the California State Board of Control released a fear-ridden 250-page report, "California and the Oriental."

What to do? The 1920 Democratic and Republican state conventions called for a constitutional amendment denying citizenship to American-born children of Japanese ancestry. In the 1920 election presidential candidates James M. Cox and Harding indirectly appealed to anti-Japanese sentiment in California, and California voters by three-to-one margins (to the disappointment of some: an even larger majority had been widely anticipated) supported a referendum provision that called for a strengthened alien land law and a poll tax on male aliens. The usual suspects—the American Legion, much of the press (though Henry Ford's *Dearborn Independent* defended the Japanese)—vigorously supported these proposals. So did the *New Republic,* which warned against "the complete Orientalization of the Pacific states" and argued that the nation should be free to determine who owned its agricultural lands.[85]

A poll tax was quickly passed—and as expeditiously struck down by the state supreme court. And while six western states adopted anti-alien laws in 1921, five rejected them, leading some to conclude that anti-Japanese antipathy was fading. "Immigration restriction means efficiency; discriminations result only in friction," warned one observer. Another held that "the racial discrimination in our naturalization law is entirely out of harmony with the general tenor of our law as a whole." The Supreme Court in 1924 decided that a Seattle ordinance limiting pawnbroking to citizens violated the 1911 treaty with Japan. And a federal circuit court struck down a Hawaii statute restricting sessions in Japanese-language schools to an hour a day and regulating their texts and curriculum. "You cannot make good citizens by oppression," the judge warned.[86]

But in Ozawa v. U.S. (1922) the Supreme Court upheld the exclusion of a foreign-born Japanese from eligibility for American citizenship. The plaintiff had come to the United States as a boy, and studied for three years at the University of California. Justice George Sutherland insisted that the denial did not involve a judgment of racial superiority or inferiority. But he noted that the great majority of Americans wanted the yellow and brown races excluded from the country, and that identifying whites as Caucasians established "a zone of more or less debatable ground . . . [inside] of which, upon the one hand, are those clearly eligible, and outside of which, upon the other hand, are those clearly ineligible for citizenship."[87]

When the first California Alien Land Law was passed in 1913, one authority thought that it was sure to fall if the Court delved into its real, racial purpose: "To hold otherwise would mean a new departure for the Supreme Court and the way would then be opened up for making classifications based upon the possession, or lack of possession, of other political privileges." But in 1923 the Court upheld the California and Washington alien land laws as proper exercises of the police power. Much was made of the lesser social stake of persons who could not become citizens, and of the danger (in the words of the lower court) that "if one incapable of citizenship may lease or own real estate, it is within the realm of possibility that every foot of land within the state may pass to the ownership or possession of non-citizens." Constitutional law expert Thomas Reed Powell caustically observed: "One who is curious about constitutional issues might well wish to speculate on the hypothetical question whether the police power of the state extends to excluding a class from some pursuit for the reason that in that particular calling they have shown themselves unusually efficient."[88]

That efficiency, and the ongoing legal problem of enforcing severe constraints on the ownership, use, and disposition of property, reduced the effect of the land laws. California's attorney general ordered a crackdown on violators in 1925. But a 1930 review of the Washington state statute concluded: "Through technicalities and construction the courts have to a large extent 'taken the teeth out of the act.'" In any event, the impact of the law faded as native-born children of Japanese ancestry grew in numbers. The impact of anti-Japanese legislation was lessened, too, by the play of economic interest. Thus, when the California senate passed a law barring Japanese fishermen from the state's coastal waters, cannery interests fearful of its effect on their business saw to it that the bill was killed in the assembly.[89]

The high racial consciousness of the 1920s also fueled legal conflict over the meaning of the "free white persons" clause in the 1790 naturalization law. Was "white" synonymous with "Caucasian"? If so, were Mediterranean peoples under the ban? Surely the drafters of the original act did not have such persons in mind; but then surely the 1907 codification of the law *must* have had them in mind. Were high-caste Hindus—ethnologically speaking, quintessential Aryans—eligible for citizenship? And what about those of mixed European and Asian origins?

The courts frequently wrestled with these questions. A New York judge decided in 1909 that a petitioner with an English father and a half-Chinese, half-Japanese mother was not sufficiently white to be a citizen. In U.S. v. Thind (1923) the Supreme Court applied the general ban on Asians to a high-caste Hindu. A Federal district judge had held that he was eligible for citizenship as a Caucasian. But the high court noted that modern science rejected the concept of Aryan or Caucasian races, and adhered to the view that Hindus were not included in the original conception of potential citizens. Only European immigrants familiar to Americans of 1790 were eligible.[90]

A 1934 opinion by Benjamin Cardozo explained further: "'White persons' within the meaning of the statute are members of the Caucasian race, as 'Caucasian' is defined in the understanding of the mass of men." Africans were eligible for citizenship under the 1870 naturalization law, but those of mixed black and other nonwhite ancestry were subject, as one authority put it, to "the ordinary rules concerning half-breeds." By the mid-1930s the courts had compiled a long (but hardly self-explanatory) list of who was in and who was out. Afghans, Arabians, Burmese, Chinese, Filipinos, 'half-breeds,' Hindus, Japanese, and Koreans were excluded; Armenians, Syrians, and other Mediterranean peoples were not.[91]

This line of decision making had limited practical effect. There were 3,357,528 naturalization petitions recorded between 1913 and 1934; 3,073,116 were granted and 284,412 denied—206 of these on racial grounds. Latin American migrants were exempt from the restriction laws, and by 1930 about 1.5 million first- and second-generation Mexicans were living in the country (over the objections of the AFL, the American Legion, the Ku Klux Klan, and southwestern state legislatures).[92]

Still, it was estimated in 1923 that almost a quarter of a million American residents were racially ineligible for naturalization. And many faced other restrictions. By 1932, thirteen states limited the freedom of Filipinos to marry partners of other races. A Los Angeles superior court judge, voiding such a marriage in 1925, declared: "I am quite satisfied in my own mind . . . that the Filipino is a Malay and that the Malay is a Mongolian"—though another judge held otherwise.[93]

In April 1933 Franklin D. Roosevelt asked the attorney general and the secretaries of state and labor to review the nation's nationality laws. Their proposals, modified and enacted by Congress as the Citizenship Act of 1934, cleared away some of the anomalies regarding the citizenship status of native-born children of alien parents, and put wives more nearly on a plane of equality with their husbands. But immigration law and policy remained for decades to come "the realm in which government authority is at the zenith and individual entitlement is at the nadir." Only with the Immigration Reform Act of 1965 was the national origins system abandoned; and only gradually did the legal vulnerability of aliens begin to be alleviated.[94]

8 · Blacks and Whites

A heightened race consciousness was one of the hallmarks of the turn-of-the-century Western world. Quasi-scientific racial theories fed on and were fed by domestic social tensions, imperialism. Old isms—chauvinism, xenophobia, militarism, anti-Semitism—became more strongly tinged with racial ideology. They came to be distinguishing features of the politics of the European right.

Historians differ over whether this political ideology stemmed primarily from still-dominant elements of the old regime—aristocrats, the officer corps, high bureaucrats—or from other social groups such as an arriviste bourgeoisie, insular peasants, and an insecure lower middle class. What does seem clear is that just as socialism assumed a variety of national forms around the turn of the century, so did race-conscious nationalism. Anti-Semitism and militarism were more conspicuous in German than in British conservatism; the British and German right were more ready than their French counterparts to accept social welfare. This new right could not be ascribed exclusively either to veneration of the past or to an antipathy to modern times: antediluvians found common ground on issues of race and nation with up-to-the-minute advocates of national efficiency.[1]

Progressivism and Race

What relation does early twentieth-century American racial policy bear to this larger context? The segregation of southern blacks was, in some ways, comparable to the situation of the Jews of eastern Europe. But to make the analogy is to suggest its limits. Race relations in America were the product of a distinctive history, and would be subject to the no less unique determinants of early twentieth-century American public policy.

251

It was in the early 1900s that American race relations reached their nadir. The social, political, legal, and (with lynchings and race riots at their height) physical situation of blacks was worse than at any time since the end of Reconstruction. Segregation laws peaked in numbers, breadth, and blatancy. Racist suppositions flourished with only peripheral challenges in both high and popular culture. One instance: students at Mississippi's Southwestern Presbyterian University, 96 percent of them professing Christians and 40 percent preparing for the ministry, were polled in 1908 on their racial views. Overwhelmingly they supported segregation, believed in black racial inferiority, and opposed education and social equality for blacks.[2]

Changing economic and demographic conditions—realignments of black-white settlement in rural areas, an estimated 57 percent increase in black land ownership during the 1890s, the growth of the black population in southern cities—led poor whites and a new breed of southern politicians to a more assertive antiblack politics. Southern respectables accepted greater political repression of blacks as a way of easing social tensions stirred by the depression of the 1890s. A rising black migration, prevalent racial views, and the unease engendered by immigration fed similar (though less widespread and intense) sentiment in the North.[3]

Racism drew on new views of government and race. The belief in social control and state activism associated with Progressivism strengthened policies of racial subordination. Plessy v. Ferguson (1896), in which the Supreme Court upheld segregated public accommodations, was an early instance of Progressive jurisprudence in its reliance on up-to-date social theory and its readiness to accept state regulation. The idea of a regenerated, racially "homogeneous nation" strongly appealed to the reform-minded. Prudential Insurance Company demographer Frederick L. Hoffman and the novelist-historian Edward Eggleston believed that American blacks were doomed to disappear because of their manifest unfitness to compete with whites—a dénouement that Eggleston with chilling prescience called "the ultimate solution of the American Negro problem."[4]

Southern white Progressives readily supported the prevailing system of segregation and discrimination. Edgar Gardner Murphy, an Alabama minister and child labor reformer, is a conspicuous example. He organized the Southern Society for the Promotion of the Study of Race Cultures and Problems in the South, which held a bellwether (and all-white) conference in Montgomery, Alabama, in 1900. Among the proposals discussed: repealing the Fifteenth Amendment and deporting blacks to the nation's new territories of Puerto Rico and the Philippines.

The Southern Education Board (Murphy was its executive secretary from 1903 to 1908) represented the first important effort by substantial southerners to improve the region's white schools. Its work only widened the gap between white and black education. And the political disenfranchisement of blacks eroded the already minute southern commitment to their schooling. Black voters in Louisiana declined from 130,344 in 1897 to 5,320 in 1900—and New Orleans stopped paying for black education beyond the fifth grade. In 1900 South Carolina devoted one sixth as much money to a black as to a white child's education; in 1915 one twelfth as much. The ratio of black to white school spending per child in North Carolina dropped by 53 percent between 1900 and 1910.[5]

Progressive stress on the need to purify the political process substantially strengthened the turn-of-the-century effort to disenfranchise southern black voters. Exotic schemes appeared in national magazines. One was that respectable whites select slates of black voters chosen for their worth as good citizens. Their right to vote could be revoked for lawlessness or "failure to maintain a high degree of well-ordered citizenship." Another called for separate black and white voting and officeholding, with black representation in the legislature kept to an "acceptable" level by the provision that it reflect the percentage of blacks in school beyond the primary grades. The techniques adopted—voting restrictions aimed at the descendants of slaves, poll taxes, intimidation and violence—were far more extreme than the toughened registration laws of northern ballot reformers. But the goal—that politics be cleansed of a corrupting element—was the same.[6]

One of the few constraints on this process was the fact that many southerners, conservatives and Progressives alike, wanted to exclude poor whites as well. Thus, a Georgia bill requiring an "understanding" of the state constitution in order to vote was criticized for favoring educated blacks over uneducated whites, and the legislature rejected it by a 137–3 margin.[7]

Disenfranchisement was more complicated in the border state of Maryland. That state's 1901 ballot reform law followed a Massachusetts precedent by eliminating straight-ticket voting, requiring that candidates' names be listed in alphabetical order, and removing party symbols from the ballot. Its subtextual purpose was clear: almost half of the state's black voters were illiterate. But the GOP quickly schooled its black voters to recognize the word *Republican* attached to a candidate's name.

Between 1904 and 1910 Maryland Democrats sought three times more to disenfranchise black voters. Republicans, immigrants, and many local reform leaders blocked these efforts. The 1910 law declared that the Fifteenth Amendment was invalid, a proposition that the entire Baltimore press and many conservative Democrats rejected. "It is the ugliest manifestation of the anti-national and anti-liberal spirit that has come to the front in many years," said the *Nation*.[8]

These constraints paled before the larger reality of national support for or acquiescence in southern racial policy. The great twentieth-century black migration to the cities of the North was just getting under way, and new tensions came with it. Blacks in 1908 constituted 1.5 percent of Chicago's population, but were charged with 12 percent of the city's crimes. And in that year whites in Lincoln's home town of Springfield, Illinois (many of them newly arrived from the South), rioted for days, driving some six thousand blacks from their homes. A 1913 examination of race relations in Ohio found segregation and discrimination comparable to that in the South. One example: the state YMCA forced its black affiliate to change its name to the Young Boys' Christian Association.[9]

Northern racial attitudes were affected by new, Progressive views on social policy at large. An English reviewer of Booker T. Washington's *Up from Slavery* found the author's life to be a model of "efficiency"—"a word of the moment." Arguments for social control and a racial policy that transcended sectional differences could count on a sympathetic reception: "the American negro . . . would be the chief beneficiary of greater accord between the white parties to the sectionalism created by his presence."[10]

Much of what passed for the left in early twentieth-century America had little more to offer. The American Federation of Labor shunned biracial unionization: none of the forty-four largest AFL unions accepted black members. In 1902 the Federation abandoned its hollow policy of excluding unions that banned blacks. AFL president Samuel Gompers favored the exclusion (but not the expulsion) of blacks from the Federation's unions. After he gave a notably hostile speech in 1917, a group of Boston blacks found "the greatest enemy of humanity here to be organized labor." The Socialist party was not much better. Party conventions from 1901 to 1919 assiduously avoided the subject of race relations; Socialist leader Victor Berger was hostile to blacks; Eugene Debs held in 1903 that "there is no 'Negro problem' apart from the general labor problem."[11]

The embryonic Democratic liberalism of the time also had little appeal to blacks (though W. E. B. Du Bois's NAACP journal *The Crisis* endorsed Woodrow Wilson for president in 1912); the antipathies of the party's southern white and northern Irish wings were too strong. Wilson's election had devastating consequences for the tenuous black presence in the government work force. Segregation and discrimination now became explicit policy in federal agencies. Wilson assured an angry black delegation that segregation was "for the benefit and the best interests of both races in order to overcome friction."[12]

Republican leaders were only marginally less addicted to segregation. The GOP's post-1896 superiority in the North reduced its need for black voters; its Philadelphia machine sharply cut patronage handouts to black politicians. Theodore Roosevelt did invite Booker T. Washington to lunch in the White House, but the outsized reaction to this act suggests how powerful was the prevailing racism. And Roosevelt's treatment of lynching and race relations in his December 1906 annual message to Congress was caution itself: condemnation of lynching and racial intolerance as threats to social order, coupled with injunctions to blacks to remedy those deficiencies of behavior that fed racial hatred. His summary dismissal of three black army companies because of questionable accusations of rioting in Brownsville, Texas, made it clear that he well knew who voted and who did not. He toyed with, and his successor William Howard Taft openly espoused, a "lily white" southern Republicanism which abandoned black votes to court white southerners. Taft committed himself in October 1909 to a policy of "showing respect for the South by appointing men to federal offices in the South whose appointment would commend themselves in the community where they live."[13]

Former advocates of black political equality subscribed to the view that this was an idea whose time had passed. *Harper's Weekly*, owned now by the Democrat George Harvey, concluded in 1905: "The experience of some thirty-five years has shown that the colored people, considered as a whole, . . . are not qualified to possess the franchise." The president of that one-time abolitionist seedbed Bowdoin College argued that while the South should not withhold the suffrage from responsible members of either race, the North should not grant it to thriftless, irresponsible, and illiterate blacks. With majestic impartiality he blamed miscegenation on "guilty white men and negro women."[14]

Leading Republicans' support for black suffrage was all but gone. Charles Francis Adams declared: "The work done by those who were in political control at the close of our civil war was done in utter ignorance of ethnological law and total disregard of unalterable fact." *Outlook* editor Lyman Abbott called the post–Civil War amendments an "error," a view shared by Yale president Arthur T. Hadley. Elihu Root told the New York Union League Club in 1903 that, given the failure of black suffrage, the future of black citizenship was open to review; and soon after the club tabled a resolution that called on it to support the Fifteenth Amendment. The journalist Ray Stannard Baker saw little difference between the South and the North on the issue of black voting, and thought that if there were more black voters in New York City, it too would have a strong disenfranchisement movement. Harry Smith, the black editor of the *Cleveland Gazette*, was excluded from the all-white Ohio constitutional convention of 1912, and the state's voters rejected the convention's proposal to repeal the "white only" suffrage restrictions in the state constitution.[15]

The courts reinforced the prevailing view. They held that segregation was both constitutional and a reasonable public policy, that the federal government (including the judiciary) had little say over the racial policies of the states, and that the Fifteenth Amendment "really presents no very serious obstacle to the disfranchisement of the entire negro vote." The Fourteenth Amendment, designed to be a strong constitutional guarantor of black rights against the states, was equally useless. The Supreme Court handed down about 525 decisions based on that amendment from 1868 to 1911: only 27 involved black plaintiffs, and 21 of these were decided against them. In sum, "no actual and practical restraint" existed on state discrimination against blacks.[16]

State courts in the North as well as the South subscribed to these views. A New York court in 1900 denied a writ of mandamus to a black woman who wished to prevent the Queens Board of Education from compelling her children to attend an all-black school. Unlike New York, which since the 1890s had permitted segregated schools, New Jersey still forbade them. But when in 1904 the Burlington school authorities transferred all eight of their black students to a separate school (which had no grade appropriate to one of the older children), New Jersey's high court refused to intervene. This was up-to-the-minute jurisprudence, shaped by the racist teachings of the new natural and social sciences, animated by the Progressive inclination to let the legislative and administrative realms of government do their work. A sympathetic observer summed up the state of race law in 1911:

> How far a State may go in the attempt to apply a practical solution to the negro problem . . . remains to be seen. So far they have not been checked by the Federal Government. In the broad day of an enlightened public opinion, world-wide in its reach, it is not probable that backward steps will be taken. New acquisitions from the growing social and behavioral sciences are bringing to us a clearer and a saner point of view than that evolved from the philosophy and theology of the past generation.[17]

Education was at the crux of the Supreme Court's most extreme endorsement of racial segregation. Berea College v. Kentucky (1908) upheld a state law forbidding integrated education in private as well as public schools and colleges. Its rationale was that this matter fell within the state's police and corporate regulatory powers. As a defender of the decision observed: "The public policy of Kentucky is and for a long time has been opposed to the social intimacy of the races." Outraged dissenting Justice John Marshall Harlan clearly saw the larger issue at stake: "Have we become so inoculated with prejudice of race that an American government professedly based on the principles of freedom, and charged with the protection of all citizens alike, can make distinctions between such citizens in the matter of their voluntary meeting for innocent purposes simply because of their respective races?" The *Philadelphia Inquirer* asked: "What American could have dreamed forty years ago that the Supreme Court of the United States would make it illegal to teach colored children and white children under the same roof?"[18]

Alongside this potent amalgam of racism old and new, a different approach gradually won a place of sorts in public life. The years after 1900 saw dramatic growth not only in the intensity but also in the diversity of debate over racial policy. True, Progressivism gave new life to legal segregation. But it reinvigorated the American countertradition of equality before the law as well. While social and cultural pluralism fueled racial animosity, it could (and did) also reinforce policies of tolerance and inclusion. Different voices came to be heard: of disgust with lynchings not only because they were lawless but because they were cruel and degrading; of protest by coalitions of blacks and whites (whose most important voice was the National Association for the Advancement of Colored People, organized in 1909) against the more blatant forms of racism.[19]

The old radical Republican commitment to the ideal of equal citizenship had not entirely disappeared. The economist and businessman Edward Atkinson argued for greater educational opportunity and federally supported land sales to blacks as solutions to the nation's race problem. Andrew Carnegie pointed to black accomplishments in education, religion, farm ownership, savings, and business enterprise. The New York Republican Club's Committee on National Affairs declared in 1908: "We appeal to all American citizens to oppose the rising tide of race discrimination that threatens to overwhelm us. The situation is far worse than it was ten years ago."[20]

British Liberals with some influence in America had a relatively enlightened view of race relations. James Bryce hardly advocated the social or political equality of "the backward races," but he did question the view that race mixing necessarily had bad social effects. He argued that segregation fostered racial hostility and was inconsistent with the principles of democracy. The economist J. A. Hobson took note of the rise of a black middle class for whom the lack of civil equality was degrading, and thought that in the struggle over the enforceability of federal civil rights statutes American democracy itself was on trial.

New voices in American cultural life also widened the range of views regarding race. The Jewish anthropologist Franz Boas led an academic assault on linking race with culture; Jewish lawyer Max J. Kohler attacked race legislation as inconsistent with the spirit of American government. Socialist William English Walling called modern racism an assault on democracy and the brotherhood of man, a product of Europe's reactionary right and radical left.[21]

The ambiguity of the social signals emanating from the conditions of modern American life is evident in the varied readings of the place of blacks in the American military. Their presence at times led to violence and local protests, and to severe reactions. Theodore Roosevelt, as we have seen, discharged several black companies after disturbances in Brownsville. Taft similarly moved a black regiment from San Antonio to the Mexican border (though when he determined later that reports of the troops' misconduct were false, he rescinded the order). But the performance of black troops in the Spanish-American

War won praise from the journalist Oswald Garrison Villard. Another commentator suggested that American race relations would improve if more blacks, Asians, and Indians were brought into the army. And an army officer argued against segregated units: "It is contrary to the spirit of the fourteenth and fifteenth amendments to the Constitution, and to the good sense of the twentieth century."[22]

In 1912 the American Bar Association's executive committee sought to expel three new members who, it emerged, were black. It did so on the ground that the association was primarily a social organization, and that "it has never been contemplated that members of the colored race should become members." William H. Lewis, one of those challenged, was an assistant to Attorney General George Wickersham, who led an attack on the motion to expel. There was a flood of newspaper protest, and the ABA's membership voted against expulsion—but in future, candidates would have to indicate their race.[23]

Even in the South some of the sounds of the time were changing. Ray Stannard Baker's *Following the Color Line* (1908) set a new standard for relatively evenhanded and insightful reporting on the situation of southern blacks. Edgar Gardner Murphy detected a substantial shift going on in race relations by 1909. The migration from the countryside to cities South and North, and abrupt economic changes such as the Texas oil strikes, were making race a more national issue. He thought that hostility would decline as blacks spread over the nation and entered new occupations.

A new type of white southern liberal now appeared, readier to work with blacks and to look hard at racial questions (though not to challenge segregation as such). Under the prodding of Willis D. Weatherford, the YMCA began to take a more enlightened position on race issues. A University Commission on Southern Race Questions gathered in Nashville in May 1912 to condemn lynching and discuss ways of improving race relations, as did the 1913 Atlanta gathering of the Southern Sociological Congress, whose deliberations were published under the title *The Human Way*.[24]

The most striking new element in public discourse on race was a more organized and visible black opinion. The turn-of-the-century curtailment of political and social rights led to the rise of a new generation of black intellectuals and activists. Most of their efforts, such as William Monroe Trotter's militant *Guardian* (1901) or Stanley P. Mitchell's National Liberty party (ca. 1904), which sought to organize border state and northern black voters to oppose southern disenfranchisement, amounted to little. But figures such as Ida B. Wells, who did pioneering work in describing the grim reality of lynching, or the wealthy clubwoman-activist Mary Church Terrell, were new voices in black life, as was W. E. B. Du Bois, whose book *The Souls of Black Folk* (1903), Niagara movement (1905), and work as editor of the NAACP journal *The Crisis* (1909) sharply challenged the more accommodationist approach of Booker T. Washington.

The NAACP, the first significant civil rights organization, was a substantial new voice in racial policy. It became a presence in cases challenging discrimination, and helped to bring about the defeat in 1913 of antimiscegenation laws in ten northern and western states. In other ways, too, black resistance surfaced. When Virginia towns imposed legal segregation on streetcars during the early 1900s and empowered conductors and motormen to bear arms, there were numerous (if brief and unsuccessful) black boycotts of the lines.[25]

A telling comment on the complex relationship between racism and modern society came, appropriately enough, in that powerful new medium, the movies. It was quite in the spirit of the time that *The Birth of a Nation*, the first massively popular motion picture, should have glorified Confederates and portrayed black Reconstruction as an unalleviated evil. But it was revealing, too, that *The Birth of a Nation* touched off the first substantial black protest movement in this century. When it opened in Boston, blacks in the audience threw eggs at the screen and fought with the police. Seven hundred protestors descended on the State House, and the courts ordered the elimination of a scene in which a drunken black man attempts to rape a white girl. Chicago's Republican Mayor William Hale Thompson, sensitive to the growing black vote, refused to allow showings in his city. Tensions were especially high in St. Louis, which was in the throes of a campaign for a residential segregation ordinance. Black leaders sought to have the movie banned; and the city's police department, recreation division, and district attorneys combined to keep it from being shown.[26]

Lynchings were the most outrageous of racist acts. The horrific drama of these events made them grist for the mills of mass journalism. And the fact that they were the most direct challenge imaginable to the ideal of a lawful, ordered society made them the target of choice of conservatives and Progressives alike. The practice was initially regarded as more a product of the general "lynch law" American tradition than of relations between whites and blacks. The 3,317 reported instances between 1882 and 1903 included 2,060 black, 1,199 white, 45 Indian, and 13 Asian victims. It was in the early twentieth century that lynching acquired its distinctive racial connotation. The *Political Science Quarterly* began to report half-yearly on the grim totals: forty-two dead, thirty-four of them black, from November 1899 to May 1900; forty-one blacks, one white from May to November 1900; forty-four blacks (including two women), eight whites, three half-breed Indians, two Italians, and one Chinese from May to November 1901.[27]

Most early twentieth-century lynchings followed timeworn patterns: the sudden flareup of a lynch mob in a small southern town; the terrified victim (a black accused of anything from rape or murder to refusing to leave a community or to abide by a labor contract) hanged, burned, shot, tortured; or a sudden wave of rumors of crime or insurrection sweeping over the countryside, resulting in the killing, beating, and burning of blacks and their property. But there were new developments as well. Lynching spread to the lower North. In 1901 a black prisoner in Leavenworth, Kansas, was burned at the stake before a crowd of a thousand, including many women and children. A black who killed a policeman in Coatesville, Pennsylvania, was dragged from the hospital bound to his bed and burned to death, tortured the while with pitchforks. Nine of the lynchers were indicted, four were acquitted. The chief of police, under indictment for complicity in the lynching, got the Republican nomination for chief constable. The remaining cases were dismissed by a jury in 1912; the presiding judge held the outcome to be a public calamity.

Urban race riots increased as blacks began to move to cities South and North. Major outbreaks in Atlanta (1906) and Springfield, Illinois (1908), made it clear that this was a national phenomenon. The interracial Jack Johnson–Jim Jeffries prizefight on July 5, 1910, led to a number of race riots in the South, and blacks were killed in New York City and Omaha.[28]

It appeared as well that black readiness to meet violence with violence was on the upswing. A black mob in Florida lynched one of their own race for assaulting a black woman. A black college building in Seneca, South Carolina, was dynamited in October 1906; blacks retaliated by setting fire to the town. Blacks were said to have dynamited the store owned by one of the three white merchants in the black town of Taft, Oklahoma, in 1909; placards warned that unless the remaining whites left, they would be killed.[29]

Public opposition to lynching became more vocal, fed in part by humanitarian abhorrence, in part by distaste for actions so threatening to the social fabric and the rule of law. Lynching frequently was ascribed to procedural delays in the stern punishment of those accused of murder or rape. A southern observer (who attributed the prevalence of lynching to French and Spanish influence in his region) concluded, "Lynchings are the acts of a temporary social insanity." The *Nation* called the practice "a profound social disease" likely to spread to the North: "We are in the presence of a new national peril." Theodore Roosevelt warned Congress of this threat to law and order, and Taft told Howard University alumni that "the man who pulls the rope should hang by the rope." Significant, too, was the rise of organized black opposition to this most manifest expression of American racism. The Tuskegee Institute became the major source of lynching statistics, and the NAACP made a federal antilynching law its chief legislative objective.[30]

The courts' response to lynching led to some of the earliest post-1900 judicial constraints on white supremacy—but to secure law and order, not black civil rights. In 1909 the Supreme Court held that Chattanooga, Tennessee, sheriff John F. Shipp and nine other law enforcement officials were guilty of contempt of court for not preventing the lynching of Edward Johnson. The victim had been granted a new trial by the Court, and the Justices were not about to countenance this affront to their authority. (Sheriff Shipp served his brief sentence for contempt, and emerged to a public ovation.)[31]

After 1910 lynchings took on a new character. Their numbers declined to about half of what they had been at the turn of the century. And mob violence more conspicuously included other groups. Among its victims in 1915 were an Italian labor organizer, Joseph Speranzo, in Johnston City, Illinois; a white man accused of murder in Columbia, Mississippi; and most prominently the Jewish businessman Leo Frank in Georgia. At the same time, adverse public reaction appeared to be growing. In the wake of a 1912 lynching in Newark, Ohio, the mayor and sheriff resigned, and a grand jury indicted over forty of the perpetrators. Thirty-five of them were tried for first-degree murder; one was given a life sentence, and the others fifteen to twenty years. The mayor ran for reelection, seeking vindication; he was defeated.

Even in the South, acceptance of lynching slowly but ineluctably waned. The *Political Science Quarterly* reported in 1916 on the growth of serious public concern over lynchings; in 1917 the magazine dropped its annual report on these and other racial incidents. The sheriff of Spartanburg County, South Carolina, in 1915 successfully defended a black prisoner from a lynch mob. Three of its members were tried and sentenced to three-year prison terms (though Governor Cole Blease included them in a general pardon of prisoners a few months later). In 1916 Anthony Crawford, a successful black businessman in Abbeville, South Carolina, was brutally lynched for having had the temerity to get into an argument with a white. Governor Richard Manning and a unanimous state press, fearful of the rising black emigration northward, roundly condemned the crime. Facing a black boycott, the town's merchants blocked the expulsion of Crawford's family, and declared their readiness to call in state and even federal aid to enforce the law.[32]

Less manifestly brutal forms of racial discrimination also began to encounter legal checks. Before politics or public opinion showed any signs of change, courts began, however tentatively, to put some limits on the extent to which the United States would be a legally segregated society. Those limits came not from belief in a race-blind Constitution or from a policy commitment to equal rights. Rather, they derived from the fact that in some contexts legal discrimination and segregation posed a challenge to other public values: the supremacy of the federal Constitution and the judicial system, the sanctity of contract and property rights.

Courts occasionally concluded that the racist appeals of prosecuting attorneys in criminal cases could be grounds for reversal. Mississippi and Florida decisions upheld challenges by black defendants in cases with all-white jury lists. The Supreme Court decided in 1911 that it was proper in the trial of a black accused of killing a white to ask the jurors if they were racially prejudiced. (Justice James McReynolds's bizarre dissent argued that there was no doubt as to the guilt of the accused, and that the possibility of race prejudice was too remote to justify that query.) When in 1915 the Court decided that Leo Frank had not been denied due process even though he was excluded from the courtroom when the jury's verdict was read and sentence pronounced, dissenters Hughes and Holmes warned: "It is our duty . . . to declare lynch law as little valid when practiced by a regularly drawn jury as when administered by one elevated by a mob intent on death."[33]

Troubling, too, were state laws segregating railroad passenger traffic. However desirable a social policy this may have seemed, it raised sticky problems of interference with interstate commerce and the Fourteenth Amendment. Oklahoma, Arkansas, and Texas allowed railroads to provide Pullman sleeping and dining cars for whites only, on the ground that the black demand for these services was too small to be economically viable. A *Harvard Law Review* note argued that to require the lines to provide such services would deprive them of their property without due process. Nevertheless, the Supreme Court in 1914 decided that the acts denied black passengers' constitutional right to equal accommodations.[34]

Even the much-abused and frequently ignored Fifteenth Amendment showed some signs of life. Maryland's 1910 election law and the Oklahoma constitution of that year had grandfather clauses that in effect disenfranchised the descendants of slaves. Oklahoma's state court had no trouble with this policy: "The virtues and intelligence of the ancestor will be imputed to his descendants, just as the iniquity of the fathers may be visited upon the children unto the third and fourth generation." Given the certainty that Congress would pass no corrective legislation, blacks denied the vote appeared to have little recourse: "another illustration," said one observer, "of the practical death of legislation when it ceases to respond to imperative sociological demands." But the civil rights attorney Moorfield Storey, representing the NAACP, led an attack on the Oklahoma provision. And in 1915 a unanimous Supreme Court, in decisions written by its southern Chief Justice, Edward D. White, found that the Oklahoma and Maryland laws violated the Fifteenth Amendment.[35]

This hardly signified the rebirth of black suffrage. Deep South states years before had dropped the grandfather clause in favor of more effective vote-denying devices such as the poll tax. The *Independent* celebrated "a wrong righted at last," but also soothingly observed: "There was never any danger of negro domination in the states in which white men were in a full majority, and in the . . . states in which they were not a majority, superior white intelligence, with kindly consideration, might easily have controlled the situation."[36]

Southern peonage and contract labor laws had their legal problems as well. They imposed fines or jail sentences on laborers who were accused of breaking their labor contracts. The usual penalty was that they work off substantial fines through unpaid labor—labor often enforced by armed employers and local authorities. Although a federal antipeonage statute had been passed in 1867, only at the beginning of the twentieth century did a legal assault begin on this "shadow of slavery." In Clyatt v. United States (1904) the Department of Justice successfully tested the constitutionality of the 1867 law. And in 1908 South Carolina's supreme court concluded that the state contract labor law violated the Thirteenth Amendment.[37]

The Supreme Court in Bailey v. Alabama (1911) voided Alabama's contract labor law on similar grounds. By its very existence the case reflected a gradually changing social sensibility (although its effect on southern peonage was minute). Booker T. Washington was actively involved in bringing it forward; Bailey's wife was able to interest Edward S. Watts, a young white southern attorney, in the case; Fred S. Ball, a prominent Alabama lawyer, joined in.

This was not a civil rights victory. Charles Evans Hughes based his opinion on the fact that Bailey had been punished for the "crime" of quitting his job under Alabama evidence rules that made the breach of contract itself sufficient evidence of criminal intent. The burden of proof that he did not intend to defraud his employer thereby lay with him; and it was this, not the issue of race, that made the law unconstitutional. Holmes dissented on the ground that since the contract itself was legal (and this was not in dispute), it was within the power of the state to impose the "disagreeable consequence" of 116 days in jail.[38]

The most substantial legal restraint on public segregation came in the realm of urban housing. Unsurprisingly, it had little to do with race and much to do with property. The black population in southern and border state cities rapidly grew during the early years of the century. The tension between traditionalism and modernity, between cultural conformity (and, with it, racial segregation) and the realities of modern society, came to be keenly felt. Residential segregation by race was an increasingly common fact of urban life. But not until after 1910 was an attempt made to secure through law and ordinance a formal, explicit system of residential apartheid. Baltimore led the way in May 1911. Atlanta; Greenville, South Carolina; the Virginia cities of Ashland, Roanoke, Richmond, and Portsmouth; Winston-Salem in North Carolina; and Louisville, Kentucky, followed.

These attempts to legalize residential segregation were closely related to the contemporaneous movements for urban zoning and the restriction of saloons and brothels. Like these other examples of Progressive urban reform, racial segregation ordinances were justified on both economic and social policy grounds. Property values declined when blacks moved into white neighborhoods; interracial contact and consequent tension and strife was greater in mixed areas. The Louisville and Baltimore ordinances spoke of "prevent[ing] conflict and ill-feeling between the white and colored races," of "promoting the general welfare of the city."[39]

One advocate warned: "Urban segregation—in most southern cities, at least—is wise . . . but the white people . . . must . . . give [blacks] a fair share of the municipal funds for streets, lights, sewers, schools, and other community activities." Another argued that since segregation already had been approved in public conveyances, schools, and marriages, its extension to residences was both proper and logical. After all, "there is nothing to prevent the improvements in the negro sections from being made the finest in the city." When the Kentucky court upheld Louisville's ordinance, it did so on the basis of the general welfare: "The advance of civilization and the consequent extension of governmental activities along lines having their objective in better living conditions, saner social conditions, and a higher standard of human character has resulted in a gradual lessening of the dominion of the individual over private property and a consequent strengthening of the regulative power of the state."[40]

St. Louis's electorate was given the opportunity in 1916 to vote on a proposed residential segregation ordinance. It forbade additional mixed residence on blocks where 75 percent or more of the inhabitants were of one race, and prohibited blacks from using buildings in white or mixed blocks as churches, dance halls, schools, theaters, or meeting places. This was the product of a six-year effort by small property owners and real estate agents. Unable to get the city council to pass the ordinance, they turned to that favored Progressive device, the popular referendum.

Leading advocates of the initiative and referendum supported the proposal, and the local Republican leadership avoided the issue. Opposition came from a Citizen's Anti–Negro-Segregation Committee, the NAACP, the *St. Louis Post-Dispatch,* the Socialist party, and the foreign press. For days before the vote, black women stood at street corners handing out leaflets attacking the plan as a return to slavery. The *New York World* condemned this attempt "to deprive black men or property, liberty, and hope." But by a three-to-one margin a turnout of 50 percent of the city's registered voters endorsed the proposed ordinance. The *St. Louis Globe-Democrat* deplored the victory of "the overwhelming forces of power, interest, and prejudice," and a black Richmond paper counseled: "The only proper course is to agitate and contend until the latent sense of fair play ever existent in the American people is aroused."[41]

But the legality of this instrument of segregation was in serious dispute. North Carolina's supreme court held that an ordinance forbidding property owners from selling to whomever they wished was unconstitutional. With the assistance of leading white realtors, the NAACP fought Baltimore's pioneering segregation ordinance in the city council and the courts. It had a white home owner in a black neighborhood bring suit because he could not occupy his own property. The state court of appeals had no problem with the power of a city to segregate residence on the basis of race. But it could not accept a law prohibiting "one who was the owner of a dwelling when the ordinance was passed from moving into it, simply because he is a different color from the other persons using that block . . . although he might keep his premises in better sanitary condition and in every way more attractive than others."[42]

The major challenge came in an NAACP-inspired test case against the Louisville ordinance. William Warley, who headed the local NAACP chapter, offered to buy a lot on a "white block" from Charles Buchanan, a white real estate agent. The city's leading law firm was engaged by the NAACP, and Moorfield Storey joined as counsel. Seven amicus briefs were filed for the opposing sides, a reflection of the number of interested groups now being drawn into social issues. Louisville's city attorney accused the NAACP and Storey of advocating miscegenation. But a unanimous Supreme Court held that to block the purchase and sale of property solely on the ground of race "was not a legitimate exercise of the police power." At the same time, the justices carefully defined the point at issue as "the constitutional right of the white man to sell his property to a colored man," not "an attempt to prohibit the amalgamation of the races."[43]

A member of the bar welcomed Buchanan v. Warley as "the most important decision that has been made since the Dred Scott case." It blocked the establishment of a "pale" in the United States. "This . . . decision makes it certain that there will be no 'reservations' for Jews or negroes or Chinese, or any other of our racial groups." (Of course, the somewhat different 'reservations' for Native Americans had long been a fact of American life.) The black press, too, saw it as a victory "for the negro and for democracy." It meant, said the *Harvard Law Review*, "that race segregation by legal compulsion, at least in cities, must be abandoned as a vain effort." At the same time, the *Review* noted, "we are treated to the strange and disquieting spectacle of having the argument against the validity of the ordinance presented only by a white man, while a negro stands forth as its only proponent." The only constitutional right held to have been denied was the taking of property without due process: "The court does not hold that any right of the negro has been violated." The decision properly was called "a marked example of the peculiar American judicial solicitude for property rights."[44]

What is one to make of these early legal constraints on racial segregation and discrimination? It is clear that restrictions on private activities—entering into a labor contract, buying or selling a house, being a passenger on an interstate railroad car—met closer court scrutiny, and were more likely to be struck down, than were constraints on public activities such as voting or going to school. In this first stage of modern American life, the inviolability of private rights provided what few checks there were to the prevailing assumption that segregation was good social policy and discrimination was not cause for public concern. In our own time that policy formula has been reversed: racism has been more susceptible to challenge in the public than in the private realm.

Racism and Normalcy

"If the war has proved anything, it has proved that we have a national will in spite of the variety of our origins": so thought one observer in the early 1920s. But whatever spurs to national unity might have accompanied the American involvement in World War I, its larger consequence for blacks (as for immigrants) was intensified antagonism.[45]

Its most evident expression was the spread of racial violence in the North. By one count there were eighteen major race riots between 1915 and 1919. The great majority occurred in border state and northern cities, where immigrants, rural whites, and southern blacks poured in to work in industries.

East St. Louis, Illinois, a grimy industrial appendage to St. Louis, underwent a bloody explosion of racial violence in July 1917. The official count was that about 40 blacks and 9 whites died; unofficial estimates ran from 125 to 175 men, women, and children. More than 300 houses in which blacks lived were burned, and thousands fled the city. A massive influx of southern blacks and whites, job competition and a severe housing shortage, rampant gambling and prostitution, and growing social and political tension set the scene. The Democrats rode the race issue to success in the 1916 election, accusing the Republicans of colonizing the city with new black voters. Woodrow Wilson's attorney general, Thomas W. Gregory, fed the flames by staging a Justice Department investigation of black "colonization." While the northern press strongly condemned the riot, the administration refused to intervene, and it was left to Congress to institute its own investigation.[46]

A new wave of outbursts came after the war in 1919, most notably in Chicago and Washington, D.C. Blacks poured into Chicago in massive numbers during the war decade; and in familiar fashion tensions fed on compacted housing, the competition for jobs, and sensational newspaper accounts of black crime. Republican Mayor William Hale Thompson relied heavily on black voters, and two blacks were on the city council by 1919. But negrophobia was rampant: many whites called for Jim Crow streetcars on the South Side. The climax to an escalating series of interracial conflicts came when a mob of ten thousand whites swept through black areas; five thousand blacks were burned out of their homes. The Washington riot stemmed from similar demographic trends, as well as a widespread white perception that black veterans were hostile to the established racial order.[47]

Old animosities and new conditions were evident in Omaha as well. Two blacks were arrested for assaults on white women. The recently deposed political machine encouraged sensational newspaper reportage, and a mob lynched one of the prisoners, dragged his body through the streets, and almost lynched the mayor (whose law firm had represented the defendants). Federal troops under General Leonard Wood (who wanted to close down the press for inciting to riot) took over the city and quickly restored order.

In 1921 a Tulsa, Oklahoma, black youth was imprisoned on the shaky testimony of a white girl. The rumor that the accused was about to be lynched brought a black crowd to the jail to protect him. Blacks and whites confronted each other, and a pitched battle ensued. A white mob ravaged the black section of the city, destroying over a thousand homes; estimates of the dead ranged from 27 to 250. More than six thousand blacks were temporarily interned in the wake of the riot, and a new fire ordinance (later found to be unconstitutional) prohibited the building of black churches and other community structures.[48]

These riots resonated all too familiarly with past American experience. But more was involved than the classic scenario of a southern lynching. They were communal eruptions, the products of accumulating social and economic tensions, not just spastic defenses of traditional racial mores. Nor were blacks merely passive (though they were overwhelmingly the more numerous) victims. The Chicago riot began with black assaults on whites triggered by a (false) rumor of a black youth having been killed on a Chicago beach; the Washington disturbance began as a series of conflicts between armed black and white war veterans. It might well have seemed that the stage was set for an escalating politics of race, and of black-white conflicts in American cities, not unlike the conflict between right and left in postwar Germany. The *New York World* called the Washington outburst "a warning to all Americans that their race riots hereafter are going to be race wars."[49]

But the racial scenario turned out to be more complex and equivocal than that. Race relations during the 1920s saw neither the decline of discrimination implicit in late Progressive rhetoric nor the descent into continuous race war threatened by the riots of 1919. The postwar milieu that fed racial tension and violence included as well a concern for law and order, and even a sentiment for racial amity and justice, that worked against race riots as a way of American life.

This may be seen in the reaction to the Chicago riot. A state Committee on Race Relations with six black and six white members looked into its causes. The committee's report broke new ground by taking the views of blacks into account and responding sympathetically to black grievances. Here and elsewhere more attention was paid to the larger social sources of race conflict: the black migration northward, inadequate housing and jobs, the effect of the overseas experience on black veterans, a new racial pride. The mainstream sociologist Franklin H. Giddings patronizingly argued for equal opportunity and civility: "The negro responds to manners more readily than to orders." The Democratic *New York World* sharply attacked lynching and race riots, and was congratulated for this by the Republican *Tribune* and *Sun*.[50]

A large black influx into the steel mills of Johnstown, Pennsylvania, led to a 1923 race riot in which three white policemen were killed. The mayor ordered all blacks resident in the city for less than seven years to move out, "for their own safety and the safety of the public." Mexican workers, he suggested, should leave as well: with their dark complexions they ran the risk of being mistaken for blacks. He wanted also to ban black and Mexican migration to the city, to prohibit blacks from holding meetings or social functions, and to require that visitors to the city register with and report weekly to the police. The reaction was immediate and overwhelming. Newspapers North and South lambasted the mayor; the Mexican Embassy demanded an explanation from the Department of State; Pennsylvania's Governor Gifford Pinchot assured the NAACP that the Commonwealth would protect the constitutional rights of Johnstown's black citizens. And the mayor lost the next primary election.[51]

Racial violence continued to flourish—and to evoke growing regional and national indignation. A rash of lynchings—seventeen from June 1917 to June 1918—put Texas second only to Georgia in that category. Even Woodrow Wilson found it necessary to issue a statement that this was inappropriate conduct in the midst of a war to make the world safe for democracy. The *San Antonio Express* took more forceful action. It launched a campaign for an antilynching law, and the newspaper's stockholders voted a $100,000 fund to suppress lynching and a $1,000 reward for a conviction in the lynching of a black ($500 if the victim was white).[52]

A number of postwar southern political leaders took a relatively moderate stance on race relations, often because the scale of the black outmigration raised fears of a rural labor shortage. With much press and public support, North Carolina's Governor Cameron Morrison adopted the policy of sending state troops into an area at the first sign of racial violence. In February 1920 Kentucky's chief executive, Edwin P. Morrow, ordered the state militia into Lexington to stop the attempted lynching of a black held for the murder of a twelve-year-old white schoolgirl. The city was put under martial law, and the lynch mob was dispersed after six of its members were killed and twenty wounded. Newspapers in Kentucky and other southern states supported the governor's action.[53]

In response to the steadily increasing outmigration of blacks from his state, Mississippi's Governor Henry L. Whitfield spoke of the need to foster their happiness and prosperity. Prominent blacks appeared before the state legislature to call their attention to such causes of the migration as the fact that the state had one thousand white high schools and not a single black one. Governor Hugh M. Dorsey of Georgia in 1921 published a pamphlet, "The Negro in Georgia," which condemned peonage and lynching, and called for a church campaign against these evils, for compulsory education for children of both races, and for the organization of (racially separate) state committees on race relations.[54]

In general, though, like so many other realms of social policy, race relations during the 1920s was in a sort of limbo: digesting, as it were, the institutional and intellectual ferment of the Progressive years, responding to a fast-changing economy and society not with fresh approaches but with a tense, uneasy standoff between old beliefs and new ideas.

Changes were more apparent in private than in public life. The scientific basis of racism continued to lose its authority in intellectual and academic circles, and the separation of race from culture had an ever-firmer hold in the social sciences. Magazines and the press, thought one observer, were taking an increasingly benign position on racial topics. A number of important northern newspapers—the *Chicago Tribune*, the *New York Evening Post*, the *New York World*, the *St. Louis Post-Dispatch*, the *Baltimore Sun*—were relatively sensitive to the issue, and frequently compared the South's readiness to enforce the Eighteenth Amendment with its reluctance to enforce the Fourteenth and Fifteenth Amendments. When a study of race relations in Columbus, Ohio, showed how disproportionate an amount of space in the city's leading newspapers was being devoted to black crime and vice, they pledged to be fairer and to omit "Negro" and "colored" from their headlines. Southern university–sponsored magazines such as *Social Forces*, the *South Atlantic Quarterly*, and the *Quarterly Review* took a relatively liberal position on many racial issues, as did a scattering of southern newspapers: the *Raleigh News and Observer* (a pioneer in capitalizing "Negro"); Richmond's *News Leader* and *Times Dispatch*; Louis Jaffe's *Norfolk Pilot*. It was a measure of changing attitudes that the 1928–1931 volume of the *International Index to Periodicals* informed its readers: "Bigotry. See Toleration."[55]

The YMCA fostered the formation of Interracial Commissions in places such as the troubled industrial town of Gary, Indiana, and 63 of Kentucky's 120 counties. They studied housing, education, medical care, and other social determinants of race relations. Racial tensions in the South led to the formation of the Commission on Interracial Cooperation, which, under the direction of Will Alexander, did pioneering work in getting white and black community leaders to work together.

There were stirrings of concern over black education and welfare. Three states in the early 1920s appointed officials charged with improving black schooling; the welfare boards of North Carolina and Georgia created Departments of Negro welfare. Spurred by grants from northern philanthropic foundations, southern states substantially increased their expenditure for this purpose, and hundreds of new country training and high schools were built.[56]

For all this, the politics of race changed at a glacial rate, if at all. The return of the Republicans to national office in 1921 had little effect on national race policy. President Warren Harding's first annual message to Congress called for a national race commission, an idea that Oswald Garrison Villard had floated before a nonresponsive Wilson administration in 1913. And he appointed a black New Orleans controller of customs, the first federal appointment of a black official since Theodore Roosevelt's time. An antilynching bill passed the Republican-controlled House by a two-to-one margin in 1922, but Senate southern Democrats killed the measure, and even this minimal reform—the chief legislative goal of the NAACP—would be unattainable for decades to come.[57]

Harding gave a widely noted—and strikingly equivocal—address on racial policy in Birmingham, Alabama, in 1921. To a massive (and massively segregated) audience—ten thousand blacks on one side, twenty thousand whites on the other—he called for equal economic opportunity and for political equality of a sort: "Let the black man vote when he is fit to vote; prohibit the white man voting when he is unfit to vote." Harding told the whites in his audience: "Whether you like it or not, unless our democracy is a lie, you must stand for that equality." At the same time, he found nothing wrong with "absolute divergence in things social and racial," for this was "not a question of social equality, but a question of recognizing a fundamental, eternal and inescapable difference." Unreconstructed southerners criticized even this halfhearted gesture. More sophisticated southerners—and northern liberals—recognized it for what it was: a Republican appeal to the region's whites that confirmed the social reality of racial segregation.[58]

Given the range and variety of racial change in the 1920s, from the northward migration of southern blacks to growing white acceptance of jazz and other forms of black cultural expression, the lack of a political, governmental, or legal response is striking. Calvin Coolidge did speak of blacks' entitlement to full political rights. But if anything he was even less interested in his party's appeal to blacks than his predecessor, Harding. The GOP's detachment from now all but disenfranchised southern blacks continued. And apart from an occasional local politician such as Chicago's Mayor Thompson, little effort was made to appeal to the growing black population of the North. There were sixty-two black delegates to the 1912 Republican convention, thirty-two in 1924.[59]

Herbert Hoover assiduously (and successfully) sought white southern votes in his 1928 campaign against Al Smith. In doing so he further distanced himself from black support. His secretary issued a public denial that the candidate had danced with a black woman while on a flood relief visit to Mississippi. After Hoover became president, there was much noise in the South over the fact that Oscar DePriest of Chicago, the first black congressman since Reconstruction, had been invited to a White House tea. DePriest himself sought to be reassuring: "There can be no social equality question as between races. Social equality is all a matter of individual taste." The report of Hoover's Research Committee on Social Trends expected the problems of racial and nationality groups to decline in importance.[60]

There were some portents of the massive shift of blacks from Republican to Democratic party allegiance that was to come in the 1930s. Blacks in Democratic-dominated cities such as New York, Baltimore, and Kansas City began to be drawn to the majority party, just as they stayed with the regnant Republicans in Chicago and Philadelphia. Democrats expected a substantial increase of black support in Indiana and Ohio in 1924 because of the Klan's close ties with the GOP. And in that year a black Democratic candidate ran for a Chicago seat in Congress.[61]

In 1928 the Democrats made their strongest effort so far to reach out to black voters in the North. But the pressures working against a national party commitment were overpowering. When W. E. B. Du Bois observed that "in all Gov. Smith's long carer he has sedulously avoided recognizing negroes in any way," this was picked up by pro–Al Smith southern newspapers as an argument in favor of the Democratic candidate. An anti-Smith circular showed Oliver Q. Morton, New York's black civil service commissioner, dictating to a white stenographer.[62]

Most Democratic leaders concentrated on maintaining their core coalition of white southerners and northern immigrants, no easy matter in the xenophobic, group-conscious 1920s. Indeed, the exclusion of blacks appears to have been one of the ways in which the party's uneasy interregional coalition was maintained. Thus it was a Democratic gerrymander that assured the defeat of the last black member of Baltimore's city council in 1931; it remained all white until 1955. Even Robert La Follette's Progressive party of 1924, the most substantial liberal-left political effort of the decade, was subject to these pressures. Black liberals were invited to the party's July convention, which was stirred by the speech of an unofficial black delegate. A Negro Division worked in La Follette's campaign, but its platform made no reference to racial issues, and he got few black votes. One problem was that the movement's core labor supporters, the Railroad Brotherhoods and the International Association of Machinists, had strong antiblack traditions.[63]

Race policy on the state and local level was comparably unchanged in attitude and practice. Little if any Jim Crow legislation was repealed. Thus in 1927, twenty-nine states had laws prohibiting racial intermarriage; the nineteen that did not had black populations of 5 percent or less. Resistance to change was particularly evident in the realm of education. Two thirds of the students in the Gary, Indiana, high school went out on strike in 1927 to protest the presence of twenty-four black classmates, assigned there during the construction of an all-black secondary school. The authorities agreed to transfer twenty-one of the students to another, presumably more complaisant school, an action that the *Chicago Tribune* and other newspapers criticized as a surrender to prejudice. The Indiana Supreme Court held that it was proper to construct a separate black high school unless the state legislature specifically forbade it, for this involved "questions of domestic policy which are within the legislature's discretion and control."[64]

Florida, Tennessee, and Kentucky laws made it a penal offense for teachers and pupils to be of different races (or, if so, to occupy the same building in private schools). These were probably unconstitutional, thought one observer in 1933, but they had not yet been challenged. Only one in three federal grants of education aid to states specified fair distribution to both races (Mississippi, South Carolina, and Florida were required to give half of their grants to blacks). And there was little or no court oversight of the distribution of education funds by state officials.[65]

Given the judicial tendency of the 1920s to frown on government interference with private activities, one might have expected to see an increase in court restraints on officially sanctioned segregation and discrimination. But just as changes in black demography and American culture failed to have a discernible effect on the politics of race relations, so too did the law reflect the received wisdom that segregation was proper public policy, and that discrimination was perhaps regrettable but of no great moment.

The Supreme Court continued to show its displeasure with gross denials of justice—but, as before, more because the rule of law had been violated than because civil rights were being denied. Five blacks were convicted of murder in an Elaine, Arkansas, race riot by an all-white jury (who spent five minutes deliberating). They did so after a mob-dominated forty-five-minute trial, on the basis of testimony widely thought to have been extracted by torture. A majority of the Court ordered a new trial. The ever-egregious Justice McReynolds found cause to dissent on the ground of the need to sustain law enforcement: "The delays incident to enforcement of our criminal laws have become a national scandal."[66]

At the same time, the Court continued to uphold local segregation. Kentucky was permitted to require Jim Crow cars on interurban trolleys even though the cars crossed the state line into Ohio. The constitutional lawyer Thomas Reed Powell coldly observed of this decision: "It is difficult to believe that the tolerance of the majority was unaffected by tenderness towards some strongly-held sentiments." He thought it unlikely that this lenience would extend to other, non-racial forms of state interference with interstate traffic.[67]

In another instance of the Court's solicitude for local custom, Chief Justice Taft held that a native-born child of Chinese ancestry was not denied equal protection by being assigned to a black rather than a white school in Mississippi. He decided that the state's constitutional distinction between the "white and colored races" separated the "pure white or Caucasian race" from all others, brown, black, yellow, or red. Segregated schools, one authority explained, "do not rest upon any theory of racial inferiority or superiority, but upon the ground that the separate schools are necessary and desirable to maintain wholesome social relations between the races."[68]

Housing continued to be the primary racial battleground in a time of growing black geographic and social mobility. The Supreme Court's 1918 Buchanan v. Warley decision put a stop to municipal segregation ordinances. But the rise of comprehensive urban zoning led Robert Whitten of Cincinnati, the nation's leading expert on the subject, to reopen the issue. He proposed a comprehensive zoning plan for Atlanta which subdivided residential areas into three racial districts:

white, black, and undetermined. The only opposition in public hearings came from realtors whose interests were threatened, and from a judge who called it "monstrous and unsound in principle." Georgia's legislature gave Atlanta the power to segregate by race; but *Buchanan* was an obstacle that could not be surmounted, and the courts struck it down.[69]

There was another, less vulnerable instrument of segregation: restrictive covenants that put constraints on the sale or use of property. Only rarely did they come under judicial review before the 1920s, and then with mixed results. Virginia's court in 1908 allowed the sale of an amusement park to a black-owned company despite a covenant restriction, on the ground that a corporation had no race. But the Louisiana court in 1915 upheld a covenant that prohibited the sale of a property to blacks for twenty-five years.[70]

Restrictive covenants, and court challenges, rapidly increased in the wake of Buchanan v. Warley. The prevailing belief that racial segregation was socially desirable might have been expected to foster judicial acceptance of these private constraints. After all, for years the courts had allowed a variety of limits on the disposal of property. But there was also a substantial countertradition of support for the freedom to sell property as one chose, a tradition in consonance with the economic views of the judiciary in the 1920s. The tension between these social attitudes was nicely displayed in two California Supreme Court decisions: one in July 1919 holding a racial covenant void because it restricted the free alienation of realty; another in December 1919 holding a similar prohibition valid because it affected not the sale but the use of the property.[71]

In general, the courts accepted restrictive covenants as both constitutional and socially desirable. The rapid and widespread adoption of urban zoning, endorsed by the Supreme Court in Euclid v. Ambler (1926), added weight to the view that a sorting out of residents made good social sense: "A restriction excluding a class of persons from occupying a piece of property may be fairly classed with use restriction." One authority thought that "as long as the courts recognize the validity of segregation in railway cars and in the public schools they can hardly insist upon any inalienable right of a colored person to live in a white neighborhood or of a white person to live in that of the negroes." Upholding racial covenants will "aid, rather than interfere with, the marketability and exchange of land," since "the fear of a negro invasion materially interferes with the profitable sale of almost every homesite." But these restraints should be limited in time: a white area can become surrounded by a "black belt," and at some point sales will be possible only to blacks.[72]

The issue came to a head in Corrigan v. Buckley (1926), when the Supreme Court passed on the constitutionality of a District of Columbia covenant not to sell to "persons of African descent." Louis Marshall (who as a prominent Jewish lawyer had his own reasons for opposing restrictive covenants) worked with the NAACP in this case. The District's court of appeals held that segregation was not against public policy, and the Supreme Court refused to reverse, on the ground that the Fourteenth Amendment's due process and equal protection clauses applied to state, not private, action. The Court thus let stand private restrictions on the sale of property to blacks, as in Terrace v. Thompson (1923) it had allowed a state to restrict sales to Asians.[73]

And so this potent instrument of racial exclusion won if not the blessing at least the acceptance of the courts. The consequences were substantial. In 1925 Michigan's supreme court upheld a covenant restricting property use, but it struck down one that forbade sales to blacks. Two years later, after *Corrigan*, it held that a covenant restriction against transfer to anyone "whose ownership or occupancy would be injurious to the locality" applied to a black purchaser. A 1928 survey concluded: "The present tendency of the state courts on the constitutional issues [regarding racially restrictive covenants] is overwhelmingly in favor of [the] validity" of racial segregation "when motivated by the more commonly felt racial antipathies." It added reassuringly that while some courts still opposed prohibitions on the sale or lease of property, "much can be accomplished in these fields by indirection."[74]

The law continued to block explicit public zoning by race, which was advocated as late as 1934: "Segregation of residence of different races is a social problem, and the control of this matter would seem to demand a more impartial viewpoint than that possessed by the individual landowner." But private racial covenants would not be outlawed by the Supreme Court until 1948.[75]

A final example of the courts' reluctance to protect black civil rights was the sorry, drawn-out tale of the Texas white primary. That state passed a law in 1923 prohibiting blacks from voting in its Democratic primary—needless to say, the only election that mattered (the Democrats' vote in the 1926 Texas gubernatorial primary was

833,442, the Republicans' 15,289). The bill was a response to the fact that blacks, alienated by the GOP's growing "lily white" appeal to white voters, were being admitted as voting members by Democratic county committees hungry for votes in their endless factional feuds.

In a unanimous decision (with an opinion by Holmes), the Supreme Court in Nixon v. Herndon (1927) found that the law violated the equal protection clause of the Fourteenth Amendment. But the Court focused on the fact that this was discrimination by statute, and it ignored the Fifteenth Amendment guarantee of black voting rights. The Texas legislature responded with a law that in effect privatized primaries, making them the business of political parties whose executive committees were empowered to determine voting qualifications and other aspects of candidate selection. There was much talk of the danger of even greater political corruption if blacks voted in the primary.[76]

Mainstream opinion was unsympathetic: "Thus is presented the strange picture of one race disfranchising another to save itself from the consequences of its own vices." And the Supreme Court by a five-to-four margin found the law unconstitutional. But the minority accepted the argument that parties were voluntary associations and could establish their own procedural rules. According to McReynolds: "White men may organize; blacks may do likewise. A woman's party may exclude males. This much is essential to free government." And Cardozo's majority opinion was based on the lack of power of the Democratic executive committee—but not necessarily of the party itself—to set its primary rules. Taking the hint, the Democratic state convention quickly held that only whites could participate in its primary, and the legislature repealed all state laws governing the conduct of that vote. The Court thereupon accepted the constitutionality of the white primary, in Grovey v. Townsend (1935). Not until a decade later did it change its mind.[77]

Nevertheless, there were signs that even the judiciary was beginning to feel the first stirrings of a new attitude toward race relations. Herbert Hoover nominated John J. Parker, a North Carolina Republican federal judge known for his antilabor decisions and antiblack attitudes, to the Supreme Court in 1930. The AFL predictably launched a strong campaign against him. So did the NAACP, which organized mass meetings to protest the choice, and was credited at the time with making a contribution to the Senate's rejection of Parker.[78]

The Scottsboro case also gave notice that change, however slow, was under way. Nine black youths were accused in 1931 of raping two white girls in a boxcar. In the past a case such as this, in a venue such as Scottsboro, Alabama, would have had a simple and speedy result: a pro forma trial; conviction and/or a lynch mob doing its deadly work. And indeed there were quick jury verdicts of guilty, and much evidence of race hatred as the proceedings unfolded.

But new attitudes gave the trial a novel character. The NAACP was joined in the defense by two notable civil liberties lawyers, Clarence Darrow and Arthur Garfield Hays. Present, too, were the Communists, seeking to turn the case into an ideological showcase. The lives of the defendants were saved by an extended series of appeals and two Supreme Court decisions. In Powell v. Alabama (1932), Justice George Sutherland found that no real right to counsel had been afforded them. Norris v. Alabama (1935), in which Chief Justice Hughes found the race-biased jury selection process in the case equally wanting, was the first Supreme Court case to deal with racial bias in jury selection since 1910. In strictly legal terms little had changed: the Court still was more interested in the sanctity of the judicial system than in the civil rights of the black defendants. But the scale and notoriety of the Scottsboro case gave it a significant place in the emergence of a modern American civil rights consciousness.[79]

The impact of the Great Depression and the New Deal on American race relations was complex and ambiguous. The depression might have been expected to (and indeed often did) increase hostility between poor blacks and whites scrambling for work and welfare. But the national recovery and welfare programs of the New Deal, based on need, provided the first large-scale federal aid to blacks since Reconstruction. By one estimate, 40 percent of American blacks benefited from welfare during the 1930s. And the major themes of political and cultural life in the New Deal years—that class and economics mattered more than ethnicity, religion, and race in defining who Americans were and what they needed—strengthened an educated public opinion less and less able to accept the traditional rationale for racial segregation.

Still, whatever long-term implications the depression and the New Deal had for American race relations, the strong southern component in the regnant Democratic party of the 1930s, and the inertial weight of the received tradition of racial thought, meant that alterations in public policy would be slow indeed. The NAACP's prime policy goal was a federal antilynching law; but even this modest cause Franklin D. Roosevelt, ever sensitive to his southern Senate supporters, could not bring himself to support. Little apparent change occurred on the state level. Alabama ended its notorious convict leasing law in 1928—to replace it with what quickly became an equally infamous system of state-run chain gangs. A number of northern states had civil rights laws, but these often excluded clubs, institutions, and places such as dance halls and swimming pools that were considered to be "distinctly private" in nature. In any event, injunctive or other relief was exceedingly hard to come by.[80]

Not until 1940 was the Fair Employment Practices Act, the first modern federal law aimed at racial discrimination, enacted by Congress. And that was the product more of the leverage afforded by the threat of the war than of a New Deal sentiment for racial justice. The American political, legal, and governmental assault on racism is a post–World War II story. The long-term historical significance of the pre-1933 experience lies in the fact that the conditions of modern American life not only fostered but began to put some constraints on the use of public policy to secure segregation and condone discrimination.

9 · Indians and Women

In its scale and intensity, the tension between blacks and whites in early twentieth-century America was in a class by itself. True, immigration restriction had a substantial racist dimension. But once admitted and nationalized, most newcomers faced few civil disabilities. Only Asian migrants and their descendants met with racial constraints comparable to those imposed on blacks. Racial considerations also strongly affected the status of American Indians, as gender differentiation did the status of women. Yet the predominant trend in public policy toward these groups was not, as in the case of blacks and Asians, to reinforce their separate status, but (however narrowly, and for whatever motives) to lessen it.

Why was this the case? In part because Native Americans were so few in numbers, so remote in location, and so encased in national myth that they could tap a large stream of public sentimentality, and because the votelessness of women, half the population, was increasingly difficult to square with the principles of American democracy. In part, too, because of the lesser social danger that these groups seemed to pose, compared to blacks and Asians. Nevertheless, Indians continued to lose reservation lands and to remain in a twilight zone between full citzenship and wardlike dependence. As for women, while they gained the vote, they continued to face substantial legal disabilities as wives. Prevailing social attitudes toward race and gender were bent by, but hardly succumbed to, the new society's winds of change.

Assimilation

In some respects the legal situation of Indians at the turn of the century, like that of blacks, was at its nadir. Official policy toward

Indians, like that toward blacks, was deeply affected by a widespread public consciousness of racial difference (more accurately, of supposed racial inferiority and superiority). But there was one conspicuous difference: segregation was the ostensible goal of public policy toward blacks, assimilation the ostensible goal of public policy toward Native Americans. "The tendency," said one observer, "is to amalgamate Indians with the people of the United States."[1]

The assimilationist impulse had its origin in the post–Civil War belief in an all-inclusive American nationality. That attitude persisted far longer for Indians than for blacks, in good part because of the desire of agricultural, railroad, and other interests to obtain the land on which the tribes resided. The Dawes Severalty Act of 1887—which Theodore Roosevelt called "a mighty pulverizing engine to break up the tribal mass"—served both that land hunger (by exposing tribal lands to the exigencies of individual ownership) and the belief that Native Americans might (and should) become yeoman farmers and citizens. These goals were strengthened at the turn of the century by the widespread sense that the closing of the frontier marked the end of a time when Indians could live a tribal life beyond the reach of the dominant society.[2]

Indian policy during the Progressive years stemmed from a complex mix of motives. Its often conflicting sources—the land greed of white farmers and corporations; idealization of the Indian as a "noble savage" by (primarily eastern) sentimentalists; the desire to see Indians assimilated into majoritarian American culture—of course long predated the new century. But now the old, tragic drama of Indian-white relations was played out on the new stage of Progressive values: social control, cultural unity. The result was an assault on tribal autonomy so devastating as to make the reform—indeed, the reversal—of Indian policy a more clearly articulated part of the New Deal than anything affecting blacks, Asians, or women.

A commission headed by Senator Henry L. Dawes of Massachusetts, the author of the 1887 Severalty Act, found in 1893 that the Indian Territory was run by half-breeds, that tribal property was concentrated in a few hands, that tribal governments were leasing land promiscuously to cattlemen and coal companies, and that most American Indians were destitute wards of the government. The time had come, it concluded, to push tribal Indians into ordinary, widespread landownership: not helter-skelter, as under the 1887 law, but after an interim period of government protection and oversight.

The *Independent* was more impatient: "With the tribe ought to go the agent, the Indian school, and the whole machinery which distinguishes the Indian, in law, from the white man." After that, "it ought not to take many years of the coming century to close out the Indian problem, to absorb the Indian in the citizenship of the country." The reformist clergyman Lyman Abbott echoed these sentiments: "Our Indian problem is to be solved by the same process by which we have solved our immigrant problem. The imaginary wall around every reservation ought to be taken down." Assimilationist reformers and land-hungry farmers and speculators occupied common ground: they believed that distributing tribal lands by allotment would turn Indians into Americans and their land into property.[3]

Government policy was designed to implement these views. The Curtis Act of 1898, and tribal agreements in its wake, replaced the system of territorial governors, judges, and legislatures under which the Five Civilized Tribes lived in the Indian Territory by a property trustee system supervised by federal officials. Half of the roughly 20 million acres under tribal control was to be distributed in homesteads or reserved for Indian-run schools, churches, mines, and other purposes. The members of the Five Tribes were given American citizenship in 1901. The expectation was that these 84,000 new citizens would live on homesteads, averaging one hundred acres, which could not be sold or taken for debt for twenty-one years. The tribes would lose their identity, their laws would be abolished, their lands divided. One observer predicted: "The curtain will soon be rung down on what has been termed by many the greatest human tragedy of the end of the century."[4]

In 1907 Oklahoma (including the Indian Territory) was admitted to statehood, and in 1908 the federal government gave jurisdiction over the property of the Five Civilized Tribes to the probate courts of the new state. The tribes at the time owned almost half of Oklahoma's land. But within a few years more than half of that total had been dispersed to white settlers, the Indians winding up with little or nothing to show for it.

Schemes to strip the Indians of their remaining land multiplied. Oklahoma Senator Thomas P. Gore charged in 1910 that there was a plan afoot, rife with questionable land transfers and inflated legal fees, to sell the tribal lands of the Choctaw and Chickasaw to white farmers and coal companies. The state wanted as well to assess and tax the eight thousand members of these tribes who received land allotments, an action sure to strip still more land from them. In 1912 the Supreme Court decided that state taxation threatened Indian property rights vested under the Curtis Act.[5]

M. L. Mott, the Creeks' attorney, investigated the probate court records and found that legal costs and attorney and guardian fees had consumed 20 percent of the value of the estates probated; the comparable cost for white minors protected by the same courts was less than 3 percent. Kate Barnard, the head of Oklahoma's Department of Charities and Corrections, tried to intervene more actively on behalf of the Indians. The response of the legislature was to reduce her department's appropriations.[6]

The Supreme Court smoothed the path of detribalization by affirming the supremacy of the federal government over both tribes and states. In 1901 it clarified how a tribe would be recognized as such, and thus be subject to federal regulation. Then in Lone Wolf v. Hitchcock (1903) the Court ruled that Congress was not held to the terms of past treaties but had a "plenary power" over the tribes. This decision dealt the final blow to the legal fiction that the tribes were independent entities, and opened the door to massive congressional allocations of reservation lands. Justice David Brewer summed up the situation in 1905:

Of late years a new policy has found expression in the legislation of Congress—a policy which looks to the breaking up of tribal relations, the establishing of the separate Indians in individual homes, free from national guardianship and charged with all the rights and obligations of citizens of the United States. Of the power of the Government to carry out this policy there can be no doubt. It is under no constitutional obligation to perpetually continue the relationship of guardian and ward.

In 1911 the Court asserted that it was up to Congress to decide when a tribe's "release from . . . condition of tutelage" would occur.[7]

Indian autonomy now was attenuated indeed. While Indians had a certain possessory right to the soil, ultimate title resided with the American people. Treaties gave way to "agreements" such as that with the Seminole Nation on July 1, 1908, which dealt with royalties from allotted lands. And when the Pottawattamie argued that their 1795 cession of the shores of Lake Michigan did not extend to land reclaimed since then, the Supreme Court held that by abandoning their lands, they had given up their right of occupancy.[8]

These developments heightened the need to define the citizenship status of reservation Indians. And it raised questions as to the ability of the Indian Office to regulate its wards' lives and property. What followed was a classic illustration of Progressive social policy: a strong impulse to develop a uniform policy and to exercise social control, cross-grained by greed, racism, and the sheer diversity of ideas and interests at play.

The Dawes Severalty Act of 1887 granted full citizenship to recipients of land allotments or to those who voluntarily took up residence outside their tribal reservations. But the precise status of tribal Indians still was unclear: Were they the equivalent of aliens, or did they have some intermediate status? Not until 1924 would all Indians be granted citizenship.[9]

Like all social policies, assimilation proved to be difficult to enforce in practice. Most particularly, it ran afoul of two attitudes that were close bedfellows in the Progressive years: the belief that government had a guardianship responsibility, and the inclination to define that responsibility in racial terms. The Supreme Court frequently approved of protective supervision on this basis. It held in 1911 that a law requiring full-blooded Oklahoma Indians to get government approval before conveying land did not deprive them of their due process rights. Two years later the Court upheld the right of Congress to prohibit the sale of liquor to the Pueblo—"essentially a simple, uninformed and inferior people," said Justice Willis Van Devanter—despite the fact that they were citizens and now lived in the state of New Mexico. In 1916 it gave Congress broad power to regulate liquor sales to Indians. And in 1919 the Court held that the government could institute a class action to protect the "non-competent" Osage from an arbitrary and excessive Oklahoma tax.[10]

There are, of course, ample grounds for believing that the old white land hunger lay behind the continuing dissolution of the reservations. William Jones, commissioner of Indian affairs from 1897 to 1905, responded to the growing demand of white farmers for access to reservation lands by streamlining land cession procedures. He accelerated as well the allotment of tribal lands to individual Indians (and thence, all too often, to white purchasers). But something else was at play as well. The governing social assumptions of Progressivism strengthened the impulse to "assimilate" the Indians in the same sense that immigrants were to be "Americanized."[11]

Theodore Roosevelt's Indian commissioner, Francis E. Leupp (1905–6), embodied this approach. Although Leupp admired the Indian "for what is Indian in him," he thought that his charges should be treated as if they were white people with red skins. White expansion had forced the Indians back into barbarism and kept them pauperized. Though they needed help, they should be encouraged to leave the reservation and become independent laborers, merging into the larger society. *Outlook* praised Leupp as "the representative of the white people in treating the Indian as a man," and the *Nation* welcomed a policy shift from dependency to encouraging the Indian to stand on his own two feet, to help himself.[12]

Cato Sells, Woodrow Wilson's Indian commissioner, also was committed to the policy of enlarging the legal rights of Indians and giving them greater responsibility. His goal was "to hasten the disappearance of the Indian as a special problem." But he shared as well the Wilson administration's heightened race consciousness. Freedom from government restriction would be granted first to those with a preponderance of white blood, unless they were manifestly incompetent. The same liberty would be given to those with half or more Indian blood who in a test of competency showed reasonable ability to be able to handle their own affairs. After a full course of civics instruction, certificates of competency were handed out in solemn ceremony, much as in Americanization programs for immigrants, to the plaudits of that old defender of Indian rights, *Outlook*.[13]

As in the past, the government's Indian policy had its share of white critics. The Board of Indian Commissioners, a Christian humanitarian advocate of Indian rights since 1869, engaged in a new (and final) burst of activity from 1906 to 1913. It criticized the headlong assimilationism of the Interior Department and the Bureau of Indian Affairs. And the characteristic Progressive concern over political and corporate corruption found ample ground for outrage in the early twentieth-century assault on the reservations. Coal companies, Standard Oil, cattle syndicates, and the Kansas and Texas Railroad were among those accused of having large and insidious influence over Indian land policy. A journalist darkly observed: "We have ended one 'Century of Dishonor,' and are apparently about to begin another."[14]

The novelist Hamlin Garland, on the prowl for new material, visited some fifteen Indian reservations in the West. He found them to be "'corrals,' or open-air prisons, into which the original owners of the continent have been impounded by the white race." Most Indians, he thought, were communal villagers, not individualists, and the best form of social organization for them was small group settlements of four or five families. His conclusion: "The allotment of lands in severalty which began in land-lust and is being carried to the bitter end by those who believe a Stone Age man can be developed into a citizen of the United States in a single generation, is in violent antagonism to every wish and innate desire of the red man . . . We are answerable for them, just as we are answerable for the black man's future."[15]

Native Americans themselves, like blacks, took an increasingly visible place in the policy debate. And as in the case of blacks, their prescriptions varied. Fayette McKenzie, a white academic who joined with several "Red Progressives" (educated Indians sharing the values and policies of their white Progressive counterparts) to organize the Society of American Indians, thought that government policy "should be to remove as rapidly as possible . . . all differences between the red and the white man in their civil status . . . There are two words which stand for the policy which is here suggested. One is the 'vanishing policy' [the Dawes Act], and the other is 'citizenship.'" A more adversarial, less assimilative position was taken by the Civilized Indians of America at that group's first convention in October, 1911. An Indian lawyer, Hiram Chase, spoke of the travails afflicting his people, and attacked the "monstrous" doctrine that Congress could ignore treaty rights and pass laws controlling Indians and their reservations.[16]

For all its resonance, Indian policy had a smaller place in post-1900 than pre-1900 American public life. One measure of the difference: there were forty-three Senate roll calls affecting Indians from 1880 to 1900, twenty-five from 1900 to 1921. This reflected the rise of more pressing, larger-scaled economic and social issues. And it suggests, too, that here as elsewhere, the determination of policy was shifting from politics and the legislature to courts and bureaucrats.[17]

Native American issues were becoming increasingly complex, technical, legal, administrative—and thus less subject to public scrutiny and concern. Indian wars in the twentieth century were more likely to be fought before judges and in administrative agencies than on battlefields or in the halls of Congress. Litigation over land claims was perhaps the primary source of Indian-white public interaction, one of the last of the arrows, as it were, in a quiver now sadly scant.

The new legal-administrative context was evident in the dealings of the Navajo, the nation's largest tribe, with the Bureau of Indian Affairs over issues stemming from their oil-rich tribal lands. Comparable complexities attended the distribution of the Indian Trust and

Treaty Fund. The Treasury held $35 million from the sale of Indian lands in trust for 53,000 Indians in sixty tribes. Problems of distribution and inheritance constantly arose, and the danger of corruption was ever present.[18]

One consequence of the assimilation of Indians into the larger body politic and the depoliticization of Indian issues was that the courts were more ready to recognize their claims. The Supreme Court held in 1912 that the tax-exempt status of land allotments to Indians could not be repealed by subsequent legislation. This secured for the Indians of the Five Civilized Tribes over $30 million in interest on back taxes.[19]

Eastern Indians—fewer in numbers than their western counterparts but closer to the battlegrounds of law and public opinion—had some success in preserving what was left of their reservation lands. New York's Seneca were "nationals without a nation," caught in a no-man's-land between Congress, state, and tribal authority. Nevertheless, they fought a long and successful battle against the allotment of their land to individuals around the turn of the century, helped by Congressman Edward B. Vreeland of upstate New York, Episcopal Bishop William D. Walker, the part-Indian Pennsylvania Republican boss Matthew Quay, and Commissioner of Indian Affairs Francis Leupp. The Iroquois, too, preserved their immunity from allotment.[20]

Typical of the new ambience was the situation of the Minnesota Indian. He was a citizen, voted, held property, and "generally regulate[d] his life by the same rules as govern the home life of the white man." But the special legal status of Indian property constantly generated litigation: some 1,500 cases in Minnesota's federal and state courts between 1913 and 1918 alone. Under the General Allotment Acts, large amounts of land were allotted to individual Indians. Legal title remained in trust with the federal government for twenty-five years. Numerous attempts were made to separate this land (which included valuable timber tracts) from its Indian owners. But these were constantly frustrated by government suits setting aside the liens, conveyances, and other devices by which transfer was attempted.[21]

Matters were complicated further by a 1906 law affecting Minnesota's White Earth Reservation. It allowed Indians of "mixed blood" to sell their allotments. About half the reservation thereby passed into the hands of white purchasers. But then the Department of Justice, arguing that Congress meant by "mixed blood" only those Indians "as had such a quantum of white blood in their veins as would tend to make them competent to handle their own affairs," instituted equity suits to cancel these arrangements. A federal district court held that unless the allottee could be shown to have at least one-eighth white blood, he should be classified as an Indian and the lands should remain under restraint. The Eighth Circuit Court of Appeals reversed, holding that any Indian with an identifiable portion of other than Indian blood came under the definition; and the Supreme Court upheld this decision. Congress in 1915 tried to resolve the question by providing for the appointment of a commission with the power to determine the age and blood status of White Earth Reservation allottees.[22]

Legislation in the 1920s sought to tidy up the last frayed ends of assimilationist policy. The Indian Omnibus Bill of 1923 ended the special status of much Indian-held property. And the Citizenship Act of 1924 conferred citizenship (and, by implication, detribalization) on all Native Americans. Ostensibly it recognized the nine thousand Indians who served in the American army during the First World War (most, unlike blacks, in integrated units); in good part it was a reformist attempt to lessen the authority of the Bureau of Indian Affairs; in the largest sense it was the final act of an assimilationist policy that had begun with the Dawes Severalty Act of 1887. (But as late as 1938, seven states still denied tribal Indians the right to vote.)[23]

The assimilationist impulse continued to be entangled in the pervasive race consciousness of the time. The Native American was widely held to stand on a higher rung of the racial ladder than his black or brown contemporaries: "Ethnically his stock is superior, and Secretary [of the Interior Ray Lyman] Wilbur is right in stating that he could pass in the American strain to our advantage, especially if he were mixed with Nordic stocks rather than Latin." For all the stress on Indians as citizens, the courts continued to support the hardly compatible view of them as wards, that "curious combination of citizenship and tutelage, on a race basis and wholly regardless of individual competency." Guardianship, in the view of the Supreme Court, would continue until Congress expressly surrendered it. The 1924 citizenship act did little to change this situation: "The fact that they remain wards far outweighs the fact that they become voters."[24]

The California courts frequently faced issues generated by the ever-closer involvement of Indians in the larger society. Could an Indian be kept from voting on the ground that he was nonwhite and not a native citizen? No, he could not. Could an Indian girl be refused admission to a public school when there was a federal Indian school in her district? No, she could not. Could a reservation Indian, injured while on a job outside, be granted workmen's compensation despite his not having filed for it, on the ground that as an Indian he was "incapable of handling his own affairs"? No, he could not, for "while it is true that [he] displayed in his character and conduct the simple, trustful, and even childlike qualities typical of the California Indian," said the court, there was no evidence that he was unable to take care of himself.[25]

Federal-state jurisdictional disputes over Indians and their property took center stage, now that the concept of tribal independence was all but gone. An advocate of greater state supervision argued that the commonwealths were experienced in dealing with "naturalized, semi-alien citizens of different racial stocks." At the same time, federal criminal jurisdiction over the reservations—more important with the coming of national Prohibition—remained in place. Conflicts between Indian custom and state marriage and divorce laws generally were resolved in favor of the former. All taxation of Indians, too, was "within the discretion of the federal government." But a review of federal authority over tribal property as of 1930 found that it "cannot fail to strike one with its arbitrary and almost unrestrained character." In sum, the Indian-federal-state relationship "is completely impossible to define and almost equally impossible to understand."[26]

One assimilationist goal was to reduce the role of the Bureau of Indian Affairs (BIA). But in 1924 that agency still had 340,000 charges on reservations (as compared to 200,000 Indians who were American citizens) and oversaw a billion dollars' worth of property. And the government continued to be subject to the competing pressures to meet its responsibility as the Indians' guardian and to serve the interests of land-seeking farmers and corporations. Albert B. Fall, Harding's Interior secretary of Teapot Dome infamy, wanted to distribute reservation oil and gas leases on the ground that these resources were part of the public domain. In response to a public outcry, Attorney General Harlan Stone countermanded him. Indian Commissioner Charles Burke wanted Congress to authorize such leases, but Indian supporters instead secured an act that made the royalties taxable like any other property. Meanwhile, the leasing went on.[27]

A 1928–29 Senate inquiry into the Bureau of Indian Affairs made it clear how little had changed over the years. One dreary measure of the stasis (or, better, slow decay) afflicting Indian policy was that appropriations to government boarding schools for Indian children declined during the 1920s. Reports of the slow starvation of boarders led President Herbert Hoover to ask for additional funds. Outraged public opinion and Senate pressure finally forced Congressman Louis Cramton of Michigan, chairman of the appropriations subcommittee handling BIA funding, to accede.

In a further reform effort, Hoover appointed the Quakers Charles J. Rhoads and Henry Scattergood to run the bureau, an action reminiscent of Ulysses S. Grant's turn to the clergy to administer his Peace Policy in the 1870s. But now, new voices challenged the assimilationist ideal. Doctors, teachers, and social workers called for "race conservation and enhancement." The Brookings Institution–sponsored Merriam Report of 1928 supported this critique. "Equality before the law," it appeared, "may mean annihilation."[28]

The Great Depression and the New Deal made the turn of the policy wheel from assimilation to cultural pluralism something more than words. By now the record of failure was clear: two out of three American Indians in 1934 were landless, or did not own enough land on which to subsist. In 1933 Franklin D. Roosevelt appointed John Collier commissioner of Indian affairs, and Native American policy underwent its most substantial change since Grant's Peace Policy. The 1933 report of the Board of Indian Commissioners recommended that control of the reservations in effect be turned over to the states. But Collier had a different view. An advocate of Indian tribal autonomy and cultural self-determination, he set out to turn the government's Indian policy in that direction. The Wheeler-Howard Indian Reorganization Act of 1934 ended the individual allotment of Indian reservation lands, for so long a source of detribalization, corruption, and benefit to white farmers, speculators, and corporations. And the principle of cultural pluralism came to take the place in national Indian policy that assimilation had had before.[29]

Was this in fact the beginning of a new era—a New Deal—for American Indians? It is true now, some sixty years on, that Indian tribal identity has been better preserved than seemed likely in the early 1930s. But public policy would continue to oscillate between attempts to "terminate" dependency and efforts to foster tribal culture. And there would be no more agreement on the ultimate goal of Indian policy—assimilation or separatism?—than before. Ronald Reagan observed in May 1988: "Maybe we made a mistake in trying to maintain Indian cultures. Maybe we should not have humored them in wanting to stay in that primitive lifestyle. Maybe we should have said 'No, come join us. Be citizens along with the rest of us.'" The endless attempt to root out corruption in Indian affairs came to focus as much on tribal leaders as on white despoilers.[30]

Contemporary Indian activism, like that of other groups, is hardly settled in its goals. It champions both assimilation and separatism, stresses the rights of Indians as American citizens and insists on the need to maintain a separate Native American cultural identity. In so doing it reflects a century and more of national ambivalence. In any event, the present state and future prospects of that identity is likely to depend far more on its relationship to American society at large than on public policy per se.

Suffrage

The most important social policy enactments of the early twentieth-century were prohibition, immigration restriction, and woman's suffrage. They had much in common: long histories as movements; charismatic leaders and increasingly effective pressure organizations; dramatic ups and downs; and then, in the wake of the First World War, enactment as national policy. Prohibition and suffrage, it has been argued, open windows into the Progressive soul: "The adoption of prohibition and the extension of women's suffrage . . . represented interrelated aspects of cultural nationalism. Prohibition was a means of achieving social control; women's suffrage was a means of achieving enhanced social cohesion." Votes on the two issues in a 1912 Ohio referendum were closely correlated; the Indiana legislature in 1917 enacted prohibition and woman's suffrage within a two-week period; and of course the Eighteenth and Nineteenth Amendments were the two postwar additions to the nation's fundamental law.[31]

But there are distinctions to be drawn as well. Although prohibition and immigration restriction had substantial humanitarian, reformist components, they drew most heavily on xenophobic public anxieties. In the deepest sense they sought more to put a stop to than to encourage or accommodate to social change. Woman's suffrage was something else again. True, its core constituency consisted of middle-class, Protestant, native-born women; they were its strongest advocates and its most immediate beneficiaries. But eventually it served as well a much wider range of Americans: indeed, an entire gender. Woman's suffrage is one of those great extensions of citizenship—universal white male suffrage in the early nineteenth century, black enfranchisement in theory in the 1860s and in reality a century later—which define the growth of American democracy.

As was the case with other important American social movements, woman's suffrage—and beyond it a new feminism—had resonant (but differently pitched) echoes abroad. An international committee on suffrage was organized in Washington in 1902, and by 1911, twenty-four countries had female enfranchisement movements.[32]

German feminism was a broadly organized effort involving perhaps half a million women between 1890 and 1914. Much more so than its American and British counterparts, it had close ties to the socialist movement. August Bebel's *Women and Socialism* (1879) was the most widely read Social Democratic party text, and the feminist spokeswoman Clara Zetkin was an important figure in German socialism. But this identification with the left—leading the Kaiser in a 1910 speech to warn women to stay home—kept the cause from making significant inroads into the broad mass of public opinion. German women's gains prior to the First World War came not in suffrage but in property rights. The Federation of German Women's Associations, founded in 1894, moved from initial radicalism to an increasingly bourgeois, respectable—and popular—stance behind Gertrud Baumer's leadership. By 1914 the Federation had cut its links with the Social Democrats and was being consulted by the government on education and social welfare matters. It did not press for the vote; that came with the postwar Weimar Republic.[33]

From the first the French woman's movement was bourgeois and legalistic, aimed more at the family and other social constraints in a Catholic country (many French feminists were Protestants) than at political and economic issues. Nor was the time propitious for feminism. A declining birthrate and the German threat made it difficult to challenge domesticity. This was true after the war as well. The Senate defeated a suffrage bill in 1922, and Frenchwomen did not get the vote until 1945.[34]

Only in England does one find a European suffrage movement that bears comparison with that in United States. Equal rights for women was a part of nineteenth-century British, as it was of American, liberalism. Married women's property acts were passed in both countries. And continuing disabilities—in divorce and desertion law, in salaries and job prospects, in professional careers, in politics and government—were issues in turn-of-the-century British and American public life alike. The British suffrage crusade, like the American, was "essentially a political movement, run by middle-class women." Its leaders, said one observer, asked not for "Votes for Women" but "Votes for Ladies." Its chronology—mid–nineteenth-century origins, a long spell of the "doldrums," a burst of renewed activity during the early 1900s, and (partial) success with and through the First World War—closely paralleled that of its American counterpart.[35]

At the same time, the two movements reflected and were shaped by the very different political worlds in which they moved. British suffragists operated in a relatively constricted public space. Public opinion at large was less important than the views of a small group of movers and shakers. Not all Conservative leaders were opposed: Balfour favored a limited form of suffrage in bland disregard of the hostility of his party's rank and file. Keir Hardie and other Labour leaders also were supporters, though—again—there was much opposition in the Labour party membership, fed by the fear that a suffrage restricted by property would benefit the Tories.

The strongest support came from the Liberal party—though not from leaders such as Gladstone, who believed that the vote for women would "trespass upon their delicacy, their purity, their refinement, the elevation of their whole nature," or Asquith, who asked: "Would our political fabric be strengthened, would our legislation be more respected, would our domestic and social life be enriched, would our standards of manner—and in manner I include the old-fashioned virtues of chivalry, courtesy, and all the reciprocal dependence and reliance of the two sexes—would the standard be raised and refined if women were politically enfranchised?"[36]

The indifference or hostility of major political leaders hobbled the British suffrage movement and fed the growing resort to violence and direct action fostered by the Women's Social and Political Union. It was the First World War that made suffrage viable. The direct action campaign stopped; the firebrands Christabel and Emmeline Pankhurst converted to superpatriotism. Suffrage opponents such as Asquith and *Times* publisher Alfred Harmsworth now supported it; and after the Conservatives accepted unrestricted adult male suffrage, their opposition to votes for women rapidly declined. The vote came in two stages. The 1918 Representation of the People Act granted universal suffrage to men over twenty-one and to women over thirty; then in 1928 all gender distinctions were removed.[37]

The American suffrage movement was shaped by the distinctive features of the nation's political system. Federalism dictated that this would be an issue contested on the state as well as the national level. The lack of a class-defined politics all but removed that source of strength (and weakness) from the suffrage cause. Instead, ethnicity and race figured much more largely. Most of all, woman's suffrage became part of the broader context in which major social issues were fought out during the early years of the century. The Progressive fixations on cultural unity and on purity in politics offered a promising new rationale for the cause. At the same time, the scale of the effort needed to achieve woman's suffrage in the face of broad (and by no means exclusively male) opposition, and the social hopes and anxieties that it evoked, made it a particularly evocative issue.

The United States might justly lay claim to being the home of the suffrage cause. The Seneca Falls Convention of 1848 marked the beginning of the modern woman's rights movement; Utah and Wyoming in the 1870s were the first substantial political units to give women the right to vote; no other country could match the scale of America's late nineteenth-century suffrage movement. Women cast ballots before 1900 in a variety of contexts. As taxpayers they voted on local special appropriations or bond issues for public improvements in New York, Louisiana, and Montana. In seventeen states they voted for school officials, though to minor effect: normally women made up about 1 percent of that vote in Connecticut and 3 to 4 percent in Massachusetts—except when a heated issue arose, as it did when Catholics and Protestants fought over control of the Boston school board in 1888. They had occasional access to municipal suffrage, most notably in Kansas, where from 1887 they could vote for all city and town offices. And by the end of the century women could vote in general elections in a scattering of western states.

Like prohibition, the suffrage movement seemed to lose much of what forward motion it had around 1900. It won no state to its cause between 1896 and 1910. Strong majorities in Kansas defeated a general suffrage law in 1891 and a state constitutional amendment in 1894. Voters in California (1896), New Jersey (1897), South Dakota and Washington (1898), Oregon (1900), and New Hampshire (1903) followed suit. Traditionally reform-minded Massachusetts held a referendum on the issue in 1895, in which women were allowed to vote.

The male vote was 86,970 for and 186,976 against; of about 575,000 eligible women, 22,204 voted in favor, 864 opposed it.[38]

Powerful cultural predispositions stood in the way of votes for women. A considerable literature dwelt on the threat that the suffrage posed to the family, to the special nature of the sex, to the apolitical character of poverty work. Female antisuffrage associations flourished in Massachusetts, New York, and Illinois; one (woman's) tract identified the suffrage movement with both socialism and aristocracy. *Outlook* editor Lyman Abbott conceded that "necessity, born of an imperfect industrial system, may drive a few thousand women into battle with Nature in bread-winning vocations." But in general, he believed, women were more concerned with individual character building than the distractions of politics. The *New York Evening Sun* polled women in 132 areas of the United States in 1913, concentrating on four groups: schoolteachers, factory workers, stenographers and bookkeepers, and saleswomen. Two thousand responded; 571 favored, 651 opposed, and 778 were indifferent to the cause.[39]

But the increasing numbers of immigrant women in the industrial work force and of native-born women in sales and clerical work eroded the traditional perception of the sex as consigned to the domestic sphere. And as a new agenda of social issues came into being (a process in which women played a major role), the Victorian view of women as society's moral guardians became an argument for inclusion in, rather than exclusion from, public affairs. Suffrage "came to be attractive to the 'clean government' school of thought, the Americanizers of immigrants, the declared enemies of corrupt boss-ridden city politics."[40]

That appeal might be seen in Colorado. More women than men voted in the 1904 election there, though they were outnumbered by thirty thousand in the population of the state. Female voters constituted 42 percent of those registered in Denver's four "best" districts (Anna M. Scott was the "boss" of the city's aristocratic twenty-fourth ward), 35 percent in the four "worst" (that is, those characterized by common laborers, Slav and Italian immigrants, and cheap lodging houses). The state's superintendent of public instruction and the school superintendents of thirty-four of Colorado's fifty-nine counties were female. And women actively fostered a variety of social reforms. In response to the argument that the vote had led to a decline in the character of Colorado's female population, Governor Alva Adams reassuringly observed: "I have known personally at least 10,000 women voters of Colorado, and I have never known one to be less a woman, or less a mother, or less a housekeeper, or less a heart keeper, from the fact that she voted—not one."[41]

Proponents of a variety of Progressive reforms saw in woman's suffrage a congenial cause and an important new source of political strength. By the same token, interests fearing that women would support lower utility rates, stronger business regulation and social welfare laws, and most of all Prohibition and constraints on the power of party machines, actively opposed suffrage extension. Thus, a proposed Oregon equal rights amendment in 1906 won the support of the Grange, the state Federation of Labor, the Women's Christian Temperance Union, and a majority of the churches. Opposition came from seven of the state's 238 newspapers, the Southern Pacific Railroad, street railway companies, and, most strongly, brewers. In response to large contributions from these sources, the state Republican party tempered its support, and the amendment was defeated.[42]

As was the case with prohibition and immigration restriction, both woman's suffrage and the opposition to it drew on the ever-larger body of interests at play in early twentieth-century America. The conflict has been described as "a confrontation between activist women and a resistant society." But in fact the lines were more complexly drawn, cutting across class, ethnicity, and ideology.[43]

Whereas the Jesuit magazine *America* and much of the Catholic clergy opposed woman's suffrage, *Catholic World* supported it, arguing that women were more likely to back legislation favoring religion, morals, and the home. Numerous well-off women, a number of them active in philanthropic work, belonged to the New York Association Opposed to Woman Suffrage, which got eighteen thousand names on a petition in six weeks in 1905. Other society women were prominent in the Equal Franchise Society. While most Progressives favored suffrage, the pioneering muckraker (and social conservative) Ida Tarbell did not, arguing that "the husband, the child, the home, the social circle, the church, these things were infinitely more interesting and important to . . . [women] than diplomas, rights to work, rights to property, rights to vote." Tarbell took suffrage leaders to task for neglecting the problems of female domestic workers.[44]

By 1910 woman's suffrage had a prominent place on the agenda of mainstream Progressivism. A *New York Times* poll of congressmen, senators, and presidents of colleges and universities found that 49 percent favored suffrage, 28 percent opposed it. The suffrage movement (very much like its prohibition counterpart) became more and more broadly organized, politically independent, and energetic and imaginative in rousing public opinion.[45]

As in the case of prohibition, its first big successes were on the state level. A moderate home-grown effort won the day in Washington state in 1910. Mrs. Emma Smith Devoe, who headed the Washington Suffrage Association, was the wife of a telegraph operator and thus had a railroad pass, which enabled her to travel freely around the state. There and elsewhere parades, curbstone speeches, and town-to-town tours by auto or suffrage "specials" on trains and interurban trolleys became common.

California's 1911 referendum vote in favor of woman's suffrage was the product of a thoroughly modern, highly organized campaign. The Los Angeles Political Equality League alone called on the services of 2,500 volunteers. Civic and commercial federations, church organizations, and unions joined in the effort. Movies, songs, leaflets dropped from balloons, store window displays, and parade floats were used to woo voters.[46]

The cause was linked to, and drew upon, the growing public sense that this was a time of portentous social change: "With the growth of industrialism, the business of government is no longer a matter of Hamiltonian or Jeffersonian principles but a matter of vital importance to a large majority of the eight millions of American women who work for their living," a contemporary observed. By the end of 1911 only the South and a scattering of other states (Kentucky, Indiana, Pennsylvania, Maine, and Rhode Island) were without any form of woman's suffrage. And with success came power and confidence. A new Woman's Suffrage party operated in ten states, going after Neanderthals such as Artemus Ward of New York City's Twenty-fifth Assembly District, whose posters sought to make the best of the situation: "Make no mistake, all the girls like Artemus Ward—except the suffragettes."[47]

The urban-industrial-immigrant East and Midwest raised special problems for suffragists, as it did for prohibitionists. Here the opposition of (some) big businessmen, brewers, and party machines was most potent. And here, too, were masses of immigrant and Catholic voters for whom women's participation in politics was problematic. Many Protestant churches also were far from sympathetic: Frances

Willard was denied a seat at a Methodist General Conference because of her gender. The *New York Times* criticized that city's 1912 suffrage parade, and warned that women empowered to vote "will play havoc with it for themselves and society if the men are not firm and wise enough, and, it may well be said, masculine enough to prevent them." And indeed male violence marred a 1913 suffrage march in the nation's capital.[48]

Suffrage proposals continued to go down to defeat in popular referenda: in Ohio by a two-to-one margin, narrowly (and suspiciously) in Michigan (1912), and by large majorities in Nebraska and Missouri (1914) despite massive campaigns and the support of William Jennings Bryan and Champ Clark. A series of losses rocked the movement in 1915: in New Jersey, where machine Democrats and Republicans, the state AFL, Catholic leaders, and liquor interests were active (the suffragists got only 10 percent of the big city vote); in New York and Pennsylvania; and in Massachusetts, despite the endorsement of the Democratic and Progressive parties, the state labor federation, and a substantial majority vote in the legislature.[49]

But ineluctably the tide turned. The gradual but steady rise in the number of women voting and holding office increased the pressure on public opinion and male politicians, as was occurring with state and local liquor prohibition. The first major industrial state to open the suffrage to women was Illinois, in 1913. It did so by legislative act, not by popular referendum or constitutional amendment. This was hardly equal suffrage: women could vote only for president and other non-congressional federal offices, and they had to cast their ballots in separate boxes. The Democratic legislator Lee O'Neill Browne, who opposed the bill because he thought it benefited the GOP more than his party (a thought that must have occurred as well to Republican legislators), blamed its victory on the organized suffrage movement: "Search the lobby if you would find the answer. It has been the best and brainiest lobby you ever saw."[50]

State and municipal offices quickly were added. "Bathhouse John" Coughlin, the longtime boss of Chicago's first ward, thought that the 1913 suffrage law "won't make very much difference at all." In 1914 he and his partner Michael "Hinky Dink" Kenna dismissed the female Progressive party candidate for the ward's council seat as rich, Protestant, and hostile to new immigrants. (In fact she was from humble origins, had become a court stenographer, and was admitted to the Chicago bar in 1892.) A Miss Vittum ran (unsuccessfully) for the council from the seventeenth ward on a platform stressing the need for a "city mother." And a midwife, Mrs. Blazi, soon emerged as a paleo-boss able to deliver hundreds of Italian votes in the ward, though supposedly she supported Coughlin because her husband told her to.[51]

The 1915 vote for Chicago's mayor was the first big city municipal election in which women participated on a large scale. About 258,000 of 292,483 women registered cast their ballots. The winner was Republican "Big Bill" Thompson: hardly the coming of the New Jerusalem. Thompson got 67 percent of the woman's vote, slightly lower than his male support. One analyst thought that Protestant women, more likely to vote, had turned out in droves to support the Protestant Thompson over the Catholic Democratic candidate, Robert Sweitzer. On policy issues, the heaviest woman's vote was cast against a proposal to allow unionization of the fire department. It was evident that women voting en bloc were less of a force for change than women acting as a nonvoting pressure group: "The real woman vote came out of the home. Neither the social Settlement influence nor the women's partizan organizations counted for much."[52]

By the end of 1914, 3 million women in ten states and Alaska were enfranchised. But this was after sixty years of effort. So—as with prohibition—the impulse grew to escape from the grind of state-by-state approval and win quick and sweeping victory with a constitutional amendment. This was an increasingly realistic goal, made more so by the examples of the Sixteenth (income tax) and Seventeenth (direct election of senators) Amendments. Organizations such as the National Consumers League had experience in working with men on public issues, and in linking woman's suffrage to other Progressive reforms, not shared by the WCTU or the Federation of Women's Clubs. And if a third of the states had woman's suffrage, thought longtime suffragist Ida Husted Harper, then "the different parties represented in Congress will do a Marathon to see who shall have the credit of a National amendment."[53]

And indeed politics far more than ideology determined the suffrage views of leading politicians. Few bothered much with the issue before 1914. Wilson dragged his heels when it came to supporting a federal amendment but voted for suffrage in a 1915 New Jersey referendum. Theodore Roosevelt endorsed an amendment in April 1916, and that year's Republican candidate, Charles Evans Hughes, as "a strong nationalist" supported the idea with greater enthusiasm than did his party's platform. Former President Taft, who was also against a Prohibition amendment, continued to stand in opposition: "The lack of experience in affairs and the excess of emotion on the part of women in reaching their political decisions . . . would lower the average practical sense and self-restraint of the electorate in case they were admitted to it now."[54]

Initially at least, the correlation of views—both elite and popular—on the Prohibition and suffrage amendments appears to have been high. Supporters were united not by a single ideological strand—reform, social control, native middle-class status, or the like—but by the fact that both causes were attractive to the same broad pluralist coalition of ideas and interests that was the Progressive contribution to American public life. It is in this sense that a contemporary observer concluded that "to a considerable extent the sentiment for the two movements is co-extensive." Coextensive, but not coequal: of the 174 congressmen who voted for the Hobson Prohibition resolution of December 24, 1914, and/or the Modell suffrage resolution of January 12, 1915, 106 (61 percent) supported both.[55]

Antisuffrage sentiment continued to draw on substantial reserves of strength. The Minnesota state senate in 1916 defeated suffrage by one vote, a result attributed to the nonsupport of the state Federation of Labor, which feared that women's voting would hasten the advent of prohibition. Of the 204 votes cast against a February 1915 suffrage amendment resolution in the House, 171 were Democratic, reflecting widespread concern among southern Democrats that an amendment might reopen the issue of restrictions on black suffrage as well. And northern Democratic immigrant constituencies still were far from enthusiastic supporters.[56]

But there were increasingly compelling reasons for big city Democratic machines and Progressive reformers to want women in the large industrial states to vote. Tammany was studiedly neutral on a November 1917 New York referendum. The suffrage victory there led the way to a favorable House vote (with Wilson's support) on a constitutional amendment in January 1918, the Senate's endorsement in June 1919, and state ratification by August 1920.

America's involvement in the First World War fostered the view that women should be rewarded for their wartime role, just as it did the belief that returning soldiers should be protected from the evils of drink. The faster the Prohibition and suffrage political bandwagons rolled, the more likely politicians were to clamber aboard. But there was far less of an urban-rural, immigrant-native, Catholic-Protestant cleavage in the suffrage than in the prohibition issue. Woman's suffrage more than any other cause of the time rested ultimately on the Progressive impulse to unify a society severely strained by fissures of class, ethnicity, and race. That it did so not by exclusion or restriction but by inclusion in the democratic process made the Nineteenth Amendment the most lasting and substantial social policy achievement of its time.[57]

Or so it was ultimately; not at once. Female voting only gradually increased. Less than half of all eligible women voted in Illinois in 1920, compared to three quarters of eligible men; the figures in Cincinnati were 30 percent for women, 50 percent for men. Because of the predominance of the Cox-Hynicka Republican machine in that city, black women initially registered in greater proportion than their white counterparts. Upper- and middle-class women were more likely to vote in national elections, lower-class and foreign-born women in local contests. Even in the Smith-Hoover election of 1928, when the centrality of social and cultural issues largely increased the immigrant female vote, an estimated 56 percent of women voted, compared to 76 percent of men.[58]

The League of Women Voters, founded in 1919, was conceived of as an instrument similar to those serving other interests: farmers, business, labor, veterans. But its conception of women's political role was differently grounded: "Just as the Chamber of Commerce speaks for Business, so they speak for Altruism or Welfare." Needless to say, this was not the high road to political power in the 1920s; nor can it be said that women's votes noticeably raised the tenor of public life. A political humorist observed in Dooleyite tones: "Wouldn't th' way things are goin' these days make a fine argymint in favor of woman suffrage if we din't already have it?"[59]

Suffrage did not readily translate into meaningful officeholding. A mass of law and custom weighed against women as political candidates and public officials, and the Nineteenth Amendment hardly transformed that situation. Indeed, after its passage a number of state and local statutes continued to exclude women from some positions. Each branch of the Massachusetts legislature could decide for itself whether women might be elected to it. But in New Hampshire women could be elected to the legislature and hold state offices even though a constitutional amendment conferring that eligibility had been defeated.[60]

Eight women were elected to Parliament in the 1922 British election; none were elected to Congress in that year. Why the difference? One observer thought that it was due to the greater political experience and sex solidarity of British women. For a generation a Women's Local Government Authority had been training women to participate in public affairs, and they had served on local authorities since 1907.[61]

Just how difficult it was to secure popular acceptance of women running for office became clear in the early suffrage years. Half of the fourteen women who served in Congress before 1933 were widows elected to their dead husbands' seats (though a couple of them— Florence Kahn of California and Edith Nourse Rogers of Massachusetts—went on to long congressional careers). The first woman senator was eighty-seven-year-old Rebecca Felton of Georgia, sworn in in November 1922 to serve for an hour and a half to fill a vacancy caused by the death of Tom Watson, until Walter George, the regularly elected senator, could take over. Flowers and flowery rodomontade filled her brief time in office; then, after she left, the senators turned to national affairs.

"Ma" Ferguson of Texas twice stood in for her husband as governor (and was elected by greatly reduced margins) while he waited out the state's ban on serving consecutive terms. As a married woman she could not make contracts, a legal handicap that had to be removed by the courts so that she could validly sign state contracts. At about this time the controller general of the United States ruled that a married woman employed by the government had to use her husband's name in order to be carried on the payroll.[62]

Depending on how you looked at it, the glass of female officeholding during the 1920s was either nine-tenths empty or one-tenth full. True, more than eighty women served in thirty-one state legislatures in September 1923, as compared to about thirty in 1920. But there still were fourteen states without any women in their legislatures in 1927, and only a dozen women were in state senates.[63]

An issue of broader concern was the capacity of women to serve on juries. They were widely excluded before the Nineteenth Amendment. State courts differed over whether the vote automatically qualified women to be jurors or legislation was required. Several held that the exclusion of women from juries was not a denial of their equal protection rights under the Fourteenth Amendment. In the wake of the suffrage amendment's passage, challenges to jury exclusion were raised in a number of states. The defeat of one such bill in Wisconsin, and the introduction instead of an act barring women from jury service, led directly to that state's 1921 equal rights law. By 1923 women still could serve on juries in only twenty-two states. And even there a hostile atmosphere often prevailed. An Iowa jury commission wanted to give women a year's immunity "in which to render themselves competent for jury service"; a judge in 1921 limited the female half of a jury to brunettes on the ground that blondes were fickle.[64]

Suffrage, officeholding, and jury duty had a resonance that set them apart from other women's rights issues. They posed stark and simple choices: Should women vote or hold office? Should they serve on juries, or shouldn't they? There were also, as we have seen, realms of women's welfare—in the workplace, with regard to their role as mothers—that evoked policy responses. But the more general issue of social and economic equality which has made pioneering feminists such as Charlotte Perkins Gilman and Alice Paul objects of sympathetic interest today in fact had a marginal place in early twentieth-century public life and thought.

Walter Lippmann included "A Note on the Woman's Movement" in his *Drift and Mastery* (1914). The situation of women was in "a period of drift and doubt," yet another instance of "the great gap between the overthrow of authority and the creation of a substitute." But the consequent questioning and uncertainty was, he thought, limited to middle- and upper-middle-class women. As for the mass of women, their "work in the future will . . . be in the application of the arts and sciences to a deepened and more extensively organized home."[65]

Indeed, beyond the vote and some welfare legislation there was little to make the early twentieth century a time of expanding women's rights. One minor exception: American women who married aliens lost their citizenship in 1907. In the wake of immigration restriction (and the Nineteenth Amendment), the Cable Act of 1922 restored their right to remain citizens; but only about five thousand were immediately affected by this change.[66]

Contractual and other property equality for married women, expanded child guardianship, and modification of the traditionally onerous terms of divorce continued to be issues, as they had been for much of the nineteenth century. A 1930 survey of the legal status of American women found spotty progress. Married women had absolute control of their property in twenty-three states, and spouses had equal interests in each others' property in thirty-one. But in no state (including those with community property laws) did each spouse have a half-interest in and control of property acquired after the marriage. Nor could a wife anywhere claim a portion of the family income, unless she earned it outside the home.[67]

Anomalies abounded. In most jurisdictions a married woman was not responsible for a felony committed by her in the presence of her husband; the legal assumption was that she had acted under his coercion. A Maryland court said in a child custody case that the mother was "entitled to no power, only to reverence and respect." A number of southern and border states at the turn of the century allowed the father to "bequeath" his children to someone other than the mother. Only in ten states were male customers as well as female prostitutes subject to prosecution; in Maryland the white mother but not the white father of a half-black child could be sent to jail for miscegenation.[68]

The suffrage was bound to have some spinoff. Wisconsin in 1921 passed an equal rights ("blanket equity") act which began: "Women shall have the same rights and privileges under the law as men." The first challenge to this statute involved the special statutory protection granted to women in the workplace; the court held that sex remained an acceptable classification for the exercise of the state police power.[69]

The fate of the National Woman's Party (NWP) and its Equal Rights Amendment (ERA) nicely epitomizes both the range of possibilities and the constraints that shaped early twentieth-century American social policy. The amendment sought to write into the Constitution a guarantee of women's full civil equality, as some Radical Republicans tried to do for blacks during Reconstruction. The sense of need was heightened by the fact that women who took on a number of new occupations during the war were fired en masse when the servicemen returned. But a mix of internal dissolution and broader social unreadiness doomed this attempt to legislate gender equality in the 1920s, much as the attempt to legislate racial equality stood no real chance in the 1870s.

Florence Kelley, who had done much to secure protective laws for working women, feared that these safeguards would be endangered by an ERA. And indeed there was an embarrassing propinquity between the Supreme Court's rejection of the District of Columbia women's minimum wage law in Adkins v. Children's Hospital (1923) and the

Equal Rights Amendment's proclamation of women's right to contractual equality with men. Referring to the special problems of child rearing, health, and safety that plagued women in the workplace, Kelley angrily declared: "The effort to enact the blanket bill in defiance of all biological differences recklessly imperils the special laws for women as such; for wives, for mothers and for wage-earners . . . These are differences so obvious, so far-reaching, so fundamental, that it is grotesque to ignore them." Nor was there a general readiness on the part of the NWP to include the interests of black women in its call for equality. An NWP spokesperson declared that the party's 1921 platform did not contemplate enforcement of the Nineteenth Amendment in the southern states. Still, the NWP-ERA efort did carry with it insights not commonly shared at the time. By dwelling on gender discrimination, it focused attention on inequalities that might otherwise have been ignored.[70]

So gender rights, and a multitude of other social concerns besides, entered into early twentieth-century public life in forms and on a scale not seen before. Now we are in the age of the modern American polity: not necessarily in terms of policy outcomes, but very much in terms of the issues at stake. The status of major social institutions (the family, voluntary associations, religion, education); the expansion of major social issues (privacy and civil liberties, the regulation of mores, criminal justice, and social welfare); the proliferation of policies affecting major social groups (immigrants and aliens, blacks, Indians, women): this was a social agenda strikingly new and unmistakably modern in its size and diversity.

Its most notable new feature was the effort to impose uniform national standards on institutions, issues, and groups. The interplay of that impulse with the demands of an increasingly pluralist society and with traditional values, which if anything gained new vigor in the face of rapid change, gave early twentieth-century American social policy its distinctive cast. That cast was not so much the beginning of a modern American state (corporate, corporate-liberal, welfare, or social democratic) as it was a modification of the classic American state of parties, courts, and diverse policies ambiguously implemented. In this sense the early twentieth-century American polity may be thought of as a palimpsest: inscribed before 1900 with the demands of the Young Republic, the Civil War, and industrialization, now overwritten (but hardly transformed) by the issues, ideas, and interests of a new society.

Abbreviations

ABAJl	*American Bar Association Journal*
AER	*American Economic Review*
AH	*Agricultural History*
AHR	*American Historical Review*
AJIL	*American Journal of International Law*
AJLH	*American Journal of Legal History*
AJPH	*American Journal of Public Health*
AJS	*American Journal of Sociology*
AL Reg	*American Law Register*
ALLR	*American Labor Legislation Review*
ALR	*American Law Review*
AM	*Atlantic Monthly*
AMag	*American Magazine*
AMerc	*American Mercury*
Annals	*American Academy of Political and Social Science Annals*
APS Proc	*Academy of Political Science Proceedings*
APSR	*American Political Science Review*
AQ	*American Quarterly*
AR of Rs	*American Review of Reviews*
ASBJ	*American School Board Journal*
ASSP	*American Sociological Society Publications*
BHM	*Bulletin of the History of Medicine*
BULR	*Boston University Law Review*
Cal LR	*California Law Review*
Cent	*Century Magazine*
CH	*Current History*
Char	*Charities*
Chaut	*Chautauquan*
CLJ	*Central Law Journal*
CLN	*Chicago Legal News*
CLQ	*Cornell Law Quarterly*
Col LR	*Columbia Law Review*
Cont R	*Contemporary Review*

CR	Congressional Record
Ec R	Economic Review
Ed R	Education Review
FCHQ	Filson Club Historical Quarterly
FHQ	Florida Historical Quarterly
FLR	Fordham Law Review
FR	Fortnightly Review
GB	Great Britain
GLJ	Georgetown Law Journal
GM	Gunton's Magazine
GWLR	George Washington Law Review
HEQ	History of Education Quarterly
HJ	Historical Journal
HLR	Harvard Law Review
HM	Harper's Monthly
HS	U.S. Bureau of the Census, Historical Statistics of the United States, Colonial Times to 1970 (Washington, D.C., 1975)
HW	Harper's Weekly
Ia LR	Iowa Law Review
ILJ	Indiana Law Journal
ILR	Illinois Law Review
Ind	Independent
IRSH	International Review of Social History
ISHSJ	Illinois State Historical Society Journal
JAH	Journal of American History
JASoc	Journal of Applied Sociology
JCH	Journal of Contemporary History
JCL	Journal of Criminal Law
JCompLeg	Journal of Comparative Legislation
JEd	Journal of Education
JFL	Journal of Family Law
JIH	Journal of Interdisciplinary History
JNH	Journal of Negro History
JP	Justice of the Peace
JPE	Journal of Political Economy
JPH	Journal of Policy History
JPol	Journal of Politics
JR	Juridical Review
JSCL	Journal of the Society of Comparative Legislation
JSH	Journal of Southern History
JSoc H	Journal of Social History
JUH	Journal of Urban History
KH	Kansas History
KLJ	Kentucky Law Journal
La H	Louisiana History
LB	Lawyer and Banker
LCP	Law and Contemporary Problems

LD	*Literary Digest*
LH	*Labor History*
LJ	*Law Journal*
LMR	*Law Magazine and Review*
LN	*Law Notes*
LQR	*Law Quarterly Review*
LT	*Law Times*
MA	*Municipal Affairs*
MacM	*MacMillan's*
MAm	*Mid-America*
Mich LR	*Michigan Law Review*
Minn H	*Minnesota History*
Minn LR	*Minnesota Law Review*
MLR	*Monthly Labor Review*
MPP	*James D. Richardson, ed., Messages and Papers of the Presidents (Washington, D.C., 1897)*
MVHR	*Mississippi Valley Historical Review*
NAR	*North American Review*
Nat R	*National Review*
NC	*Nineteenth Century*
NCCC	*National Conference on Charities and Corrections*
NCHR	*North Carolina Historical Review*
NCLR	*North Carolina Law Review*
NCSWP	*National Conference of Social Work Proceedings*
NDQ	*North Dakota Quarterly*
NEM	*New England Magazine*
NJH	*New Jersey History*
NMR	*National Municipal Review*
NR	*New Republic*
NS	*New Statesman*
NSN	*New Statesman and Nation*
NYH	*New York History*
NYULQR	*New York University Law Quarterly Review*
OH	*Ohio History*
Outl	*Outlook*
PAH	*Perspectives in American History*
PH	*Pennsylvania History*
PHR	*Pacific Historical Review*
PNWQ	*Pacific Northwest Quarterly*
PQ	*Political Quarterly*
PRO, Cab	*Public Record Office, Cabinet Papers, 1880–1916*
PSM	*Popular Science Monthly*
PSQ	*Political Science Quarterly*
QJE	*Quarterly Journal of Economics*
QR	*Quarterly Review*
R of Rs	*Review of Reviews*
SA	*Scientific American*

SAQ	*South Atlantic Quarterly*
SCLR	*Southern California Law Review*
SCQ	*Southern California Quarterly*
SEP	*Saturday Evening Post*
SLR	*Stanford Law Review*
SM	*Scribner's Magazine*
Spect	*Spectator*
SS	*School and Society*
SSSQ	*Southwestern Social Science Quarterly*
SW	*Southern Workman*
SWPSQ	*Southwest Political and Social Science Quarterly*
TLR	*Texas Law Review*
UCLR	*University of Chicago Law Review*
UPa LR	*University of Pennsylvania Law Review*
VLR	*Virginia Law Review*
VMHB	*Virginia Magazine of History and Biography*
Wis LR	*Wisconsin Law Review*
WMH	*Wisconsin Magazine of History*
WR	*Westminster Review*
WVLR	*West Virginia Law Review*
WW	*World's Work*
YLJ	*Yale Law Journal*
YR	*Yale Review*

Notes

Introduction

1. The best overview of the enormous literature on Progressivism is Daniel Rodgers, "In Search of Progressivism," *Reviews in American History*, 10 (1982), 113–132. The classic statement of the status interpretation is Richard Hofstadter, *The Age of Reform: From Bryan to F.D.R.* (New York, 1955); the central role of big business is emphasized in Gabriel Kolko, *The Triumph of Conservatism: A Reinterpretation of American History, 1900–1916* (New York, 1964), and Martin J. Sklar, *The Corporate Reconstruction of American Capitalism, 1890–1916: The Market, Law, and Politics* (Cambridge, 1988); the leading organizational interpretation is Robert H. Wiebe, *The Search for Order, 1877–1920* (New York, 1967). See also Morton Keller, *Regulating a New Economy: Public Policy and Economic Change in America, 1900–1933* (Cambridge, Mass., 1990), pp. 3–5.
2. Jan Romein, *The Watershed of Two Eras: Europe in 1900* (Middletown, Conn., 1978); Norman Stone, *Europe Transformed, 1878–1919* (Cambridge, 1984); Morton Keller, "Anglo-American Politics, 1900–1930, in Anglo-American Perspective: A Case Study in Comparative History," *Comparative Studies in Society and History*, 22 (1980), 458–477; James Kloppenberg, *Uncertain Victory: Social Democracy and Progressivism in European and American Thought, 1870–1920* (New York, 1986).
3. Edward A. Ross, "Recent Tendencies in Sociology, II," *QJE*, 17 (1902), 82–110. See also W. F. Ogburn and Delvin Peterson, "Political Thought of Social Classes," *PSQ*, 31 (1916), 300–317.
4. Duane Mowry, "Some Thoughts on Social Welfare," *Arena*, 28 (1902), 480.
5. Joseph Jacobs, "The Middle American," *AMag*, 63 (1906–7), 522–526.
6. Dorothy Ross, *The Origins of American Social Science* (Cambridge, 1991), chap. 7; Edward A. Ross, *Social Control* (New York, 1901); Julius Weinberg, *Edward Alsworth Ross and the Sociology of Progressivism* (Madison, 1972); Morris Janowitz, *The Last Half Century* (Chicago, 1978), chap. 2.
7. Edward A. Ross, "Recent Tendencies in Sociology," *QJE*, 17 (1902), 96–97, 107.

8. John Martin, "Social Reconstruction To-Day," *AM*, 102 (1908), 293, 294.
9. Benjamin Kidd, *Social Evolution*, 2nd ed. (New York, 1902), p. viii; J. A. Hobson, *The Social Problem*, 2nd ed. (New York, 1902), pp. v–vi; Martin, "Social Reconstruction," 294; William H. Allen, "A National Fund for Efficient Democracy," *AM*, 102 (1908), 463. See also Herbert D. Croly, *The Promise of American Life* (New York, 1909).
10. William D. P. Bliss, *The Encyclopedia of Social Reform* (New York, 1897), preface.
11. Charles A. Ellwood, *The Social Problem* (New York, 1926), p. viii. On reconstruction, see F. A. Cleveland, *Democracy in Reconstruction* (Boston, 1919); Elisha M. Friedman, *American Problems of Reconstruction* (New York, 1918); idem, *America and the New Era: A Symposium on Social Reconstruction* (New York, 1920).
12. D. E. Phillip, *The New Social Civics* (Chicago, 1926), p. 492.
13. Leo Wolman, "The Frontiers of Social Control," *ALLR*, 17 (1927), 233.
14. Edward A. Ross, *World Drift* (New York, 1928), p. 84.
15. Frederick Lewis Allen, "The End of an Era," *Outl*, 154 (1930), 208–209, 239–240.
16. Committee on Social Trends, *Recent Social Trends* (New York, 1933), p. xii. See also Robert C. Angell, "Recent Social Trends in the United States," *Mich LR*, 31 (1932–33), 638–658, and Karl W. Bigelow, "Recent Social Trends," *QJE*, 48 (1933–34), 150–170.
17. Committee, *Recent Social Trends*, pp. xii, xxxi–xxxii.

1. The Family and the State

1. Ohio ex rel. Popovici v. Agler, 280 U.S. 379, 384 (1930).
2. Albert Levitt, "French Marriage Law," *CLJ*, 97 (1924), 87.
3. Morton Keller, *Affairs of State: Public Life in Late Nineteenth-Century America* (Cambridge, Mass., 1977), pp. 468–470; Michael Grossberg, *Governing the Hearth: Law and the Family in Nineteenth-Century America* (Chapel Hill, 1985).
4. "Polygamy in Congress," *Arena*, 23 (1900), 113–131; Julius C. Burrows, "Another Constitutional Amendment Necessary," *Ind*, 62 (1907), 1074–78.
5. Sydney Brooks, "Marriage and Divorce in America," *FR*, 84 (1905), 333; "Eugenic Marriage Laws," *Outl*, 105 (1913), 342.
6. A. C. Rogers, "Recent Attempts at Restrictive Marriage Legislation," *NCCC* (1901), 200–203; Anna G. Spencer, "The Age of Consent and Its Significance," *Forum*, 49 (1913), 406–420.
7. "The New Marriage Law of New York," *Outl*, 70 (1902), 104–105; In re Hinman, 147 App. Div. 452 (3rd Dept., 1911). On a similar law proposed in Minnesota, see "The Regulation of Marriage," *Ind*, 53 (1901), 971–972. On judicial recognition of marriage regulation, see Joseph H. Beale, "Marriage and the Domicil," *NAR*, 44 (1930–31), 527.
8. Charles H. Haberich, "Venereal Disease in the Law of Marriage and Divorce," *ALR*, 37 (1903), 226–236; Jacob Lippman, "The Sexual Aspect of

Juridical Marriage," *ALR*, 65 (1931), 136–153; "Eugenics in Pennsylvania," *LD*, 47 (1913), 306; "Getting Married in Wisconsin," *LD*, 47 (1913), 52–53; Paterson v. Widule, 147 N.W. 966, 968 (Wisc., 1914); Lyannes v. Lyannes, 177 N.W. 683 (Wisc., 1920).

9. G. J. Bayles, *Woman and the Law* (New York, 1901), p. 28; Lelia Robinson, *The Law of Husband and Wife Compiled for Popular Use* (Boston, 1890), p. 6. See also Edward W. Spencer, "Some Phases of Marriage Law and Legislation from a Sanitary and Eugenic Standpoint," *YLJ*, 25 (1915–16), 58–73; Isidor Loeb, *The Legal Property Relations of Married Parties* (New York, 1900), pp. 32–34; Grossberg, *Governing the Hearth*, chap. 8.

10. Edith M. Hadley, "Legal Status of Women in the United States," *Gunton's*, 24 (1903), 307–315; Joseph Warren, "Husband's Right to Wife's Services," *HLR*, 38 (1925), 421–446, 622–650.

11. Ex parte Warfield, 50 S.W. 933 (Texas, 1899); Vanderbilt v. Mitchell, 67 Atl. 97 (N.J. 1907).

12. Hodecker v. Stricker, 39 N.Y.S. 515 (1896).

13. Snedaker v. King, 145 N.E. 15 (Ohio, 1924). See also Roy Moreland, "Injunctive Control of Family Relations," *KLJ*, 18 (1930), 207–224.

14. Robert M. Hutchins and Donald Slesinger, "Some Observations on the Law of Evidence: Family Relations," *Minn LR*, 13 (1928–29), 675–686; "Liability of One Spouse to the Other for Personal Torts under the Married Women's Acts," *HLR*, 38 (1924–25), 383–389; Drake v. Drake, 177 N.W. 624, 625 (Minn., 1920).

15. Fred S. Hall, *Marriage Laws in Their Social Aspects* (New York, 1919), pp. 18–21; "Our Colossal Hodgepodge of Marriage Laws," *LD*, 75 (November 11, 1922), 34; Joseph H. Beale et al., "Marriage and the Domicil," *HLR*, 44 (1930–31), 501–529; Richard F. Cleveland, "Status in Common Law," *HLR*, 38 (1924–25), 1074–95. See also Chester G. Vernier, *American Family Laws* (Stanford, 1931), 1:15.

16. Mary E. Richmond and Fred S. Hall, *Marriage and the State* (New York, 1929), p. 87; Fred S. Hall, "Marriage and the Law," *Modern American Family, Annals*, 160 (1932), 110–115. See also Geoffrey May, *Marriage Laws and Decisions in the United States: A Manual* (New York, 1929); Vernier, *Family Laws*, vol. 1, passim.

17. Boardman Wright, "Community Property in Europe and America," *ABAJl*, 11 (1925), 703–706; Harriet S. Daggett, "The Modern Problem of the Nature of the Wife's Interest in Community Property: A Comparative Study," *Cal LR*, 19 (1930–31), 567–701.

18. Fred S. Hall, "Common Law Marriage in New York State," *Col LR*, 30 (1930), 10–11; "Common Law Marriage Again Abolished in New York," *ALR*, 67 (1933), 275–276; Otto E. Koegel, "Common Law Marriage," *The Family*, 4 (1923), 172–175.

19. Jacob Lippmann, "The Breakdown of Consortium," *Col LR*, 30 (1930), 651–673; Evans Holbrook, "The Change in the Meaning of Consortium," *Mich LR*, 22 (1923), 1–9.

20. Nathan P. Feinsinger, "Legislative Attack on 'Heart Balm,'" *Mich LR*, 33 (1935), 997–1000, 1009; RMJ, "Abolition of Actions for Breach of Promise,

Enticement, Criminal Conversation, and Seduction," *VLR*, 21 (1935), 205–218.

21. J. P. Chamberlain, "Changes in the Law of the Family, Persons, and Property," *Annals*, 136 (1928), 15–25; Vernier, *Family Laws*, 1:16.

22. Gail Savage, "Divorce and the Law in England and France Prior to the First World War," *JSH*, 21 (1988), 499–514; E. S. P. Haynes, "The Anomalies of the English Divorce Law," *FR*, 86 (1905), 1115–22; Arthur Barratt, "The English Divorce Reports from an American Standpoint," *ALR*, 48 (1914), 493–529. See also Frederick Payler, "The Divorce Court and the Public," *MacM*, 92 (1905), 351–357.

23. Keller, *Affairs of State*, pp. 470–472. See also William L. O'Neill, *Divorce in the Progressive Era* (New Haven, 1967); Lynne C. Halem, *Divorce Reform: Changing Legal and Social Perspectives* (New York, 1980), chap. 2.

24. Roosevelt quoted in Evans Holbrook, "Divorce Laws and the Increase of Divorce," *Mich LR*, 8 (1909–10), 386; Sydney Brooks, "Marriage and Divorce in America," *FR*, 84 (1905), 329–341; Frederick C. Hicks, "Marriage and Divorce Provisions in the United States," *Annals*, 26 (1905), 133–136.

25. Cleveland Cabler, "Marriage and Divorce," *ALR*, 59 (1925), 467; Edward A. Ross, "The Significance of Increasing Divorce," *Cent*, 78 (1909), 149–152; Elaine T. May, "The Pressure to Provide: Class, Consumerism, and Divorce in Urban America, 1880–1920," *JSoc H*, 12 (1978), 180–193; idem., *Great Expectations: Marriage and Divorce in Post-Victorian America* (Chicago, 1980).

26. E. Ray Stevens, "Divorce in America: The Problem," and "Divorce in America: The Solution," *Outl*, 86 (1907), 239, 287–293; Henry F. Harris, "Marriage and Divorce," *Arena*, 29 (1903), 170; Elizabeth C. Stanton, "Are Homogeneous Divorce Laws in All the States Desirable?" *NAR*, 170 (1900), 405–409.

27. George E. Howard, "The Problem of Uniform Divorce Laws in the United States," *American Lawyer*, 14 (1906), 16; Holbrook, "Divorce Laws and Increase of Divorce," 386–395.

28. George E. Howard, "Divorce and the Public Welfare," *McClure's*, 34 (1909–10), 232–242; Vernier, *Family Laws*, 1:3. See also Wilbur Larremore, "American Divorce Law," *NAR*, 183 (1906), 70–81.

29. Amasa M. Eaton, "Proposed Reforms in Marriage and Divorce Laws," *Col LR*, 4 (1904), 263.

30. James P. Davenport, "Our American Letter," *LT*, 104 (1898), 574–575.

31. Haddock v. Haddock, 201 U.S. 562, 628 (1906); Joseph H. Beale, "Haddock Revisited," *HLR*, 39 (1926), 429; idem, "Constitutional Protection for Decrees of Divorce," *HLR*, 19 (1905–6), 584–597; "The Divorce Decision," *Outl*, 82 (1906), 919–920; Morton L. Lewis, "Divorce and the Federal Constitution," *ALR*, 49 (1915), 852–879; Henry T. Blake, "Judicial Tendencies in Impairment of the Marriage Relation," *ILR*, 10 (1915–16), 574–583.

32. Malcolm M'Ilwraith, "Separation and Divorce," *LQR*, 33 (1917), 335–341; J. E. G. Montmorency, "Divorce Law in England," *UPa LR*, 75 (1926–27), 36–49; Nancy M. Schoonmaker, "The Divorce Laws of America and Europe," *CH*, 20 (1924), 249–253.

33. *HS*, 1:64; Richmond and Hall, *Marriage and the State*, pp. 330–331; on Minnesota, see Mildred D. Mudgett, "Where Courts Interlock," *The Family*, 4 (1923), 51–55; Leon C. Marshall and Geoffrey May, *The Divorce Court* (Baltimore, 1932–33), p. 57; Alfred Cahen, *Statistical Analysis of American Divorce* (New York, 1932), pp. 15–16, 21.

34. Anthony M. Turano, "The Conflict of Divorce Laws," *AMerc*, 17 (1929), 459–462; J. P. Chamberlain, "Divorce and the Legislatures," *ABAJl*, 18 (1932), 870–873; Marshall and May, *Divorce Court*, p. 15.

35. Charlotte P. Gilman, "Divorce and Birth Control," *Outl*, 148 (1928), 130–131, 153; Robert Grant, "Marriage and Divorce," *YR*, 14 (1924–25), 223–228; "The New Freedom in Divorce: Can It Be Secured by Uniformity in Marriage Laws?" *Forum*, 76 (1926), 321–328.

36. N. P. Feinsinger and Kimball Young, "Recrimination and Related Doctrines in the Wisconsin Law of Divorce as Administered in Dane County," *Wis LR*, 6 (1930–31), 196–216.

37. J. P. Lichtenberger, "Divorce Legislation," *Annals*, 160 (1932), 116–132; *LD*, 93 (April 9, 1927), 13–14; *LD*, 109 (April 4, 1931), 11; "Divorce—Our Growing Divorce 'Racket' and Its Legal, Social, and Economic Consequences," *Minn LR*, 17 (1932–33), 638–653.

38. Halem, *Divorce Reform*, chap. 4; Karl Llewellyn, "Behind the Law of Divorce—The Decay of the Traditional Marriage Pattern," *Col LR*, 32 (1932), 1281–1308; *Col LR*, 33 (1933), 249–294.

39. "The Rights and Duties of Parents," *JP*, 87 (1923), 687; "Legal Changes Affecting the Family," *LT*, 134 (1913), 319; Charles Gans, "The Organization of the Family in the French Civil Code," *JR*, 14 (1902), 283.

40. Sophinisba Breckinridge, *The Family and the State* (Chicago, 1934), p. 1.

41. Ernst Freund, *Standards of American Legislation* (Chicago, 1917), pp. 12–13.

42. Albert Levitt, "The Interests Secured by the Law Governing the Contracts of an Infant," *CLJ*, 94 (1922), 4–10; Joseph H. Beale, "The Status of the Child and the Conflict of Laws," *UCLR*, 1 (1933–34), 13–27; Stark v. Hamilton, 99 S.E. 861 (Ga., 1919); Roscoe Pound, "Individual Interests in the Domestic Relations," *Mich LR*, 14 (1915), 181; "The Right to Recover for Malicious Alienation of a Child's Affections," *HLR*, 40 (1926–27), 771–774.

43. "Support of Children in Absence of Provision Therefore in Decree Awarding Custody to Divorced Wife," *YLJ*, 17 (1907–08), 284; "Extent of a Parent's Duty of Support," *YLJ*, 32 (1922–23), 825–829; Dougherty v. Engler, 211 Pac. 619 (Kan., 1923). See also "Reciprocity of Rights and Duties between Parent and Child," *HLR*, 42 (1928–29), 112–115.

44. Grossberg, *Governing the Hearth*, pp. 234–253; Cardozo in Finlay v. Finlay, 148 N.E. 624, 625 (N.Y., 1925).

45. *Ex parte* Tillman, 84 S.C. 552 (1909); Edna Kenton, "The Ladies' Next Step: The Case for an Equal Rights Amendment," *HM*, 152 (1925–26), 367, 368 (*Narramore* case).

46. Mary A. Greene, "The American Mother's Right to Her Child," *ALR*, 52 (1918), 371–382; Logan Morrill, "Divergent Points of View in the Law of

Persons and Domestic Relations," *University of Cincinnati Law Review*, 8 (1934), 321.

47. Frank E. Wade, "The Prosecution of Parents for the Delinquencies of Their Children," *NCCC* (1909), 297–307; idem, "Some Practical Results of the New Family Desertion Law," *Char*, 17 (1906–07), 708–711; People v. Joyce, 98 N.Y.S. 863 (1906).

48. Carl Zollman, "Parental Rights and the Fourteenth Amendment," *Marquette Law Review*, 18 (1923–24), 53–60; "Parens Patriae," *Oregon Law Review*, 4 (1925), 233–566; Meyer v. Nebraska, 262 U.S. 390 (1923); Pierce v. Society of Sisters, 268 U.S. 510 (1925). See also "Developments in the Law—The Constitution and the Family," *HLR*, 93 (1980), 1162.

49. Keller, *Affairs of State*, pp. 463–464; Grossberg, *Governing the Hearth*, chap. 6, pp. 268–280; Stephen B. Presser, "The Historical Background of the American Law of Adoption," *JFL*, 11 (1971–72), 443–516. See also Joseph C. Ayer, Jr., "Legitimacy and Marriage," *HLR*, 16 (1902–03), 22–42.

50. Everett L. Dodrill, "The Status of Legitimation and Adoption," *WVLR*, 31 (1924–25), 258; Herbert F. Goodrich, "Legitimation and Adoption in the Conflict of Laws," *Mich LR*, 22 (1924), 637–651; "Legitimation by Subsequent Marriage," *LQR*, 36 (1920), 255.

51. "The Illegitimate Child," *Survey*, 43 (1919–20), 654–655; Ernst Freund, *Illegitimacy Laws of the United States* (Washington, D.C., 1919), pp. 10, 18; on mothers' pensions laws, see Ruth Reed, *Negro Illegitimacy in New York City* (New York, 1926), p. 23.

52. Ernst Freund, "A Uniform Illegitimacy Law," *Survey*, 49 (1922), 104, 127, 129; "The Uniform Illegitimacy Act and the Present Status of Illegitimate Children," *Col LR*, 24 (1924), 909–915; "Inheritance By, From, and Through Illegitimate," *UPa LR*, 75 (1935–36), 531–542.

53. "Legislation and Decisions on Inheritance Rights of Adopted Children," *Ia LR*, 22 (1936–37), 145–154; Joseph W. Newbold, "Jurisdictional and Social Aspects of Adoption," *Minn LR*, 11 (1926–27), 605–634; Horace H. Robbins and Francis Déak, "The Familial Property Rights of Illegitimate Children: A Comparative Study," *Col LR*, 30 (1930), 308–329; Earl D. Meyers, "The English Adoption Law," *Social Service Review*, 4 (1930), 56–63.

54. Richard A. Solloway, *Birth Control and the Population Question in England, 1877–1930* (Chapel Hill, 1982), chap. 3; C. P. B. Blacker, *Birth Control and the State: A Plan and a Forecast* (London, 1926).

55. C. Thomas Dienes, *Law, Politics, and Birth Control* (Urbana, 1972), p. 25; J. C. Ruppenthal, "Criminal Statutes on Birth Control," *JCL*, 10 (1919), 48–61.

56. David M. Kennedy, *Birth Control in America: The Career of Margaret Sanger* (New Haven, 1970), p. 68 and chaps. 2–3; "Films and Births and Censorship," *Survey*, 34 (1915), 4–5. See also James Reed, *From Private Vice to Public Virtue: The Birth Control Movement and American Society* (New York, 1978).

57. Eden Paul and Cedar Paul, *Population and Birth Control* (New York, 1917), pp. 146, 138; Kennedy, *Birth Control*, pp. 106–107; S. Adolphus

Knopf, "Birth Control in Its Medical, Social, Economic, and Moral Aspects," *AJPH*, 7 (1917), 152–172.

58. "Some Legislative Aspects of the Birth-Control Problem," *HLR*, 45 (1932–33), 723–729; on the AFL, see Kennedy, *Birth Control*, p. 235; Louis I. Dublin, "The Fallacious Propaganda for Birth Control," *AM*, 137 (1926), 186–194.

59. Helene H. Smith, "Birth Control and the Law," *Outl*, 149 (1928), 686–687, 718; Gladys Gaylord, "Restrictions in Regard to Regulation of Birth Imposed by Laws of the Various Civilized Nations," *NCSWP* (1931), 136–142; Mary W. Dennett, *Birth Control Laws* (New York, 1926).

60. Young's Rubber Co. v. C. I. Lee, 45 Fed. 2d 103 (2d Circ., 1930); Davis v. U.S., 62 Fed. 2d 473 (6th Circ., 1933); U.S. v. One Package, 86 Fed. 2d 737 (2d Circ., 1936); Griswold v. Connecticut, 381 U.S. 478 (1965); Peter Smith, "The History and Legal Future of the Legal Battle over Birth Control," *CLQ*, 42 (1964), 275–303.

61. James C. Mohr, *Abortion in America* (New York, 1978); "A Functional Survey of Existing Abortion Laws," *Col LR*, 36 (1936), 87–97; Fred Taussig, *Abortion* (St. Louis, 1936); "Developments in the Law—The Constitution and the Family," *HLR*, 93 (1980), 1156–1383.

62. Michael Freeden, "Eugenics and Progressive Thought: A Study in Ideological Affinity," *HJ*, 22 (1979), 645–671; G. R. Searle, *Eugenics and Politics in Britain, 1900–1914* (Leyden, 1976). See also Richard A. Solloway, *Demography and Degeneration: Eugenics and the Declining Birthrate in Twentieth-Century Britain* (Chapel Hill, 1990).

63. Edward A. Ross, Introduction to Paul Popenoe and Roswell H. Johnson, *Applied Eugenics* (New York, 1922), pp. xvi, xi; Loren R. Graham, "Science and Values: The Eugenics Movement in Germany and Russia in the 1920s," *AHR*, (1977), 1133–64.

64. G. P. Mudge, "The Menace to the English Race and Its Traditions of Present-Day Immigration and Emigration," *Eugenics Review*, 11 (1919–20), 205; J. B. S. Haldane, "Eugenics and Social Reforms," *Nation* (GB), 35 (1924), 291–292; "The Sterilization Bill," *Spect*, 147 (1931), 105. See also Herbert Brewer, "Eugenics and Socialism: Their Common Ground and How It Should Be Sought," *Eugenics Review*, 24 (1932–33), 19–21; Greta Jones, "Eugenics and Social Policy Between the Wars," *HJ*, 25 (1982), 717–728; Michael Freeden, "Eugenics and Ideology," *HJ*, 26 (1983), 959–962.

65. Charles A. Boston, "A Protest against Laws Authorizing the Sterilization of Criminals and Imbeciles," *JCL*, 4 (1913–14), 327; on Pennypacker, see Daniel J. Kevles, *In the Name of Eugenics: Genetics and the Uses of Human Heredity* (New York, 1985), p. 109; "Shall We Legalize Homicide?" *Outl*, 82 (1906), 253; "Euthanasia Once More," *Ind*, 60 (1908), 291–292; "Jury of Scientists Hung on Sterilization," *Survey*, 39 (1917–18), 206; "Eugenics and Common-Sense," *Nation*, 97 (1913), 526.

66. Smith v. Board of Examiners, 88 Atl. 963, 966–967 (N.J., 1913). See also "The Constitutionality of the Compulsory Asexualization of Criminals and Insane Persons," *HLR*, 26 (1912–13), 163–165; Joseph P. Chamberlain, "Eugenics in Legislatures and Courts," *ABAJl*, 15 (1929), 165–169.

67. "The Indiana Mode of Extinguishing the Unfit," *Current Literature,* 43 (1907), 328; Boston, "Protest," 357.

68. Paul Popenoe, "Eugenic Sterilization in California," *Journal of Social Hygiene,* 13 (1927), 257–268, 321–330, 468–477, 14 (1928), 23–32, 271–285; Frank C. Richmond, "Sterilization in Wisconsin," *JCL,* 25 (1934–35), 586–593; J. H. Landman, "The History of Human Sterilization in the United States—Theory, Statute, Adjudication," *ILR,* 23 (1928–29), 473; Leon F. Whitney, *The Case for Sterilization* (New York, 1934), p. 302.

69. Smith v. Comm., 204 N.W. 140, 145 (Mich., 1925). See also Burke Shartel, "Sterilization of Mental Defectives," *JCL,* 16 (1925–26), 541, 552; Landman, "History," 480.

70. Landman, "History," 465; Buck v. Bell, 274 U.S. 200, 207 (1927).

71. Jacob B. Aronoff, "The Constitutionality of Asexualization Legislation in the United States," *St. John's Law Review,* 1 (1927–28), 159; Kevles, *In the Name of Eugenics,* p. 111; Landman, "History," 480.

72. Clarence J. Ruddy, "Compulsory Sterilization: An Unwarranted Extension of the Powers of Government," *Notre Dame Lawyer,* 3 (1927), 1. See also J. H. Landman, "The Human Sterilization Movement," *JCL,* 24 (1933–34), 400–408; Harry F. J. Schroeder, "Genetics and the Law," *JCL,* 7 (1932–33), 253–286, for a Catholic critique, with a rebuttal by Dr. Alex S. Wiener, *JCL,* 8 (1933–34), 70–80; and Raymond W. Murray, "Eugenic Legislation and the Lawyer," *Notre Dame Lawyer,* 8 (1932–33), 327–337.

2. Church and State, School and Society

1. Zechariah Chafee, Jr., "The Internal Affairs of Associations Not for Profit," *HLR,* 43 (1930), 993–1029. See also "Legal Status of Voluntary Associations," *HLR,* 33 (1919–20), 298–300; Olcott O. Partridge, "The Legal Status of a College Fraternity Chapter," *ALR,* 42 (1908), 168–191; Morton Keller, *Affairs of State: Public Life in late Nineteenth-Century America* (Cambridge, Mass., 1977), pp. 517–518.

2. Joseph R. Long, "Equitable Jurisdiction to Protect Personal Rights," *YLJ,* 33 (1923), 127–129; Choate v. Logan, 133 N.E. 582 (Mass., 1921); Barker v. Bryn Mawr, 122 Atl. 220 (Pa., 1923).

3. James Murphy, *Church, State, and Schools in Britain, 1800–1970* (London, 1971), pp. 90, 96; G. W. Kekewich, "The Church and the Education Act," *Cont R,* 83 (1903), 779; "The Nonconformists and the Education Bill," *Cont R,* 82 (1902), 429–434; "Politics and Education," *Cont R,* 82 (1902), 479.

4. John McManners, *Church and State in France, 1870–1914* (New York, 1972), chaps. 13–14, p. 132; Véronique Bédin, "Briand et la séparation des Eglises et l'Etat: la commission des Trentetrois," *Revue historique moderne contemporaire,* 24 (1977), 364–392.

5. "Reading the Bible in Common Schools," *YLJ,* 12 (1902–03), 103; State v. Board, 44 N.W. 967 (Wisc., 1890), and Thomas C. Hunt, "The Egerton Book Decision: The End of an Era," *Catholic Historical Review,* 67 (1981), 589–619; Carl Zollmann, "Religious Education," *ALR,* 56 (1922),

436–447; idem, "The Constitutional and Legal Status of Religion in Public Education," *Journal of Religion*, 2 (1922), 236–244. See also Lawrence A. Stith, "Bible Reading in the Public Schools," *LN*, 32 (1928), 225–228.

6. Edwin C. Goddard, "The Law in the United States in Its Relation to Religion," *Mich LR*, 10 (1912), 176; W. A. Coutts, "Constitutionality of the Rule Excluding Atheists as Witnesses," *CLJ*, 72 (1911), 22–27; B. H. Hartogensis, "Denial of Equal Rights to Religious Minorities and Non-Believers in the United States," *YLJ*, 39 (1929–30), 659–681; "Taxation—Exemption of Property Owned or Used by Religious Organizations," *Minn LR*, 11 (1926–27), 541–551.

7. Andrew A. Bruce, "Religious Liberty in the United States," *CLJ*, 74 (1912), 285; Samuel W. Brown, "Present Legal Status: New and Proposed Legislation Concerning Religious Instruction in Public Schools," *Religious Education*, 11 (1916), 103–108; on the Salvation Army, see Carl Zollmann, "Religious Liberty in American Law," *ILR*, 10 (1915–16), 197. See also Carl Zollmann, "Religious Liberty in the American Law," *Mich LR*, 17 (1929), 355–377, 456–478.

8. On New Jersey, see George J. Bayules, "Notes on the Development of American Civil Church Law," *PSQ*, 14 (1899), 519; Carl Zollmann, "Religious Charities in the American Law," *Marquette Law Review*, 9 (1925), 131–148; idem, "Classes of American Religious Corporations," *Mich LR*, 13 (1914–15), 566–583; "Powers of American Religious Corporations," *Mich LR*, 13 (1914–15), 646–666.

9. Epaphroditus Peck, "American versus British Ecclesiastical Law," *YLJ*, 15 (1905–06), 255–262; "The Right of a Majority in a Church to Change the Doctrine and Retain Property against a Dissentient Minority," *YLJ*, 14 (1904–5), 400. See also John W. Patton, "The Civil Courts and the Churches," *ALReg*, n.s., 45 (1906), 391–423.

10. "The Independence of Church Courts," *Ind*, 67 (1909), 1089–99; "When Will Civil Courts Investigate Ecclesiastical Doctrine and Laws?" *HLR*, 39 (1925–26), 1079–84.

11. State v. Buswell, 40 Neb. 158 (1894); Edward W. Dickey, "Christian Science and Religious Liberty," *Mich LR*, 4 (1905), 264; Irving E. Campbell, "Christian Science and the Law," *Virginia Law Register*, 10 (1904), 292; American School of Healing v. McAnnulty, 187 U.S. 94, 104 (1902).

12. In re First Church of Christ Scientist, 55 Atl. 536, 539 (Pa., 1903); "The Power of the State over Christian Science," *YLJ*, 13 (1903–4), 42–44.

13. "The Dictatorship of the Sabbatariat," *Nation*, 111 (1920), 681; Albert Levitt, "Compulsory Bible Reading in Public Schools," *CLJ*, 99 (1926), 77, 81; Raymond M. Hudson, "Rights of Religion and the Bible in Public and Private Schools," *LB*, 20 (1927), 357.

14. PRO, Cab 37, vol. 28 (1890), no. 63; "World-Politics," *NAR*, 187 (1908), 622–628.

15. Murphy, *Church, State, and Schools*, p. 84; J. Edward Graham, "State-Aided Education in England and Scotland," *JR*, 14 (1902), 365–377; Cloudesley Brereton, "A National System of Education," *FR*, 75 (1901), 834; John E. Gorst, "The Education Bill," *NC*, 52 (1902), 584.

16. "World-Politics," *NAR*, 182 (1906), 933; Brian Simon, *Education and the Labour Movement, 1870–1920* (London, 1965), pp. 203–204.

17. "World-Politics," *NAR*, 182 (1906), 931; James E. Russell, "The Trend in American Education," *Ed R*, 32 (1906), 39; W. P. W. Phillimore, "The Rights—and Wrongs—of Parents under the Education Acts," *LMR*, 37 (1912), 399. See also "The English Education Bill," *Ind*, 60 (1906), 1056–58; "The Education Bill," *QR*, 204 (1906), 590–612; W. T. Stead, "The Education Controversy in England," *AR of Rs*, 34 (1906), 722–727.

18. James E. Russell, "The Trend in American Education," *Ed R*, 32 (1906), 35; Friedrich Paulsen, "Old and New Fashioned Notions about Education," *Ed R*, 35 (1908), 480. For a Catholic critique, see "Our Public Schools," *Outl*, 75 (1903), 441–443.

19. Lawrence A. Cremin, *The Transformation of the School: Progressivism in American Education, 1876–1957* (New York, 1961); David B. Tyack, *The One Best System: A History of American Urban Education* (Cambridge, Mass., 1974), pt. 4.

20. Luther H. Gulick, "Why 250,000 Children Quit School," *WW*, 20 (1910), 13285–94

21. George C. Fox, "The Injustice of the Free High School to the Wage-Earning Class," *SS*, 1 (1915), 852; Wilford E. Talbert, "Efficiency in State School Systems," *NMR*, 6 (1917), 585–590; C. A. Prosser, "Vocational Education: Legislation of 1910–1911," *APSR*, 6 (1912), 586–595; Robert W. Selvidge, "State Control of Entrance to the Industries," *Vocational Education*, 3 (1913–14), 338–343; Sol Cohen, "The Industrial Education Movement, 1906–1917," *AQ*, 20 (1968), 95–110. See also Edward A. Krug, *The Shaping of the American High School, 1880–1920* (Madison, 1969).

22. James P. Munroe, *New Demands in Education* (New York, 1912), p. 2, quoted in Raymond E. Callahan, *Education and the Cult of Efficiency* (Chicago, 1962), p. 62; Leonard P. Ayres, "An Index of Efficiency for Public School Systems," *JEd*, 70 (1909), 426–427; William Estabrook, "Criteria for Determining the Relative Efficiency of City School Systems," *JEd*, 75 (1912), 610; Samuel M. Lindsay, "The State and Education," *Teachers' College Record*, 17 (1916), 311–329.

23. John Dewey, "Nationalizing Education," *JEd*, 84 (1916), 425–428; William J. Reese, "Progressive School Reform in Toledo, 1898–1921," *Northwest Ohio Quarterly*, 47 (1975), 44–59; Selwyn K. Troen, *The Public and the Schools: Shaping the St. Louis School System, 1838–1920* (Columbia, Mo., 1975), pp. 187–190.

24. S. P. Orth, "The Cleveland Plan of School Administration," *PSQ*, 19 (1904), 403.

25. James T. Young, "The Administration of City Schools," *Annals*, 15 (1900), 171–185; Howard J. Rogers, "Educational Organization and Progress in American Cities," *Annals*, 25 (1905), 157–188; "Cleveland," *Annals*, 17 (1901), 145–147; Orth, "Cleveland Plan," 402–416.

26. Elwood P. Cubberly, "Politics and the Country School Problem," *Ed R*, 47 (1914), 10–21; Young, "Administration," 178.

27. Peter J. Harder, "Politics, Efficiency, and Rural Schools in Connecticut,

1866–1919," *Connecticut Historical Society Bulletin,* 44 (1979), 52–60; E. A. Kirkpatrick, "The Drift from Town to State Administration of Education in Massachusetts," *JEd,* 78 (1913), 852–854; James H. Harris, "Is Efficiency an Adequate Statement of the Aim of Education?," *JEd,* 82 (1915), 339–340; Troen, *Public and the Schools,* chap. 9.

28. David Spencer, "School Reform in Boston," *AM,* 99 (1907), 46; George A. D. Ernst, "The Movement for School Reform in Boston," *Ed R,* 28 (1904), 433–443; G. W. Anderson, "Politics and the Public Schools," *AM,* 87 (1901), 433–447.

29. "Public School Legislation in Illinois," *Dial,* 30 (1901), 129–131; "Free Text-Books in Chicago," *Outl,* 68 (1901), 517–518; Joan K. Smith, "Progressive School Administration: Ella Flagg Young and the Chicago Schools, 1905–1915," *ISHSJ,* 73 (1980), 30.

30. Dominic Candeloro, "The Chicago School Board Crisis of 1907," *JSHSJ,* 68 (1975), 396–406; "The Dismissal of Chicago Teachers Belonging to the Teachers' Federation," *SS,* 4 (1916), 93–94; Glen Edwards, "Schools and Politics in Chicago," *Survey,* 42 (1919), 724–726. See also Julia Wrigley, *Class, Politics, and Public Schools: Chicago, 1900–1950* (New Brunswick, N.J., 1982).

31. George D. Strayer, "The Baltimore School Situation," *Ed R,* 42 (1911), 325–345.

32. Quoted in Diane Ravitch, *The Great School Wars: New York City, 1805–1973* (New York, 1974), p. 166.

33. "Epoch-Making School Legislation for New York City," *Ed R,* 20 (1900), 99–102; "Revolution but Not Reform," *Outl,* 98 (1911), 522–524; A. Emerson Palmer, "New York's Education Law Revised," *AR of Rs,* 56 (1917), 78; "Control of New York City's Schools," *SS,* 1 (1915), 525–526; "The Crime of Motherhood," *LD,* 47 (1913), 802; "Restoring the Family," *NR,* 1 (November 28, 1914), 8–9. See also Ravitch, *Great School Wars,* pp. 107–108; David C. Hammack, *Power and Society: Greater New York at the Turn of the Century* (New York, 1982), chap. 9.

34. Ravitch, *Great School Wars,* pp. 189–190; Moses Stambler, "The Effect of Compulsory Education and Child Labor Laws on High School Attendance in New York City, 1898–1917," *HEQ,* 8 (1968), 184–214; "The Opening of Schools," *Outl,* 96 (1910), 146–147; "A Salutary Measure," *Dial,* 38 (1905), 255–257; William H. Maxwell, "School Achievements in New York," *Ed R,* 44 (1912), 275–309.

35. Cremin, *Transformation,* pp. 154–158; Ida G. Sargeant, "Is the Gary System the Panacea for Our Educational Ills?" *Forum,* 56 (1916), 323–326; on Tarbell, see *LD,* 55 (November 3, 1917), 27.

36. Bourne in *NR,* 2 (1915), passim, and quoted in Ravitch, *Great School Wars,* p. 202; Paul Shorey, "The Bigotry of the New Education," *Nation,* 105 (1917), 252–256; H. de W. Fuller, "The Gary System: A Summary and a Criticism," *Nation,* 102 (1916), 698–699.

37. Joseph W. McKee, "The Gary System," *Catholic World,* 102 (1915–16), 514, 516; Ravitch, *Great School Wars,* pp. 192–193, 210–211, 223, 227; "Politics against the Schools," *NR,* 6 (1916), 32–33; John Martin, "The

Gary School Issue in New York City," *NMR*, 6 (1917), 730–731; "What Is the Gary System?" *LD*, 55 (November 3, 1917), 27–28.

38. Dewey quoted in Victor S. Yarros, "Human Progress, The Idea and The Reality," *AJS*, 21 (1915), 23; David Rosenstein, "Social and Educational Standards in a Democracy at War," *SS*, 7 (1918), 421–423; J. Montgomery Gambrill, "Nationalism and Civic Education," *Teachers' College Record*, 23 (1922), 120. See also Charles W. Eliot, "Defects in American Education Revealed by the War," *SS*, 9 (1919), 1–10; Charles A. Ellwood, "The Reconstruction of Education on a Social Basis," *Ed R*, 57 (1919), 91–109.

39. "Who Is John J. Tigert?" *Survey*, 46 (1921), 489; "New York's Disloyal School-Teachers," *LD*, 55 (December 8, 1917), 32–33.

40. "German in the Schools," *SS*, 7 (1918), 645, 673–674.

41. Brian Simon, *The Politics of Educational Reform, 1920–1940* (London, 1974), pp. 37–38.

42. Charles H. Judd, "A National Educational System," *YR*, 8 (1919), 559; idem, "Federal Department of Education," *ABAJl*, 7 (1921), 63–64. See also John H. MacCracken, "A National Department of Education," *Nation*, 106 (1918), 356–357.

43. "Federal Control Urged to Meet the Crisis in Education," *Current Opinion*, 70 (1921) 76–77; George D. Strayer, "Why the Smith-Towner Bill Should Become a Law," *Ed R*, 60 (1920), 271–284; Samuel P. Capen, "Arguments against the Smith-Towner Bill," *Ed R*, 60 (1920), 285–295; Hugh S. Magill, "Education and the Federal Government," *SS*, 14 (1921), 259–263; "The Fight against Federal Aid for Schools," *LD*, 69 (April 16, 1921), 26; "Dictatorial Education," *Commonweal*, 11 (1929), 209–210.

44. "Proposed Federal Department of Education," *SS*, 17 (1923), 210–211; David Kinley, "The Relation of State and Nation in Education Policy," *SS*, 14 (1921), 600.

45. "Opposition to the Sterling-Towner Bill," *SS*, 17 (1923), 181; "Opposition to the Federal Education Bill," *SS*, 19 (1924), 457–458; U.S., *CR*, 71st Cong, 1st sess, House (April 15, 1929).

46. "Expenditures for Education and Other Things," *Bankers' Magazine*, 98 (1919), 12; Callahan, *Education and Cult of Efficiency*, p. 95; Ernest C. Witham, "Public-School Progress of the States," *ASBJ*, 75 (1927), 37–39.

47. Commission on the Reorganization of Secondary Education, *Cardinal Principles of Secondary Education*, U.S. Bureau of Education, Bulletin no. 35, (Washington, D.C., 1918); Krug, *Shaping*, pp. 385–393; Francis P. Donnelly, "A Federal Revolution in the High School," *Catholic World*, 109 (1919), 331–337.

48. Robert J. Taggert, "Pierre S. du Pont and the Great School Fight of 1919–1921," *Delaware History*, 17 (1977), 155–177.

49. *HS*, 1:375–376, 370–372, 2:1120–21. See also Ward G. Reeder, "Trends of State and National Expenditures for Education in Terms of Wealth," *ASBJ*, 73 (1926), 43–45.

50. "Tendencies in Educational Legislation," *SS*, 30 (1929), 735; "New York's Falling School Population," *SS*, 24 (1926), 176–177.

51. "Consolidated Rural Schools," *Survey*, 44 (1920), 447. See also Horace M. Kallen, "The American Public School," *NR*, 42 (1925), 117–120.

52. Glen H. Kelly, "The Constitutional and Legal Basis of Transporting Pupils to and from School," *ASBJ*, 75 (December 1927), 64–65, 76; Duncan v. People, 299 Pac. 1,060 (Colo., 1931); Sherman E. Walrod, "Power of School Boards to Discontinue Schools," *Rocky Mountain Law Review*, 5 (1932–33), 210–214.

53. Don C. Rogers, "Legal Status of the City Superintendent of Schools," *Educational Administration and Supervision*, 9 (1923), 76–77; "The Social Composition of Boards of Education," *ASBJ*, 76 (April 1928), 41.

54. Philip N. Racine, "A Progressive Fights Efficiency: The Survival of Willis Sutton, School Superintendent," *SAQ*, 76 (1977), 103–116: Howard E. Wilson, "The Trial of William McAndrew," *AR of Rs*, 77 (1928), 405–411; "A Review of School Matters of Moment," *Ed R*, 73 (1927), 233–239.

55. Stephen Ewing, "Blue Laws for School-Teachers," *HM*, 156 (1927–28), 334; "The Crime of Motherhood," 802; "Restoring the Family," *NR*, 1 (November 28, 1914), 8–9.

56. J.K.H., "School Politics in California," *Survey*, 46 (1921), 442.

57. Henry R. Linville, "Yellow-Dog Contracts for Teachers," *Nation*, 133 (1931), 13–14; "The Seattle School Case and a Court Decision," *ASBJ*, 77 (July 1928), 56; American Federation of Teachers v. Sharples, 293 Pac. 994, 998 (Wash., 1931).

58. Pugsley v. Sellmeyer, 250 S.W. 538 (Ark., 1923); Hardwick v. Board, 205 Pac. 49 (Ct. of App., 3rd Dist., Cal., 1921); Valentine v. School District, 183 N.W. 434 (Iowa, 1921); C. C. Liebler, "Legal Aspects of Residence for School Purposes," *ASBJ*, 75 (1927), 45–46, 148. See also I. N. Edwards, "Recent Judicial Decisions Relating to the Powers of Boards of Education," *School Review*, 32 (1924), 445–454.

59. Anthony v. Syracuse Univ., 231 N.Y.S. 435 (1928); Barker v. Bryn Mawr College, 122 Atl. 220 (Pa., 1923). See also James D. Hurley, "Colleges: Nature of Relation to Student: Right of Dismissal," *CLQ*, 13 (1927–28), 85–88; "Expulsion of Students from Private Educational Institutions," *Col LR*, 35 (1935), 898–905.

60. People v. N.Y. Central R.R., 119 N.E. 299 (Ill., 1918); Charles G. Howard, "School Law in Illinois," *Illinois Law Quarterly*, 5 (1922–1923), 168–175.

61. "Making Teaching Efficient and Patriotic," *Outl*, 122 (1919), 100; "Governor Smith and the New York Schools," *SS*, 21 (1925), 72.

62. Fletcher H. Swift, "The Declining Importance of State Funds in Public-School Finance," *School Review*, 29 (1931), 534–539; Robert J. Taggart, "The Modernization of Delaware's School Tax System during the 1920s," *Delaware History*, 18 (1979), 153–179.

63. "The San José School Bond Campaign," *ASBJ*, 68 (March 1924), 94; on Los Angeles, see *ASBJ*, 74 (May 1927), 70–80. See also Callahan, *Education and Cult of Efficiency*, chap. 9.

64. Swift, "Declining Importance," 540.

65. William F. Russell, "Who Shall Mould the Mind of America?," *SS*, 22

(1925), 186; W. A. Shumaker, "Legislative Power over School Curriculum," *LN*, 29 (1925), 85–87.

66. "The Segregation of Negro Children at Toms River, N.J.," *SS*, 25 (1927), 365; "Negro Students in a Gary High School," *SS*, 26 (1927), 563–564.

67. Kate Sargent, "Catholicism in Massachusetts," *Forum*, 74 (1925), 521–532, 730–742; David H. Pierce, "May Catholics Teach School?" *Nation*, 120 (1925), 485–486.

68. Robert C. Dexter, "The Gallic War in Rhode Island," *Nation*, 117 (1923), 215–216.

69. Meyer v. Nebraska, 262 U.S. 390, 403, 412 (1923). See also Kenneth B. O'Brien, Jr., "Education, Americanization, and the Supreme Court in the 1920s," *AQ*, 13 (1961), 161–171.

70. "Oregon's Outlawing of Church Schools," *LD*, 76 (January 6, 1923), 34. See also David B. Tyack, "The Perils of Pluralism: The Background of the Pierce Case," *AHR*, 74 (1968), 74–98; Lloyd P. Jorgenson, "The Oregon School Law of 1922: Passage and Sequel," *Catholic Historical Review*, 54 (1968), 455–466; M. Paul Holsinger, "The Oregon School Bill Controversy, 1922–1925," *PHR*, 37 (1968), 327–341.

71. Pierce v. Society of Sisters, 268 U.S. 510 (1925); *LD*, 85 (June 13, 1925), 7–8.

72. Ray Ginger, *Six Days or Forever? Tennessee v. John Thomas Scopes* (Boston, 1958).

73. William J. Bryan, "The Control of the Schools," *Forum*, 74 (August 1925), xxvi, xxviii; Arthur W. Page, "The Meaning of the Dayton Trial," *Spect*, 135 (1925), 134–135.

74. Virginia Gray, "Anti-Evolution Sentiment and Behavior: The Case of Arkansas," *JAH*, 57 (1970), 352–366; Cal Ledbetter, Jr., "The Antievolution Law: Church and State in Arkansas," *Arkansas Historical Quarterly*, 76 (1977), 219–233, Epperson v. Arkansas, 389 U.S. 266 (1968).

75. Dudley G. Wooten, "The Scopes Case," *Notre Dame Lawyer*, 1 (1925–26) 11–24; David E. Lilienthal, "The Tennessee Case and State Autonomy," *Outl*, 140 (1925), 453–454.

76. "Saving the Bible by Education," *Religious Education*, 20 (1925), 221–225; Robert S. Keebler, "Limitations upon the State's Control of Public Education: A Critical Analysis of State of Tennessee v. John Thomas Scopes," *Tennessee Law Review*, 6 (1928), 153–177; William Waller, "The Constitutionality of the Tennessee Anti-Evolution Act," *YLJ*, 35 (1925–26), 195. See also Charles E. Carpenter, "The Constitutionality of the Tennessee Anti-Evolution Law," *Oregon Law Review*, 6 (1926–27), 130–147.

77. Hugh R. Fraser, "Missouri Votes Down the Anti-Evolutionists," *Outl*, 145 (1927), 432–433; Willard B. Gatewood, Jr., "Politics and Piety in North Carolina: The Fundamentalist Crusade at High Tide, 1925–1927," *NCHR*, 42 (1965), 275–290; David T. Hites, "Recent Legislation on Religion and the Public Schools," *Religious Education*, 20 (1925), 292–297; "Religion and the Public Schools," *Catholic World*, 122 (1925–26), 842–844.

78. Scopes v. State, 289 S.W. 363, 367 (1927).
79. David Tyack, *Public Schools in Hard Times: The Great Depression and Recent Years* (Cambridge, Mass., 1984), p. 190.
80. Ibid., pp. 59–61.
81. Ibid., pp. 63, 65–67.
82. Ibid., pp. 32–33, 37–40.
83. Ibid., pp. 50, 81–84.
84. "The Financial Condition of the Schools of Chicago," *SS*, 31 (1930), 82; Tyack, *Public Schools*, p. 91.
85. Ibid., pp. 92–103, 110–111.

3. *Private Rights and Civil Liberties*

1. Roscoe Pound, "Interests of Personality," *HLR*, 28 (1915), 359, 349.
2. William F. Walsh, "Equitable Protection of Personal Rights," *NYULQR*, 7 (1929–30), 878–896; Zechariah Chafee, Jr., "The Progress of the Law, 1919–1920: Equitable Relief against Torts," *HLR*, 34 (1920–21), 407. See also Joseph R. Long, "Equitable Jurisdiction to Protect Personal Rights," *YLJ*, 33 (1923), 115–132.
3. Pound, "Interests of Personality," 344; idem, *Selected Essays on the Law of Torts* (Cambridge, Mass., 1924), 87n.
4. Van Vechten Veeder, "Freedom of Public Discussion," *HLR*, 23 (1910), 413; Roscoe Pound, "Equitable Relief against Defamation and Injuries to Personality," *HLR*, 29 (1915–16), 640–682.
5. William J. Gaynor, "Libel in England and America," *Cent*, 82 (1911), 824–831; Frank Carr, "The English Law of Defamation: With Especial Reference to the Distinction between Libel and Slander," *LQR*, 71 (1902), 256; Hulton v. Jones (1910) A.C. 20.
6. *ALReg*, n.s., 30 (1891), 565; George D. Watrous, "The Newspaper before the Law," *YLJ*, 9 (1899–1900), 1–16.
7. "The New Pennsylvania Libel Law," *Outl*, 74 (1903), 202–203; Alfred H. Kelly, "Constitutional Liberty and the Law of Libel: A Historian's View," *AHR*, 74 (1968), 437; Samuel W. Pennypacker, "Sensational Journalism and the Remedy," *NAR*, 190 (1909), 587–597. See also Henry Schofield, "Freedom of the Press in the United States," *American Sociological Society Publications*, 9 (1914), 102n.
8. "Is Criminal Libel Freedom of the Press?" *Outl*, 91 (1909), 415–416; "Roosevelt's Law of Libel," *Nation*, 90 (1910), 104–105; U.S. v. Press Publishing Co., 219 U.S. 1 (1911); L.F.A., "The Roosevelt Libel Suit," *Outl*, 104 (1913), 325–329; Melvin Holli, "Roosevelt vs. Newett: The Politics of Libel," *Minn H*, 47 (1963), 338–356; George T. Blakley, "Calling a Boss a Boss: Did Roosevelt Libel Barnes in 1915?" *NYH*, 60 (1979), 195–216.
9. Lawrence Vold, "Defamation by Radio," *Journal of Radio Law*, 2 (1932), 673–707; Joseph E. Keller, "Federal Control of Defamation by Radio," *Notre Dame Lawyer*, 12 (1936–37), 15–39, 134–178; Swenson v. Wood, 243 N.W. 82 (Neb., 1932).

10. Theodore Schroeder, "Presumptions and Burden of Proof as to Malice in Criminal Libel," *ALR*, 49 (1915), 199–216.

11. John E. Hallen, "The Texas Libel Law," *TLR*, 5 (1926–27), 336; *Illinois Law Bulletin*, 2 (1918–1920), 452–457; Wettach, "Recent Developments," 6.

12. "Liability for Defamation of a Group," *Col LR*, 34 (1934), 1322–35; Gordon Stoner, "The Influence of Social and Economic Ideals on the Law of Malicious Torts," *Mich LR*, 9 (1909–10), 471, 479.

13. Robert H. Wettach, "Recent Developments in Newspaper Libel," *NCLR*, 7 (1928–29), 16–17; "Statutory Extension of the Scope of Defenses in Civil Libel," *HLR*, 43 (1929–30), 131; Fowler V. Harper, "Privileged Defamation," *VLR*, 22 (1935–36), 642.

14. Samuel D. Warren and Louis D. Brandeis, "The Right to Privacy," *HLR*, 4 (1890–91), 192–220; "The Right to Privacy in Nineteenth Century America," *HLR*, 94 (1981), 1892–1910. See also Walter F. Pratt, "The Warren and Brandeis Argument for a Right to Privacy," *Public Law* (Summer 1975), 161–179; James H. Barron, "Warren and Brandeis, *The Right to Privacy*, 4 Harv. L. Rev. 193 (1890): Demystifying a Landmark Citation," *Suffolk University Law Review*, 13 (1979), 875–922; Richard F. Hixson, *Privacy in a Public Society: Human Rights in Conflict* (New York, 1987), chaps. 1–2.

15. Cases in H. C. Guttridge, "The Comparative Law of the Right to Privacy," *LQR*, 47 (1931), 219–228, and F. P. Walton, *LQR*, 47 (1931) 203–218; George Ragland, Jr., "The Right of Privacy," *KLJ*, 17 (1929), 105–110.

16. J. A. Jameson, "The Legal Relation of Photographs," *ALReg*, n.s., 8 (1869), 1; Atkinson v. Dougherty, 80 N.W. 285 (1899); Schuyler v. Curtis, 142 N.Y. 22 (1895); Corliss v. Walker, 57 Fed. Rep. 434 (1893).

17. Marks v. Jaffa, 26 N.Y.S 908, 909 (1893). See also Wilbur Larremore, "The Law of Privacy," *Col LR*, 12 (1912), 693–708.

18. Quoted in Denis O'Brien, "The Right of Privacy," *Col LR*, 2 (1902), 9; Roberson v. Rochester Folding Box Co., 64 N.E. 442 (1902); Perry L. Edwards, "Right of Privacy and Equity Relief," *CLJ*, 55 (1902), 123–127.

19. Rhodes v. Sperry & Hutchinson, 95 N.E. 1097 (1903); O'Brien, "Right of Privacy," 445. See also Elbridge L. Adams, "The Law of Privacy," *NAR*, 175 (1902), 361–369; "No Right to Privacy," *Chaut*, 35 (1902), 540–541.

20. Edison v. Edison Polyform Co., 67 Atl. 392, 394 (N.J., 1907); Pavesich v. New England Life Ins. Co., 50 S.E. 68 (Ga., 1905).

21. Vassar College v. Loose-Wiles Biscuit Co., 197 Fed. 983 (U.S.C.C, Mo., 1912).

22. George J. Leicht, "The Law Relating to a Right of Privacy," *LB*, 7 (1914), 338–339; Adams, "Law of Privacy," 363.

23. "Moving Pictures and the Right of Privacy," *YLJ*, 28 (1918–19), 271.

24. Melvin v. Reid, 297 Pac. 91 (Cal. D.C.A. 4th, 1931).

25. Byfield v. Candler, 125 S.E. 905 (Ga., 1924); Brents v. Morgan, 299 S.W. 967 (Kent., 1927).

26. Ragland, "Right of Privacy," 85; Calvert Magruder, "Mental and Emotional Disturbance in the Law of Torts," *HLR*, 49 (1936), 1067.

27. "Necessity of Statutory Protection of the Right of Privacy," *UPa LR*, 81 (1932–33), 327–332; Roscoe Pound, *Interpretations of Legal History* (New York, 1923), p. 137; Gerald Dickler, "The Right of Privacy: A Proposed Redefinition," *United States Law Review*, 70 (1936), 456; Griswold v. Connecticut, 381 U.S. 479 (1965). See also Leon Green, "The Right of Privacy," *ILR*, 27 (1932), 237–260; Basil W. Kacedon, "The Right of Privacy," *BULR*, 12 (1932), 353–395, 600–647.

28. Lynch v. Knight, 9 H.L. Cas. 577 (1861); Francis H. Bohlen, "Right to Recover for Injury Resulting from Negligence Without Impact," *ALReg*, n.s., 41 (1902), 143; Huston v. Freemansburg, 212 Pa. 548, 550 (1905). See also Archibald H. Throckmorton, "Damages for Fright," *HLR*, 34 (1920–21), 260–281; James M. Kerr, "Future Mental Suffering as an Element of Danger," *ALR*, 51 (1917), 203–214.

29. Ralph S. Bauer, "Mental Suffering as an Element of Damage in Contract," *CLJ*, 91 (1920), 141; Howard C. Joyce, "Mental Suffering in Actions for Negligence in Delivering Telegrams," *LN*, 22 (July 1918), 67–71; Martha Chamallas with Linda K. Kerber, "Women, Mothers, and the Law of Fright: A History," *Mich LR*, 88 (1990), 834.

30. Mitchell v. Rochester Railway Co., 151 N.Y. 107, 110 (1896).

31. Cohn v. Ansonia Realty Co., 148 N.Y. Supp. 39 (1915).

32. Comstock v. Wilson, 251 N.Y. 231 (1931).

33. William L. Prosser, "Intentional Infliction of Mental Suffering: A New Tort," *Mich LR*, 37 (1939), 874–892; Magruder, "Mental and Emotional Disturbance," 1035. See also Herbert F. Goodrich, "Emotional Disturbance as Legal Damage," *Mich LR*, 20 (1921–22), 497–513; Francis H. Bohlen and Harry Polikoff, "Liability in New York for the Physical Consequences of Emotional Disturbance," *Col LR*, 32 (1932), 409–419; Philip V. Manning, Jr., "The Development of the Rule of Damages for Fright in New York," *St. John's Law Review*, 6 (1931), 101–106.

34. Roscoe Pound, "Courts and Legislation," *CLJ*, 71 (1913), 228–229; Maxwell v. Dow, 176 U.S. 581 (1900). See also Norman L. Rosenberg, "The Law of Political Libel and Freedom of the Press in Nineteenth-Century America: An Interpretation," *AJLH*, 17 (1973), 336–352; Alexis J. Anderson, "The Formative Period of First Amendment Theory, 1870–1915," *AJLH*, 24 (1980), 56–75; Michael T. Gibson, "The Supreme Court and Freedom of Expression from 1791 to 1917," *FLR*, 55 (1986), 263–333.

35. Edward A. Ross, "Freedom of Communication and the Struggle for Right," *ASSP*, 9 (1914), 7.

36. Anderson, "Formative Period," 64–65; Eugene McQuillin, "Some Observations on State Laws and Municipal Ordinances in Contravention of Common Rights, Interfering with Individual Liberty, and Attempting to Regulate Personal Association and Employment," *CLJ*, 64 (1907), 210.

37. Holmes in Commonwealth v. Davis, 39 N.E. 113 (Mass., 1895); Davis v. Massachusetts, 167 U.S. 43, 47 (1897). See also P. L. Edwards, "Free

Speech and Free Press in Relation to the Police Power of the State," *CLJ*, 58 (1904), 383–386; "Free Speech and Law," *Outl*, 112 (1916), 364–365.

38. "On New York, Regulating the Press," *Nation*, 100 (1915), 348–349; on California, see Henry B. Brown, "The Liberty of the Press," *ALR*, 34 (1910), 329; on Missouri, see "Free Speech Sustained," *Outl*, 89 (1908), 355–356.

39. Coleman v. MacLennan, 98 Pac. 281, 283–284 (Kan., 1908). See also Norman L. Rosenberg, *Protecting the Best Men: An Interpretive History of the Law of Libel* (Chapel Hill, 1986), and Alfred H. Kelly, "Constitutional Liberty and the Law of Libel: A Historian's View," *AHR*, 74 (1968), 437, 440–442.

40. Thomas R. White, "Constitutional Provisions Guaranteeing Freedom of the Press in Pennsylvania," *ALReg*, n.s., 52 (1904), 12; Van Vechten Veeder, "Freedom of Public Discussion," *HLR*, 23 (1910), 433–434. On the lack of strong judicial protection of free speech in this period, see David M. Rabban, "The First Amendment in Its Forgotten Years," *YLJ*, 90 (1980–81), 514–595.

41. State v. McKee, 46 Atl. 409, 413–414 (Conn., 1900).

42. *Arena*, 35 (1906), 66–67; Morris E. Cohn, "The Censorship of Radical Materials by the Post Office," *St. Louis Law Review*, 17 (1932), 115; "Extent of the Postmaster General's Right to Regulate the Use of the Mails," *YLJ*, 12 (1902–3), 241–242; B. O. Flower, "The Postal Bureaucracy Rebuked by the Higher Courts," *Arena*, 29 (1903), 200–202; American School of Magnetic Healing v. McAnnulty, 187 U.S. 94 (1902).

43. Lewis Publishing Company v. Morgan, 229 U.S. 288, 316 (1913). See Lindsay Rogers, "The Extension of Federal Control through the Regulation of the Mails," *HLR*, 27 (1913–14), 27–44; Rogers, "Federal Interference," 579; "Freedom of the Press," *Outl*, 102 (1912), 830; Edwin C. Madden, *The U.S. Government's Shame: The Story of the Great Lewis Case* (Detroit, 1908); Sidney Morse, *The Siege of University City, The Dreyfus Case of America* (St. Louis, 1912).

44. State v. McKee, 46 Atl. 409, 411 (Conn., 1910); George W. Alger, "Sensational Journalism and the Law," *AM*, 91 (1903), 149–150; George D. Watrous, "The Newspapers before the Law," *YLJ*, 19 (1899–1900), 11–12.

45. Crow v. Shepard, 76 S.W. 79 (Mo., 1903); State v. Pioneer Press, 110 N.W. 867, 868 (Minn., 1907).

46. "Locking Up the Idaho Editors," *LD*, 46 (1913), 122; Patterson v. Colorado, 205 U.S. 454 (1907); Fox v. Washington, 236 U.S. 273, 278 (1915).

47. Toledo Newspaper Co. v. U.S., 247 U.S. 402, 419–420, 422–426 (1918); "Regulating the Press," *Nation*, 100 (1915), 348.

48. Henry F. May, *The End of American Innocence* (New York, 1959), pts. 2, 3; Christopher Lasch, *The New Radicalism in America* (New York, 1965), chap. 4; on Schroeder, see Rabban, "First Amendment," 1213; Alden Freeman, comp., *The Fight for Free Speech* (East Orange, N.J., 1909); "Birth Control and Free Speech," *Outl*, 129 (1921), 507; "Upton Sinclair and the Sunday Law," *Ind*, 71 (1911), 326–328.

49. Sidney S. Grant and S. E. Angoff, "Massachusetts and Censorship," *BULR*, 10 (1930), 36–60, 147–194; idem, "Recent Developments in Censorship," *BULR*, 10 (1930), 488–509; Gerald Glenn, "Censorship at Common Law and Under Modern Dispensation," *UPa LR*, 82 (1933–34), 114–128.

50. Forrest R. Black, "The Vanishing Bill of Rights," *ALR*, 61 (1927), 227–245.

51. Olmstead v. U.S., 277 U.S. 439, 464, 470 (1928).

52. Ibid., 455–457, 465, 452–455.

53. Frederic C. Howe, "What to Do with the Motion-Picture Show: Shall It Be Censored?," *Outl*, 107 (1914), 412–416; William Inglis, "Morals and Moving Pictures," *HW*, 54 (June 30, 1910), 13; Rev. H. A. Jump, "The Social Influence of the Moving Picture," *Playground*, 5 (1911–12), 74–84.

54. Bertram Clayton, "The Cinema and Its Censor," *FR*, 115 (1921), 222–228.

55. "The Prize Fight Moving Pictures," *Outl*, 95 (1910), 541–542; Weber v. Freed, 239 U.S. 325 (1915).

56. John Collier, "Censorship and the National Board," *Survey*, 35 (1915–16), 9–14, 31–33; idem, "Censorship in Action," *Survey*, 34 (1915), 423–427; "The Regulation of Films," *Nation*, 100 (1915), 486–487. See also p. 260 of this volume, and Robert Sklar, *Movie-Made America: A Social History of American Movies* (New York, 1975), pp. 58–61.

57. "Censorship for Moving Pictures," *Survey*, 22 (1909), 8–9; John Collier, "The Learned Judges and the Films," *Survey*, 34 (1915), 513–516; Sklar, *Movie-Made America*, pp. 31, 126–127.

58. Howe, "What to Do," 415–416; William Inglis, "Morals and Moving Pictures," *HW*, 54 (July 30, 1910), 12–13; "The Morals of the Movies," *Outl*, 107 (1914), 387–388; Sklar, *Movie-Made America*, pp. 31–32.

59. John Collier, "'Movies' and the Law," *Survey*, 27 (1911–12), 1628–29.

60. John Collier, "Film Shows and Lawmakers," *Survey*, 29 (1912–13), 643–644; "Motion Pictures: Safety and Decency," *Outl*, 103 (1913), 103; Sonya Levien, "New York's Motion Picture Law," *American City*, 9 (1913), 319–321.

61. Mutual Film Corpn. v. Industrial Commn., 236 U.S. 230, 244, 243 (1915).

62. Collier, "Learned Judges," 513–516; Gilbert H. Montague, "Censorship of Motion Pictures before the Supreme Court," *Survey*, 34 (1915), 82–83; *Col LR*, 15 (1915), 546. See also Sklar, *Movie-Made America*, pp. 127–130.

63. "Censorship," *Survey*, 46 (1921), 231–232; Joseph Leverson, "Censorship of the Movies," *Forum*, 69 (1923), 1404–14.

64. James N. Rosenberg, "Censorship in the United States," *LN*, 32 (1928), 49–53, 67–70; New York judge in Leverson, "Censorship," 1408; "The Legal Aspect of Motion-Picture Censorship," *HLR*, 44 (1930–31), 113–117; on Hays Office, see Sklar, *Movie-Made America*, pp. 90–91.

65. Edwin W. Hallinger, "Free Speech for Talkies?" *NAR*, 227 (1929), 737–

743; In re Fox Film Corp., 145 Atl. 514 (Pa., 1929); Stephen Vaughn, "Morality and Entertainment: The Origins of the Motion Picture Production Code," *JAH*, 77 (1990), 39–65. See also Leonard J. Leff and Jerold L. Simmons, *The Dame in the Kimono: Hollywood, Censorship, and the Production Code from the 1920s to the 1960s* (New York, 1990).

66. *HS*, 2:796; Morton Keller, *Regulating a New Economy: Public Policy and Economic Change in America, 1900–1933* (Cambridge, Mass., 1990), pp. 81–84.

67. "The Freedom of Radio Speech," *HLR*, 46 (1932–33), 987–993; KRKB Broadcasting Co. v. F.R.C., 47 Fed. 2d. 670 (App. D.C. 1931); "Indirect Censorship of Radio Programs," *YLJ*, 41 (1930), 967–973.

68. Paul Hutchinson, "The Freedom of the Air," *Christian Century*, 48 (1931), passim; Hilda Matheson, "Politics and Broadcasting," *PQ*, 5 (1934), 179–196; Robert W. McChesney, "Free Speech and Democracy! Louis G. Caldwell, The American Bar Association and the Debate over the Free Speech Implications of Broadcast Regulation, 1928–1938," *AJLH*, 35 (1991), 351–392; Terence N. Hickey, "Television Broadcasts of Boxing Matches," *Marquette Law Review*, 16 (1931–32), 260–266.

69. William Preston, Jr., *Aliens and Dissenters: Federal Suppression of Radicals, 1903–1933* (Cambridge, Mass., 1963), p. 67. See also Henry W. Biklé, "The Jurisdiction of the United States over Seditious Libel," *ALReg*, n.s., 41 (1902), 13.

70. "Anarchism and the Law," *Ind*, 53 (1901), 2189; "Freedom of Speech," *Ind*, 53 (1901), 2367–68; "Legislating Anarchists," *Nation*, 74 (1902), 243; Hoar quoted in Preston, *Aliens*, p. 32; Joseph W. Folk, "The Limitations of Reform," *SEP*, 182 (February 12, 1910), 1–11, 243.

71. Lindsay Rogers, "Federal Interference with Freedom of the Press," *YLJ*, 23 (1913–14), 575; Ernest Crosby, "How the United States Curtails Freedom of Thought," *NAR*, 178 (1904), 605–616; Turner v. Williams, 194 U.S. 279 (1904); Preston, *Aliens*, pp. 33–34.

72. Mary A. Hill, "The Free-Speech Fight at San Diego," *Survey*, 28 (1912), 192–194; "San Diego's Free Speech Troubles," *LD*, 46 (1913), 1146; Preston, *Aliens and Dissenters*, pp. 51, 54. See also John G. Brooks, "Freedom of Assemblage and Public Security," *ASSP*, 9 (1914), 11–28.

73. On Dayton, see "Free Speech Victories," *Arena*, 40 (1908), 345, 350–351; on Los Angeles, see Brooks, "Freedom of Assemblage," 18; on Schenectady, "The Constitution and the Police," *Survey*, 29 (1912–13), 93–94; "Disfranchising a Socialist," *LD*, 46 (1913), 1083–84.

74. "What Is Hostility to Government?" *Outl*, 104 (1913), 351; "New Jersey's Journalistic Perils," *LD*, 46 (1913), 1366–67; "In the Interpreter's House," *AMag*, 66 (1908), 208; Arthur Woods, "Reasonable Restrictions upon Freedom of Assemblage," *ASSP*, 9 (1914), 29–45.

75. Fredrick M. Davenport, "American Virility in Convention Assembled," *Outl*, 115 (1917), 229.

76. Paul L. Murphy, *World War I and the Origins of Civil Liberties in the United States* (New York, 1979), chap. 2; David M. Kennedy, *Over Here: The First World War and American Society* (New York, 1980), chap. 1.

77. Jerrold Auerbach, "Woodrow Wilson's 'Prediction' to Frank Cobb: Words Historians Should Doubt Ever Got Spoken," *JAH*, 54 (1967), 608–617; Wilson quoted in Murphy, *World War I*, 52, and "Freedom of Speech in War Time," *Nation*, 105 (1917), 220; Frederick L. Allen, "The American Tradition and the War," *Nation*, 104 (1917), 484–485.

78. James R. Mock and Cedric Larson, *Words That Won the War: The Story of the Committee on Public Information, 1917–1919* (Princeton, 1939); Stephen Vaughn, "First Amendment Liberties and the Committee on Public Information," *AJLH*, 23 (1979), 95–199; idem, *Holding Fast the Inner Lines: Democracy, Nationalism, and the Committee on Public Information* (Chapel Hill, 1980).

79. Dicey quoted in "The Right of Free Speech," *LT*, 108 (1900), 556–557; Alice G. Marquis, "Propaganda in Britain and Germany during the First World War," *JCH*, 13 (1978), 467–498. See also J. Andrew Strahan, "Is the Press Free?" *LMR*, 23 (1898), 83–92.

80. Colin Lovelace, "British Press Censorship during the First World War," in G. Boyce et al., eds, *Newspaper History from the Seventeenth Century to the Present Day* (London, 1978), pp. 307–319; Sidney Webb, "Conscience and the Conscientious Objector," *NAR*, 205 (1917), 403–420; Herbert Samuel, "The War and Liberty, III, Liberty of Speech and of the Press," *NS*, 9 (1917), 223–225; on Lloyd George, see Lovelace, "Press Censorship," 313.

81. Holford Knight, "The Restoration of Civil Liberty," *Cont R*, 116 (1919), 60; Rex v. Halliday (1917) A.C. 260.

82. Quotations in Lindsay Rogers, "The War and the English Constitution," *Forum*, 54 (1915), 31, 36. See also Arthur Marwick, *The Deluge: British Society and the First World War* (Boston, 1965), pp. 36–37.

83. Burleson quoted in "Must We Go to Jail?" *NAR*, 206 (1917), 674–675; Harold M. Hyman, *To Try Men's Souls: Loyalty Tests in American History* (Berkeley, 1959), chap. 11; Harry N. Scheiber, *The Wilson Administration and Civil Liberties, 1917–1921* (Ithaca, 1960), pp. 21–22; Murphy, *World War I*, p. 76.

84. "Must We Go to Jail?" 673–675; "Post-Office Census Under Fire," *LD*, 55 (July 28, 1917), 19; Thomas F. Carroll, "Freedom of Speech and of the Press in War Time," *Mich LR*, 17 (1919), 630–633; Scheiber, *Wilson Administration*, pp. 30–33.

85. Baruch quoted in Richard Barry, "'Freedom' of the Press," *NAR*, 208 (1918), 707, 702–709. See also David M. Rabban, "The Emergence of Modern First Amendment Doctrine," *UCLR*, 56 (1983), 1227–1228.

86. Scheiber, *Wilson Administration*, pp. 14–18, 33, 47; "An Impressive Record," *Nation*, 108 (1916), 112–113; Murphy, *World War I*, pp. 55n, 74n.

87. Davenport, "American Virility," 227–229; Hyman, *To Try Men's Souls*, chap. 11; Kennedy, *Over Here*, pp. 81–83.

88. "Loafing a Crime," *LD*, 56 (March 30, 1918), 19; State v. McClure, 105 Atl. 712 (Del., 1919). See also Ex parte Hudgins, 103 S.E. 327 (W. Va., 1920).

89. Burns and Landis quoted in Forrest R. Black, "Debs v. the United

States—A Judicial Milepost in the Road to Absolutism," *UPa LR*, 81 (1932–33), 171; Thomas F. Carroll, "Freedom of Speech and of the Press in War Time: The Espionage Act," *Mich LR*, 17 (1918), 621–665.

90. "The Espionage Cases," *HLR*, 32 (1918–19), 417–420.

91. "Ten Years for Criticism," *LD*, 57 (June 15, 1918), 13; "Mr. Hearst's Loyalty," *LD*, 57 (May 25, 1918), 12–13.

92. Star Co. v. Brush, 172 N.Y.S 851 (1918); on Amidon, see Murphy, *World War I*, p. 203; on Anderson, see J. C. Furnas, *Great Times: An Informal Social History of the United States, 1914–1929* (New York, 1974), p. 239; *Masses* Publication Co. v. Patten, 244 Fed. 535, 538 (S.D.N.Y., 1917); 246 Fed. 24, 37 (C.C.A. 2d, 1917).

93. Ernst Freund, "Freedom of Speech and Press," *NR*, 25 (1921), 346; Murphy, *World War I*, pp. 154n, 166. See also Paul L. Murphy, *The Meaning of Freedom of Speech* (Westport, Conn., 1972), chap. 3.

94. Edward S. Corwin, "Freedom of Speech and Press under the First Amendment: A Résumé," *YLJ*, 30 (1920–21), 48, 55. See also James P. Hall, "Free Speech in War Time," *Col LR*, 21 (1921), 526–537; Henry W. Taft, "Freedom of Speech and the Espionage Act," *ALR*, 55 (1921), 695–721.

95. John A. Ryan, "Freedom of Speech in War Time," *Catholic World*, 106 (1918), 577–588.

96. William R. Vance, "Freedom of Speech and of the Press," *Minn LR*, 2 (1918), 239–260.

97. Schenck v. U.S., 249 U.S. 47, 52 (1919); Fred D. Ragan, "Justice Oliver Wendell Holmes, Jr., Zechariah Chafee, Jr., and the Clear and Present Danger Test for Free Speech: The First Year, 1919," *JAH*, 58 (1971), 24–45.

98. Zechariah Chafee, Jr., "Freedom of Speech in War Time," *HLR*, 32 (1918–19), 941; idem, *Freedom of Speech* (New York, 1920).

99. "British Liberty and Arbitrary Power," *Weekly Review*, 3 (1920), 613–614; Knight, "Restoration of Civil Liberty," 63.

100. Robert Ferrari, "Political Crime," *Col LR*, 20 (1920), 308; Scheiber, *Wilson Administration*, pp. 52–53; Robert K. Murray, *Red Scare: A Study of National Hysteria, 1919–1920* (New York, 1955). See also Stanley Coben, "A Study in Nativism: The American Red Scare of 1919–1920," *PSQ*, 79 (1964), 52–75.

101. Stanley Coben, *A. Mitchell Palmer: Politician* (New York, 1963), chaps. 11–12; David Williams, "The Bureau of Investigation and Its Critics, 1919–1921: The Origins of Federal Political Surveillance," *JAH*, 68 (1981), 560–579.

102. F. G. Franklin, "Anti-Syndicalist Legislation," *APSR*, 14 (1920), 291–298; William Seagle, "The Technique of Suppression," *AMerc*, 7 (1926), 35–42.

103. Richard Roberts, "The Restoration of Civil Liberty," *Survey*, 43 (1919–20), 109–110; "The Dead-Line of Sedition," *LD*, 64 (March 6, 1920), 17–19.

104. "Labor's Attitude toward the 'Red' Agitators," *LD*, 64 (March 20, 1920), 21–23; "Forgiving War-Offenders," *LD*, 67 (October 2, 1920), 18–19.
105. "Arresting the Reds," *Outl*, 124 (1920), 53; William G. Hale, "Freedom of Speech and of the Press—Resolution of the Missouri Bar Association," *Illinois Law Bulletin*, 2 (1918–1920), 452; "The Anderson Decision," *NR*, 23 (1920), 189–191.
106. William Hard, "Perhaps the Turn of the Tide," *NR*, 21 (1919–20), 313–316; "Alien and Sedition Bills of 1920," *LD*, 64 (February 7, 1920), 11–13.
107. Franklin H. Giddings, "Three Vicious Bills," *Ind*, 102 (1920), 53, 55; John Spargo, "Aliens and the Political Party System," *WR*, 2 (1920), 175–177; "Mock Hysteria," *WR*, 2 (1920), 43–44. See also Thomas Wadney, "The Politics of Repression: A Case Study of the Red Scare in New York," *NYH*, 49 (1968), 56–75; Harold Josephson, "The Dynamics of Repression: New York during the Red Scare," *MAm*, 59 (1977), 131–141.
108. "Voters Vindicate Socialists," *Ind*, 104 (1920), 17–18; "Even If Lawful, Is It Wise?" *Outl*, 124 (1920), 94–95; "Dangerous Methods of Destroying Sedition," *Outl*, 124 (1920), 232–233, 688–689; "Albany's Ousted Socialists," *LD*, 64 (January 24, 1920), 19; *LD*, (February 7, 1920), 14–15. See also Frederick M. Davenport in *Outl*, 125 (1920), 14–15, 65–66, 126 (1920), 222–223.
109. *Massachusetts Acts*, 1913, c. 678; ibid., 1915, c. 255; Franklin, "Anti-Syndicalist Legislation," 292.
110. ACLU quoted in Hyman, *To Try Men's Souls*, p. 322.
111. Harwood v. Trembley, 116 Atl. 430, 432 (N.Y., 1922).
112. Charles A. Beard and Mary R. Beard, *American Citizenship*, rev. ed. (New York, 1921), p. 52; on Johnstown, see Oswald G. Villard, "The New Fight for Old Liberalism," *HM*, 151 (1925), 445, and pp. 270–271 in this volume.
113. On Baldwin, see Villard, "New Fight," 442, and private information.
114. "Liberalism," *Spect*, 143 (1929), 76.
115. Charles Warren, "The New 'Liberty' under the Fourteenth Amendment," *HLR*, 39 (1925–26), 433; Paterson v. Colorado, 205 U.S. 454, 464–465 (1907); Gilbert v. Minnesota, 254 U.S. 325 (1920); Gitlow v. New York 268 U.S. 652 (1925). See also M. B. Carrott, "The Supreme Court and Minority Rights in the Nineteen-Twenties," *Northwest Ohio Quarterly*, 41 (1969), 144–156.
116. Fiske v. Kansas, 274 U.S. 380 (1927); Richard C. Cortner, "The Wobblies and Fiske v. Kansas: Victory Amid Disintegration," *KH*, 4 (1981), 30–38.
117. "The Present Status of Freedom of Speech under the Federal Constitution," *HLR*, 41 (1927–28), 528; Whitney v. California, 274 U.S. 357 (1927); "The Jailing of Anita Whitney," *LD*, 87 (November 14, 1925), 15; "Criminal Syndicalism Statutes before the Supreme Court," *UPa LR*, 76 (1927–28), 203; Stromberg v. California, 283 U.S. 359 (1931). See also David W. Ryder, "California: Ashamed and Repentant," *NR*, 51 (1927), 41–44.
118. Henry W. Taft, "The Press and the Courts," *ALR*, 58 (1924), 595–617; State v. Shumaker, 164 N.E. 272, 408 (Ind., 1928); Robert W. Winston,

"How Free Is Free Speech?" *SM*, 77 (1925), 583. See also Robert H. Wettach, "Recent Developments in Newspaper Libel," *Minn LR*, 13 (1928–29), 21–38; Walter Nelles and Carol W. King, "Contempt by Publication in the United States," *Col LR*, 28 (1928), 401–431, 525–562; Frederick S. Siebert, *The Rights and Privileges of the Press* (New York, 1934).

119. State v. Guilford, 219 N.W. 770, 772 (Minn., 1925). See also Fred W. Friendly, "Censorship and Journalists' Privilege: The Case of Near versus Minnesota—A Half Century Later," *Minn H*, 46 (1978), 147–151; "The War on the Minnesota 'Gag Law,'" *LD*, 104 (February 1, 1930), 13.

120. Near v. Minnesota, 283 U.S. 697, 723, (1931).

121. "Privilege of Newspapermen to Withhold Sources of Information from the Court," *YLJ*, 45 (1935), 357–360; "Freedom of the Press to Publish Reports of Current Judicial Proceedings," *YLJ*, 45 (1935), 360–363; "Academic Freedom and the Law," *YLJ*, 46 (1936–37), 670–686.

4. Private Vices, Public Mores

1. Christopher G. Tiedeman, "Suppression of Vice: How Far a Proper and Efficient Function of Government?" *Brief*, 3 (1900), 17–28. See also John R. Dos Passos, "Gambling and Cognate Vices," *YLJ*, 14 (1904–05), 9–17.

2. Joseph W. Folk, "The Limitations of Reform," *SEP*, 182 (February 12, 1910), 10–11, 46.

3. W. A. Purrington, "The Police Power and the Police Force," *NAR*, 174 (1902), 505. See David J. Pivar, *Purity Crusade: Sexual Morality and Social Control, 1868–1900* (Westport, Conn., 1973); Paul Boyer, *Urban Masses and Moral Order in America, 1820–1920* (Cambridge, Mass., 1978); John C. Burnham, *Bad Habits: Drinking, Smoking, Taking Drugs, Gambling, Sexual Misbehavior, and Swearing in American History* (New York, 1993).

4. Morton Keller, *Affairs of State: Public Life in Late Nineteenth-Century America* (Cambridge, Mass., 1977), 515–516; John Collier, "Anthony Comstock—Liberal," *Survey*, 35 (1915–16), 127–130, 152–153. Collier listed—from who knows what source—the religious backgrounds of those arrested during the forty-three-year period of the Comstock laws, until 1916: 964 Catholics, 1,078 Jews; 954 Protestants; 564 of no religion; 12 Free Lovers; 13 Spiritualists; 27 Atheists; 6 Greeks; 22 Heathen.

5. Frank R. Kent, "Filth on Main Street," *Ind*, 114 (1925), 686.

6. U.S. v. Limehouse, 285 U.S. 424 (1932); New York judge quoted in William McAdoo, "The Theatre and the Law," *SEP*, 194 (January 25, 1922), 6; Cropsey, J., in People v. Byrne, 163 N.Y. Supp. 682, 684, 686 (1917).

7. U.S. v. Dennett, 39 Fed. 2d 564 (C.C.A. 2d, 1930); U.S. v. One Obscene Book, Entitled 'Married Love,' 48 Fed. 2d 821 (D.C.N.Y., 1931); U.S. v. One Book Entitled *Ulysses*, 72 Fed. 2d 705, 707 (C.C.A. 2d, 1934). See also Harry G. Balter, "Some Observations Concerning the Federal Obscenity Statutes," *SCLR*, 8 (1935), 267–287.

8. "A Sunday Law in France," *Ind*, 61 (1906), 180–181; on Britain, see

A. A. Strong, "The Law as to Sunday Amusements," *LMR*, 24 (1899), 155–166.

9. *Ind*, 64 (1908), 254–255.

10. Hilla v. State, 124 Md 385 (1914); decisions in L. A. Wilder, "Baseball and the Law," *Case and Comment*, 19 (1902), 151–162; Gaynor in Poole v. Hestenberg, 89 N.Y.S. 498 (1904). See also Alvin W. Johnson, "Sunday Legislation," *KLJ*, 23 (1934–35), 131–166.

11. "Can the Puritan Sunday Be Restored?" *Current Literature*, 70 (1921), 74–75.

12. C. Sidney Newhoff, "The Exception as to Works of Necessity and Charity in Sunday Labor Laws," *St. Louis Law Review*, 12 (1927), 123–138.

13. Leonhard F. Fuld, *Police Administration* (New York, 1909), pp. 401–402; Adolf Hepner, *Gambling Communities, Authorities of Law and Law Authorities under the Character of "Nickel Slots" in St. Louis* (St. Louis, 1894); Barton W. Currie, "The Transformation of the Southwest," *Cent*, 75 (1907–8), 905–910.

14. PRO, Cab 37, vol. 116, no. 49 (July 18, 1913). The *Westminster Review* in 1907 printed a number of articles dealing with aspects of social morality; these faded out by 1909.

15. Champion v. Ames, 188 U.S. 321 (1903); Ah Sim v. Wittman, 198 U.S. 500, 507 (1905); Lamar in Murphy v. California, 225 U.S. 623, 629 (1912); Morgan v. State, 90 N.W. 108 (Neb., 1902).

16. On Arkansas, see *ALReg*, n.s., 35 (1896), 100–105; Columbia Athletic Club v. State, 40 N.E. 914 (Ind., 1895); on Cincinnati, see *AR of Rs*, 23 (1901), 264–265. See also Lon B. Rogers, "The Use of the Injunction to Prevent Crime in Cases Involving Houses of Ill Fame, Gambling Houses, Bull Fights, Prize Fights, and Saloons," *KLJ*, 20 (1931–32), 329–342.

17. U.S. v. Johnston, 232 Fed. 970, 974, 975 (D. Ct. N.D.N.Y., 1916).

18. Edgar G. Sisson, "Race-Track Gambling: Its Allies and Its Foes," *World To-Day*, 7 (1904), 1528–35; *Outl*, 89 (1908), 354–355, 494–495; on New Jersey, see "Race-Track Gambling," *Outl*, 88 (1908), 151–152; George D. Smith, "Gambling in Illinois," *ILR*, 16 (1921–22), 23–45. See also Almond G. Shepard, "Horse Racing and the Courts," *Case and Comment*, 19 (1912), 176–183.

19. "The Fight against Race Track Gambling," *Outl*, 82 (1906), 483–484; "A Plain Duty for the New York Legislature," *Outl*, 85 (1907), 729–730; "Notes on Current Legislation," *APSR*, 2 (1907), 420–425; Robert F. Wesson, *Charles Evans Hughes: Politics and Reform in New York, 1905–1910* (Ithaca, 1967), pp. 189–208.

20. Franklin Hichborn, "California's Capture by Entrenched Vice," *Survey*, 32 (1914), 430.

21. "Kentucky to Choose between Beckham and Betting," *LD*, 94 (August 27, 1927), 13; Robert F. Sexton, "The Crusade against Pari-Mutual Gambling in Kentucky: A Study of Southern Progressivism in the 1920's," *FCHQ*, 50 (1976), 47–57.

22. Colin P. Campbell, "Advertising Schemes and the Lottery Law," *CLJ*, 82 (1916), 389–393.

23. J. C. Furnas, *Great Times: An Informal Social History of the United States, 1914–1929* (New York, 1974), 35; "The Anti-Cigarette Crusade," *Outl*, 67 (1901) 607–608; F. J. Munagle, "Voting Out the Streetcar Smoker," *HW*, 56 (July 20, 1912), 23; Charles A. Boyers, "A City Fights the Cigarette Habit," *American City*, 14 (1916), 369–370; Austin v. Tennessee, 179 U.S. 343 (1900). See also Thomas A. Sims, "The Constitutionality of Indiana's Anti-Cigarette Law," *MLR*, 4 (1905–06), 124–137.

24. William J. Schieffelin, "Safeguarding the Sale of Narcotics," *NCCC* (1909), 209; David F. Musto, *The American Disease: Origins of Narcotic Control* (New Haven, 1973), pp. 5–7, chap. 5. See also David T. Courtwright, *Dark Paradise: Opiate Addiction in America before 1940* (Cambridge, Mass., 1982).

25. H. Wayne Morgan, *Drugs in America: A Social History, 1800–1980* (Syracuse, 1981), pp. 102–110.

26. "Drug Addiction and the Harrison Law," *AR of Rs*, 56 (1917), 435–436; Doremus v. U.S., 253 U.S. 487 (1919); "Federal Encroachment on the Police Power: Harrison Anti-Narcotic Act," *HLR*, 32 (1918–19), 846–848.

27. Charles B. Towns, "The National Drug Problem," *Survey*, 37 (1916–17), 169–170; Jeannette Marks, "Narcotism and the War," *NAR*, 206 (1917), 882; Morgan, *Drugs in America*, pp. 111–113.

28. "Drug Prohibition," *Survey*, 41 (1918–19), 728; Gabriel G. Nahas, *Cocaine: The Great White Plague* (Middlebury, Vt., 1989); Musto, *American Disease*, chap. 8, and "Lessons of the First Cocaine Epidemic," *Wall Street Journal*, June 11, 1986.

29. Lippmann quoted in Mark T. Connolly, *The Response to Prostitution in the Progressive Era* (Chapel Hill, 1980), pp. 11–12. See also David J. Pivar, *Purity Crusade: Sexual Morality and Social Control, 1868–1900* (Westport, Conn., 1973); Ruth Rosen, *The Lost Sisterhood: Prostitution in America, 1900–1918* (Baltimore, 1982).

30. Roy Lubove, "The Progressives and the Prostitute," *Historian*, 24 (1962), 308–330; Leslie Fishbein, "Harlot or Heroine? Changing Views of Prostitution, 1870–1920," *Historian*, 43 (1980), 23–35.

31. Egal Feldman, "Prostitution, the Alien Woman, and the Progressive Imagination, 1910–1915," *AQ*, 19 (1967), 192–206.

32. Edward J. Bristow, *Vice and Vigilance: Purity Movements in Britain since 1700* (Dublin, 1977); Richard J. Evans, "Prostitution, State, and Society in Imperial Germany," *Past and Present*, 70 (1976), 106–129.

33. PRO, HO 45, 10430/A, 55693/21; ibid., B13517/39; Bristow, *Vice and Vigilance*, p. 145. See also "Do the Contagious Diseases Acts Succeed?" *WR*, 152 (1899), 608–627; 153 (1900), 135–158.

34. Eliot quoted in "The American Social Hygiene Association," *Journal of Social Hygiene*, 1 (1914), 3, and "New Methods of Grappling with the Social Evil," *Current Literature*, 54 (1913), 308–309; Albert W. Elliott, *The Cause of the Social Evil and Its Remedy* (Atlanta, 1914), pp. 21, 25.

35. John DeWitt Warner, "The Raines Liquor Tax Law: State Promotion of Vice," *Municipal Affairs*, 5 (1901), 842–851; Rev. John P. Peters, "Sup-

pression of the 'Raines Law Hotels,'" *Annals*, 32 (1908), 556–566; on the 1905 law, see *PSQ*, 20 (1905), 754–755. See also Richard L. McCormick, *From Realignment to Reform: Political Change in New York State, 1893–1910* (Ithaca, 1981), pp. 94–98.

36. New York City Committee of Fifteen, *The Social Evil*, (New York, 1902), pp. 136–137; Abraham Flexner, *Prostitution in Europe* (New York, 1914), p. 266.

37. Connelly, *Response to Prostitution*, p. 183; "Organized Vice as a Vested Interest," *Current Literature*, 52 (1912), 292–294; "The Vice Report and the Mails," *Outl*, 98 (1911), 353–354.

38. Fuld, *Police Administration*, p. 401; Thomas A. Bingham, "The Girl That Disappears," *Hampton's*, 25 (1910), 559–573.

39. L'Hote v. New Orleans, 177 U.S. 587, 596–597 (1900); City of New Orleans v. Miller, 70 So. 596 (La., 1917).

40. Joseph Mayer, "The Passing of the Red Light District—Vice Investigations and Results," *Social Hygiene*, 4 (1918), 197–209. "'Red Light' and Abatement Acts," *Col LR*, 20 (1920), 605–608; "Chicago's Morals Court," *LD*, 46 (1913), 1228–29; on New York, see Graham Taylor, "Morals Commission and Police Morals," *Survey*, 30 (1913), 62–64; "Commercialized Vice in Pittsburgh," *Survey*, 36 (1916), 215–216. See also "Putting Out the Red Lights," *LD*, 51 (1915), 1086–87; "The Social Evil," *NMR*, 5 (1916), 698–702.

41. Jeremy P. Felt, "Vice Reform as a Political Technique: The Committee of Fifteen in New York, 1900–1901," *NYH*, 54 (1973), 24–51.

42. Willoughby C. Waterman, *Prostitution and Its Repression in New York City* (New York, 1932), p. 15; Arthur B. Spingarn, *Laws Relating to Sex Morality in New York City* (New York, 1916), xi; Frederick H. Whitin, "Cleaning Up New York," *NMR*, 12 (1923), 655–662; "The Wreck of Commercialized Vice," *Survey*, 35 (1915–16), 532–533. See also Raymond B. Fosdick, "Prostitution and the Police," *Journal of Social Hygiene*, 2 (1915–16), 11–19; David C. Hammack, *Power and Society: Greater New York at the Turn of the Century* (New York, 1982), pp. 154–156.

43. On Chicago, see Robert McCurdy, "The Use of the Injunction to Destroy Commercialized Prostitution," *JCL*, 19 (1928–29), 513–517; on Cleveland, see Newton D. Baker, "Law, Police, and Social Problems," *AM*, 116 (1915), 19; on Baltimore, see "Closing a Vice District by Strangulation," *Survey*, 35 (1915–16), 229; on Portland, see Graham Taylor, "The War on Vice," *Survey*, 29 (1912–13), 137, 811–812; Harry G. Lefever, "Prostitution, Politics, and Religion: The Crusade against Vice in Atlanta, 1912," *Atlanta Historical Journal*, 24 (1980), 7–29; "Buffalo's Waning Red Lights," *Survey*, 36 (1916), 218.

44. *HW*, 109 (October 10, 1911), 740–744; "The Hand That Rocked Seattle," *LD*, 44 (1912), 577; *LD*, 48 (1914), 607–608; Norman H. Clark, *The Dry Years: Prohibition and Social Change in Washington* (Seattle, 1965), p. 72; "Seattle Changed Its Mind about Hi Gill," *AMag*, 80 (September 1915), 51–52.

45. Neil L. Shumsky, "Vice Responds to Reform: San Francisco, 1910–1914," *JUH*, 7 (1980), 31–47; Franklin Hichborn, "California's Fight for a Red Light Abatement Law," *Journal of Social Hygiene*, 1 (1914), 6–8, 194–206; "California's Campaign against Entrenched Vice," *Survey*, 32 (1914), 430; "California Red-Light Law Still in Doubt," *Survey*, 33 (1914–15), 167.

46. S. S. McClure, "The Tammanyizing of a Civilization," *McClure's*, 34 (1909–10), 117–128; "The Slave Traffic in America," *Outl*, 93 (1909), 528–529; Jane Addams, "A New Conscience and an Ancient Evil," *McClure's*, 38 (1911–12), 3–13, 232–240, 338–344, 471–478, 592–598; Brand Whitlock, "The White Slave in America," *English Review*, 16 (1913–14), 379–400; Orison S. Marsden, *The Crime of Silence* (New York, 1915).

47. Edward J. Bristow, *Prostitution and Prejudice: The Jewish Fight against White Slavery, 1870–1939* (New York, 1983); U.S. v. Keller, 213 U.S. 318 (1909); "May the United States Prevent the Importation of Vice?" *Outl*, 92 (1909), 250–251; J. Howard Whitehouse, "Parliament and the White Slave Traffic Bill," *Cont R*, 102 (1912), 688–672; Hoke v. U.S., 227 U.S. 308, 321 (1913); Lubove, "Progressives and the Prostitute," 310–315.

48. David J. Pivar, "Cleansing the Nation: The War on Prostitution, 1917–21," *Prologue*, (Spring 1980), 29–40; Harry A. Rider, "Regulation of Social Disease," *APSR*, 14 (1920), 298–302; Edith Picton-Turbervill, "America and the Social Evil," *NC*, 86 (1919), 153–163.

49. George Creel, "Where Is the Vice Fight?" *HW*, 59 (October 10, 1914), 340–341; "Popular Gullibility as Exhibited in the New White Slavery Hysteria," *Current Literature*, 56 (1914), 129; "The Futility of the White Slave Agitation as Brand Whitlock Sees It," *Current Literature*, 56 (1914), 287–288.

50. Lyman B. Stone, "Vice, Crime, and the New York Police," *AR of Rs*, 48 (1913), 73–78; Berkeley Davids, "Applications of Mann Act to Commercialized Vice," *LN*, 20 (November 1916), 146; Moll v. Morrow, 253 Pa. 442 (1916); "Commercialized Vice in Pittsburgh," *Survey*, 36 (1916), 215–216; Hedden v. Hand, 107 Atl. 285 (N.J., 1919).

51. James B. Reynolds, "A Revolution in Morals," *NMR*, 12 (1923), 586–591; poll results in "Prostitution," *Survey*, 47 (1922), 571–572; C. C. Pierce, "Prostitution: A Community Problem," *American City*, 27 (1922), 217–218; George F. Worthington, "Vice in Atlantic City," *NMR*, 13 (1924), 515–522.

52. Henry F. Pringle, "Vice and the Volstead Act," *HM*, 157 (1928), 760–768; Waterman, *Prostitution and Its Repression*, p. 149; Bascom Johnson and Paul M. Kinsie, "Prostitution in the United States," *Journal of Social Hygiene*, 19 (1933), 467–491.

53. George E. Worthington and Ruth Topping, "Summary and Comparative Study of the Special Courts in Chicago, Philadelphia, Boston, and New York," *Journal of Social Hygiene*, 9 (1923), 350; Connelly, *Response to Prostitution*, 79.

54. Helen Buckler, "Sex and the Law," *SM*, 90 (1931), 240–248. For a similar

British police scandal, see "Prostitutes and the Police," *JP*, 87 (1923), 178–179.

55. Edward Lissner, "Liquor and Common Sense in Iowa," *HW*, 53 (June 19, 1909), 13; Robert J. Sprague, "The Prohibition Crisis in Maine," *NEM*, n.s., 45 (1911), 81–88; Charles F. Thwing, "A Study of the 'Maine Law,'" *Ind*, 54 (1902), 2054–56; "New Hampshire Abandons Prohibition," *Outl*, 73 (1903), 699; on Vermont, see *AM*, 95 (1905), 302–308.

56. Clement L. M. Sites, *Centralized Administration of Liquor Laws in the American Commonwealth* (New York, 1899); C. E. Littlefield, "Anti-Canteen Legislation and the Army," *NAR*, 178 (1904), 398–413, 582–596; "Liquor Licenses for Patent Medicine Dealers," *Outl*, 81 (1905), 147.

57. *Outl*, 73 (1903), 858; *AM*, 95 (1905), 308.

58. Frank Foxcroft, "The Drift Away from Prohibition," *Outl*, 81 (1905), 69; *AM*, 95 (1905), 303.

59. Treatments of prohibition as religious moralism may be found in Richard Hofstadter, *The Age of Reform: From Bryan to F.D.R.* (New York, 1955), pp. 286–291, and Joseph Gusfield, *Symbolic Crusade: Status Politics and the American Temperance Movement* (Urbana, 1963).

60. Jack S. Blocker, *Retreat from Reform: The Prohibition Movement in the United States, 1890–1913* (Westport, Conn., 1976), p. 241; John J. Rumbarger, *Profits, Power, and Prohibition: Alcohol Reform and the Industrializing of America, 1800–1930* (Albany, 1989); Norman H. Clark, *Deliver Us from Evil: An Interpretation of American Prohibition* (New York, 1976); James H. Timberlake, *Prohibition and the Progressive Movement, 1900–1920* (Cambridge, Mass., 1963); Blocker, *Retreat*, chap. 1.

61. "Foreign Anti-Liquor Movements," *Nation*, 86 (1908), 230; "Europe's Reaction against Alcoholism," *AR of Rs*, 50 (1914), 212–216. See also Jan Romein, *The Watershed of Two Eras: Europe in 1900* (Middletown, Conn., 1978), pp. 201–204.

62. A. E. Dingle, *The Campaign for Prohibition in Victorian England: The United Kingdom Alliance, 1872–1895* (New Brunswick, N.J., 1980), p. 74, chap. 1; "The Liquor Problem in Great Britain," *Outl*, 88 (1908), 246–247. See also Brian Harrison, *Drink and the Victorians* (Pittsburgh, 1971).

63. Robert Hunter, "The Present Position of the Licensing Question," *NC*, 53 (1903), 695–707; J. E. Allen, "The Temperance Manifesto," *Ec R*, 14 (1904), 83–86; Philip Snowden, *Socialism and the Drink Question* (London, 1908), pp. 27–28 and passim; Burns quoted in Charles M. Sheldon, "Great Britain and the Liquor Business," *Ind*, 64 (1908), 648.

64. Quote in "The Government and Parties," *Blackwood's*, 173 (1903), 721; "The Temperance, Justice, and the Licensing Bill," *QR*, 208 (1908), 568–592; Edwin A. Pratt, "Sobriety by Act of Parliament," *NC*, 63 (1908), 582–594, and *The Licensed Trade* (London, 1907); Sydney Brooks, "England and Drink," *NAR*, 209 (1919), 600–613.

65. Samuel J. Barrows, "The Temperance Tidal Wave," *Outl*, 89 (1908), 557–

564. On the WCTU, see Ruth Bordin, *Woman and Temperance: The Quest for Power and Liberty, 1873–1900* (Philadelphia, 1981).

66. Barrows, "Temperance Tidal Wave," 515; W. B. Ferguson, "Temperance Teaching and Recent Legislation in Connecticut," *Ed R*, 23 (1902), 238, 240. See also Timberlake, *Prohibition*, chap. 2.

67. Simon N. Patten, "The Social Basis of Prohibition," *Char*, 20 (1908), 707–708.

68. W. Frank McClure, "The Work of the Anti-Saloon League," *World To-Day*, 11 (1906), 848–850; Norman A. Clark, *The Dry Years: Prohibition and Social Change in Washington* (Seattle, 1965), pp. 80–81. See also Timberlake, *Prohibition*, chap. 3.

69. Quotes from A. J. McKelway, "State Prohibition in Atlanta and the South," *Outl*, 86 (1907), 949; John Corrigan, "The Prohibition Wave in the South," *AR of Rs*, 36 (1907), 328; Ferdinand C. Iglehart, "The Nation's Anti-Drink Crusade," *AR of Rs*, 37 (1908), 474; on *Collier's* article, see Paul E. Isaac, *Prohibition and Politics: Turbulent Decades in Tennessee, 1885–1920* (Knoxville, 1965), pp. 147–148.

70. Iglehart, "Anti-Drink Crusade," 474; Booker T. Washington, "Prohibition and the Negro," *Outl*, 88 (1908), 587–589; idem, "Negro Crime and Strong Drink," *JCL*, 3 (1912–13), 384–392; Rev. John E. White, "Prohibition: The New Task and Opportunity of the South," *SAQ*, 7 (1908), 131, 135–139. See also C. Vann Woodward, *Origins of the New South, 1877–1913* (Baton Rouge, 1951), pp. 389–392. Clark, *Deliver*, p. 111, argues that the control of blacks was not the major purpose of southern Prohibition.

71. "New Liquor Law for South Carolina," *Outl*, 85 (1907), 492; Freeman Tilden, "The State Dispensary of South Carolina: A Lesson in Liquor Legislation," *World To-Day*, 11 (1906), 739–743; James B. Sellers, *The Prohibition Movement in Alabama, 1702–1943* (Chapel Hill, 1943), pp. 86–95, 123, 129–130.

72. Isaac, *Prohibition and Politics*; R. S. Keebler, "Prohibition in Tennessee," *NMR*, 6 (1917), 675–688; Eric R. Lacy, "Tennessee Teetotalism: Social Forces and the Politics of Progressivism," *Tennessee Historical Quarterly*, 24 (1965), 219–240.

73. Daniel J. Whitener, *Prohibition in North Carolina, 1715–1945* (Chapel Hill, 1946), pp. 141, 155–157; Josiah W. Bailey, "The Political Treatment of the Drink Evil," *SAQ*, 6 (1907), 111–124.

74. Lewis L. Gould, *Progressives and Prohibitionists: Texas Democrats in the Wilson Era* (Austin, 1973), p. 49.

75. *Current Literature*, 44 (1908), 347–350; Edward Lissner, "Dry Days in the South," *HW*, 51 (1907), 1057.

76. Peter H. Odegard, *Pressure Politics: The Story of the Anti-Saloon League* (New York, 1928); K. Austin Kerr, *Organized for Prohibition: A New History of the Anti-Saloon League* (New Haven, 1985); Robert E. Wagner, "The Anti-Saloon League in Nebraska Politics, 1898–1910," *Nebraska History*, 52 (1971), 267–292; Blocker, *Retreat*, chaps. 1, 6, 8, 9; Timberlake, *Prohibition*, chap. 5.

77. Blocker, *Retreat*, p. 14. See also Kerr, *Organized for Prohibition*, p. 80; Odegard, *Pressure Politics*, p. 5; Burton J. Hendrick, "'Frightfulness' against the Saloon," *HM*, 137 (1918), 568; and Rumbarger, *Profits*, chap. 9.

78. On Rockefeller, see David Kyvig, *Repealing National Prohibition* (Chicago, 1979), p. 96; W. M. Burke, "The Anti-Saloon League as a Political Force," *Annals*, 32 (1908), 497; J. Fanning O'Reilly, "The Growth of Prohibition and Local Option," *Ind*, 63 (1907), 567.

79. On Ohio, see W. Frank McClure, "The Work of the Anti-Saloon League," *World To-Day*, 11 (1906), 848–850; Hendrick, "Frightfulness," 569–570; on Newark, see Burke, "Anti-Saloon League," 504.

80. Barrows, "Temperance Tidal Wave," 513–521. See also "Notes on Current Legislation," *APSR*, 3 (1908–9), 66–68 and passim; Thomas P. Pegram, "The Dry Machine: The Formation of the Anti-Saloon League of Illinois," *Illinois Historical Journal*, 83 (1990), 173–186.

81. Barrows, "Temperance Tidal Wave," 513; "Politics and Temperance in the Middle West," *Ind*, 65 (1908), 906–908; "Elections and the Liquor Law," *Outl*, 87 (1907), 144–145.

82. J. Fanning O'Reilly, "The Growth of Prohibition and Local Option," *Ind*, 63 (1907), 564–567; Harold T. Smith, "Prohibition in Nevada," *Nevada Historical Society Quarterly*, 19 (1976), 227–250; Nancy T. Clarke, "The Demise of Demon Rum in Arizona," *Journal of Arizona History*, 18 (Spring 1977), 69–92; "Why Arizona Went Dry," *NR*, 1 (January 16, 1915), 20.

83. Ohio, *Constitution of 1851*, art. 15, sec. 9; Lloyd Sponholtz, "The Politics of Temperance in Ohio, 1880–1912," *OH*, 85 (1976), 4–27; "High License in Ohio," *Outl*, 82 (1906), 820.

84. R. E. Pritchard, "The Failure of Prohibition in the South," *HW*, 55 (March 18, 1911), 12–13; R. S. Keebler, "Prohibition in Tennessee," *NMR*, 6 (1917), 675–688; John Koren, "Government and Prohibition," *AM*, 117 (1916), 532; on Kansas City, see "The Sunday Closing Movement," *Outl*, 81 (1905), 693; William W. Rose, "My Fight against the Ring," *Ind*, 61 (1906), 681–684.

85. L. Ames Brown, "Prohibition's Legislative Efforts," *NAR*, 205 (1916), 590, 589–593. On the bitter cultural conflict in the Illinois legislature, see John D. Buenker, "The Illinois Legislature and Prohibition, 1907–1919," *ISHSJ*, 62 (1969), 363–384.

86. John Koren, "Drink Reform in Europe," *AM*, 116 (1916), 739; Harry Jones, "What Lloyd George Accomplished against Liquor," *WW*, 30 (1915), 433–437; Henry Carter, *The Control of the Drink Trade: A Contribution to National Efficiency, 1915–1917* (London, 1918); Thomas N. Carver, *Government Control of the Liquor Business in Great Britain and the United States* (New York, 1919); Arthur Shadwell, "The Liquor Trade in War," *NC*, 81 (1917), 332–347; idem, *Drink in 1914–1922: A Lesson in Control* (London, 1923).

87. L. Ames Brown, "The Election and Prohibition," *NAR*, 204 (1916), 852–853.

88. Larry Engelmann, "Dry Run: The Local Option Years, 1889–1917," *Michigan History*, 59 (1975), 69–90; "The Tidal Wave of Prohibition," *Ind*, 88 (1916), 299; Brown, "Election and Prohibition," 850–856.

89. John Koren, "The Status of Liquor-License Legislation," *NMR*, 2 (1913), 629–638; on Worcester, see *PSQ*, 25 (1910), 374.

90. Leisy v. Hardin, 135 U.S. 100 (1890); American Express Co. v. Iowa, 196 U.S. 133 (1905); Clifford R. Snider, "Growth of State Power under Federal Constitution to Regulate Traffic in Intoxicating Liquors," *WVLR*, 21 (1917–18), 52; quote in Charles Warren, *The Supreme Court in United States History* (Boston, 1922), 2:732.

91. Winfred T. Denison, "States' Rights and the Webb-Kenyon Liquor Law," *Col LR*, 14 (1914), 321–329; Lindsay Rogers, "State Legislation under the Webb-Kenyon Act," *CLQ*, 12 (1916–17), 225–236; Clark Distilling Co. v. Western Md./Mich. R.R., 242 U.S. 311 (1917); Wayne B. Wheeler, "General Welfare v. States' Rights," *CLJ*, 97 (1924), 282; L. Ames Brown, "Prohibition's Legislative Efforts," *NAR*, 205 (1916), 590.

92. Kerr, *Organized for Prohibition*, p. 1.

93. Bailey quoted in Gould, *Progressives and Prohibition*, p. 24; O. H. Myrick, "May Prohibition Laws Authorize the Taking of Property without Compensation?" *CLJ*, 68 (1909), 2–9.

94. George C. Sikes, "The Liquor Question and Municipal Reform," *NMR*, 5 (1916), 411–418; John Koren, "Drink Reform in the United States," *AM*, 116 (1915), 588–594; idem, "Some Aspects of the Liquor Problem," *NMR*, 3 (1914), 505–516; Whidden Graham, "After National Prohibition—What?" *NAR*, 205 (1917), 577–583.

95. Vanderlip quoted in "The Problem of War Prohibition," *Outl*, 116 (1917), 51; L. Ames Brown, "National Prohibition," *AM*, 115 (1915), 743.

96. Kerr, *Organized for Prohibition*, p. 186; Robert A. Woods, "Winning the Other Half: National Prohibition a Leading Social Issue," *Survey*, 37 (1916–17), 349.

97. *Outl*, 116 (1917), 358; "The Anti-Alcohol Movement," *Outl*, 117 (1917), 240–241; Kerr, *Organized for Prohibition*, 188; data from Arthur Newsholm, *Prohibition in America* (London, 1921), 15, and Odegard, *Pressure Politics*, 75; Joy Jackson, "Prohibition in New Orleans: The Unlikeliest Crusade," *Louisiana History*, 19 (1978), 261.

98. Robert A. Woods, "Massachusetts Ratifies," *Survey*, 40 (1918), 59–62.

99. Woods, "Massachusetts," 62; Hendrick, "Frightfulness," 563; S.K.R., "Bone Dry?" *NS*, 12 (1918–19), 461–462.

100. Charles E. Russell, "Is the World Going Dry? The Relation of Big Business to Prohibition," *Cent*, 107 (1923–24), 323–331.

101. Hawke v. Smith, 253 U.S. 221 (1920); Rhode Island v. Palmer, 253 U.S. 350 (1920); "Decisions without Opinions," *HLR*, 34 (1920–21), 314–316.

102. C. W. Saleeby, "Prohibition in North America," *Outl*, (GB), 51 (1923), 99–103, 112–113, 116; B. H. Spence, "Prohibition Enforcement in Canada," *Annals*, 109 (1923), 230–264; on Johnson, see "Prospects for Prohibition in Britain," *LD*, 64 (February 28, 1920), 34–35; F. J. P. Veale, "Restrictive Legislation," *NC*, 102 (1927), 356.

103. Arthur Newsholme, *Prohibition in America* (London, 1922), p. 62; Wayne B. Wheeler, "General Welfare v. State's Rights," *CLJ*, 97 (1924), 280–283; "Labor's Verdict on Prohibition," *LD*, 64 (March 13, 1920), 13–15; Richard T. Jones, "The Wet Drive and the A.F. of L.," *NR*, 35 (1923), 41–42; "What Some Mayors Think of Prohibition," *American City*, 27 (1922), 295–298.

104. Harry S. Warner, *Prohibition: An Adventure in Freedom* (Westerville, Ohio, 1928), pp. 254–255. See also Paul A. Carter, "Prohibition and Democracy: The Noble Experiment Reassessed," *WMH*, 56 (1973), 189–201.

105. On map, see *LD*, 60 (January 25, 1919), 1; "Wet Hopes in the Elections," *LD*, 63 (November 22, 1919), 17–18; "State Attacks on Prohibition," *LD*, 64 (March 27, 1920), 23–24; Larry Englemann, *Intemperance: The Lost War against Liquor* (New York, 1979), pp. 44–55, and *LD*, 60 (March 15, 1919), 85–90.

106. *LD*, 60 (January 25, 1919), 9–11; Kyvig, *Repealing National Prohibition*, p. 43.

107. Fabian Franklin, *What Prohibition Has Done to America* (New York, 1922), p. 29; "The Political Effects of Prohibition," *NR*, 46 (1926), 318; Robert C. Flack, "The Soul of American Prohibition," *English Review*, 47 (1928), 441.

108. Franklin, *What Prohibition Has Done*, p. 120; Everett P. Wheeler, "General Welfare and the Rights of Individuals," *CLJ*, 97 (1924), 319; Wheeler, "General Welfare," 280–283; Kyvig, *Repealing Prohibition*, p. 43.

109. Charles Steizle, "What America Thinks about Prohibition," *WW*, 55 (1928), 282–288.

110. Ernest W. Mandeville, "Prohibition in Chicago and Cincinnati," *Outl*, 140 (1925), 21–24; Gilman M. Ostrander, *The Prohibition Movement in California, 1848–1933* (Berkeley, 1957), p. 173; Clark, *Deliver*, p. 159.

111. Mandeville, "Prohibition," 22–24; Jackson, "Prohibition in New Orleans," 281; Debra P. Sansoucy, "Prohibition and Its Effect on Western Massachusetts, 1919–1920," *Historical Journal of Western Massachusetts*, 4 (1975), 27–39.

112. On Detroit, see Engelmann, *Intemperance*, pp. 122–123; Harold T. Smith, "Prohibition in Nevada," *Nevada Historical Society Quarterly*, 19 (1976), 227–250; James E. Hansen II, "Moonshine and Murder: Prohibition in Denver," *Colorado Magazine*, 50 (1973), 1–23; James A. Carter III, "Florida and Rumrunning during National Prohibition," *FHQ*, 48 (1969), 47–56.

113. Kyvig, *Repealing Prohibition*, p. 21; Rogers quote in Steizle, "What America Thinks," 282.

114. H. L. Mencken in *AMerc*, 1 (1924), 161–164.

115. Ostrander, *Prohibition Movement*, pp. 179–180; Dorothy M. Brown, *Mabel Walker Willebrandt: A Study of Power, Loyalty, and Law* (Knoxville, 1984); Harold D. Wilson, *Dry Laws and Wet Politicians* (Boston, 1922); "Gary's Bootlegging Administration," *LD*, 77 (April 21, 1923), 15–16.

116. Charles G. Ross, "The Power behind Prohibition," *Ind*, 119 (1927), 30–32; Robert B. Smith, "Politics and Prohibition Enforcement," *Ind*, 115 (1925), 381–383; Ray T. Tucker, "Seven Years of Prohibition," *NR*, 51 (1927), 68. See also Charles Merz, *The Dry Decade* (New York, 1930).

117. W. G. Clugston, "The Anti-Saloon League's Lost Virtue," *Nation*, 122 (1926), 203–205; Louis F. Budenz, "Indiana's Anti-Saloon League Goes to Jail," *Nation*, 125 (1927), 177–278; "The Court and Its Critics," *Christian Century*, 44 (1927), 990–991.

118. "Biased Justice in Ohio," *Outl*, 145 (1927), 359; Tumey v. Ohio, 273 U.S. 510 (1927); "Ohio Kills the Kangaroo Courts," *LD*, 95 (November 19, 1927), 12.

119. Frank R. Kent, "Prohibition in America," *Spect* (GB), 130 (1923), 92; on New York, see "Liquor Laws and the Constitution," *Outl*, 134 (1923), 73–74.

120. Kent, "Prohibition," 91–92; Howard L. McBain, *Prohibition, Legal and Illegal* (New York, 1928), pp. 16–17.

121. "Wet or Dry?" *Nation*, 123 (1926), 497; "The American Elections and Prohibition," *NS*, 28 (1926–27), 38–39; "The Problem of Dry America," *Nation* (GB), 38 (1925–26), 109–110; "The Dry Battle of 1928," *Christian Century*, 44 (1927), 41; "Prohibition Sectism," *Christian Century*, 45 (1928), 103–104; Reinhold Niebuhr, "Protestantism and Prohibition," *NR*, 56 (1928), 265–267.

122. McBain, "Prohibition," 14; Allan J. Lichtman, *Prejudice and the Old Politics: The Presidential Election of 1928* (Chapel Hill, 1979). See also Kyvig, *Repealing Prohibition*, pp. 134–135.

123. *NSN*, n.s., 3 (1932), 11.

124. Clark, *Deliver*, p. 187; Wilson quoted in Ostrander, *Prohibition Movement*, p. 197; "Alien Representation," *Outl*, 156 (1930), 609–610.

125. Samuel Crowther, *Prohibition and Prosperity* (New York, 1930), p. vi; "Reports of the National Commission on Law Observance and Enforcement," *MLR*, 30 (1931–32), 1–132; Bartlett C. Jones, "Prohibition and Prosperity, 1920–1930," *Social Science*, 50 (1975), 78–86.

126. "Prohibition Repeal—Practical Politics," *NR*, 63 (1930), 84–86; Kyvig, *Repealing Prohibition*, p. 191.

127. "The End of Prohibition," *NSN*, n.s., 4 (1932), 398.

128. Kyvig, *Repealing Prohibition*, pp. 152, 178.

129. Dayton E. Heckman, "Contemporary State Statutes for Liquor Control," *APSR*, 28 (1934), 628–636; "A Comparative Survey of Post-Repeal Liquor Legislation," *UPa LR*, 83 (1934–35), 510–521.

5. Crime and Punishment

1. David J. Rothman, *Conscience and Convenience: The Asylum and Its Alternatives in Progressive America* (New York, 1980), pt. 2; Lawrence J. Friedman and Robert V. Percival, *The Roots of Justice: Crime and Punishment in Alameda County, California, 1870–1910* (Chapel Hill, 1981);

Edward S. Shapiro, "Progressives and Violence," *North Dakota Quarterly*, 46 (Spring 1978), 47–55.

2. Harry A. Foster, "Do Our Laws Protect Criminals?" *ALR*, 51 (1917), 241; on Chicago, see James W. Garner, "Lynching and the Criminal Law," *SAQ*, 5 (1906), 331–341.

3. James E. Brown, "The Increase of Crime in the United States," *Ind*, 62 (1907), 831–834; Frederick Bauman, "The Cause of Crime in the United States," *ALR*, 542–550; judge's estimate in Garner, "Lynching and the Criminal Law," 340.

4. John D. Lawson and Edwin R. Keedy, "Criminal Procedure in England," *JCL*, 1 (1910–11), 766; "Criminal Procedure in England," *ALR*, 45 (1911), 161–193. See also Frederic R. Coudert, "French Criminal Procedure," *YLJ*, 19 (1909–10), 326–340; James W. Garner, "Criminal Procedure in France," *YLJ*, 25 (1915–16), 255–284.

5. Mark Sullivan, *Our Times: The United States, 1900–1925* (New York, 1930), 3:944–951; "Leaden-Heeled Justice," *Outlook*, 85 (1907), 730; Edwin R. Reedy, "Criminal Law Reform in England and the United States," *APS Proc*, 1 (1900–1901), 667–675.

6. Julius Goebel, Jr., "The Prevalence of Crime in the United States and Its Extent Compared with That in the Leading European States," *JCL*, 3 (1912–13), 754–769; Benjamin F. Martin, "Law and Order in France, 1980 and 1912," *Contemporary French Civilization*, 5 (1981), 205–212; "Children and Crime," *JP*, 88 (1924), 585–587.

7. George W. Alger, "The Irritating Efficiency of English Criminal Justice," *AM*, 142 (1928), 218–226; Cicely M. Craven, "The Progress of English Criminology," *JCL*, 24 (1933–34), 230–247.

8. Pendleton Howard, "The Rise of Summary Jurisdiction in English Criminal Law Administration," *Cal LR*, 19 (1930–31), 488; "The Criminal Law, 1910–1935," *LJ*, 79 (1935), 314–315; T. R. Fitzwalter Butler, "Developments in Criminal Law—1910–1935," *LT*, 179 (1935), 325–327.

9. Edith R. Spaulding and William Healy, "Inheritance as a Factor in Criminality," *JCL*, 4 (1913–14), 858; Carl Murchison, "American White Criminal Intelligence," *JCL*, 15 (1924–25), 253; Maurice F. Parmelee, *Criminology* (New York, 1918), pp. v, 38. See also Travis Hirschl and David Rudisill, "The Great American Search: Causes of Crime, 1876–1976," *Annals*, 423 (976), 14–22; Ethan A. Dausman, "Crime and Criminals," *ALR*, 36 (1902), 612–680; Philip Jenkins, "Eugenics, Crime, and Ideology: The Case of Progressive Pennsylvania," *PH*, 51 (1984), 64–78.

10. David A. Orebaugh, *Crime, Degeneracy, and Immigration* (Boston, 1929); E. H. Sutherland, "Public Opinion as a Cause of Crime," *JASoc*, 9 (1924–25), 51–56; "Causes of America's Crime Wave," *LD*, 63 (December 27, 1919), 14; Raymond B. Fosdick, "The Crime Wave in America," *NR*, 26 (1921), 150–152; "Cities Helpless in the Grip of Crime," *LD*, 73 (April 22, 1922), 10–11.

11. Linda C. Bowler, "Law Enforcement and the Alien," *NCSWP* (1931), 479–494; Marcus Kavanagh, *The Criminal and His Allies* (Indianapolis, 1928),

pp. ix, xii; Lawrence Veiller, "The Rising Tide of Crime," *WW*, 51 (1925–26), 133–147; on the Wickersham Committee, see Samuel Walker, *Popular Justice: A History of American Criminal Justice* (New York, 1980), pp. 173–175.

12. Louis N. Robinson, "History of Criminal Statistics (1908–1933)," *JCL*, 24 (1933–34), 125–139; S. S. McClure, "The Increase of Lawlessness in the United States," *McClure's*, 24 (1904–5), 163–171; "Crime in America," *LT*, 118 (1905), 471; Charles A. Ellwood, "Has Crime Increased in the United States since 1880?" *JCL*, 1 (1910–11), 378–385; Harold E. Pepinsky, "The Growth of Crime in the United States," *Annals*, 423 (1976), 23–30. See also Eric H. Monkkonen, "A Disorderly People? Urban Order in the Nineteenth and Twentieth Centuries," *JAH*, 68 (1981), 539–559; idem, "The Organized Response to Crime in Nineteenth- and Twentieth-Century America," *JIH*, 14 (1983), 113–128.

13. Samuel J. Barrows, *New Legislation Concerning Crimes, Misdemeanors and Penalties* (Washington, D.C., 1900), pp. xv–xxii; idem, "New Crimes and Punishments," *Ind*, 55 (1903), 720–723; on Chicago, see Edward Lindsey, "Legislation on Crime in Twenty-Five Years," *JCL*, 24 (1933–34), 110–111.

14. Lawrence J. Friedman, "Crimes of Mobility," *SLR*, 43 (1991), 637–658; Arthur C. Hall, *Crime in Its Relations to Social Progress* (New York, 1902), pp. 331–332; on automobile-induced crime, see Francis W. Laurent, *The Business of a Trial Court* (Madison, 1959), pp. 35–36, 49, 78–79; Arch Mandel, "Analysis of Arrests and Police Court Cases in Detroit," *JCL*, 11 (1920–21), 413–418; Arthur E. Wood, "A Study of Arrests in Detroit, 1913 to 1919," *JCL*, 21 (1930–31), 168–200.

15. Dwight C. Smith, Jr., "Mafia: The Prototypical Alien Conspiracy," *Annals*, 423 (1976), 75–88; Luciano Iorizzo and Salvatore Mondello, "Origins of Italian-American Criminality: From New Orleans through Prohibition," *Italian Americana*, 1 (1975), 217–237.

16. George K. Turner, "Tammany's Control of New York by Professional Criminals," *McClure's*, 33 (1909), 117–134; Thomas A. Bingham, "Foreign Criminals in New York," *NAR*, 188 (1908), 383–394; rebuttal by Francis J. Oppenheim, "Jewish Criminality," *Ind*, 64 (1908), 640–642. See also Maynard Shipley, "Effects of Immigration on Homicide in American Cities," *PSM*, 69 (1906), 160–174, and rebuttal by Morris Loeb, 375–379.

17. John Landesco, "The Criminal Underworld of Chicago in the 80s and 90s," *JCL*, 25 (1934–35), 341–357, 928–940; Maynard Shipley, "Crimes of Violence in Chicago and Greater New York," *PSM*, 73 (1908), 127–134.

18. Francis B. Sayre, "Criminal Responsibility for the Acts of Another," *HLR*, 43 (1930), 719; Lindsey, "Legislation on Crime," 109; *Recent Social Trends in the United States* (New York, 1933), 1:lviii, 2: chap. 22.

19. Lindsey, "Legislation on Crime," 110–111; Edward Rubin, "A Statistical Study of Federal Criminal Prosecutions," *LCP*, 1 (1934), 494–503.

20. Arthur V. Lashly, "The Illinois Crime Survey," *JCL*, 20 (1929–30), 588.

21. Clarence S. Darrow, "Crime and the Alarmists," *HM*, 153 (1926), 535–544.

22. Kenneth E. Barnhart, *A Study of Homicide in the United States* (Birmingham, Ala., 1932), p. 23; on Chicago, see Richard E. Enright, "Our Biggest Business—Crime," *NAR*, 228 (1929), 385; Florence M. Warner, *Juvenile Detention in the United States* (London, 1933), p. 147; Joint Committee on Negro Child Study in New York City, *A Study of Delinquent and Neglected Negro Children before the New York Children's Court* (New York, 1927).

23. John R. Brazil, "Murder Trials, Murder, and Twenties America," *AQ*, 33 (1981), 163–184.

24. Robert D. Highfill, "The Effect of News of Crime and Scandal upon Public Opinion," *ALR*, 62 (1928), 93; "The Part Newspapers Play in the Administration of Justice," *CLJ*, 98 (1925), 145–159; Leon R. Yankwich, "Sensationalism in Crime News: Newspapers and the Administration of Justice," *ABAJl*, 19 (1933), 51–53.

25. John Gunther, "The High Cost of Hoodlums," *HM*, 159 (1929), 530–531; R. L. Duffus, "The Function of the Racketeer," *NR*, 58 (1929), 166–168; Louis Adamic, "Racketeers and Organized Labor," *HM*, 161 (1930), 404–416; "The Rackets of New York," *NS*, 30 (1930), 262–264. See also Katherine O. McCarthy, "Racketeering: A Contribution to a Bibliography," *JCL*, 22 (1931–32), 578–586.

26. Lashly, "Illinois Crime Survey," 591.

27. John Landesco, "Crime and the Failure of Institutions in Chicago's Immigrant Areas," *JCL*, 23 (1932–33), 238–248; on the ethnic breakdown, see Mark H. Haller, "Urban Crime and Criminal Justice: The Chicago Case," *JAH*, 57 (1970), 620; Daniel Bell, "Crime as an American Way of Life," in *The End of Ideology* (New York, 1960), pp. 127–150.

28. Richard E. Enright, "Our Biggest Business—Crime," *NAR*, 228 (1929), 385, 388. See also Lawrence Veiller, "The Rising Tide of Crime," *WW*, 51 (1925–26), 133–147.

29. *HS*, 1:420; Ray M. Simpson, "Unemployment and Prison Commitments," *JCL*, 23 (1932–33), 404–414; Albert C. Wagner, "Crime and Economic Change in Philadelphia, 1924–1934," *JCL*, 27 (1936–37), 483–490.

30. Martin Mooney, *Crime Incorporated* (New York, 1935), p. 5; Gordon L. Hostetter and Thomas Q. Beasley, "The Rising Tide of Racketeering," *PQ*, 4 (1933), 406.

31. Mooney, *Crime*, pp. 37–38.

32. Samuel J. Barrows, *New Legislation Concerning Crimes, Misdemeanors, and Penalties* (Washington, D.C., 1900), pp. xii–xiii; Rothman, *Conscience and Convenience*; Herbert L. Packer, "Two Models of the Criminal Process," *UPa LR*, 113 (1964), 1–68.

33. Richard M. Brown, "Legal and Behavioral Perspectives on American Vigilantism," in *PAH*, 5 (1971), 95–144; "Administration of Justice in the United States," *Annals*, 36 (1910); Samuel Walker, *Popular Justice: A History of American Criminal Justice* (New York, 1980), pts. 2 and 3.

34. "The Proposed Model Statute on Insanity and Criminal Responsibility," *HLR*, 30 (1916–17), 179.

35. Samuel J. Barrows, *The Criminal Insane in the United States and Foreign*

Countries (Washington, D.C., 1898); William E. Mitchell, "McNaghten's Case and Beyond," *ALReg*, n.s., 4 (1902), 265–282; E. Bowen-Edwards, "The Criminal Law and the Insane," *FR*, 114 (1920), 316–327; Winfred Overholser, "The History and Operation of the Briggs Law of Massachusetts," *LCP*, 2 (1935), 436–447; Anthony M. Turano, "Insanity and the Law," *AMerc*, 19 (1930), 487–495; L. A. Tulin, "The Problem of Mental Disorder in Crime: A Survey," *Col LR*, 32 (1932), 933–963.

36. Mark H. Haller, "Urban Crime and Criminal Justice: The Chicago Case," *JAH*, 57 (1970), 629, 639; *WW*, 51 (1925–26), passim; "The Necessity of Gun-Toting," *LD*, 70 (August 6, 1921), 33–34; Joseph P. Chamberlain, "Legislatures and the Pistol Problem," *ABAJl*, 11 (1925), 596–598; "Federal Cooperation in Criminal Law Enforcement," *HLR*, 48 (1935), 489–498.

37. Holmes in Kepner v. U.S., 195 U.S. 100, 134 (1904); William H. Taft, "The Administration of Criminal Law," *YLJ*, 15 (1905–6), 1–17. See also E. M. Grossman, "The Growing Disrespect for the Law," *ALR*, 45 (1911), 25–46.

38. George W. Alger, "American Discontent with Criminal Law," *Outl*, 86 (1907), 327; on Amidon, see George W. Moore, "The Quest for Error and the Doing of Justice," *Outl*, 84 (1906), 75–78.

39. Moore, "The Quest for Error," 75–78; Edward Lindsey, "Appeals in Homicide Cases in Pennsylvania, 1905–1910," *UPa LR*, 59 (1911), 623–642; on Wigmore, see "The Law's Delay," *UPa LR*, 59 (1911), 387–388; on Pound, see "The Courts and the Criminal," *UPa LR*, 59 (1911), 251–252; Chester G. Vernier, "Legislative and Judicial Tendencies in the Field of Criminal Law," *ILR*, 11 (1916), 69–90.

40. Samuel J. Barrows, "The Projected Criminal Code of the United States," *AM*, 53 (1901), 1730–33; D. K. Watson, *The Growth of the Criminal Law of the United States*, U.S., 57th Cong., 1st sess., House, Doc. 362 (Washington, D.C., 1902).

41. Sheldon Glueck and Eleanor T. Glueck, "Predictability in the Administration of Criminal Justice," *HLR*, 42 (1928–29), 297, 329; Raymond Moley, "Politics and Crime," *Annals*, 125 (1926), 78–84; Sheldon Glueck, "Significant Transformations in the Administration of Criminal Justice," *Mental Hygiene*, 14 (1930), 288–291; Fred E. Haynes, "What Is Crime Today?" *Ind*, 114 (1925), 316.

42. Samuel J. Barrows, "Recent Tendencies in American Criminal Legislation," *Annals*, 23 (1904), 494; Jerome Michael and Mortimer Adler, *Crime, Law, and Social Science* (London, 1933), p. xxviii; Edwin S. Mack, "The Revival of Criminal Equity," *HLR*, 16 (1902–3), 389–403.

43. Champe S. Andrews, "Private Societies and the Enforcement of the Criminal Law," *Forum*, 36 (1904–5), 280–288.

44. *ABA Reports*, 47 (1922), 424–432; James B. Reynolds, "Proposed Reforms of American Criminal Law," *YLJ*, 32 (1922–23), 368–375.

45. J. Hugo Grimm, "Developments in the Criminal Law of Missouri," *St. Louis Law Review*, 15 (1929–30), 65; Edwin R. Keedy, "Administration of the Criminal Law," *YLJ*, 31 (1921–22), 240–262.

46. Raymond Moley, "Some Tendencies in Criminal Law Administration," *PSQ*, 42 (1927), 497–523.

47. "The Administration of Bail," *YLJ*, 41 (1932), 293–300; Jay Wishingrad, "The Plea Bargain in Historical Perspective," *Buffalo Law Review*, 23 (1974), 499–527. On the large number of nolle prosequi cases in Georgia counties, see "Crime and the Georgia Courts: A Statistical Analysis," *JCL*, 16 (1925–26), 213.

48. Roscoe Pound, "Criminal Justice in the American City," *Survey*, 47 (1921), 154; idem, "The Future of the Criminal Law," *Col LR*, 21 (1921), 9; idem, *Criminal Justice in America* (New York, 1930), pp. 175–176, 179.

49. Walter Lippmann, "The Underworld: A Stultified Conscience," *Forum*, 85 (1931), 68.

50. John A. Fairlie, "Police Administration," *PSQ*, 16 (1901), 1–23.

51. District of Columbia, *Police Regulations* (Washington, D.C., 1910). See also Leonhard F. Fuld, *Police Administration* (New York, 1909).

52. James F. Richardson, *The New York Police* (New York, 1970), chap. 11; A. G. Warner, "Politics and Crime," *AJS*, 1 (1895–96), 290–298; Eugene Watts, "The Police in Atlanta, 1890–1905," *JSH*, 39 (1973), 165–182. See also a *World To-Day* series in 1910 on police brutality and corruption.

53. Gene E. Carter and Elaine H. Carter, *Police Reform in the United States: The Era of August Vollmer, 1905–1932* (Berkeley, 1975).

54. "Policewomen in Chicago," *LD*, 47 (1913), 271.

55. Walker, *Popular Justice*, p. 145; "Pennsylvania's State Constabulary," *Nation*, 81 (1905), 49–50; "Policing a State," *Nation*, 98 (1914), 5–6; "The State Constabulary," *Nation*, 98 (1914) 5–6; "State Constabularies Needed," *Outl*, 106 (1914), 145.

56. J.W.G., "Veto of the New York Anti-Mugging Bill," *JCL*, 2 (1911–12), 343–345; Newton D. Baker, "Law, Police, and Social Problems," *AM*, 116 (1915), 14.

57. August Vollmer, "Police Progress in the Past Twenty-Five Years," *JCL*, 24 (1932–33), 161–175; idem, *The Police and Modern Society* (Berkeley, 1936). See also Raymond Fosdick, *American Police Systems* (New York, 1921).

58. Bruce Smith, *The State Police* (New York, 1925); Margaret M. Corcoran, "State Police in the United States: A Bibliography," *JCL*, 13 (1923–24), 544–545; Milton Conover, "State Police," *APSR*, 15 (1921), 82–93; idem, "State Police Developments," 779.

59. St. Louis Board of Police Commissioners, *Official Manual of the St. Louis Police Department* (St. Louis, 1920); Smedley D. Butler, "Making War on the Gangs: A Plan to Take the Police Out of Politics," *Forum*, 85 (1931), 131–141; on the FBI, see Justin Miller, "Criminal Law—An Agency for Social Control," *YLJ*, 43 (1933–34), 691–715.

60. Milton Conover, "State Police Developments: 1921–1924," *APSR*, 18 (1924), 773–781; August Vollmer and Alfred E. Parker, *Crime and the State Police* (Berkeley, 1936), p. 143.

61. Ernest J. Hopkins, *Our Lawless Police* (New York, 1931), p. 67, and "The

Lawless Arm of the Law," *AM*, 148 (1931), 279–287; H. L. Mencken, *The American Language*, 4th ed. (New York, 1937), p. 577; Edwin R. Keedy, "The Third Degree and Legal Interrogation of Suspects," *UPa LR*, 85 (1937), 761–777; "The Third Degree and the Privilege against Self Incrimination," *CLQ*, 13 (1928), 211; "The Third Degree," *HLR*, 43 (1929–30), 617–623; People v. Doran, 159 N.E. 379 (N.Y., 1927); People v. Sweeney, 136 N.E. 687 (Ill., 1922); David v. U.S., 32 F. 2d 860 (C.C.A. 9th, 1929).

62. Friedman and Percival, *Roots of Justice*, pp. 310–314; "The Virginia Court Massacre," *LD*, 44 (1912), 627–628; Ernest Poole, "The Story of Manuel Levine," *Outl*, 87 (1907), 413–419; Thomas L. Woolwine, "A Story of Law Enforcement," *WW*, 18 (1909), 1828–33.

63. Mary E. Paddon, "The Inferior Criminal Courts of New York City," *JCL*, 11 (1920–21), 10; Robert Ferrari, "The Immigrant in the New York County Criminal Courts," *JCL*, 3 (1912–13), 194–219.

64. J.W.G., "The Success of the Chicago Municipal Court," *JCL*, 1 (1910–11), 655–656; William B. Herle, "A Court That Does Its Job," *WW*, 21 (1910), 14,198–199.

65. William E. Barton, "Judge Cleland and Chicago's Four Hundred," *Ind*, 64 (1908), 141–147.

66. Walker, *Popular Justice*, p. 156.

67. On Milwaukee, see Steven L. Schlossman, *Love and the American Delinquent: The Theory and Practice of 'Progressive' Juvenile Justice, 1825–1920* (Chicago, 1977), chap. 4; Bernard Flexner, "The Juvenile Court, Its Legal Aspects," *Annals*, 36 (1910), 49–50; Friedman and Percival, *Roots of Justice*, p. 316. See also Anthony M. Platt, *The Child-Savers: The Invention of Delinquency* (Chicago, 1969); Ellen Ryerson, *The Best-Laid Plans: America's Juvenile Experiment* (New York, 1978), chap. 4; Sanford J. Fox, "Juvenile Justice Reform: An Historical Perspective," *SLR*, 22 (1970), 1187–1239.

68. Justin Miller, "General Progress in Criminal Procedure," *Annals*, 136 (1928), 112–118; F. R. Aumann, "Where To with Criminal Equity?" *ALR*, 62 (1928), 355–370. See also Charles K. Burdick, "Criminal Justice in America," *ABAJl*, 11 (1925), 510–515.

69. Ryerson, *Best-Laid Plans*, p. 96; Grace Abbott, "Trends in Juvenile Delinquency Statistics," *JCL*, 17 (1926–27), 168; "Criminal Appeals in Southern States," *MLR*, 21 (1922–23), 584–586; Justin Miller, "Appeals by the State in Criminal Cases," *YLJ*, 36 (1926–27), 485–512; "Lawless Enforcement of Law," *HLR*, 33 (1919–20), 956–960.

70. Moseley v. State, 73 So. 791 (Miss., 1916); Skuy v. U.S., 261 Fed. 316, 320 (1919).

71. James D. Barnett, "Executive, Legislative, and Judiciary in Pardon," *ALR*, 49 (1915), 684–734; "The 'Probation System' in the United States," *LT*, 114 (1903), 407; Sir Evelyn Ruggles-Brise, "An English View of the American Penal System," *JCL*, 2 (1911–12), 363–364.

72. Herbert C. Parsons, "Probation—Eight Years After," *Survey*, 52 (1924), 231–233; Dorothy W. Burke, *Youth and Crime* (Washington, D.C., 1930),

p. 4. See also Charles L. Chute, "The Progress of Probation and Social Treatment in the Courts," *JCL*, 24 (1933–34), 60–73.

73. Ex parte United States, 242 U.S. 27, 37 (1916); Anthony A. Goerner, "Criminal Law: Probation: The Federal Probation Act," *CLQ*, 12 (1926–27), 83–97.

74. Ruggles-Brise, "English View," 358–359, 360–362; T.H., "Pardon and Parole in America," *LT*, 114 (1903), 423; Eugene Smith, "The Old Penology and the New," *NAR*, 184 (1907), 80–86; L. C. Stoors, "The Indeterminate Sentence Law in Michigan," *Char*, 10 (1903), 37–38. See also Charlton T. Lewis, "The Indeterminate Sentence," *YLJ*, 9 (1899–1900), 17–30.

75. A. K. McNamara, "The Constitutionality of the Federal Parole Law," *ALR*, 45 (1911), 401–414; Robert H. Gault, "The Parole System a Means of Protection," *JCL*, 5 (1914–15), 799–806. See also Edward Lindsey, "Historical Sketch of the Indeterminate Sentencing and Parole System," *JCL*, 16 (1925–26), 9–126; John P. Bramer, *A Treatise Giving the History of Parole* (New York, 1926).

76. Amos W. Butler, "The Indeterminate Sentence and Parole Law in Indiana," *JCL*, 4 (1913–14), 924–926; idem, "The Operation of the Indeterminate Sentence and Parole Law," *JCL*, 6 (1915–16), 885–893.

77. Gault, "Parole System," 799–802; on Ohio, see Harris R. Cooley, "The Criminal Treatment of Crime," *Arena*, 30 (1913), 617–622; Tirey L. Ford, "Purpose, Operation, and Result of the Parole Law of California," *LB*, 5 (1912), 36–41.

78. Illinois Parole Board, *The Workings of the Indeterminate Sentencing Law and the Parole System in Illinois* (Chicago, 1928), p. 71; on Pennsylvania, see "Availability of Pardons and Commutations as Means of Conditional Release," *HLR*, 39 (1925–1926), 112n.

79. John C. Charney, "Work of the Board of Pardons in Indiana," *ILJ*, 2 (1926–27), 170–173; Howard McClellan, "A Panic in Crookdom," *AR of Rs*, 75 (1927), 155–163; Luther S. Cressman, "New York's Bludgeon Law," *AR of Rs*, 77 (1928), 77–80.

80. S. J. Barrows, *The Reformatory System in the United States* (Washington, D.C., 1900), p. 14; E. H. Pickersgill, "Prisons in England and America: A Contrast," *LMR*, 24 (1899), 408–421.

81. Charles H. Reeve, *The Prison Question* (Chicago, 1890); Rothman, *Conscience and Convenience*, chap. 4.

82. "A Revolutionary Appointment," *Outl*, 106 (1914), 118–119; "Labor on Prison Reform," *NR*, 10 (1917), 9–10.

83. Bryant Smith, "Efficiency v. Reform in Prison Administration," *JCL*, 11 (1920–21), 587–597; Mary C. Terrell, "Peonage in the United States: The Convict Lease System and the Chain Gangs," *NC*, 62 (1907), 306–322; "The End of the Convict Lease System in Georgia," *Outl*, 90 (1908), 238–239.

84. Henry C. Mohler, "Convict Labor Policies," *JCL*, 15 (1924–25), 530–597; Blake McKelvey, "The Prison Labor Problem: 1875–1900," *JCL*, 25 (1934–

35), 254–270; E. T. Hiller, "Development of the Systems of Control of Convict Labor in the United States," *JCL*, 5 (1914–15), 241–269; Florence L. Sanville, "Social Legislation in the Keystone State," *Survey*, 34 (1915), 84–88. See also "The Convict Labor Problem," *Nation*, 70 (1900), 332–333.

85. "County Jail System in New Jersey Condemned: A Report on Its Abuses and Absurdities," *Char*, 10 (1903), 70–76; George W. Kirchway, "Report of the New Jersey Prison Inquiry Commission," *JCL*, 9 (1918), 207–239.

86. E. H. Pickersgill, "Prisons in England and America: A Contrast," *LMR*, 24 (1899), 417; "Graft, Vice, Murder in Nebraska Prison," *Survey*, 28 (1912), 111–112; Jack M. Holl and Roger A. Pederson, "The Washington State Reformatory at Monroe: A Progressive Ornament," *PNWQ*, 67 (1976), 21–28.

87. Ray M. During Simpson, "Prison Stagnation since 1900," *JCL*, 26 (1935–36), 870, 887; "Abominable Conditions in County Jails," *American City*, 33 (1925), 606–608; Thorsten Sellin, "Prison Tendencies in Europe," *NCSWP* (1930), 118–132; idem, "A Quarter Century's Progress in Penal Institutions for Adults in the United States," *JCL*, 24 (1933–34), 142. See also Joseph Fishman, *The Crucibles of Crime: The Shocking Story of the American Jail* (New York, 1923); Chicago Community Trust, *Reports Comprising the Survey of the Cook County Jail* (Chicago, 1922).

88. Rothman, *Conscience and Convenience*, chap. 11.

89. A. L. Bowen, "The Joliet Prison and the Riots of June 5th," *JCL*, 8 (1917–18), 576–585; "The Bloodiest Prison Mutiny," *LD*, 103 (November 19, 1929), 8–9; Milton MacKaye, "Riots in Our Prisons," *Outl*, 153 (1929), 325–328, 356; "New York State's Prison Revolts," *LD*, 102 (August 10, 1929), 8–9; "Desperation Will Out," *Survey*, 63 (1929–30), 451–452; George W. Alger, "The Revolt of the Convicts," *AM*, 145 (1930), 688–697.

90. Maynard Shipley, "Should Capital Punishment be Abolished?" *JCL*, 2 (1911–12), 48–55.

91. Maynard Shipley, "Does Capital Punishment Prevent Convictions?" *ALR*, 43 (1909), 321–334. See also Samuel J. Barrows, "Legislative Tendencies as to Capital Punishment," *Annals*, 29 (1907), 618–662.

92. Richard B. Dressner and Glenn C. Altschuler, "Sentiment and Statistics in the Progressive Era: The Debate on Capital Punishment in New York," *NYH*, 56 (1975), 191–209; "Crime and Capital Punishment: A Symposium," *Annals*, 29 (1907), 601–629; E. H. Sutherland, "Murder and the Death Penalty," *JCL*, 15 (1924–25), 522–529.

93. "Cruel and Unusual Punishments," *YLJ*, 11 (1901–2), 55–56; on Colorado, see Raymond T. Bye, *Capital Punishment in the United States* (Philadelphia, 1919), p. 9.

94. On Hunt, see "The New Criminology," *Hearst's*, 22 (September 1912), 88–96; "Why the People of Arizona Voted to Keep Their Hangman," *Survey*, 33 (1915), 585.

95. Jacob Goldstein, "Shall Capital Punishment Be Abolished?—How Pennsylvania Is Answering the Question," *Outl*, 117 (1917), 18–19; Bye, *Capi-*

tal Punishment, pp. 12–13; Raymond T. Bye, "Recent History and Present Status of Capital Punishment in the United States," *ALR*, 50 (1926), 905–920.

96. "Reports of the National Commission on Law Observance and Enforcement," *Mich LR*, 30 (1931–32), passim; Walker, *Popular Justice*, pp. 173–175.

6. Social Welfare

1. Peter Flora et al., *State, Economy, and Society in Western Europe, 1815–1975* (Frankfurt, 1983), 1:454. See also Peter Flora and Arnold J. Heidenheimer, *The Development of Welfare States in Europe and America* (New Brunswick, N.J., 1981); Charles W. Pipkin, *The Idea of Social Justice: A Study of Legislation and Administration and the Labor Movement in England and France between 1900 and 1926* (New York, 1927), and *Social Politics and Modern Democracies*, 2 vols. (New York, 1931).

2. W. J. Mommsen, ed., *The Emergence of the Welfare State in Britain and Germany, 1850–1950* (London, 1981); William H. Dawson, "The Legal Position of German Workmen," *PSQ*, 21 (1906), 264–287; John H. Weiss, "Origins of the French Welfare State: Poor Relief in the Third Republic, 1871–1914," *French Historical Studies*, 13 (1983), 47–78.

3. Bentley Gilbert, "Winston Churchill versus the Webbs: The Origins of British Unemployment Insurance," *AHR*, 71 (1966), 854–855; PRO, Cab 37, vol. 96 (1908), no. 159, 1; Asa Briggs, "The Welfare State in Historical Perspective," *Archives européennes de sociologie*, 2 (1961), 234–235, 241. See also C. L. Mowat, "Social Legislation in Britain and the United States in the Early Twentieth Century: A Problem in the History of Ideas," in *Historical Studies: Papers Read before the Irish Conference of Historians*, ed. J. C. Beckett (New York, 1969), 6:81–96.

4. H. A. Mess, *Factory Legislation and Its Administration, 1891–1924* (London, 1926); Bentley B. Gilbert, *British Social Policy, 1914–1939* (Ithaca, 1970); Derek Fraser, *The Evolution of the British Welfare State*, 2nd ed. (London, 1984); Philip Abrams, "The Failure of Social Reform, 1918–1920," *Past and Present*, no. 24 (1963), 43–64.

5. Mowat, "Social Legislation," 90.

6. Gaston Rimlinger, *Welfare Policy and Industrialization in Europe, America, and Russia* (New York, 1971), pp. 7–8; David B. Robertson, "The Bias of American Federalism: The Limits of Welfare-State Development in the Progressive Era," *JPH*, 1 (1989), 261–291. See also Ann S. Orloff, "The Political Origins of America's Belated Welfare State," in *The Politics of Social Policy in the United States*, ed. Margaret Weir et al. (Princeton, 1988), pp. 37–80; Theda Skocpol and John Ikenberry, "The Political Function of the American Welfare State in Historical and Comparative Perspective," *Comparative Social Research*, 6 (1983), 87–148; Edwin Amenta and Theda Skocpol, "Taking Exception: Explaining

the Distinctiveness of American Public Policies in the Last Century," in *The Comparative History of Public Policy*, ed. Francis G. Castles (Oxford, 1989), pp. 292–333.

7. Edward T. Devine, "The Department of Public Welfare," *Survey*, 46 (1921), 299; "Nationalism in Social Work," *Ind*, 98 (1919), 466–467; Thomas I. Parkinson, "A Federal Department of Public Welfare," *APS Proc*, 9 (1921), 510–515.

8. Katrina L. Tiffany, "The Social Unit at Cincinnati—Is It A Soviet?" *Review*, 2 (1920), 12. See also Ida C. Clarke, *The Little Democracy* (New York, 1918); "The Social Unit Plan," *Outl*, 122 (1919), 460–461.

9. Charles A. L. Reed, "The 'Social Unit' in Cincinnati," *AR of Rs*, 59 (1919), 523–524; "Social Work by Blocks," *LD*, 63 (December 6, 1919), 34–35, 90–91; "Who Makes Bolshevism in Cincinnati?" *NR*, 18 (1919), 365–367; Gertrude M. Shelby, "Extending Democracy: What the Cincinnati Social Unit Has Accomplished," *HM*, 140 (1919–20), 688–695. See also Patricia M. Melvin, "'A Cluster of Interlacing Communities': The Cincinnati Social Unit Plan and Neighborhood Organization, 1900–1920," in *Community Organization for Urban Social Change*, ed. Robert Fisher and Peter Romanofsky (Westport, Conn., 1981), pp. 59–88.

10. Robert Moses, "Reconstruction of State Welfare Agencies," *Survey*, 44 (1920), 74–76.

11. I. M. Rubinow, "A National Dependency Index: Its Place in the Program of Reconstruction," *Survey*, 42 (1919), 77–79; Florence Dubois, *A Guide to Statistics of Social Welfare in New York* (New York, 1920); Shelby M. Garrison and Allen Eaton, *Welfare Problems in New York City . . . 1915 through 1925* (New York, 1926); New York City Department of Public Welfare, *Directory of Activities of Public and Private Welfare Agencies*, 2nd ed. (New York, 1921); James N. Giglio, "Voluntarism and Public Policy between World War I and the New Deal: Herbert Hoover and the American Child Health Association," *Presidential Studies Quarterly*, 13 (1983), 430–452.

12. "Social Policies and the English Public," *Char*, 16 (1906), 160. See Michael B. Katz, *In the Shadow of the Poorhouse: A Social History of Welfare in America* (New York, 1986), pt. 1; Daniel Levine, *Poverty and Society: The Growth of the American Welfare State in International Comparison* (New Brunswick, N.J., 1988).

13. Kathleen Woodroofe, "The Royal Commission on the Poor Laws, 1905–9," *IRSH*, 22 (1977), 137–164; Gilbert Slater, *Poverty and the State* (New York, 1930), p. 22.

14. Geoffrey Drage, *The State and the Poor* (London, 1914), pp. 8, 248, 235.

15. Amos G. Warner, *American Charities* (New York, 1894), pp. 402, 395; idem, *American Charity*, 2nd ed., (New York, 1919), p. 464.

16. Warner, *American Charity*, pp. 133–134, 477–478; Devine quoted in Walter I. Trattner, *From Poor Law to Welfare State: A History of Social Welfare in America* (New York, 1974), p. 92.

17. Edward T. Devine and Lillian Brandt, *American Social Work in the Twentieth Century* (New York, 1921), pp. 19–20. See also Frank D. Wat-

son, *The Charity Organization Movement in the United States* (New York, 1922).

18. Raymond A. Mohl, "Three Centuries of American Public Welfare: 1600–1932," *CH*, 65 (July 1973), 38; H. A. Mills, "The Law Relating to the Relief and Care of Dependents," *AJS*, 3 (1897–98), 378–391, 479–489, 631–648, 777–794; ibid., 4 (1898–99), 51–68, 178–186. See also Katz, *In the Shadow of the Poorhouse*, pt. 1.

19. Edmond Kelly, *The Elimination of the Tramp* (New York, 1908), pp. xviii, 1; Orlando F. Lewis, *Vagrancy in the United States* (New York, 1907), pp. 7, 13; "Methods Employed by American Cities to Eradicate Vagrancy," *NCCC* (1903), 414–415.

20. "Subsidies," *NCCC* (1901), 118–131; Florence L. Sanville, "Social Legislation in the Keystone State," *Survey*, 34 (1915), 7–12; Alexander Fleisher, "Pennsylvania's Appropriations to Privately-Managed Charitable Institutions," *PSQ*, 30 (1915), 15–36; on Connecticut, see "State Boards and Commissions," *Char*, 8 (1902), 308.

21. William D. Foulke, "Political Patronage in State Institutions," *NCCC* (1902), 324–328; James Leiby, "State Welfare Administration in California, 1879–1929," *PHR*, 41 (1972), 169–187. See also C. R. Henderson, "Politics in Public Institutions of Charity and Correction," *AJS*, 4 (1898–99), 202–234.

22. *APSR*, 10 (1916), 327–335; Amos W. Butler, "A Decade of Official Poor-Relief in Indiana," *AJS*, 11 (1905–6), 763–783.

23. People v. New York S.P.C.C., 55 N.E. 1063 (N.Y., 1900); "Inspection of Charities," *Outl*, 64 (1900), 482–483.

24. William C. Graves, "The Problem of State Supervision of Charities in Illinois," *NCCC* (1909), 430–439. See also Thomas R. Peagram, *Partisans and Progressives: Private Interest and Public Policy in Illinois, 1870–1922* (Urbana, 1992), pp. 158–173.

25. *HS*, 2:1128; N.Y. State Library Bulletin, *Index to Legislation* (Albany, 1900–1901, 1906–7), S.V. "Charities."

26. John Haynes Holmes, "Poverty—The Crime of Society," *Bankers' Magazine*, 80 (1910), 396; Louis D. Brandeis, "The Road to Social Efficiency," *Outl*, 98 (1911), 291; D. Frank Garland, "The Municipality and Public Welfare," *NCCC* (1916), 306. See also Edward T. Devine, "Municipal Reform and Social Welfare in New York," *AR of Rs*, 28 (1903), 433–448.

27. Robert W. Kelso, *The Science of Public Welfare* (New York, 1928), p. 407.

28. *HS*, 2:1128.

29. Edwin D. Solenberger, "Pennsylvania Poor Laws—A Tangle of Good Intent," *Survey*, 54 (1925), 81–83; Abraham Epstein, "After Four Lean Years," *NR*, 51 (1927), 239–241.

30. Arlien Johnson, *Public Policy and Private Charities: A Study of Legislation in the United States and of Administration in Illinois* (Chicago, 1931).

31. Elsie M. Bond, "New York's New Public Welfare Law," *Social Service Review*, 3 (1929), 412–421.

32. Hugh Heclo, *Modern Social Policies in Britain and Sweden: From Relief to Income Maintenance* (New Haven, 1974), pp. 156, 175; Clarence Perkins, "Old Age Pensions—French Act of 1910," *APSR*, 4 (1910), 565–569; Robert F. Foerster, "The French Old Age Insurance Law of 1910," *QJE*, 24 (1909–10), 763–770.

33. Theda Skocpol, *Protecting Soldiers and Mothers: The Political Origins of Social Policy in the United States* (Cambridge, Mass., 1992), chap. 2.

34. *HS*, 2:1149; Frank J. Goodnow, "The Constitutionality of Old Age Pensions," *APSR*, 5 (1911), 194–212. See also F. Spencer Baldwin, "Old Age Pension Schemes: A Criticism and a Program," *QJE*, 24 (1909–10), 713–742; Skocpol, *Protecting Soldiers and Mothers*, chap. 5.

35. Abraham Epstein, "Present Status of Old-Age Pension Legislation in the United States," *Mich LR*, 19 (1924), 26–33; Murray W. Latimer, "Old Age Pensions in America," *ALLR*, 19 (1929), 55–66. See also National Industrial Conference Board, *Industrial Pensions in the United States* (New York, 1925).

36. Latimer, "Old Age Pensions," 36; "Old Age Security—A Problem of Modern Industrialism," *HLR*, 46 (1932–33), 1012–18. See also David McCahan, *State Insurance in the United States* (Philadelphia, 1929).

37. Rubinow, "Public and Private Interests," 189; William E. Leuchtenberg, *Franklin D. Roosevelt and the New Deal, 1932–1940* (New York, 1963), p. 132.

38. Jeanne L. Brand, *Doctors and the State: The British Medical Profession and Government Action in Public Health, 1870–1912* (Baltimore, 1965); PRO, Cab 37, 108 (1906), no. 189, p. 5; Ann-Louise Shapiro, "Private Rights, Public Interest, and Professional Jurisdiction: The French Public Health Law of 1902," *BHM*, 54 (1980), 4–22. For a (rare) American expression of concern, see Percy S. Grant, "Physical Deterioration among the Poor in America and One Way of Checking It," *NAR*, 184 (1907), 254–267.

39. Manfred Wasserman, "The Quest for a National Health Department in the Progressive Era," *BHM*, 49 (1975), 353–380; *Char*, 21 (1908–9), 169–170; on Fisher, see Earl Mayo, "The Problem of National Health," *Outl*, 102 (1912), 764–772; S. Adolphus Knopf, "The Owen Bill for the Establishment of a Federal Department for Medical Health, and Its Opponents," *PSM*, 77 (1910), 373–378; "The Government and Health," *Outl*, 95 (1910), 453; "A National Health Service," *Nation*, 95 (1912), 78. See also Fitzhugh Mullan, *Players and Politics: The Story of the United States Public Health Service* (New York, 1989), chap. 2.

40. *JP*, 87 (1923), 717; PRO, Cab, HO 45, 10284/10739.

41. Oscar Anderson, *The Health of a Nation: Harvey W. Wiley and the Fight for Pure Food* (Chicago, 1958); Peter Temin, *Taking Your Medicine: Drug Regulation in the United States* (Cambridge, Mass., 1980), pp. 27–29; Gabriel Kolko, *The Triumph of Conservatism* (Glencoe, Ill., 1963), pp. 108–110. James H. Young, *Pure Food: Securing the Federal Food and Drug Act of 1906* (Princeton, 1989).

42. "'Pure Food' Corruption in Missouri," *Outl*, 73 (1903), 940; "Pure Food Laws for Private Purposes," *Ind*, 55 (1903), 1224–25.

43. Margaret R. Wolfe, *Lucius Polk Brown and Progressive Food and Drug Control: Tennessee and New York City, 1908–1920* (Lawrence, Kans., 1978). See also Edward A. Morse, "Public Health and Politics," *Annals*, 64 (1916), 134–145.

44. Wainwright Evans, "Raids on the Pantry: The Pure Food Law after 23 Years," *Outl*, 153 (1929), 443–445, 474–475.

45. "The Decline of Caveat Emptor in the Sale of Food," *FLR*, 4 (1935), 295–306; Davis v. Van Camp Packing Co., 189 Iowa 775 (1920); "The Consumer's Protection under the Federal Pure Food and Drugs Act," *Col LR*, 32 (1932), 735.

46. Hipolite Egg Co. v. U.S., 220 U.S. 45 (1911), upholding 1906 act; Holmes in U.S. v. Johnson, 221 U.S. 488 (1911); McDermott v. Wisc, 228 U.S. 115 (1913); "Supreme Court Upholds the Pure Food Law," *Survey*, 35 (1915–16), 598; Temin, *Taking Your Medicine*, chap. 2.

47. Robert W. Bruère, "The New Meaning of Public Health," *HM*, 124 (1912), 694; Carl E. McCombs, "Relative Functions of State and Local Health Departments," *AJPH*, 10 (1920), 393–399; on New York, see "Commission Government for Public Health," *WW*, 27 (1913–14), 495–496; U. G. Dubach, "Quasi-Judicial Powers of the State Boards of Health," *APSR*, 10 (1916), 80–95.

48. *APSR*, 7 (1913), 419–420; Martin V. Melosi, *Garbage in the Cities: Refuse, Reform, and the Environment* (College Station, Tex., 1981); John B. C. Kershaw, "The Public Health Act of 1926," *FR*, 129 (1928), 687–698; Eugene M. McQuillin, "Municipal Ordinances and Contracts for the Removal and Disposition of Garbage," *CLJ*, 62 (1906), 64–70.

49. Marion M. Torchia, "The Tuberculosis Movement and the Race Question, 1890–1950," *BHM*, 49 (1975), 152–168; Marilyn T. Williams, "Philanthropy in the Progressive Era: The Public Baths of Baltimore," *Maryland Historical Magazine*, 72 (1977), 118–131; Alan I. Marcus, "Disease Prevention in America: From a Local to a National Outlook, 1880–1910," *BHM*, 53 (1979), 184–203. See also Judith W. Leavitt, *The Healthiest City: Milwaukee and the Politics of Health Reform* (Princeton, 1982); Samuel H. Adams, "Guardians of the Public Health," *McClure's*, 31 (1908), 241–252.

50. "Trends in Health Legislation," *AJPH*, 15 (1925), 710–711; Milton Conover, "National, State, and Local Cooperation in Food and Drug Control," *APSR*, 22 (1928), 910–928; "Foods Getting Purer," *LD*, 75 (October 7, 1922), 72–73.

51. "Compulsory Vaccination," *YLJ*, 12 (1902–3), 504–506; Leavitt, *Healthiest City*, p. 101; People ex rel. Jenkins v. Board of Education, 84 N.E. 1046 (Ill., 1908), and Henry B. Hemenway, "Legal Aspect of Public Health Work in Illinois," *ILR*, 5 (1910–11), 157–172; Wong Wai v. Williamson, 103 Fed. 1 (C.C.A., Cal., 1900); Austin Lewis, "Municipal Boards of Health and Quarantine Regulations," *ALR*, 34 (1900), 722–725; Jacobson v. Mass., 197 U.S. 11 (1905).

52. *HS*, 1:84; Gerald N. Grob, *Mental Illness and American Society, 1875–1940* (Princeton, 1983), pp. 180, 188.

53. *HS*, 2:1128; Charles E. Rosenberg, *The Care of Strangers: The Rise of America's Hospital System* (New York, 1987); Rosemary Stevens, *In Sickness and In Wealth: American Hospitals in the Twentieth Century* (New York, 1989).

54. Harry A. Austin, "The Protection of Our 'Infant Industry,'" *Forum*, 45 (1911), 457–463; "Our New Mother—the Government," *Outl*, 105 (1913), 60. See also Skocpol, *Protecting Soldiers and Mothers*, chaps. 6–9.

55. Quoted in Trattner, *From Poor Law to Welfare State*, p. 18; Mark H. Leff, "Consensus for Reform: The Mothers' Pension Movement in the Progressive Era," *Social Service Review*, 47 (1973), 397–417; J. Stanley Lemons, "The Sheppard-Towner Act: Progressivism in the 1920s," *JAH*, 55 (1968–69), 776–786.

56. "Capital and Labor on Each Other's Necks," *Survey*, 37 (1916–17), 495–496; I. M. Rubinow, "20,000 Miles over the Land: A Survey of the Spreading Health Insurance Movement," *Survey*, 37 (1916–17), 631–635.

57. I. M. Rubinow, "Public and Private Interests in Social Insurance," *ALLR*, 21 (1931), 181; Charles J. Hastings, "Democracy and Public Health Administration," *AJPH*, 9 (1919), 81–86, 172–179; "Labor Getting behind Health Insurance," *Survey*, 39 (1917–18), 708–709; "Health Insurance," *APSR*, 13 (1919), 89–92.

58. Data from New York State Library, *Legislation Bulletin* (Albany, 1890–1909); Irene Osgood, "A Review of Labor Legislation in the United States for the Year 1909," *APSR*, 4 (1910), 170.

59. Samuel Rosenbaum, "Labour Legislation in the United States," *JComp Leg*, n.s., 16 (1916), 13–23.

60. Osgood, "Review," 172, 177; *Survey*, 34 (1915), 142–144; Mary Chamberlain, "The Tammany Tiger's Paw on Labor Laws in New York State," *Survey*, 32 (1914), 449–502, 514; Dorothy Kenyon, "Using Political Machinery for Social Ends," *ALLR*, 26 (1936), 141–142.

61. Robert H. Wettach, "Labor Law Administration in Pennsylvania," *UPa LR*, 70 (1922–23), 277–302. See also Henry R. Seager, "Progress of Labor Legislation, 1900–1925," *ALLR*, 15 (1925), 289–294.

62. Clarence A. Lightner, "Economic Aspects of the Law of Master and Servant, in Its Relation to Industrial Accidents," *Mich LR*, 7 (1909), 461–462.

63. William Graebner, *Coal-Mining Safety in the Progressive Period: The Political Economy of Reform* (Lexington, Ky., 1976).

64. Thomas G. Shearman and Amasa A. Redfield, *A Treatise on the Law of Negligence*, 5th ed. (New York, 1898), pp. iii, vi; James Boyle, "Organized Labor and Court Decisions," *Forum*, 42 (1909), 551; Andrew A. Bruce, "Employers' Liability in the United States," *Forum*, 33 (1902), 46–52.

65. On Europe, see "Employers' Liability," 256–283, and "After the Common Law—What?" *Survey*, 28 (1912), 232–249; Donald MacKay,

"Workmen's Compensation Questions in the British Courts," *CLJ,* 79 (1914), 202–203.

66. George E. Barnett, "The End of the Maryland Workmen's Compensation Act," *QJE,* 19 (1904–5), 320–322; Mondoux v. N.Y., New Haven & Hartford R.R., 223 U.S. 1 (1912); Seaboard Air Line Railway v. Horton, 233 U.S. 492 (1914); "Judicial Acceptance of Workmen's Compensation," *HLR,* 29 (1915–16), 199–201.

67. Ives v. South Buffalo Railway Co., 94 N.E. 431, 436 (N.Y., 1911); Ernst Freund, "Constitutional Status of Workmen's Compensation," *ALLR,* 2 (1912), 43. See also Charles H. Hamil, "Constitutional Chaos," *Forum,* 48 (1912), 45–46; Eugene Wambaugh, "Workmen's Compensation Acts: Their Theory and Their Constitutionality," *HLR,* 25 (1911–12), 129–139.

68. "Economy, Philosophy and Morals v. the Court of Appeals," *Survey,* 26 (1911), 77; *Outl,* 98 (1911), 709–711, 807; Ernst Freund, "Constitutional Status of Workmen's Compensation," *ALLR,* 2 (1912), 43, 53. See also Barbara C. Steidle, "'Reasonable' Reform: The Attitude of Bench and Bar towards Liability Law and Workmen's Compensation," in *Building the Organizational Society,* ed. Jerry Israel (New York, 1982), pp. 31–41.

69. *Nation,* 97 (1913), 526; Jensen v. Southern Pacific R.R. Co., 215 N.Y. 514 (1915); Powell, "Workmen's Compensation Cases," 553; N.Y. Central R.R. Co. v. White, 243 U.S. 188, 198 (1917); Edward S. Corwin, "Social Insurance and Constitutional Limitations," *YLJ,* 26 (1916–17), 443.

70. William F. Ogburn, *Social Change with Respect to Culture* (New York, 1923), p. 231; Joseph F. Tripp, "An Instance of Labor and Business Cooperation: Workmen's Compensation in Washington State (1911)," *LH,* 17 (1976), 530–550; Patrick D. Reagan, "The Ideology of Social Harmony and Efficiency: Workmen's Compensation in Ohio, 1904–1919," *OH,* 90 (1981), 317–331; Robert Asher, "The Origins of Workmen's Compensation in Minnesota," *Minn H,* 44 (1974), 142–153; idem, "The 1911 Wisconsin Workmen's Compensation Law: A Study in Conservative Labor Reform," *WMH,* 57 (1973–74), 123–140; Paul Kennaday, "Big Business and Workmen's Compensation," *Survey,* 29 (1912–13), 809–810. See also *APSR,* 7 (1913), 247–254.

71. Quoted in P. Tecumseh Sherman, "Jurisprudence of Workmen's Compensation Laws," *UPa LR,* 63 (1914–15), 826; "Employers' State Compensation Laws Reviewed," *Survey,* 38 (1917), 259; Willard C. Fisher, "The Scope of Workmen's Compensation in the United States," *QJE,* 30 (1915–16), 22–63.

72. Willard C. Fisher, "American Experience with Workmen's Compensation," *AER,* 10 (1920), 18–47; Walter M. Glass, "Farm Laborers as Statutory Employees," *Case and Comment,* 20 (1913–14), 765–769; Robert Asher, "Radicalism and Reform: Workmen's Compensation in Minnesota, 1910–1933," *LH,* 14 (1973), 40.

73. Frank A. Ross, "The Applicability of Common Law Rules of Evidence in Proceedings before Workmen's Compensation Commissions," *HLR,* 36 (1922–23), 263–298; James M. Rosenthal, "The Chronological Story of a

Workmen's Compensation Case," *Massachusetts Law Quarterly,* 8 (1923), 40–49; William L. Crow, "A History of the Legislative Control of Workmen's Compensation in Wisconsin," *ILR,* 27 (1932–33), 137–153.

74. Ralph H. Swan, "Workmen's Compensation and the Conflict of Laws," *Minn LR,* 11 (1926–27), 329–353; Lester P. Schoene and Frank Watson, "Workmen's Compensation on Interstate Railways," *HLR,* 47 (1934), 389–424.

75. F. J. Stimson, *Labor in Its Relation to Law* (New York, 1895), pp. 21–22, 36; George W. Alger, "The Courts and Factory Legislation," *AJS,* 6 (1900–1901), 396–406.

76. Holden v. Hardy, 169 U.S. 366 (1898); Florence Kelley, "The United States Supreme Court and the 'Eight Hours' Law," *AJS,* 4 (1898–99), 22.

77. Henry R. Seager, "The Attitude of American Courts towards Restrictive Labor Laws," *PSQ,* 19 (1904), 611; People v. Orange County Construction Co., 67 N.E. 129 (N.Y., 1903); Stange v. Cleveland, 114 N.E. 261 (N.Y., 1916); "Legislative Restraints upon Hours of Labor as a Health Regulation," *YLJ,* 13 (1903–4), 316. See also Charles M. Kneier, "Regulation of Conditions of Employment on Municipal Public Works," *SWPSQ,* 11 (1931), 377–392.

78. Lochner v. N.Y., 198 U.S. 45, 63, (1905); David J. Brewer, "The Legitimate Exercise of the Police Power in the Protection of Health," *Char,* 21 (1908–9), 240–241. See also Frank L. Story, "The Economic Philosophy of Lochner: Emergence, Embrasure, and Emasculation," *Arizona Law Review,* 15 (1973), 419–455; Sydney Tarrow, "Lochner versus New York: A Political Analysis," *LH,* 5 (1964), 277–312; Paul Kens, *Judicial Power and Reform Politics: The Anatomy of Lochner v. New York* (Lawrence, Kans., 1990).

79. People v. Williams, 81 N.E. 778, 780 (N.Y., 1907) Ernst Freund, "Limitation of Hours of Work and the Supreme Court," *JPE,* 13 (1904–5), 598–599. See also Charles Warren, *The Supreme Court in American History* (Boston, 1926), 2:741.

80. Muller v. Oregon, 208 U.S. 412 (1908); Brewer, "Legitimate Exercise," 240–241.

81. Quoted in Philippa Strum, *Louis D. Brandeis: Justice for the People* (Cambridge, Mass., 1984), p. 114.

82. Josephine Goldmark, "The Illinois Ten-Hours Decision," *APS Proc,* 1 (1910–11), 185–187; Ritchie v. Wayman, 91 N.E. 695 (Ill., 1910); People v. Charles Schweinler Press, 214 N.Y. 395 (1915); Bunting v. Oregon, 243 U.S. 426 (1917). See also Thomas R. Powell, "The Oregon Minimum-Wage Cases," *PSQ,* 32 (1917), 296–311; Ernst Freund, "The Constitutional Aspect of the Protection of Women in Industry," *APS Proc,* 1 (1910–11), 162–184; Judith A. Baer, *The Judicial Response to Women's Labor Legislation* (Westport, Conn., 1978).

83. George K. Behlmer, *Child Abuse and Moral Reform, 1870–1908* (Stanford, 1981); Owen J. Lovejoy, "Child Labor Legislation in England," *Chaut,* 46 (1907), 217–225.

84. Holland Thompson, "Life in a Southern Mill Town," *PSQ,* 15 (1900), 1–13.

85. Stephen B. Wood, *Constitutional Politics in the Progressive Era: Child Labor and the Law* (Chicago, 1968), chap. 1.

86. *PSQ,* 18 (1903), 369; "Factory Inspection," *Char,* 10 (1903), 493–494.

87. Florence L. Sanville, "Pennsylvania: A Graveyard for Social Legislation," *Char,* 18 (1907), 247–248; Florence Kelley, "Judge-Made Ignorance in Pennsylvania," *Char,* 16 (1906), 189–190.

88. Theresa Wolfson, "How Our Courts Interpret Child Labor Laws," *American Child,* 1 (1919), 133–137.

89. Walter I. Trattner, "The First Federal Child Labor Law (1916)," *Social Science Quarterly,* 50 (1969), 507–524.

90. Thomas I. Parkinson, "The Federal Child Labor Law: Another View of Its Constitutionality," *PSQ,* 31 (1916), 531–540; Henry Hull, "The Federal Child-Labor Law: The Question of Its Constitutionality," *PSQ,* 31 (1916), 519–530; "Federal Power and Child Labor," *Nation,* 98 (1914), 150–151.

91. Hammer v. Dagenhart, 247 U.S. 251 (1918); *Survey,* 38 (1917), 96–97, 122–123.

92. Bailey v. Drexel Furniture Co., 259 U.S. 20 (1922); Wood, *Constitutional Politics,* chaps. 6–8.

93. On Wheeler, see p. 140 of this volume; John A. Ryan, "The Supreme Court and Child Labor," *Catholic World,* 108 (1919–20), 212–223; idem, "The Proposed Child Labor Amendment," *Catholic World,* 120 (1924–25), 166–174. See also J. H. Lawson, "Child Labor and the Constitution," *ALR,* 56 (1922), 733–746.

94. Ross L. Finney, "What Is Behind Child Labor Opposition?" *Christian Century,* 42 (1925), 89; Powell in *APSR,* 19 (1925), 305.

95. William L. Chenery, "Child Labor: The New Alignment," *Survey,* 53 (1924–25), 379; Wood, *Constitutional Politics,* 300–301; U.S. v. Darby Lumber Co., 312 U.S. 100 (1941). See also Thomas F. Cadwalader, "The Defeat of the Twentieth Amendment," *Annals,* 129 (1927), 65–69; W. A. Robinson, "Advisory Referendum in Massachusetts on the Child Labor Amendment," *APSR,* 19 (1925), 69–73; Vincent A. McQuade, *The American Catholic Attitude on Child Labor since 1891* (Washington, D.C., 1938), p. 97.

96. "The Unemployed," *QR,* 202 (1905), 645; Gilbert, "Winston Churchill versus the Webbs," 855–858.

97. PRO, Cab 37, 106 (1911), no. 40; Robert F. Foerster, "The British National Insurance Act," *QJE,* 26 (1911–12), 276.

98. William Hard, "Unemployment as a Coming Issue," *ALLR,* 2 (1912), 93–100; W. M. Leiserson, "The Problem of Unemployment Today," *PSQ,* 31 (1916), 1–24; Donald A. Ritchie, "The Gary Committee: Businessmen, Progressives, and Unemployment in New York City, 1914–1915," *New York Historical Society Quarterly,* 57 (1973), 327–347. See also Alexander Keyssar, *Out of Work: The First Century of Unemployment in Massachusetts* (Cambridge, 1986).

99. William M. Leiserson, "The Theory of Public Employment Offices and the Principles of their Practical Administration," *PSQ*, 29 (1914), 39; Francis Kellor, *Out of Work: A Study of Unemployment* (New York, 1904).

100. William A. Berridge, *Cycles of Employment in the United States, 1903–22* (Boston, 1923); Sir William Beveridge, "Unemployment Insurance in the War and After," in *War and Insurance*, ed. Sir Norman Hill (London, 1927), 229–252; Leo Wolman, "English Experience with Unemployment Insurance," *ALLR*, 16 (1926), 32–44. See also Daniel Nelson, *Unemployment Insurance: The American Experience, 1915–1935* (Madison, 1969), chap. 1.

101. J. Mark Jacobson, "The Wisconsin Unemployment Compensation Law of 1932," *APSR*, 26 (1932), 300–311; idem, "The Wisconsin Unemployment Compensation Law," *Col LR*, 32 (1932), 442; Nelson, *Unemployment Insurance*, chap. 6. See also Udo Sautter, "Government and Unemployment: The Use of Public Works before the New Deal," *JAH*, 73 (1986), 59–86.

102. Leon M. Despres, "The New Poor Law: A Study of Fraud in Illinois Unemployment Relief," *UCLR*, 1 (1933–34), 592–601; Carl A. Heisterman, "Constitutional Limitations Affecting State and Local Funds," *Social Service Review*, 6 (1932), 1–20.

103. "Unemployment Insurance: Federal and State Legislation," *Col LR*, 35 (1935), 1262–92; Nelson, *Unemployment Insurance*, chap. 9.

104. Scott Nearing, *Wages in the United States, 1908–10* (New York, 1911), 4; Arthur N. Holcombe, "The Legal Minimum Wage in the United States," *AER*, 2 (1912), 21–37; J. Tyrell Baylee, "The Minimum Wage and the Poor Law," *WR*, 152 (1899), 628–640.

105. Ryan v. New York, 177 N.Y. 271 (1904); Rinehart J. Swenson, *Public Regulation of the Rate of Wages* (New York, 1917). See also W. J. Ghent, "The Movement for a Minimum Wage," *HW*, 58 (April 25, 1914), 18; "The Case for the Minimum Wage," *Survey*, 33 (1914–15), 487–504.

106. James Boyle, *The Minimum Wage and Syndicalism: An Independent Survey of the Two Latest Movements Affecting American Labor* (Cincinnati, 1913), p. 4; "The Legislative Minimum Wage," *HLR*, 31 (1917–18), 1013–17.

107. Arthur F. Lucas, *The Legal Minimum Wage in Massachusetts* (Philadelphia, 1927); James T. Patterson, "Mary Dewson and the American Minimum Wage Movement," *LH*, 5 (1964), 134–152; Holcombe v. Creamer, 231 Mass. 99 (1918); newspaper provision voided in Commonwealth v. Boston Transcript Co., 249 Mass. 477 (1924); Ethel M. Johnson, "Fifteen Years of Minimum Wage in Massachusetts," *American Federationist*, 35 (1928), 1469–77.

108. V. O'Hara, *A Living Wage by Legislation: The Oregon Experience* (Salem, Ore., 1916); Stettler v. O'Hara, 139 Pac. 743 (Ore., 1914); Roland M. Miller, "California's Reasonable Minimum Wage," *JASoc*, 11 (1926–27), 541–552; Joseph F. Tripp, "Toward an Efficient and Moral Society: Washington State Minimum-Wage Law, 1913–1925," *PNWQ*, 67 (1976),

97–112; Thomas J. Kerr IV, "The New York Factory Investigating Commission and the Minimum Wage Movement," *LH*, 12 (1971), 373–391.

109. Adkins v. Children's Hospital, 261 U.S. 525, 569–570 (1923); Felix Frankfurter, *District of Columbia Minimum Wage Cases* (New York, 1920); E.M.B., "The Supreme Court and the Minimum Wage," *YLJ*, 32 (1922–23), 829–831. See also Edwin E. Witte, "The Effects of Special Labor Legislation for Women," *QJE*, 42 (1927–28), 153–164; Elizabeth F. Baker, *Protective Labor Legislation* (New York, 1925).

110. Atkin v. Kansas, 191 U.S. 207 (1903); Connally v. General Construction Co., 269 U.S. 385 (1926); "Constitutionality of Minimum Wage Laws for Labor on Public Works," *HLR*, 39 (1925–26), 875.

111. "Constitutionality of the New York Minimum Wage Law," *YLJ*, 42 (1933), 1250–59; Morehead v. Tipaldo, 298 U.S. 587 (1936); on Hoover, see Paul L. Murphy, *The Constitution in Crisis Times, 1918–1969* (New York, 1972), p. 151; West Coast Hotel v. Parrish, 300 U.S. 379 (1937); U.S. v. Darby, 312 U.S. 100 (1941).

7. *Immigrants and Aliens*

1. Quoted in PRO, Cab 37, no. 88 (1907), and no. 48, Appendix Ib; Edward L. de Hart, "The English Law of Nationality and Naturalization," *JSCL*, 2, n.s. (1900), 11–26.

2. Hugh H. Lusk, "Chinese Exclusion in Australia," *NAR*, 174 (1902), 368–375. For complaints against South African laws directed at Indian and Asian entrants, see PRO, Cab 37, nos. 88, 90, 94 (1907).

3. PRO, Cab 37, no. 31 (1892); Great Britain, Board of Trade (Alien Immigration), *Reports on the Volume and Effects of Recent Immigration from Eastern Europe to the United Kingdom* (London, 1894), pp. 91–94, 134–135.

4. "Foreign Undesirables," *Blackwood's*, 169 (1901), 285; M. J. Lande, "The Case for the Alien," *FR*, 83 (1905), 1094–1105. See also Bernard Gainer, *The Alien Invasion: The Origin of the Aliens Act of 1905* (London, 1972); John A. Garrard, *The English and Immigration, 1880–1910* (Oxford, 1971); Lloyd P. Gartner, *The Jewish Immigrant in England, 1870–1914* (London, 1960).

5. "World-Politics," *NAR*, 180 (1908), 294; An Observer, "The Aliens Act," *Nation* (GB) 81 (1905), 141; Alfred E. Zimmern, "The Aliens Act: A Challenge," *Ec R*, 2 (1911), 187–188. See also William E. Gordon, "The Attack on the Aliens Act," *Nat R*, 48 (1906), 460–471.

6. PRO, Home Office 45, 110326/131787 (February 26, 1907); Jasper Kemmis, "Our Immigration Laws," *FR*, 96 (1911), 146–159; Garrard, *English and Immigration*, chap. 7.

7. Arthur A. Baumann, "Nationality and Naturalization," *FR*, 103 (1915), 495–505; F. T. Piggott, "'The Ligeance of the King': A Study of Nationality and Naturalization," *NC*, 78 (1915), 729–754. See also Richard W. Flournoy, Jr., "The New British Imperial Law of Nationality," *AJIL*, 9 (1915), 870–882.

8. Albert Shaw, *Political Problems of American Democracy* (New York, 1907), pp. 73–74; William S. Rossiter, "A Common Sense View of the Immigrant Problem," *NAR*, 188 (1908), 371; John Higham, *Strangers in the Land* (New Brunswick, N.J., 1955), p. 107; Larry C. Miller, "William James and Twentieth-Century Ethnic Thought," *AQ*, 31 (1979), 533–555.

9. T. V. Powderly, "Immigration's Menace to the National Health," *NAR*, 175 (1902), 53–60; Delber L. McKee, "'The Chinese Must Go,' Commissioner General Powderly and Chinese Immigration, 1897–1902," *PH*, 44 (1977), 37–51; on Hardie, see Garner, *Alien Invasion*, p. 192; Julius Weinberg, "E. A. Ross: The Progressive as Nativist," *WMH*, 50 (1967), 242–253; Barbara M. Solomon, *Ancestors and Immigrants* (Cambridge, Mass., 1956), chaps. 5–7.

10. O. P. Austin, "Is the New Immigration Dangerous to the Country?" *NAR*, 178 (1904), 558–570; William S. Bennet, "The Effect of Immigration on Municipal Politics," *Conference for Good City Government* (1909), 142–147.

11. Edward A. Ross, "Immigrants in Politics," *Cent*, 87 (1913–14), 396. See also Grace Abbott, "The Immigrant and Municipal Politics," *Conference for Good City Government* (1909), 148–156.

12. W. F. Willcox, "Popular Delusions about Immigration," *Ind*, 72 (1912), 304–307; Isaac A. Hourwitch, "The Economic Aspects of Immigration," *PSQ*, 26 (1911), 615–642, and *Labor and Immigration* (New York, 1912); Henry B. Leonard, "Louis Marshall and Immigration Restriction, 1906–1924," *American Jewish Archives*, 24 (1972), 24. See also "Discussion," *AER* (Supplement), 2 (1912), 64–78.

13. Francis E. Hamilton, "Restriction of Immigration," *Forum*, 42 (1909), 558; Henry P. Fairchild, "The Restriction of Immigration," *AER* (Supplement), 2 (1912), 60. See also Robert DeC. Ward, "The Restriction of Immigration," *NAR*, 179 (1904), 226–237.

14. Alcott W. Stockwell, "What Is the Problem of Immigration?" *World To-Day*, 19 (1910), 1006–1010; Paul S. Pierce, "The Control of Immigration as an Administrative Problem," *APSR*, 4 (1910), 374–389. See also the frequent articles on the subject in *PSM:* e.g., 62 (1902–3), 230–236; 64 (1904–5), 232–248; 66 (1904–5), 243–255; 83 (1913), 313–338.

15. Robert Hutcheson, "Why the Chinese Should Be Admitted," *Forum*, 33 (1902), 61; "The Chinese Exclusion Bill," *Nation*, 74 (1902), 303–304; "The Problem of Immigration," *Arena*, 27 (1902), 260–266.

16. Boies Penrose, "Chinese Exclusion and the Problem of Immigration," *Ind*, 54 (1902), 12; O. O. Howard, "Our Suicidal Chinese Policy," *Ind*, 54 (1902), 858–860; Truxton Beale, "Why the Chinese Should Be Excluded," *Forum*, 33 (1902), 53–58; E. P. Hutchinson, *Legislative History of American Immigration Policy, 1798–1965* (Philadelphia, 1981), chap. 4.

17. Oscar Handlin, *Race and Nationality in American Life* (Garden City, N.Y., 1957), chap. 5; James S. Pula, "American Immigration Policy and the Dillingham Commission," *Polish-American Studies*, 37 (1980), 5–30.

18. "Restriction of Immigrants," *Ind*, 72 (1912), 1068–69; Jane Addams, "Pen and Book as Tests of Character," *Survey*, 29 (1912–13), 419–420.

19. A. Piatt Andrew, "The Crux of the Immigration Question," *NAR*, 199 (1914), 866–867; Joseph Lee, "Democracy and the Literacy Test," *Survey*, 29 (1912–13), 497–499.

20. Horace M. Kallen, *Cultural Democracy in the United States* (New York, 1924), p. 23; William S. Rossiter, "What Are Americans?" *AM*, 126 (1920), 270–280.

21. "The War and Immigration: An Unintentional Experiment in Restriction," *SA*, 113 (1915), 244; "Immigration after the War," *NR*, 4 (1915), 250–251; "Americanization," *NR*, 5 (1916), 322–323; "Wanted—An Immigration Policy," *NR*, 1 (December 26, 1914), 10–11.

22. Frances A. Kellor, "Immigration in Reconstruction," *NAR*, 209 (1919), 199–208; Cannon quoted in "The Native American," *Outl*, 112 (1916), 788; Randolph S. Bourne, "Trans-National America," *AM*, 118 (1916), 86–97.

23. George Makgill, "The Law and the Alien," *NC*, 83 (1918), 971. See also Gisela C. Lebzelter, *Anti-Semitism in England, 1918–1939* (London, 1978), chap. 1.

24. "Canada," *Round Table*, 11 (1921), 662, 665; "The Alien and Legal History," *LT*, 163 (1927), 497–498. See also George Godwin, "Canada's Racial Problem," *Outl* (GB), 61 (1928), 575–576.

25. J. W. Garner, "The New French Code of Nationality," *AJIL*, 22 (1928), 379; Gary S. Cross, "To Assimilate or Regulate: French Immigration Policy in the 1920s," *Journal of Ethnic Studies*, 10, no. 3 (1982), 1–20; idem, "Toward Prosperity and Social Peace: The Politics of Immigration in the Era of World War I," *French Historical Studies*, 11 (1980), 612–632; Ambroise Got, "L'assimilation des étrangers," *Mercure de France*, 170 (1924), 611; Ralph Schor, "Le parti communiste et les immigrés (1921–1937)," *Histoire*, 35 (1981), 84–86.

26. Sidney L. Gulick, *American Democracy and Asiatic Citizenship* (New York, 1919), pp. ix–x, 107; idem, "A New Oriental Policy for America," *Asia*, 17 (1917), 720–721; idem, "An Intelligent Guard at the Gate," *Ind*, 105 (1921), 208–209. See also Sandra C. Taylor, *Advocate of Understanding: Sidney Gulick and the Search for Peace with Japan* (Kent, Ohio, 1984), chaps. 7–9.

27. "A Truce to Immigration," *NR*, 25 (1920), 95–96.

28. *Survey*, 45 (1920–21), 416–417; Reuben Fink, "Visas, Immigration, and Official Anti-Semitism," *Nation*, 112 (1921), 870; "The Immigration Bill," *Nation*, 108 (1919), 185; *LD*, 60 (February 8, 1919), 17–18; *LD*, 62 (July 5, 1919), 28–29; on foreign press, see *LD*, 69 (May 28, 1921), 19–20, 48–60. See also Higham, *Strangers*, chap. 11.

29. *LD*, 68 (February 26, 1921), 7–9; *LD*, 75 (April 22, 1922), 15.

30. On Dillingham, see Henry P. Fairchild, "The Immigration Law of 1924," *QJE*, 38 (1923–24), 658; on Johnson, see Mark Sullivan, "Congress and the Alien Restriction Law," *WW*, 47 (1923–24), 438.

31. Robert A. Divine, *American Immigration Policy 1924–1952* (New Haven, 1957), pp. 5–6; George E. Haynes, "The Negro Laborer and the Immigrant," *Survey*, 46 (1920), 209–210; Hutchinson, *Legislative History*, pp. 178–181.

32. Frances Kellor, "Humanizing the Immigration Law," *NAR*, 217 (1923), 780–784; Herbert W. Horwill, "America's New Immigration Policy," *Cont R*, 121 (1922), 468–474.

33. Henry H. Curran, "Fewer and Better, or None," *SEP*, 196 (April 26, 1924), 8; Herbert F. Sherwood, "Wanted—A Policy for New Americans," *Outl*, 134 (1923), 455.

34. "America Wants No Wide-Open Immigration," *American Federationist*, 30 (1923), 657–659; *LD*, 75 (November 18, 1922), 18–19; "No Immigrant Flood," *NR*, 33 (1922), 58–59.

35. Higham, *Strangers*, pp. 155–157; Lowell quoted in Roy L. Garis, "The Immigration Problem: A Practical American Solution," *SM*, 72 (1922), 366–367.

36. Harding quoted in "Desirable Immigration," *Ind*, 111 (1923), 30; Ruth Crawford, "Standing Pat on the Quota Law," *Survey*, 49 (1923), 771–772; Peter H. Wang, "Farmers and the Immigration Act of 1924," *AH*, 49 (1975), 649–650; Edward A. Filene, "Immigration, Progress and Prosperity," *SEP*, 196 (June 28, 1923), 8, 70–71.

37. "The Immigration Question," *NR*, 38 (1924), 6–7. See also Ernest Greenwood, "The Quota Law," *Outl*, 134 (1923), 311–313.

38. Sullivan, "Congress and Alien Restriction Law," 440; on Coolidge, see Roy L. Garis, "How the New Immigration Law Works," *SM*, 76 (1924), 183–184.

39. "The Progress of the World," *AR of Rs*, 69 (1924), 451–456; Sidney L. Gulick, "American-Japanese Relations: The Logic of the Exclusionists," *Annals*, 122 (1925), 186–187; A. Warner Parker, "The Quota Provisions of the Immigration Act of 1924," *AJIL*, 18 (1924), 737–754. See also Higham, *Strangers*, pp. 316–324; Hutchinson, *Legislative History*, pp. 187–192.

40. Philip C. Jessup, "Some Phases of the Administration and Judicial Interpretation of the Immigration Act of 1924," *YLJ*, 35 (1925–26), 724, 705; Mark Sullivan, "Behind the Convention Scenes," *WW*, 47 (1923–24), 535; Robert DeC. Ward, "Our New Immigration Policy," *Foreign Affairs*, 3 (1924–25), 110.

41. *LD*, 87 (October 17, 1925), 10–11.

42. "Where New Americans Come From," *Outl*, 143 (1926), 10; Rufus S. Tucker, "The Old Americans in 1920," *QJE*, 37 (1922–23), 761.

43. "National Origins," *Survey*, 62 (1929), 441–442; Divine, *Immigration Policy*, p. 40.

44. S.K.R., "The New American Quotas," *NS*, 33 (1929), 398–399; Butler quoted in Elmer Murphy, "American for Americans," *Commonweal*, 10 (1929), 330; *LD*, 101 (April 6, 1929), 10, and (June 29, 1929), 10. See also J. J. Spengler, "The Merits and Demerits of the National Origins Provisions for Selecting Immigrants," *SWPSQ*, 10 (1929), 149–170.

45. Harold Fields, "Closing Immigration throughout the World," *AJIL,* 26 (1932–33), 674; *NR,* 66 (1931), 338–339.
46. Emory S. Bogardus, "The Mexican Immigrant and the Quota," *Sociology and Social Research* 12, (1927–28), 371–378; Mark Reisler, *By the Sweat of their Brow: Mexican Immigrant Labor in the United States, 1900–1940* (Westport, Conn., 1976), chaps. 7–9.
47. Alexander M. Bickel, "Citizenship in the American Constitution," *Arizona Law Review,* 15 (1973), 369–387; Albert Shaw, "Puerto Ricans as Citizens," *AR of Rs,* 63 (1921), 483–491.
48. Frederick Dwight, "Proper Names," *YLJ,* 20 (1910–11), 387–392.
49. Henry B. Hazard, "The Trend toward Administrative Naturalization," *APSR,* 21 (1927), 342–344; Frederick Van Dyne, *A Treatise on the Law of Naturalization of the United States* (Washington, D.C., 1907).
50. Louis F. Post, "Administrative Decision in Connection with Immigration," *APSR,* 10 (1916), 253; "Will Congress Pass a Citizenship Law?" *Outl,* 85 (1907), 152–153; Gaillard Hunt, "The New Citizenship Law," *NAR,* 185 (1907), 530–539.
51. "The Deportation of Aliens," *Col LR,* 20 (1920), 680–684; William Preston, *Aliens and Dissenters* (Cambridge, Mass., 1963), chap. 1.
52. Post, "Administrative Decision," 261; Lewis v. Frick, 233 U.S. 291 (1914); Carfora v. Williams, 186 Fed. 354 (D.C., S.D.N.Y., 1911); Gegiow v. Uhl, 239 U.S. 3 (1915); "Statutory Construction in Deportation Cases," *YLJ,* 40 (1931), 1290–1291, 1288. See also Thomas R. Powell, "Judicial Review of Administrative Action in Immigration Proceedings," *HLR,* 22 (1908–9), 360–366; Clement L. Bouvé, "The Immigration Act and Returning Resident Aliens," *UPa LR,* 59 (1911), 359–372.
53. Hattie P. Williams, "The Road to Citizenship: A Study of Naturalization in a Nebraska County," *PSQ,* 27 (1912), 399–427; "The Passing of Alien Suffrage," *APSR,* 25 (1931), 114–116.
54. "The Arizona Alien Labor Law," *Outl,* 109 (1915), 109–110; Truax v. Raich, 239 U.S. 33, 43 (1915); "The Alien's Right to Work," *LD,* 51 (1915), 1070; "The Supreme Court and Human Rights," *Nation,* 101 (1915), 564.
55. Heim v. McCall, 239 U.S. 175 (1915); Cardozo in People v. Crane, 214 N.Y. 154, 164 (1915); "A Decline of Legicide," *NR,* 2 (March 6, 1915), 116–117; "Aliens May Be Barred from Public Works," *Survey,* 35 (1915–16), 284; "New York's Way with Alien Labor," *LD,* 51 (1915), 1340; "A Bad Law and Big Problem," *Outl,* 109 (1915), 548.
56. Thomas R. Powell, "The Right to Work for the State," *Col LR,* 16 (1916), 112–113. See also Lee v. Lynn, 111 N.E. 700 (Mass., 1915).
57. U.S. v. Uhl, 271 Fed. 676, 677 (C.C.A. 2nd, 1921); Minor Bronaugh, "Exclusion of Aliens because of Anarchistic or Similar Political Belief," *LN,* 29 (1925), 106–109; Frederic C. Howe, "Lynch Law and the Immigrant Alien," *Nation,* 110 (1920), 194–195; Harry Rider, "Americanization," *APSR,* 14 (1920), 110–115; "American Fascismo—A New Kind of Hyphenism," *WW,* 46 (1921), 240–241.
58. Hugo Wall, "The Use of the License Laws in the Regulation of Businesses

and Professions," *SWPSQ*, 12 (1931), 124; Imogen B. Oakley, "When Is a Citizen Not a Citizen?" *AM*, 135 (1925), 19–27; Henry B. Hazard, "Naturalization and the Prohibition Amendment," *GLJ*, 18 (1929–30), 199–214; "Crimes Involving Moral Turpitude," *HLR*, 43 (1929–30), 117–121.

59. The Inquiry, *Alien Registration, A Study Outline* (New York, 1926); Olive McKee, Jr., "Town and Country," *Commonweal*, 10 (1929), 354–356.

60. Norman Alexander, *Rights of Aliens under the Federal Constitution* (Montpelier, Vt., 1931), pp. 78–87; Luella Gettys, "'Preliminary Hearings' in Naturalization Administration," *APSR*, 30 (1936), 288–294; Max J. Kohler, "Legal Disabilities of Aliens in the United States," *ABAJl*, 16 (1930), 113–117.

61. Gegiow v. Uhl, 239 U.S. 3, 10 (1915); Henry B. Hazard, "The Right of Appeal in Naturalization Cases in the Federal Courts," *AJIL*, 21 (1927), 40–52. See also "Right of an Alien to a Fair Hearing in Exclusion Proceedings," *HLR*, 41 (1927–28), 522–525.

62. Jane P. Clark, "Administrative Standards in Deportation Procedure," *PSQ*, 44 (1929), 202–214.

63. William C. Van Vleck, "Administrative Justice in the Enforcement of Quasi-Criminal Law," *GWLR*, 1 (1932–33), 29; Charles A. Enslow, "Alien Deportation Law," *LB*, 19 (1925), 146–153, 233–247; "Statutory Construction in Deportation Cases," *YLJ*, 40 (1931), 1283n. See also Edwin M. Borchard, "Decadence of the American Doctrine of Political Expatriation," *AJIL*, 25 (1931), 312–316; Reuben Oppenheimer, "The Deportation Terror," *NR*, 69 (1932), 231–234; Reuben H. Klainer, "Deportation of Aliens," *BULR*, 15 (1935), 663–722.

64. "Shall Aliens Be Registered?" *Survey*, 64 (1931), 179; Gardner Jackson, "Doak the Deportation Chief," *Nation*, 132 (1931), 295–296.

65. Harold Fields, "Unemployment and the Alien," *SAQ*, 30 (1931), 60–78; Maurice Sugar, "Michigan Passes the Spolansky Act," *Nation*, 133 (1931), 31–33.

66. "The Making of Americans," *Outl*, 67 (1901), 481–482; "A Factor in Americanization," *Ind*, 55 (1901), 415–416.

67. Frances A. Kellor, "Needed—A Domestic Insurance Policy," *NAR*, 193 (1911), 561–573; Paul McBride, "Peter Roberts and the YMCA Americanization Program, 1907–World War I," *PH*, 44 (1977), 145–162; Frances Cahn, *Welfare Activities of Federal, State, and Local Government in California, 1850–1934* (Berkeley, 1936), p. 363.

68. Henry J. Fletcher, "Our Divided Country," *AM*, 117 (1916), 224; "The Hyphen Must Go," *NAR*, 203 (1916), 343–344.

69. Agnes Repplier, "Americanism," *AM*, 117 (1916), 289–297. See also Robert L. Schuyler, "The Movement for Americanization," *Columbia University Quarterly*, 128 (1915–16), 181–192; Leonard Wood, "Heat Up the Melting Pot," *Ind*, 87 (1916), 15; Higham, *Strangers*, chap. 9.

70. John F. McClymer, "The Federal Government and the Americanization Movement, 1915–1924," *Prologue*, 10 (Spring 1978), 23–41; Howard C. Hill, "The Americanization Movement," *AJS*, 24 (1918–19), 613.

71. Luther D. Burlingame, "Americanizing a Thousand Men," *Industrial Management*, 53 (1917), pp. 385–392; Gregory Mason, "An Americanization Factory," *Outl*, 123 (1916), 439–448.

72. James D. Whelpley, "The Naturalised American," *FR*, 108 (1917), 594–603; John M. Maguire, "Naturalization of Aliens," *HLR*, 32 (1918–19), 165.

73. Frances A. Kellor, "What Is Americanization?" *YR*, 8 (1918–19), 285; Sidney Ratner, "Horace M. Kallen and Cultural Pluralism," in *The Legacy of Horace M. Kallen*, ed. Milton R. Konvitz (Cranbury, N.J., 1987), pp. 48–63; George Creel, "The Hope of the Hyphenated," *Cent*, 91 (1915–16), 350–363. See also M. E. Ravage, "Standardizing the Immigrant," *NR*, 19 (1919), 145–147; Henry P. Fairchild, "Americanizing the Immigrant," *YR*, 5 (1916), 731–740; Esther E. Lape, "Americanization," *Columbia University Quarterly*, 20 (1918), 59–80.

74. Julius Drachsler, *Democracy and Assimilation* (New York, 1920), p. 29; Rider, "Americanization," 110–115; "Americanization: Its Meaning and Function," *AJS*, 25 (1919–20), 695–730; "Nationalism in Social Work," *Ind*, 98 (1919), 466–467.

75. Vernon Kellog, "Race and Americanization," *YR*, 10 (1921), 729. See also Ellwood Griscom, *Americanization* (New York, 1921); Robert W. Bruère, "Do Americans Want Americanization?" *Survey*, 50 (1923), 75–77.

76. Carman F. Randolph, "Constitutional Aspects of Annexation," *HLR*, 12 (1898–99), 302; Fuller in Downes v. Bidwell, 182 U.S. 244, 373–374 (1901), Harlan at 379.

77. DeLima v. Bidwell, 182 U.S. 1 (1901); Frederic R. Coudert, "The Evolution of the Doctrine of Territorial Incorporation," *Col LR*, 26 (1926), 832, 850. See also articles in *HLR*, 12 (1898–99), 291–315, 365–392, 393–416, and 13 (1899–1900), 155–176, 371–399; Charles E. Littlefield, "The Insular Cases," *HLR*, 15 (1901–2), 169–190, 281–301; John W. Burgess, "The Decisions in the Insular Cases," *PSQ*, 16 (1901), 486–504.

78. Howard, "Suicidal Chinese Policy," 858–860; John W. Foster, "The Chinese Boycott," *AM*, 97 (1906), 288; "Chinese Exclusion," *Outl*, 76 (1904), 963–965; on Portland, see "The Progress of the World," *R of Rs*, 32 (1905), 144; Max J. Kohler, "Un-American Character of Race Legislation," *Annals*, 34 (1909), 275–293.

79. Raymond L. Buell, "The Development of the Anti-Japanese Agitation in the United States," *PSQ*, 37 (1922), 605–638; *Outl*, 91 (1909), 315–316, 367–368; "California and Japan," *Ind*, 66 (1909), 203–204. See also James J. Lorence, "Business and Reform: The American Asiatic Association and the Exclusion Laws, 1905–7," *PHR*, 39 (1970), 421–438; Thomas L. James, "A Revival of the 'Know-Nothing' Spirit," *NAR*, 184 (1907), 268–274.

80. Wong Wai v. Williamson, 103 Fed. 1 (C.C.N.D. Cal., 1900); Charles M. Kneier, "Discrimination against Aliens by Municipal Ordinances," *GLJ*, 16 (1927–28), 155; Ex parte Quong Wo, 118 Pac. 714 (Cal., 1911); Raymond L. Buell, "The Development of the Anti-Japanese Agitation in the United States," *PSQ*, 38 (1923), 58.

81. U.S. v. Tu Joy, 198 U.S. 253 (1905); Ex parte Shahid, 205 Fed. 812

(D.C.E.D. S.C., 1913); Max J. Kohler, "Nationalization and the Color Line," *American Asiatic Association Journal,* 7 (February 1907), 9–11; Chin Yow v. U.S., 208 U.S. 8 (1908).

82. Harriette M. Dilla, "The Constitutional Background of the Recent Japanese Anti-Alien Land Bill Controversy," *Mich LR,* 12 (1913–14), 573–584.

83. Buell, "Development of Anti-Japanese Agitation," 57–64; "The Anti-Alien Land Law Problem," *Outl,* 104 (1913), 86–87.

84. William H. Taft, "Shall the Federal Government Protect Aliens in Their Treaty Rights?" *Ind* 77 (1914), 156–158; "Secretary Bryan in California," *HW,* 57 (May 3, 1913), 3; William Inglis, "Playing with Dynamite," *HW,* 57 (May 3, 1913), 7. See also Herbert P. Le Pore, "Prelude to Prejudice: Hiram Johnson, Woodrow Wilson, and the California Alien Land Law Controversy of 1913," *Southern California Quarterly,* 61 (1979), 99–110.

85. Buell, "Development of Anti-Japanese Agitation," 71–72; Walter G. Beach, "Facts about San Francisco's Alien Population as Gleaned from the Poll Tax Registration of 1921," *Journal of Social Forces,* 3 (1925), 321–325; Maurice E. Harrison, "Legal Aspects of Alien Land Legislation on the Pacific Coast," *ABA Jl,* 8 (1922), 467–469; *LD,* 67 (October 9, 1920), 14–15, (November 20, 1920), 16–17; "Discrimination against the Japanese," *NR,* 24 (1920), 134–136. See also Yuji Ichioka, "Japanese Immigrant Response to the 1920 California Alien Land Law," *AH,* 58 (1984), 157–178.

86. Payson J. Treat, "California and the Japanese," *AM,* 127 (1921), 543; Ex parte Kotta, 200 Pac. 957 (Cal., 1921); K. K. Kawakami, "California and the Japanese," *Nation,* 112 (1921), 173–174, and *The Real Japanese Question* (New York, 1921), pp. 80, 94–95, 97–110; McGovney, "Race Discrimination," 241; Asakura v. City of Seattle, 265 U.S. 332 (1924); Farrington v. Tokushigii, 11 F2d 710, 714 (C.C.A. 9th Circ., 1926).

87. Ozawa v. U.S., 260 U.S. 178, 198 (1922); "The Supreme Court and the Japanese Question," *Outl,* 132 (1922), 554–555.

88. Charles W. Collins, "Will the California Alien Land Law Stand the Test of the Fourteenth Amendment?" *YLJ,* 23 (1913–14), 338; Terrace v. Thompson, 263 U.S. 197, 220–221 (1923); Thomas Reed Powell, "Alien Land Cases in United States Supreme Court," *LR,* 12 (1924), 281. See also "The Constitutionality and Scope of the Alien Land Laws," *UPa LR,* 72 (1923–24), 148–158; Raymond L. Buell, "Some Legal Aspects of the Japanese Question," *AJIL,* 17 (1923), 29–49.

89. Jack D. Freeman, "The Rights of Japanese and Chinese Aliens in Land in Washington," *Washington Law Review,* 6 (1930–31), 131; "California and Its Japanese Problem," *Outl,* 139 (1925), 168; on the fishing bill, see Buell, "Anti-Japanese Agitation," 72–73.

90. In re Knight, 171 Fed. 299 (E.D. N.Y. 1909); U.S. v. Thind, 261 U.S. 203 (1923).

91. Morrison v. Cal., 291 U.S. 82, 85 (1934); George W. Gold, "The Racial Prerequisite in the Naturalization Law," *BULR,* 15 (1935), 466. See also D. O. McGovney, "Race Discrimination in Naturalization," *Iowa Law Bulletin,* 8 (1923), 120–161, 211–244

92. Gold, "Racial Prerequisite," 466; Mark Reisler, *By the Sweat of Their*

Brow: Mexican Immigrant Labor in the United States, 1900–1940 (Westport, Conn., 1976), pp. 56, 151–197.

93. McGovney, "Race Discrimination," 216; Nellie Foster, "Legal Status of Filipino Intermarriages in Colorado," *Sociology and Social Research*, 15 (1932), 446. See also Henry B. Hazard, "The Right of Appeal in Naturalization Cases in the Federal Courts," *AJIL*, 21 (1927), 40–52.

94. Peter H. Schuck, "The Transformation of Immigration Law," *Col LR*, 84 (1984), 1; Lester B. Orfield, "The Citizenship Act of 1934," *UCLR*, 2 (1934–35), 99–118.

8. Blacks and Whites

1. Paul Kennedy, "The Pre-War Right in Britain and Germany," and Geoffrey Searle, "The 'Revolt from the Right' in Edwardian England," in *Nationalist and Racialist Movements in Britain and Germany before 1914*, ed. Paul Kennedy and Anthony Nicholls (London, 1981); Arno J. Mayer, *The Persistence of the Old Regime: Europe to the Great War* (New York, 1981).

2. Rayford W. Logan, *The Betrayal of the Negro: From Rutherford B. Hayes to Woodrow Wilson* (New York, 1965); George M. Fredrickson, *The Black Image in the White Mind* (New York, 1971), chaps. 8–10; Carl Holliday, "The Young Southerner and the Negro," *SAQ*, 8 (1908), 117–131. Gilbert S. Stephenson, in "The Segregation of the Races in Public Conveyances," *APSR*, 3 (1908–9), 180–204, and *Race Distinctions in American Law* (New York, 1910), suggests that Jim Crow legislation built steadily from the 1870s, whereas C. Vann Woodward, in *The Strange Career of Jim Crow* (New York, 1955), argues that this legislation was peculiarly the product of the turn of the century. But when it reached its flowering is not in dispute.

3. R. P. Brooks, "A Local Study of the Race Problem: Race Relations in the Eastern Piedmont Region of Georgia," *PSQ*, 26 (1911), 193–221; James W. Garner, "Recent Agitation on the Negro Question in the South," *SAQ*, 7 (1908), 11–22.

4. Plessy v. Ferguson, 163 U.S. 537 (1896); Richard A. Epstein, "Race and the Police Power: 1890 to 1937," *Washington and Lee Law Review*, 46 (1989), 746–747; William P. Pickett, *The Negro Problem* (New York, 1909), p. 517; on Hoffman, see Fredrickson, *Black Image*, pp. 249–252; Edward Eggleston, *The Ultimate Solution of the American Negro Problem* (Boston, 1913), 265–271. See also Charles A. Lofgren, *The Plessy Case: A Legal-Historical Interpretation* (New York, 1987).

5. On Murphy, see Fredrickson, *Black Image*, pp. 284, and Morton P. Sosna, *In Search of the Silent South: Southern Liberals and the Race Question* (New York, 1977), p. 124; *PSQ*, 15 (1900), 368; Louis R. Harlan, *Separate and Unequal: Public School Campaigns and Racism in the Southern Seaboard States, 1901–1915* (Chapel Hill, 1958), pp. ix, 14–15, 69; Paul L. Haworth, "Negro Disfranchisement in Louisiana," *Outl*, 71 (1902), 163–166; J. Morgan Kousser, "Progressivism—For Middle-Class Whites Only:

North Carolina Education, 1880–1910," *JSH*, 46 (1980), 179. See also C. Vann Woodward, *Origins of the New South, 1877–1913* (Baton Rouge, 1951), chap. 14; Dewey Grantham, "The Progressive Movement and the Negro," *SAQ*, 54 (1955), 461–477; and Bruce Clayton, *The Savage Ideal: Intolerance and Intellectual Leadership in the South, 1890–1914* (Baltimore, 1972).

6. T. B. Edgington, "The Repeal of the Fifteenth Amendment," *NAR*, 188 (1908), 92–100; Ernest G. Dodge, "A New Suggestion on the Race Problem," *SAQ*, 8 (1908), 311–315; J. Morgan Kousser, *The Shaping of Southern Politics: Suffrage Restriction and the Establishment of the One-Party South, 1880–1910* (New Haven, 1974).

7. "Disenfranchisement Defeated in Georgia," *Ind*, 51 (1899), 3306–7.

8. "Nullification in Maryland," *Nation*, 90 (1910), 334; "The Maryland Disenfranchisement Law," *Outl*, 67 (1901), 933; "Negro Disenfranchisement in Maryland," *Nation*, 78 (1904), 6–7; "The Franchise in Maryland," *Nation*, 81 (1905), 4–5; "Negro Suffrage in Maryland," *Outl*, 94 (1910), 820.

9. On Chicago, see Garner, "Recent Agitation," 13n; William E. Walling, "The Race War in the North," *Ind*, 64 (1908), 529–534; Frank U. Quillin, *The Color Line in Ohio* (Ann Arbor, 1913), p. 128.

10. H. C. Foxcroft, "A Negro on Efficiency," *FR*, 86 (1906), 461; Alfred H. Stone, *Studies in the American Race Problem* (New York, 1908), p. xi.

11. "The Negro and the Unions," *Nation*, 91 (1910), 515–516; on Gompers, see "The Negro and the Nation," *Nation*, 105 (1917), 86; Sally M. Miller, "The Socialist Party and the Negro, 1900–1920," *JNH*, 56 (1971), 220–229; Nick Salvatore, *Eugene V. Debs: Citizen and Socialist* (Urbana, 1982), pp. 225–227.

12. "President Wilson and the Color Line," *LD*, 47 (1913), 270–271; *LD*, 49 (1914), 1052–54; Oswald G. Villard, "The President and the Segregation at Washington," *NAR*, 198 (1913), 800–807. See also Harry Blumenthal, "Woodrow Wilson and the Race Issue," *JNH*, 48 (1963), 1–21; and Nancy J. Weiss, "The Negro and the New Freedom: Fighting Wilsonian Segregation," *PSQ*, 84 (1969), 61–79.

13. On Philadelphia, see *Charities Magazine, The Negro in the Cities of the North* (New York, 1905), p. 33; *MPP*, 7029–33; Paul D. Casdorph, *Republicans, Negroes, and Progressives in the South, 1900–1912* (University, Ala., 1981), p. 9.

14. "New Light from a Southern Source on the Negro Problem," *HW*, 49 (1905), 303; Alfred H. Stone, *Studies in the American Race Problem* (New York, 1908), p. xi.

15. Adams quoted in John M. Macklin, *Democracy and Race Friction* (New York, 1914), pp. 145n, 246n; Root quoted in "The 'Failure' of Negro Suffrage," *Chaut*, 37 (1903), 230–231; Ray S. Baker, "The Negro in a Democracy," *Ind*, 67 (1909), 584–588, and "Negro Suffrage in a Democracy," *AM*, 106 (1910), 612–619; Lloyd L. Sponholtz, "Harry Smith, Negro Suf-

frage and the Ohio Constitutional Convention: Black Frustration in the Progressive Era," *Phylon*, 35 (1974), 165–180.

16. Edgington, "Repeal of the Fifteenth Amendment," 3; "Present Views of the Fifteenth Amendment," *HW*, 47 (1903), 873–874. See also William C. Colman, "The Fifteenth Amendment," *Col LR*, 10 (1910), 416–450 (a defense), and Arthur W. Machen, Jr., "Is the Fifteenth Amendment Void?" *HLR*, 23 (1909–10), 169–193 (objecting to its validity).

17. Cisco v. School Board, 61 N.Y. Supp. 330 (1899), and "Comment," *YLJ*, 9 (1900–1901), 227–229; Linton Satterthwaite, "The Color Line in New Jersey," *Arena*, 35 (1906), 394–400; Charles W. Collins, "The Fourteenth Amendment and the Negro Race Question," *ALR*, 45 (1911), 853.

18. Berea College v. Kentucky, 211 U.S. 45, 69 (1908); Andrew A. Bruce, "The Berea College Decision and the Segregation of the Colored Races," *CLJ*, 68 (1909), 137.

19. For examples of relatively balanced media discussion, see "Have We an American Race Question?" *Arena*, 24 (1900), 449, and George H. White, "The Injustice to the Colored Voter," *Ind*, 52 (1900), 176–180. See also George Packard, "Fellow Citizens—A Civic Problem and a Social Duty," *CLN*, 45 (1912–13), 154–156, 158–160, by a white lawyer who championed black civil rights.

20. Edward Atkinson, *The Race Problem: Its Possible Solution* (Baltimore, 1901); Andrew Carnegie, *The Negro in America* (Inverness, Scotland, 1907); New York Republican Club, *Report of the Committee on National Affairs* (New York, 1908).

21. A. V. Dicey, "Mr. Bryce on the Relation between Whites and Blacks," *Nation*, 75, (1902), 26–28; John A. Hobson, "The Negro Problem in the United States," *NC*, 54 (1903), 581–594; Franz Boas, "Race Problems in America," *Science*, n.s., 29 (1909), 839–849; Max J. Kohler, "Un-American Character of Race Legislation," *Annals*, 34 (1909), 275–293; William E. Walling, "Science and Human Brotherhood," *Ind*, 66 (1909), 1318–27, and *Progressivism and After* (New York, 1914), app. F ("The American Socialists and the Race Problem").

22. On Taft, see *PSQ*, 26 (1911), 367; Oswald G. Villard, "The Negro in the Regular Army," *AM*, 91 (1903), 721–729; John T. Bramhall, "The Red, Black, and Yellow," *Overland*, 37 (1901), 722–726; Captain Matthew F. Steele, "The Color Line in the Army," *NAR*, 183 (1906), 1286.

23. "The Bar Association and the Negro," *Outl*, 102 (1912), 1–2; "The Color Line at the Bar," *Nation*, 94 (1912), 509–510; "Lawyers and the Color Line," *LD*, 45 (1912), 36.

24. Ray S. Baker, *Following the Color Line* (New York, 1908), and "Gathering Clouds Along the Color Line," *WW*, 32 (1916), 234–236; Edgar G. Murphy, "Backward or Forward?" *SAQ*, 8 (1909), 19–38; "A Southern Protest against Lynching," *Outl*, 112 (1916), 124–125; Sosna, *In Search*, chap. 2; George B. Tindall, *The Emergence of the New South, 1913–1945* (Baton Rouge, 1967), pp. 175–177.

25. August Meier and Elliott M. Rudwick, *From Plantation to Ghetto* (New

York, 1966), pp. 182–188; George E. Taylor, "The National Liberty Party's Appeal," *Ind*, 57 (1904), 844–846; August Meier and Elliott M. Rudwick, "Negro Boycotts of Segregated Streetcars in Virginia, 1904–1907," *VMHB*, 81 (1973), 479–487.

26. "Progressive Protest against Anti-Negro Film," *Survey*, 34 (1915), 209–210; on St. Louis, see "Progressive Protest," *NR*, 3 (1915), 125. See also Joan M. Silverman, "*The Birth of a Nation:* Prohibition Propaganda," *Southern Quarterly*, 19 (Spring-Summer 1981), 23–30; Robert Sklar, *Movie-Made America: A Social History of American Movies* (New York, 1975), pp. 58–61.

27. *PSQ*, 15 (1900), 368; *PSQ*, 16 (1901), 379, 747.

28. "The Leavenworth Lynching," *AR of Rs*, 23 (1901), 262–263; on Coatesville, see *PSQ*, 26 (1911), 754–755, *PSQ*, 27 (1912), 366; on the prizefight, see *PSQ*, 25 (1910), 743–744.

29. *PSQ*, 18 (1903), 733; 21 (1906), 74; 24 (1909), 747.

30. John C. Kilgo, "An Inquiry Concerning Lynching," *SAQ*, 1 (1902), 7; "How to Put Down Lynching," *Nation*, 77 (1903), 86; James W. Garner, "Lynching and the Criminal Law," *SAQ*, 5 (1906), 331–341; Taft in *PSQ*, 27 (1912), 366; William H. Glasson, "The Statistics of Lynchings," *SAQ*, 5 (1906), 342–348.

31. U.S. v. Shipp, 214 U.S. 386 (1909); *PSQ*, 21 (1906), 367; 24 (1909), 746; 25 (1910), 377–378. See also "In Contempt of the Supreme Court," *Outl*, 92 (1909), 301.

32. On Newark, see "Wiping Off a Smirch," *Outl*, 100 (1912), 7–8; *PSQ*, 31 (1916), 36; on Spartanburg, see "Punishment for Lynching," *Nation*, 100 (1915), 330–332; Roy Nash, "The Lynching of Anthony Crawford," *Ind*, 88 (1916), 456–462.

33. Beirne Stedman, "Appeals to Race Prejudice by Counsel in Criminal Cases," *Virginia Law Register*, n.s., 4 (1918), 241–247; Hampton v. State, 40 So. 545 (Miss., 1906); Montgomery v. State, 45 So. 879 (Fla., 1908); Farrow v. State, 45 So. 619 (Miss., 1908); Aldridge v. U.S., 283 U.S. 308, 317–318 (1911); Frank v. Mangum, 237 U.S. 309, 350 (1915). See also "Equal Protection of the Laws Relating to Juries because of Discrimination on Account of Race or Color," *CLJ*, 66 (1908), 481–482.

34. "Statutory Discriminations against Negroes with Reference to Pullman Cars," *HLR*, 28 (1914–15), 419; McCabe v. Atchison, Topeka & Santa Fe R.R., 235 U.S. 151 (1914). See also Newton D. Baker, "The Segregation of White and Colored Passengers in Interstate Trains," *YLJ*, 19 (1909–10), 445–452.

35. Atwater v. Hassett, 111 Pac. 802, 812 (Okla., 1910); Julien C. Monnet, "The Latest Phase of Negro Disfranchisement," *HLR*, 26 (1912–13), 62; Guinn & Beal v. U.S., 238 U.S. 347 (1915); Myers v. Anderson, 238 U.S. 368 (1915); Moorfield Storey, "The 'Grandfather Clause' Attack on the Constitutionality of the Oklahoma Law in the Highest Court," *LB*, 6 (1913), 358–367. See also "The Grandfather Clause and the Fifteenth Amendment," *HLR*, 24 (1910–11), 388–389; "The Grandfather Clause in

Oklahoma," *Outl*, 95 (1910), 853–854; "The Grandfather Clause in Oklahoma," *Ind*, 96 (1910), 655–656.

36. "A Wrong Righted at Last," *Ind*, 83 (1915), 304; James C. Hemphill, "The South and the Negro Vote," *NAR*, 202 (1915), 213–219.

37. Daniel A. Novak, *The Wheel of Servitude: Black Forced Labor after Slavery* (Lexington, Ky., 1978); Pete Daniel, *The Shadow of Slavery: Peonage in the South, 1901–1969* (Urbana, 1972); Clyatt v. U.S., 197 U.S. 209 (1904); Ex parte Hollman, 60 S.E. 19 (S.C., 1908).

38. Bailey v. Alabama, 219 U.S. 219, 246 (1911); Daniel, *Shadow of Slavery*, chap. 4; "A Blow at Peonage," *Outl*, 97 (1911), 47–48; Ray S. Baker, "A Pawn in the Struggle for Freedom," *AMag*, 72 (1911), 608–610; Thomas I. Parkinson, "Constitutional Aspects of Compulsory Arbitration," *APS Proc.*, 7 (1917–18), 49–56.

39. Garrett Power, "Apartheid Baltimore Style: The Residential Segregation Ordinances of 1910–1913," *Maryland Law Review*, 42 (1983), 289; Gilbert T. Stephenson, "The Segregation of the White and Negro Races in Cities by Legislation," *NMR*, 3 (1914), 504.

40. T. B. Benson, "Segregation Ordinances," *Virginia Law Register*, n.s., 1 (1915), 331; Warren B. Hunting, "The Constitutionality of Race Distinctions and the Baltimore Negro Segregation Ordinance," *Col LR*, 11 (1911), 35; Harris v. Louisville, 177 S.W. 472 (Kent., 1915). See also "Constitutionality of Segregation Ordinances," *Virginia Law Register*, 18 (1912), 561–576, and 19 (1913), 427–448; *CLJ*, 81 (October 22, 1915), 290.

41. Newspapers quoted in "Negro Segregation in St. Louis," *LD*, 52 (1916), 702; "A Popular Vote on a Black Ghetto," *Survey*, 35 (1915–16), 627; "Negro Segregation Adopted by St. Louis," *Survey*, 35 (1915–16), 694; Roger N. Baldwin, "Negro Segregation by Initiative Election in St. Louis," *American City*, 14 (1916), 356; Roland G. Usher, "Negro Segregation in St. Louis," *NR*, 6 (1916), 176–178.

42. State v. Darnell, 81 S.E. 338 (N. Car., 1914); Power, "Apartheid Baltimore Style," 302, 310; State v. Gurry, 88 Atl. 546, 553 (Md., 1913). See also "The Segregation of the Negro in Separate Residential Districts," *HLR*, 27 (1913–14), 270–271.

43. Buchanan v. Warley, 245 U.S. 60, 82, 81 (1917); George C. Wright, "The NAACP and Residential Segregation in Louisville, Kentucky, 1914–1917," *Kentucky Historical Society Register*, 78 (1980), 39–54; Roger L. Rice, "Residential Segregation by Law, 1910–1917," *JSH*, 34 (1968), 179–199. See also Alexander M. Bickel and Benno C. Schmidt, Jr., *The Judiciary and Responsible Government, 1910–21*, vol. 9 of *The Oliver Wendell Holmes Devise History of the Supreme Court* (New York, 1984), pp. 789–817, which emphasizes the relative racial liberalism of the decision.

44. "The Negro's Right of Residence," *LD*, 55 (November 24, 1917), 17–18; "A Momentous Decision," *Nation*, 105 (1917), 526; "Race Segregation Ordinance Invalid," *HLR*, 31 (1917–18), 476, 478.

45. Edward A. Steiner, "America and the New Race," *Christian Century*, 40 (1923), 1226.

46. "The Illinois Race War and Its Brutal Aftermath," *Current Opinion*, 63 (1917), 75–77; "The Riots in East St. Louis," *Pan-American*, 24 (1917), 173; Moorfield Storey, "The Negro Question" (pamphlet, Widener Library, Harvard University); Elliott M. Rudwick, *Race Riot at East St. Louis, July 2, 1917* (Carbondale, Ill., 1964).

47. Herbert J. Seligmann, "What Is behind the Negro Uprisings?" *Current Opinion*, 67 (1919), 154–155; "Racial Tension and Race Riots," *Outl*, 122 (1919), 532–534; Carl Sandburg, *The Chicago Race Riots, 1919* (New York, 1919); Charles W. Holman, "Race Riots in Chicago," *Outl*, 122 (1919), 566–567; on Washington, see "Mob Fury and Race Hatred as a National Danger," *LD*, 69 (June 18, 1921), 7–9.

48. "Omaha," *LD*, 63 (October 11, 1919), 16; Herbert J. Seligmann, *The Negro Faces America* (New York, 1920), p. 162; Scott Ellsworth, *Death in a Promised Land: The Tulsa Race Riot of 1921* (Baton Rouge, 1982), passim.

49. *LD*, 62 (August 16, 1919), 17–18. On greater black assertiveness, see Robert T. Kerlin, *The Voice of the Negro, 1919* (New York, 1920).

50. Franklin H. Giddings, "The Black Man's Rights," *Ind*, 99 (1919), 153; Chicago Committee on Race Relations, *The Negro in Chicago* (Chicago, 1923); *LD*, 75 (October 28, 1922), 11–12; Glenn Frank, "The Clash of Color: The Negro in American Democracy," *Cent*, 99 (1919–20), 86–98; "The Blunder of Race Riots," *Cent*, 99 (1919), 176, 178.

51. "Johnstown's Flood of Negro Labor," *LD*, 79 (October 6, 1923), 178; and see p. 105 in this volume.

52. *LD*, 69 (June 4, 1921), 19; Mary White Ovington, "Is Mob Violence the Texas Solution of the Race Problem?" *Ind*, 99 (1919), 320.

53. Edward E. Lewis, "The Southern Negro and the American Labor Supply," *PSQ*, 48 (1933), 172–183; "Why the Negro Comes North," *Homiletic Review*, 87 (1924), 32–33; William H. Richardson, "No More Lynchings: How North Carolina Has Solved the Problem," *AR of Rs*, 69 (1924), 401–404; "The Kentucky Cure for Lynching," *LD*, 61 (February 28, 1920), 20–21.

54. Lester A. Walton, "Whitfield—Apostle of Racial Good Will," *Outl*, 136 (1924), 589–591; on Dorsey, see *LD*, 69 (May 14, 1921), 17–18. See also Virginius Dabney, *Liberalism in the South* (Chapel Hill, 1932).

55. P. B. Young, "Contribution of the Press in the Adjustment of Race Relations," *SW*, 57 (1928), 147–154; Nimrod B. Allen, "Interracial Relations in Columbus, Ohio," *SW*, 55 (1926), 161–169; Tindall, *Emergence of New South*, pp. 177–183.

56. Thyra J. Edwards, "The Gary Interracial Program," *SW*, 54 (1925), 545–554; James Bond, "Interracial Work in Kentucky," *SW*, 54 (1925), 254–256; W. T. B. Williams, "The South's Changing Attitude toward Negro Education," *SW*, 54 (1925), 398–400; on welfare, see "Race Barriers Slowly Crumbling," *LD*, 92 (February 12, 1927), 34.

57. *LD*, 73 (June 10, 1922), 14; "A Race Commission—A Constructive Plan," *Nation*, 112 (1921), 612; on the appointment, see *LD*, 77 (June 2, 1923), 17–18; David O. Walter, "Proposals for a Federal Anti-Lynching Law," *APSR*, 28 (1934), 436–442.

58. *Outl,* 129 (1921), 380, *Current Opinion,* 71 (1921), 704–708; *Nation,* 113 (1921), 561; *LD,* 71 (November 19, 1921), 7–9.

59. "Coolidge on Colored Candidates," *LD,* 82 (August 30, 1924), 13; William F. Nowlin, *The Negro in American National Politics* (Boston, 1931), 174. See also Harold F. Gosnell, *Negro Politicians* (Chicago, 1935); Richard B. Sherman, *The Republican Party and Black Americans from McKinley to Hoover, 1896–1933* (Charlottesville, 1973).

60. *LD,* 101 (June 29, 1929), 10; *LD,* 99 (November 3, 1928), 15; Research Committee on Social Trends, *Recent Social Trends in the United States* (New York, 1933) 1:xli.

61. Lester A. Walton, "The Negro in Politics," *Outl,* 137 (1924), 472–473; on Chicago, see *WW,* 47 (1923–24), 536; on the Klan, see *Ind,* 113 (1924), 268.

62. *LD,* 99 (November 3, 1928), 15; *LD,* 101 (June 29, 1929), 10. See also James W. Johnson, "A Negro Looks at Politics," *AMerc,* 18 (1929), 88–94.

63. Suzanne E. Green, "Black Republicans on the Baltimore City Council, 1890–1931," *Maryland Historical Magazine,* 74 (1979), 213, 220; Abram L. Harris, "A White and Black World in American Labor and Politics," *Journal of Social Forces,* 4 (1925), 376–383.

64. "Intermarriage with Negroes—A Survey of State Statutes," *YLJ,* 36 (1926–27), 858–866; on Gary, see *LD,* 95 (October 22, 1927), 14; Greathouse v. Bd., 151 N.E. 411, 414 (Ind., 1926).

65. Hoke F. Henderson, "Separation of Races in Schools," *LN,* 32 (1928), 147–149; "Legality of Race Segregation in Educational Institutions," *UPa LR,* 82 (1933–34), 157–164.

66. "Mob Domination of a Trial as a Violation of the Fourteenth Amendment," *HLR,* 37 (1923–24), 247–250; "Judge Lynch Reversed," *Outl,* 136 (1924), 173–174; Moore v. Dempsey, 261 U.S. 86, 93 (1923).

67. South Covington & Cincinnati Street Railway Co. v. Kentucky, 252 U.S. 399 (1920); Powell in *PSQ,* 35 (1920), 423.

68. Gong Lum v. Rice, 275 U.S. 78, 79, 82 (1927); Robert E. Cushman, *APSR,* 23 (1929), 96.

69. "The Atlanta Zoning Plan," *Survey,* 48 (1922), 114–115; reply by Whitten, *Survey,* 48 (1922) 418; "No Laws May Part White and Black," *LD,* 92 (March 26, 1927), 12; "Statutory Segregation Illegal," *Outl,* 145 (1927), 388.

70. People's Pleasure Park v. Rohleder, 61 S.F. 794 (Va., 1908); Queensborough Land Co. v. Cazeaux, 67 So. 641 (La., 1915).

71. Title Guaranty & Investment Co. v. Garrott, 183 Pac. 470 (Cal., 1919); Los Angeles Investment Co. v. Gary, 186 Pac. 596 (Cal., 1919). See also Harold W. Bowman, "The Constitutional and Common Law Restraints on Alienation," *BULR,* 8 (1928), 14; Clement E. Vose, *Caucasians Only: The Supreme Court, the NAACP, and the Restrictive Covenant Cases* (Berkeley, 1959).

72. Alfred E. Cohen, "Racial Restrictions in Covenants in Deeds," *Virginia Law Register,* n.s., 6 (1921), 742; Euclid v. Ambler, 272 U.S. 365 (1926); F. D. G. Ribble, "Legal Restraints on the Choice of a Dwelling," *UPa LR,* 69 (1929–30), 851; Andrew A. Bruce, "Racial Zoning by Private Contract

in the Light of the Constitution and the Rule against Restraints on Alienation," *ILR*, 21 (1926–27), 711, 715, 716. See also George D. Hott, "Constitutionality of Municipal Zoning and Segregation Ordinances," *West Virginia Law Quarterly*, 33 (1926–27), 332–349.

73. "The Supreme Court's 'Jim Crow' Case," *LD*, 89 (June 12, 1926), 14; Corrigan v. Buckley, 271 U.S. 323 (1926); Terrace v. Thompson, 263 U.S. 197 (1923).

74. Parmalee v. Morris, 218 Mich. 625 (1925); Porter v. Barrett, 206 N.W. 532 (Mich., 1925); Schulte v. Starks, 213 N.W. 102 (Mich., 1927); M. T. Van Hecke, "Zoning Ordinances and Restrictions in Deeds," *YLJ*, 37 (1928), 412. See also *CLQ*, 12 (1926–27), 400–405; Helen C. Monchow, "Conditions and Restrictions Dealing with Alienation, Occupancy, Duration, and Racial Conditions," *LB*, 22 (1929), 169–174.

75. Arthur T. Martin, "Segregation of Residence of Negroes," *Mich LR*, 32 (1934), 726; Shelley v. Kraemer, 334 U.S. 1 (1948).

76. Joseph R. Burcham, "Discriminations against Negroes in Primary Elections," *St. Louis Law Review*, 12 (1927), 199–204; Roy W. McDonald, "Negro Voters in Democratic Primaries," *TLR*, 5 (1926–27), 393–400; Nixon v. Herndon, 233 U.S. 536 (1927); "Right of Negroes to Vote in State Primaries," *HLR*, 43 (1929–30), 467–471. See also O. Douglas Weeks, "The White Primary," *Mississippi Law Journal*, 8 (1935), 135–153. See also Darlene C. Hine, *Black Victory: The Rise and Fall of the White Primary in Texas* (Millwood, N.Y., 1979).

77. "The Negro's Right to Be a Democrat," *LD*, 92 (March 19, 1927), 10; "Nixon v. Condon—Disenfranchisement of the Negro in Texas," *YLJ*, 41 (1932), 1215; Nixon v. Condon, 286 U.S. 73, 104 (1932); "The White Primary in Texas since Nixon v. Condon," *HLR*, 46 (1933), 812–818; Luther H. Evans, "Primary Elections and the Constitution," *Mich LR*, 32 (1934), 451–477; Grovey v. Townsend, 295 U.S. 45 (1935); Smith v. Allwright, 321 U.S. 649 (1944). See also O. Douglas Weeks, "The Texas Direct Primary System," *SSSQ*, 13 (1932), 95–120.

78. Walter White, "The Negro and the Supreme Court," *HM*, 162 (1930–31), 241–242. See also Richard L. Watson, "The Defeat of Judge Parker: A Study in Pressure Groups and Politics," *MVHR*, 50 (1963), 213–234; William C. Burris, *The Senate Rejects a Judge: A Study of the John J. Parker Case* (Chapel Hill, 1962).

79. Dan T. Carter, *Scottsboro: A Tragedy of the American South* (New York, 1969); Powell v. Alabama, 287 U.S. 45 (1932); Norris v. Alabama, 294 U.S. 587 (1935).

80. "The End of Convict Leasing in Alabama," *LD*, 98 (July 21, 1928), 11; "Race Equality by Statute," *UPa LR*, 75 (1935–36), 75–84.

9. Indians and Women

1. "Legal State of the Indians—Validity of Indian Marriages," *YLJ*, 13 (1903–4), 252. See also David G. Taylor, "Cultural Pluralism versus Assimilation: New Perspectives on the American Indian in the Twentieth Cen-

tury," *MAm*, 64 (1982), 3–16, which characterizes the period from 1887 to 1928 as one of assimilation, and Frederick E. Hoxie, *A Final Promise: The Campaign to Assimilate the Indians, 1880–1920* (Lincoln, Neb., 1984).

2. Morton Keller, *Affairs of State: Public Life in Late Nineteenth-Century America* (Cambridge, Mass., 1977), pp. 153–156, 457–461; Roosevelt quoted in Robert F. Berkhofer, Jr., *The White Man's Indian: Images of the American Indian from Columbus to the Present* (New York, 1978), p. 175.

3. Colonel Richard J. Hinton, "The Indian Territory—Its Status, Development, and Future," *AR of Rs*, 23 (1901), 451–478; "The Approaching End of the Indian Problem," *Ind*, 52 (1900), 2586–87; Lyman Abbott, "The Rights of Man: A Study in Twentieth-Century Problems," *Outl*, 68 (1901), 350. See also Janet A. McDonnell, *The Dispossession of the American Indian, 1887–1934* (Bloomington, Ind., 1991).

4. W. R. Draper, "The Reconstruction of the Indian Territory," *Outl*, 68 (1901), 444; Hoxie, *Final Promise*, pp. 153–154.

5. Francis E. Leupp, "The Indian Land Troubles and How to Solve Them," *AR of R*, 42 (1910), 468–472; Choate v. Trapp, 224 U.S. 665 (1912).

6. *Outl*, 108 (1914), 62–63; Kate Barnard, "For the Orphans of Oklahoma," *Survey*, 33 (1914–15), 154–155, 161–164.

7. Montoya v. U.S., 180 U.S. 261 (1901); Lone Wolf v. Hitchcock, 187 U.S. 553 (1903); In re Heff, 197 U.S. 488, 499 (1905); Tiger v. Western Investment Co., 221 U.S. 286, 315 (1911).

8. Dudley O. McGoveny, "American Citizenship," *Col LR*, 11 (1911), 326–337; Williams v. Chicago, 242 U.S. 434 (1917).

9. William W. Quinn, Jr., "Federal Acknowledgment of American Indian Tribes: The Historical Development of a Legal Concept," *AJLH*, 34 (1990), 352, 354.

10. Tiger v. Western Investment Co., 221 U.S. 286 (1911); U.S. v. Sandoval, 231 U.S. 28, 39 (1913); U.S. v. Nice, 241 U.S. 591 (1916); U.S. v. Board of Commissioners, 251 U.S. 128 (1919). See Hoxie, *Final Promise*, chap. 7.

11. Hoxie, *Final Promise*, pp. 152–162; "An Indian Policy," *Ind*, 52 (1900), 3058–59; "Shall the Indian Be Made A Citizen," *Chaut*, 34 (1901–2), 360–361.

12. "Mr. Leupp and Mr. Valentine," *Outl*, 92 (1909), 421; Francis E. Leupp, "Outline of an Indian Policy," *Outl*, 79 (1905), 946–950; "Our 'New Policy' with the Red Brother," *Nation*, 79 (1904), 211–212; Hoxie, *Final Promise*, pp. 163–164. See also John F. Berens, "Old Campaigners, New Realities: Indian Policy Reform in the Progressive Era, 1900–1912," *MAm*, 59 (1977), 51–64.

13. "A New Step in Our Indian Policy," *Outl*, 116 (1917), 136; on the ceremony, see *Case and Comment*, 23 (1917), 701. See also Janet McDonnell, "Competency Commissioners and Indian Land Policy, 1913–1920," *South Dakota History*, 11 (Winter 1980), 21–34.

14. George Kennan, "Have Reservation Indians Any Vested Rights?" *Outl*, 70 (1902), 765; Henry E. Fritz, "The Last Hurrah of Christian Humanitarian Indian Reform: The Board of Indian Commissioners, 1909–1918," *West-*

ern Historical Quarterly, 16 (1985), 147–162; H. Craig Miner, *The Corpo-ration and the Indian: Tribal Sovereignty and Industrial Civilization in Indian Territory, 1865–1907* (Columbia, Mo., 1976).

15. Hamlin Garland, "The Red Man's Present Needs," *NAR*, 174 (1902), 476, 479, 488.

16. Hazel W. Hertzberg, *The Search for an American Indian Identity: Mod-ern Pan-Indian Movements* (Syracuse, 1971), p. 33; Hiram Chase, "The Law and the American Indian in Amebic," *Ohio Law Reporter*, 9 (1911), 345–349; Peter Iverson, *Carlos Montezuma and the Changing World of American Indians* (Albuquerque, 1982).

17. On Senate roll calls, see Hoxie, *Final Promise*, pp. 245–256.

18. Lawrence C. Kelly, *The Navajo Indians and Federal Indian Policy, 1900–1935* (Tucson, 1968); John M. Oskison, "Remaining Causes of Indian Dis-content," *NAR*, 184 (1907), 486–493.

19. Choate v. Trapp, 224 U.S. 665 (1912); Grant Foreman, "The U.S. Court and the Indian," *Overland*, 61 (1913), 573–579; Frank J. Goodnow, "The Nature of Tax Exemptions," *Col LR*, 13 (1913), 104–120.

20. Cuthbert W. Pound, "Nationals without a Nation: The New York State Tribal Indians," *Col LR*, 22 (1922), 97–106; Lawrence M. Hauptman, "Senecas and Subdividers: Resistance to Allotment of Indian Lands in New York, 1875–1906," *Prologue*, 9 (1977), 105–117; on the Iroquois, see Arthur C. Parker, "The New York Indians," *SW*, 50 (1921), 155–160. See also Karl J. Knoepfler, "Legal Status of American Indian and His Prop-erty," *Iowa Law Bulletin*, 7 (1921–22), 232–249.

21. Gordon Cain, "Indian Titles in Minnesota," *Minn LR*, 2 (1918), 177–191.

22. Ibid., 187; U.S. v. First National Bank of Detroit, 234 U.S. 245 (1914).

23. Michael L. Tate, "From Scout to Doughboy: The National Debate over Integrating American Indians into the Military, 1891–1918," *Western Historical Quarterly*, 17 (1986), 417–457; "If the Red Man Can Fight, Why Can't He Vote?" *LD*, 59 (December 21, 1918), 36–37; Gary C. Stein, "The Indian Citizenship Act of 1924," *New Mexico Historical Review*, 47 (1972), 257–274; Theodore Haas, "The Legal Aspects of Indian Affairs from 1887 to 1957," *Annals*, 311 (1957), 12–13, 16. See also N. D. Houghton, "The Legal Status of Indian Suffrage in the United States," *Cal LR*, 19 (1931), 508–520.

24. Mary Austin, "Why Americanize the Indian?" *Forum*, 82 (1929), 170; Chauncey S. Goodrich, "The Legal Status of the California Indian," *Cal LR*, 14 (1926), 178, 179.

25. Anderson v. Matthew, 163 Pac. 902 (Cal., 1917); Piper v. Big Pine School District, 226 Pac. 926 (Cal., 1924); Francisco v. Industrial Accident Com-mission, 221 Pac. 373, 376 (Cal., 1923).

26. Goodrich, "Legal Status," 187; Ray A. Brown, "The Indian Problem and the Law," *YLJ*, 39 (1930), 307–331; Robert C. Brown, "The Taxation of Indian Property," *Minn LR*, 15 (1930–31), 207, 182.

27. Brown, "Indian Problem," 327–329. See also Jennings C. Wise, "Indian Law and Needed Reforms," *ABAJl*, 12 (1926), 37–40.

28. Ruby A. Black, "A New Deal for the Red Man," *Nation*, 130 (1930), 388–

390; Mary Ross, "The New Indian Administration," *Survey*, 64 (1930), 268–269; Brown, "Indian Problem," 307–308.

29. McDonnell, *Dispossession*, p. 120; W. G. Rice, "The Position of the American Indian in the Law of the United States," *JComp Leg*, 3rd ser., 16 (1934), 78–95; Leonard A. Carson, "Federal Policy and Indian Land: Economic Interests and the Sale of Indian Allotments, 1900–1934," *AH*, 57 (1983), 33–45. See also Lawrence C. Kelly, *The Assault on Assimilation: John Collier and the Origins of Indian Policy Reform* (Albuquerque, 1983); Kenneth R. Philip, *John Collier's Crusade for Indian Reform, 1920–1954* (Tucson, 1977).

30. "In the Red," *Economist*, February 25, 1989, 25–26.

31. Ross E. Paulson, *Women's Suffrage and Prohibition: A Comparative Study of Equality and Social Control* (Glenview, Ill., 1973), pp. 167–168; C. E. Gehlke, "On the Correlation between the Vote for Suffrage and the Vote on the Liquor Question: A Preliminary Study," *American Statistical Association Journal*, n.s., 15 (1916–17), 524–532; Oliver M. Sayles, "Indiana's Double Somersault," *NR*, 10 (1917), 192–194.

32. Ida H. Harper, "The World Movement for Woman Suffrage," *AR of Rs*, 44 (1911), 725–729; "Woman Suffrage throughout the World," *NAR*, 186 (1907), 55–71. See also Jan Romein, *The Watershed of Two Eras: Europe in 1890* (Middletown, Conn., 1978), pp. 601–617; Richard J. Evans, *The Feminists: Women's Emancipation Movements in Europe, America, and Australasia, 1840–1920* (London, 1977).

33. Richard J. Evans, *The Feminist Movement in Germany, 1894–1933* (London, 1976); idem, "Liberalism and Socialism: The Feminist Movement and Social Change," in *Society and Politics in Wilhelmine Germany*, ed. Richard J. Evans (London, 1978), pp. 188–224; Jean H. Quatert, *Reluctant Feminists in German Social Democracy, 1885–1917* (Princeton, 1979).

34. Karen Offen, "Depopulation, Nationalism, and Feminism in Fin-de-Siècle France," *AHR*, 89 (1984), 648–676; Steven C. Hause and Anne R. Kenney, "The Limits of Suffrage Behavior: Legalism and Militancy in France, 1876–1922," *AHR*, 86 (1981), 781–806, and *Women's Suffrage and Social Politics in the Third Republic* (Princeton, 1984). See also Evans, *Feminist Movement*, 124–134.

35. "Ignota," "The Present Legal Position of Women in the United Kingdom," *WR*, 163 (1905), 513–529; Constance Rover, *Women's Suffrage and Party Politics in Britain, 1866–1914* (London, 1967), p. 12; Sheridan Jones, "The Future of Feminism," *Outl* (GB), 56 (1925), 87–88. See also David Morgan, *Suffragists and Liberals: The Politics of Woman Suffrage in England* (Totawa, N.J., 1975); Sandra S. Holton, *Feminism and Democracy: Women's Suffrage and Reform Politics in Britain, 1900–1918* (Cambridge, 1986), pp. 4–7; Brian Harrison, *Separate Spheres: The Opposition to Women's Suffrage in Britain* (London, 1978); David Morgan, "Woman Suffrage in Britain and America in the Early Twentieth Century," in *Contrast and Connection: Bicentennial Essays in Anglo-American History*, ed. H. C. Allen and Roger Thompson (Athens, Ohio, 1976), pp. 272–295.

36. Gladstone quoted in John Grigg, *Lloyd George: The People's Champion*,

1902–1911 (Berkeley, 1978), p. 165; Asquith quoted in Stephen Koss, *Asquith* (London, 1976), p. 132. See also Martin D. Pugh, *Electoral Reform in War and Peace, 1906–1918* (London, 1978), chap. 2.

37. Martin D. Pugh, "Politicians and the Women's Vote, 1914–1918," *Historian*, 59 (1974), 358–374; John D. Fair, "The Political Aspects of Women's Suffrage during the First World War," *Albion*, 8 (1976), 274–295; Helen Archdale, "Ten Years of the Woman's Vote," *Spect*, 140 (1928), 148.

38. Susan B. Anthony, "The Outlook for Woman Suffrage," *Cosmopolitan*, 28 (1899–1900), 621–623; Frank Foxcroft, "The Check to Woman Suffrage in the United States," *NC*, 56 (1904), 833–841. See also Eleanor Flexner, *Century of Struggle: The Woman's Rights Movement in the United States* (Cambridge, Mass., 1959), chap. 19.

39. Lyman Abbott, "Why Women Do Not Wish the Suffrage," *AM*, 92 (1903), 296; Helen K. Johnson, *Woman and the Republic* (New York, 1897); on the poll, see *Outl*, 104 (1913), 268–269.

40. Morgan, "Woman Suffrage," 274. See also Theda Skocpol, *Protecting Soldiers and Mothers: The Political Origins of Social Policy in the United States* (Cambridge, Mass., 1992).

41. "Ignota," "How the Vote Has Affected Womanhood in Colorado," *WR*, 163 (1905), 268; Alfred D. Runyon, "The Woman Boss of Denver," *HW*, 52 (December 26, 1908), 8–9, 28. See also "Woman Suffrage in Colorado," *NAR*, 183 (1906), 1203–6.

42. Alice H. Chittenden, "The Counter-Influence to Woman Suffrage," *Ind*, 67 (1909), 246–249; Ida H. Harper, "Status of Woman Suffrage in the United States," *NAR*, 189 (1909), 501–512; idem, "Evolution of the Woman Suffrage Movement," *World To-Day*, 19 (1910), 1017–21; on Oregon, see Alice S. Blackwell, "An Object Lesson," *Ind*, 61 (1906), 198–199.

43. Steven M. Buechler, *The Transformation of the Woman Suffrage Movement: The Case of Illinois, 1850–1920* (New Brunswick, N.J., 1986), p. 1.

44. Helen Haines, "Catholic Womanhood and the Suffrage," *Catholic World*, 102 (1915–16), 55–67; Mrs. Barclay Hazard, "New York State Association Opposed to Woman Suffrage," *Chaut*, 59 (1910), 84–89; William Hemmingway, "Campaigning for Equal Franchise," *HW*, 53 (March 13, 1909), 15–16; Ida M. Tarbell, *The Business of Being a Woman* (New York, 1912), p. 21. See also Robert Stinson, "Ida M. Tarbell and the Ambiguities of Feminism," *Pennsylvania Magazine of History and Biography*, 101 (1977), 217–239.

45. On the poll, see Dora B. Montefiore, "The Woman Suffrage Movement in England and in America," *Ind*, 69 (1910), 32–34.

46. "Women's Victory in Washington," *Collier's*, 46 (January 7, 1911), 25, 28; Bertha D. Knobe, "Spectacular Woman Suffrage in America," *Ind*, 71 (1911), 804–810; Jane A. Stewart, "The Winning of California," *JEd*, 74 (1911), 480–481.

47. J. O. P. Bland, "Woman Suffrage in the United States," *NC*, 74 (1913), 1338; Bertha Rembaugh, *The Political Status of Women in the United States* (New York, 1911); on Ward, see Bertha D. Knobe, "Recent Strides of Woman Suffrage," *WW*, 22 (1911), 14,734.

48. On Willard, see Elbert Hubbard, "A Setback for Woman Suffrage," *Hearst's*, 22 (1912), 155–157; *LD*, 44 (1912), 1024–25.

49. Ida H. Harper, "The Recent Elections and Woman Suffrage," *NAR*, 200 (1914), 893–899; on Ohio, see Hubbard, "Setback for Woman Suffrage," 155–157; on New Jersey, see Joseph F. Mahoney, "Woman Suffrage and the Urban Masses," *NJH*, 87 (1969), 131–172; Sharon H. Strom, "Leadership and Tactics in the American Suffrage Movement: A New Perspective from Massachusetts," *JAH*, 62 (1975), 296–315.

50. *LD*, 46 (1913), 1410; "Woman Suffrage at Work in America," *NC*, 75 (1914), 415–433.

51. Katherine Buell, "How Women Vote," *HW*, 58 (April 15, 1914), 20–23; John D. Buenker, *Urban Liberalism and Progressive Reform* (New York, 1973), p. 157.

52. Hugh S. Fullerton, "How the Women Voted in Chicago," *AMag*, 79 (June 1915), 57–58.

53. Ida H. Harper, "The National Constitution Will Enfranchise Women," *NAR*, 199 (1914), 720; Florence Kelley, "Women and Social Legislation in the United States," *Annals*, 56 (1914), 62–70.

54. Taft in L. Ames Brown, "Suffrage and Prohibition," *NAR*, 203 (1916), 94; "The New Status of Suffrage," *Nation*, 103 (1916), 28–29.

55. Brown, "Suffrage and Prohibition," 97, 99. See Eileen L. McDonagh, "Issues and Constituencies in the Progressive Era: House Roll Call Voting on the Nineteenth Amendment, 1913–1919," *JPal*, 51 (1989), 119–135, for a discussion that emphasizes the differences in congressional support for the two causes.

56. "Labor's Position on Woman Suffrage," *NR*, 6 (1916), 150–152; Christine A. Lunardini and Thomas J. Knock, "Woodrow Wilson and Woman Suffrage: A New Look," *PSQ*, 95 (1980–81), 655–676; Buenker, *Urban Liberalism*, pp. 156–160.

57. Sally H. Graham, "Woodrow Wilson, Alice Paul, and the Woman Suffrage Movement," *PSQ*, 98 (1983–84), 665–679; David Morgan, *Suffragists and Democrats: The Politics of Woman Suffrage in America* (Lansing, Mich., 1972); on the ratification process, see Flexner, *Century of Struggle*, passim.

58. Joel M. Goldstein, *The Effects of the Adoption of Woman Suffrage: Sex Differences in Voting Behavior—Illinois, 1914–21* (New York, 1984), pp. 96, 111, 165; Brian Williams, "Petticoats in Politics: Cincinnati Women and the 1920 Election," *Cincinnati Historical Society Bulletin*, 35 (Spring 1977), 61; Margaret M. Wells, "Some Effects of Woman Suffrage," *Annals*, 143 (1929), 207–216.

59. Emily Blair, "Are Women a Failure in Politics?" *HM*, 151 (1925), 519; James C. Furnas, *Great Times: An Informal Social History of the United States, 1914–1929* (New York, 1974), p. 414.

60. Gladys Wells, "A Critique of Methods for Alteration of Women's Legal Status," *Mich LR*, 21 (1923), 723–724.

61. Anne Martin, "Political Methods of American and British Feminists," *CH*, 20 (1924), 396–401. See also Frances Kellor, "Women in British and American Politics," *CH*, 17 (1922–23), 831–835.

62. Office of the Historian, U.S. House of Representatives, *Women in Congress, 1917–1990* (Washington, D.C., 1991); on Ferguson, see Edna Kenton, "The Ladies' Next Step: The Case for the Equal Rights Amendment," *HM*, 152 (1925–26), 366–367.

63. On Felton, see *LD*, 82 (September 6, 1924), 16; *LD*, 78 (September 22, 1923), 50, 52; Dorothy A. Moncure, "Women in Political Life," *CH*, 29 (1928–29), 639–643.

64. Wells, "Critique of Methods," 721–722; Blanche Crozier, "Constitutionality of Discrimination Based on Sex," *BULR*, 15 (1935), 725–733; Minor Bronagh, "Jury Service as Incidental to Grant of Women's Suffrage," *LN*, 27 (1923), 147–150; on Wisconsin, see Zona Gale, "What Women Won in Wisconsin," *Nation*, 115 (1922), 184–185; on Iowa, see Sue S. White, "Women and the Law," *Nation*, 112 (1921), 402; on the exclusion of brunettes, see *New York Times*, March 17, 1921, p. 17.

65. Walter Lippmann, *Drift and Mastery* (New York, 1914), pp. 126–127.

66. John M. Maguire, "Suffrage and Married Women's Nationality," *ALR*, 54 (1920), 646–661; Ernest J. Hover, "Citizenship of Women in the United States," *AJIL*, 26 (1932), 700–719; "Personal Citizenship for Women," *LD*, 75 (October 21, 1922), 14.

67. National League of Women Voters, *A Survey of the Legal Status of Women in the Forty-Eight States* (Washington, D.C., 1930), pp. 9–18.

68. Kenton, "Ladies' Next Step," 367; Burnita S. Matthews, "Women Should Have Equal Rights with Men: A Reply," *ABAJl*, 12 (1926), 117–120.

69. Carroll R. Heft, "Women's Equality Legislation in Wisconsin," *Wis LR*, 2 (1922–1924), 350–362.

70. Florence Kelley, "Should Women Be Treated Identically with Men by the Law?" *American Review*, 1 (1923), 277; "Shall Women Be Equal before the Law?" *Nation*, 114 (1922), 419–421; Joan G. Zimmerman, "The Jurisprudence of Equality: The Women's Minimum Wage, the First Equal Rights Amendment, and *Adkins v. Children's Hospital*, 1905–23," *JAH*, 78 (1991), 188–225. See also "Feminism in the Federal Constitution," *WW*, 45 (1922–1923), 20–21; "Doctrinaire Equality," *NR*, 59 (1929), 249; Nancy Cott, *The Grounding of Modern Feminism* (New Haven, 1987); J. Stanley Lemons, *The Woman Citizen: Social Feminism in the 1920s* (Urbana, 1973); Christine A. Lunardini, *From Equal Suffrage to Equal Rights: Alice Paul and the National Woman's Party, 1910–1928* (New York, 1986).

Index